Present Tense

Contemporary Themes for Writers

Lee Bauknight *and* Brooke Rollins

WADSWORTH
CENGAGE Learning™

Australia • Brazil • Japan • Korea • Mexico • Singapore • Spain • United Kingdom • United States

WADSWORTH
CENGAGE Learning™

Present Tense: Contemporary Themes for Writers
Lee Bauknight, Brooke Rollins

Publisher: Lyn Uhl

Acquisitions Editor: Kate Derrick

Development Editor: Laurie Runion Dobson

Senior Assistant Editor: Kelli Strieby

Editorial Assistant: Jake Zucker

Media Editor: Cara Douglass-Graff

Marketing Manager: Jennifer Zourdos

Marketing Coordinator: Ryan Ahern

Senior Marketing Communications Manager: Stacey Purviance

Senior Content Project Manager: Michael Lepera

Senior Art Director: Jill Ort

Senior Print Buyer: Betsy Donaghey

Senior Permissions Editor, Text: Margaret Chamberlain-Gaston

Text Researcher: Sarah D'Stair

Production Service/Compositor: Pre-PressPMG; Beth Kluckhohn, Senior Project Manager

Text Designer: Yvo Riezebos, Riezebos Holzbaur Design Group

Photo Manager: Leitha Etheridge-Sims

Photo Researcher: Catherine Schnurr, Pre-PressPMG

Cover Designer: Hahn Luu

Cover Image: collage by Amy Wasserman

For product information and technology assistance, contact us at **Cengage Learning Customer & Sales Support, 1-800-354-9706**

For permission to use material from this text or product, submit all requests online at **www.cengage.com/permissions**. Further permissions questions can be emailed to **permissionrequest@cengage.com**.

Library of Congress Control Number: 2008939814

ISBN-13: 978-1-4130-3067-9

ISBN-10: 1-4130-3067-X

Wadsworth
20 Channel Center Street
Boston, MA 02210
USA

Cengage Learning products are represented in Canada by Nelson Education, Ltd.

For your course and learning solutions, visit **www.cengage.com**.

Purchase any of our products at your local college store or at our preferred online store **www.ichapters.com**.

Printed in Canada
1 2 3 4 5 6 7 12 11 10 09

table of contents

Can we talk? Too often these days, it seems the answer is no. We can yell and point fingers, we can plug our ears and convince ourselves that we're right. But, individually and as a nation, we seem to be losing the ability to discuss difficult issues. So, what can we do? For starters, we can take a brief look back at the rich rhetorical tradition behind argumentation and the vital links between rhetoric, citizenship, and democracy in ancient Greece to better understand where we've gone wrong. Then, we can revive a more constructive definition of "argument" that foregrounds listening and exploring rather than winning at any cost. We'll do all of this to help you understand how mastering the skills of reasoned argument will make you a better writer and communicator in college and beyond.

You probably won't be surprised to hear that the reading you have to do in college will be vastly different from your pleasure reading—and even from most of what you read in high school. And we're not just talking about what you read, but also about how you read it. Your teachers are going to expect you to do something smart with the texts you encounter in college, and this chapter introduces a few strategies that will help you focus your reading for particular kinds of thinking and writing tasks.

Chapter 3: Writing Rhetorically............................ 45

If you think about it, you've been dealing with arguments for most of your life—whether as a target for advertisers or a member of a committee, at home, on the job, or in any number of other situations. Sometimes you read, watch, or listen to these arguments; other times you make them yourself. To help you prepare to write effective arguments, this chapter begins with an overview of related writing tasks that will come in handy in many different writing situations. Next, we examine a handful of important ideas about rhetoric and argumentation from ancient Greece, and then we show you how to apply these concepts to modern ideas and situations—all to get you ready to write your own arguments.

Chapter 4: Genres of Argument 81

As you begin to understand the tradition behind and uses for well-reasoned arguments, you'll also begin to see more clearly the need for rhetorical adaptability and versatility. Think, for example, of the arguments you encounter every day: Some may involve issues of definition and evaluation, others may focus on causes and consequences, while still others may involve questions of policy and procedure. Often, arguments that touch on all of these points swirl around a single issue (freedom of speech, for instance, or abortion). In this chapter, you'll learn to distinguish different types of argumentative claims and how these claims are often intertwined in the arguments you read and write.

PART 2: READINGS FOR WRITING

Chapter 5: Reading and Writing 119

What does it mean to be able to read and write? The authors in this chapter all have plenty to say about literacy and how it is changing. Some bemoan the rapid move away from traditional literacy, rooted in the reading of "Great Books." Others see reading and writing undergoing an evolution, driven by changes in technology and the habits of children and young adults. Whatever their positions, these authors may offer a point of reference as you think about your own reading and writing.

Chapter 6: Defining a Generation 157

Who are the Millennials? Are they mutant narcissists born of the self-esteem rush of the 1990s, nurtured on Facebook, MySpace, and YouTube, and unable or unwilling to care about anything beyond themselves? Or are they self-confident, technologically savvy citizens who have as much passion about the world around them—and more ability to get things done—than any generation before them? As with most complicated questions, the answer lies somewhere in between, according to the readings in this chapter.

Chapter 7: The Heat Is On

"Are humans like frogs in a simmering pot, unaware that temperatures have reached the boiling point?" asks writer Andrew C. Revkin. "Or has global warming been spun into an 'alarmist gale'. . ." The answer is difficult to gauge, given that so much about our relationship with and effects on the environment is up for debate. But one thing is certain, as these readings show: Global warming, ignored for so long by the public and government at all levels, demands our immediate attention.

Chapter 8: Body Images

"If you ever want to make people visibly uncomfortable," writes columnist Wendy Shanker, "say the f-word"—fat—"out loud." Although most experts agree that America has problems with food, weight, and body image, there's less consensus over the nature of these problems, their causes and consequences, and how to deal with them. These essays and articles may help you see the problems in a different light.

Chapter 9: Modern Love . . . and Other Social Studies

Henry Fountain reports in "The Lonely American Just Got a Bit Lonelier" that adults have fewer close relationships than ever. In "Love in the Digital Age," Alice Mathias worries about the effects that technology is having on the ways we interrelate. What's happening here? These and the other pieces in this chapter examine how friendship and love are faring in the 21st century.

Chapter 10: Air Waves 283

The writers in this chapter investigate different kinds of media we consume—what we watch and listen to; why and how we watch and listen to it; and the effect all of this has on us. And while these writers may reach different conclusions, they share a common understanding of the influence that pop culture has in our lives.

Chapter 11: The Arguing "I" 323

The essays in this chapter are proof that writing in the first person—using your own voice and talking about your own experiences—can be a compelling way to present an argument on just about any subject.

table of contents

BY GENRE

Although few essays fit neatly into a single category, we've included this alternate table of contents to help you find examples of texts that incorporate the argumentative genres we cover in Part 1. All of these pieces present arguments in one way or another, but some do so more explicitly than others. As you read the list, keep in mind that many texts contain elements of more than one genre of writing. George Saunders' satirical essay "My Amendment," for example, makes an argument of policy but also deals with issues of definition, evaluation, and cause and effect. Thus, it—like most of the pieces in this book—appears in more than one of the categories below.

Texts That Analyze

Like exploratory writing, analysis involves investigation and explanation. Its ultimate goal, however, is to examine in great detail how and why the subject functions the way it does.

Texts That Address Causal Issues

You'll notice that this category is the largest (with Definitional Issues a close second). That's because, no matter what the genre, argumentative essays often address problems, and problems have causes and effects. Sometimes—as in J. Eric Oliver's "Why We Hate Fat People"—the causal questions are the focus of the argument; just as often, however, the causal issues are secondary.

Texts That Address Definitional Issues

Whether they make explicit definitional arguments—see Wendy Shanker's "From 'fat' to 'Fat'"— or, as is more often the case, make definitional claims as part of larger arguments, these texts deal with definitions in one way or another.

Texts That Address Evaluative Issues

These essays and articles may present straightforward evaluations—see A. O. Scott's review of Iron Man—or may use evaluative claims to support other kinds of arguments, especially policy arguments.

Texts That Explore

Though they may also present arguments—often implicitly—the primary purpose of these texts is to investigate, explain, and explore specific issues. These kinds of essays and articles are common in newspapers and magazines that want to keep readers informed about many different topics.

Texts That Incorporate Humor

In these essays, the authors use one of the most powerful pathetic appeals—humor—to help them make their arguments. In different ways, the authors incorporate humor to make us think about topics we might not otherwise be interested in addressing; to help us see things from different perspectives; or to make talking about difficult issues a little easier.

Personal Narratives

In these essays and articles, the authors use their own experiences and stories to connect with readers. In some pieces, these narratives are part of the evidence the authors present to support their arguments; in others, they serve as a framework on which the essays are built. Whatever strategy the authors use, these essays show how powerful and effective the personal narrative can be in argumentative writing.

Texts That Address Policy Issues

As we explain in Chapter 4, these kinds of essays argue for a course of action to deal with a specific problem. In doing so, they often incorporate definitional, evaluative, and causal claims, as well.

Texts Written by Students

These authors were students—in high school or college—when they wrote these essays. You can find more student writing, completed in response to the questions and assignments we mention throughout Present Tense, on our companion website.

preface

WHY WE WROTE THIS BOOK

The basic argument we make in *Present Tense: Contemporary Themes for Writers* is that composition classes can best serve students by helping them learn how to respond thoughtfully and appropriately to whatever rhetorical situations they encounter. So it seems only fitting, as we think back to the origins of this book, that it was itself a response.

When we were involved, as teachers and administrators, in the University of South Carolina's First-Year English Program, we found that most composition texts dealing with contemporary issues were readers with broad introductions and general discussions of ways to approach various issues. Our experience teaching composition and training graduate teaching assistants showed us that this focus on hot-button issues often produced interesting classroom discussions that made students want to respond. But it did little to teach them how to respond. The result, too often, was frustration—for the students and their teachers. After a great deal of trial and error, practice, and tweaking in our classes at South Carolina and, later, at Louisiana State University, we have responded—with *Present Tense*. And we think our book addresses several common challenges in writing classes:

- Students who don't know what to write about (the rhetoric helps students learn how to engage with topics, while the reader provides a range of perspectives on several important public issues).
- Students who have ideas but don't know how to write about them (the rhetoric teaches them strategies for figuring out what they want to write and the best way to write it).
- Students who don't like to read (the rhetoric is written in a conversational and humorous tone, and the reader includes current texts that are by turns exciting, compelling, and funny).
- Instructors who are intimidated by rhetoric and argument—but who have to teach it to their students (the book foregrounds the accessibility and usefulness of rhetoric and argument).
- The common perception that composition courses have no content (the rhetoric provides students and instructors a classical foundation upon which they can build a course that is truly about writing).

KEY FEATURES

We've designed *Present Tense* as a rhetoric and reader that will provide a brief but thorough grounding in argumentation, analytical reading, and critical thinking to help students become more confident and effective readers and writers. Here's a quick look:

- The Table of Contents walks the reader logically through the story of the book, from the discussion and definitions of argument and rhetoric in Part 1 to the thematic chapters in Part 2.

- The Rhetorical Table of Contents organizes the readings—articles and essays—by genre of argument and rhetorical approach. This will be especially useful when students look for particular kinds of arguments and when teachers design their syllabi.
- Part 1, the concise rhetoric, prepares students to respond effectively and creatively to the reading and writing tasks they will encounter by introducing them to a handful of important rhetorical concepts and giving them a thorough grounding in argumentative writing.
- Part 2, the reader, presents an array of perspectives, ideas, and opinions about some of the most compelling issues of the day.
- Appendix 1 gives students a rhetorically based perspective on doing research and finding, using, and documenting sources in their essays.
- Appendix 2 provides examples of researched papers—an annotated bibliography, an exploratory essay, and a policy argument—written in response to specific assignments.
- The reading and writing apparatus—including head notes, discussion questions, writing prompts, and assignments—will help students figure out how to engage with the texts we present more productively.
- The instructional support material includes an online instructor's manual and other resources (sample syllabi, assignments, and student papers).

WHAT MAKES *PRESENT TENSE* DIFFERENT

In the pages that follow, we begin with classical rhetoric and focus on argument to give students a productive base from which to launch their encounters with the issues that interest them. After trying out a number of different pedagogical approaches, we found this blending of classical rhetoric with modern issues to be the most successful—for our students as writers and for us as teachers. And as we developed this approach in our own classrooms, we came to notice fewer and fewer students who experienced that all-too-familiar frustration of having no idea what to write. It seemed that engaging the modern issues rhetorically proved to be an inventive process. Rather than struggling to decide what topic to propose for a definitional argument, for example, one recent student knew that she wanted to argue about the quiet activism of many members of the so-called "Y Generation."

And while we found that the current issues helped pique students' interest in the power of writing arguments, we also came to see how the grounding in rhetoric provided them with focused and sophisticated ways to enter public discourse. It's not uncommon for composition courses to slip into prolonged discussions of social issues that can turn the class's attention away from writing. But we found that bringing classical theory to bear on modern issues gave our classes a focused trajectory. So, we included the rhetoric in this book to give students and teachers alike an intellectually demanding tradition that can guide intervention into public discourse and allow for thoughtful approaches to important issues. And along the way, we gathered plenty of evidence confirming our belief that learning these approaches will continue to serve students long after their writing courses end.

Perhaps the most important reason for the rhetorical approach in Part 1 of our book is precisely this point: We strongly believe that understanding and practicing the rhetorical approaches outlined by classical rhetoricians help students develop their capacities to respond appropriately to the professional and intellectual situations they will face both in and beyond the college classroom. In short, what we try to provide here is a kind of training in how to assess and respond to rhetorical situations. Students will become accustomed to asking questions such as "Who is the audience?" "How can I appeal to this audience?" "What approach is appropriate for this situation?" And, we hope, students will come to understand that there is no one answer to these questions. Every rhetorical situation is unique, and there is no single way to respond to it. But students can gain practice; they can gain sophistication and prowess in asking and answering these questions as they formulate their responses.

HOW WE CHOSE THE READINGS

Although we felt confident, based on our own classroom hits and misses, developing the pedagogical approach in Part 1, we turned to students and other teachers to help us decide which issues to cover in Part 2. During our time at South Carolina, we were involved in the development and production of four editions of the reader used each year by the 3,000 or so students in English 101. Our mandate was simple: to produce a collection of readings that served the needs of the First-Year English Program's students and teachers better than any other on the market. With that in mind, we set out to create a reader that tapped into the interests of students and teachers; that was topically engaging and up to date; and that gave students the best chance possible to become better and more confident readers, thinkers, and writers.

The first step in doing this was to ask students and teachers what they would like to be reading, thinking, talking, and writing about. In addition to receiving lists of specific topics, articles, and essays, we found—through informal surveys, listserv discussions, and program meetings—that students and teachers alike wanted to engage with issues that had some bearing on their lives. Both groups also liked the idea of being able to bring their own interests and knowledge to the classroom; this gave them a sense of confidence that they said made the teaching and learning experiences more enjoyable and effective. And, finally, we found that controversy was king, especially among students. From this base of responses—and with additional surveys each year—we developed a kind of current-issues database that we continue to update. The result, *Present Tense*, is a collection of readings that we think will spark curiosity and intellectual investigation while providing students with models of the rhetorical approaches outlined in Part 1.

WHY USE THIS BOOK?

We wrote *Present Tense* to help take the mystery—and some of the frustration—out of writing. Make no mistake, we understand that writing is hard work and that becoming a confident and effective writer takes time. Part of our mission in *Present Tense* is to persuade students to put forth that time and effort, and we believe the book will help students by giving them a handful of key rhetorical skills that they can practice in their composition courses, in other classes, and in their personal writing. We also think *Present Tense* is a great book because:

- **It's accessible.** Because we've worked with a lot of writing students and teachers, we know that the study of rhetoric is unfamiliar to most people. Thus, we provide an easy-to-follow introduction to the basic elements of classical rhetoric that we believe will help students bring weight to their writing without bogging them down with dense historical or theoretical instruction.
- **It's current.** Since one of our goals is to give students fresh takes on issues that they care about, most of the essays and articles we've selected are less than five years old, and many were written within the past two years.

- **It's inclusive.** We've worked hard to find a broad range of social, cultural, and political perspectives by a diverse cast of writers.
- **It's cost effective.** We like to think of *Present Tense* as a greatest-hits package: For one affordable price, students get the best of classical rhetoric and current writing on contemporary issues.

ACKNOWLEDGMENTS

We do not exaggerate when we say we owe our greatest debt to our students and fellow teachers at the University of South Carolina and Louisiana State University. There are many others who helped make this book possible, as well: Steve Lynn and Bill Rivers gave us the administrative and professional support we needed; Christy Friend inspired us to keep becoming better teachers; and Elizabeth Smith, John Muckelbauer, Eme Crawford, and Eric Bargeron were simply irreplaceable as colleagues and friends. We also want to thank Lyn Uhl, Publisher; Megan Power, Editorial Assistant; Michael Lepera, Senior Content Project Manager; Mandee Eckersley, Executive Marketing Manager; Jennifer Zourdos, Marketing Manager; Cate Rickard Barr, Senior Art Director; Amy Wasserman, Cover Designer; and the rest of the team at Cengage Learning that helped see this project through. To Beth Kluckhohn, your patience and attention to detail have been extraordinary; thank you for both. And, finally, to our development editor, Laurie Runion: Thank you for everything; this is as much your book as it is ours.

We also wish to thank our helpful reviewers whose insights helped shape this book:

Trela N. Anderson, *Fayetteville State University*
Carlos E. Bolton, *University of Memphis*
Lindsay Lewan, *Arapahoe Community College*
Kathleen Mayberry, *Lehigh Carbon Community College*
Jim McKeown, *McClennan Community College*
Bryan Moore, *Arkansas State University*
Lyle W. Morgan, *Pittsburg State University*
Michael Morris, *Eastfield College*
Laura Raffaelli, *DeAnza College*
Sharrón Eve Sarthou, *University of Mississippi*
Michael J. Schofield, *California State University at Northridge*
Susan Shibe Davis, *Arizona State University*
Anne Stockdell-Giesler, *University of Tampa*
Evert Villarreal, *University of Texas at Pan American*
Carmaletta M. Williams, *Johnson County Community College*

DEDICATION

For our families

a brief rhetoric

arguing america

"Is it possible in America today to convince anyone of anything he doesn't already believe?"

—**Matt Miller,** *"Is Persuasion Dead?"*

"Perhaps one of the hardest things to do these days is to convince people that what they have believed all their lives might be wrong. And it's just as difficult to get people to simply listen to anything or anyone that doesn't support their beliefs."

—**Shirien Elamawy,** *"My Struggle to Share the Light"*

WHERE ARE WE NOW?

Remember those childhood disagreements—over a favorite toy, perhaps, or control of the television remote, or who was cuter or stronger or faster or smarter—that seemed so vital to your existence in the moment but that could be fought and forgotten in a matter of minutes? They usually went something like this, right?

"You had it last time."

"No, I didn't."

"Yes, you did."

"No. I didn't."

"YES. You did!"

"NO. I DID NOT!"

"Shut up!"

"You shut up."

"Jerk."

"Stupid."

"MOM!"

The pattern is worth noting. There's the initial accusation ("You had it last time.") and denial ("No, I didn't."), followed by repetitions of both, just in case one side or the other isn't clear on the positions. Next come the accusation and denial with emphasis (usually indicated by raised voices). Here is usually where frustration starts to set in because either or both sides get the feeling that their original assertions are going nowhere, but both still feel that winning the disagreement is vital. Attempts to cut off the conversation ("Shut up!") are followed by name-calling ("Jerk." "Stupid.") and, finally, by the invocation of a greater authority (in this case, Mom).

Even as children, we quickly learn the futility inherent in this kind of exchange—rarely is anything constructive accomplished. Indeed, more often than not, the most we achieve is the occasional moment of smug self-congratulation when the greater authority (Mom) rules in our favor. Still, for reasons that linger through adulthood, we seem unable to abandon this mode of engagement—or the overwhelming desire to "win" any kind of disagreement at any cost, even the most juvenile of name-calling.

For an even more public example, consider the following excerpt from *The O'Reilly Factor*, a Fox News television program that purports to balance the liberal-leaning tendencies of the mainstream news media. One of the show's guests that day was Jeremy Glick, described by host Bill O'Reilly as an "American who lost his father in the World Trade Center attack" on September 11, 2001, and who later "signed an anti-war advertisement that accused the USA itself of terrorism." The excerpt picks up as Glick is explaining why he signed the ad in question:

Bill O'Reilly: I don't want to debate world politics with you.

Jeremy Glick: Well, why not? This is about world politics.

O'Reilly: Because, Number 1, I don't really care what you think.

Glick: Well, OK.

The exchange deteriorates rapidly as Glick tries to accuse O'Reilly of using the terrorist attacks as a means to justify "everything from domestic plunder to imperialistic aggression." O'Reilly, for his part, does everything he can to keep his guest from completing a sentence, shouting Glick down and cutting him off at every turn. Finally, after Glick claims that O'Reilly uses "the 9/11 families" in the same fashion, the host snaps back:

O'Reilly: That's a bunch of crap. I've done more for the 9/11 families by their own admission—I've done more for them than you will ever hope to do.

Glick: OK.

O'Reilly: So you keep your mouth shut when you sit here exploiting those people.

Although the pattern of exchange between O'Reilly and Glick has evolved some from the classic childhood spat, it—like so much other public discourse today—starts to sound remarkably like a couple of kids bickering after a few lines. Notice the accusatory and aggressive tone, the jockeying for control, and, above all, the unwillingness to listen (not just O'Reilly's admission that "I don't really care what you think," but also the constant interruptions by both speakers). And while O'Reilly and Glick managed to avoid that most juvenile of argument strategies—name-calling—things do often get personal during this type of public discourse. O'Reilly himself famously called one guest a "vicious son of a bitch" (he apologized almost immediately), while author and Air America radio host Al Franken titled one book *Lies and the Lying Liars Who Tell Them: A Fair and Balanced Look at the Right* and another *Rush Limbaugh Is a Big, Fat Idiot.* Columnist Ann Coulter, among the most distinct voices in the cacophonous world of public punditry, is also among the most frequent name-callers: She has listed among the traits of Democrats "incessant lying, utter shamelessness, criminal behavior and lots of crying"; has called the Democratic party "Spawn of Satan"; and has said that, in addition to being "stupid," most journalists "are also catty, lazy, vengeful and humorless."

Make no mistake: This is not simply a case of political discourse run amok. We, as a country and individually, have begun to argue like this on many issues, from sports and entertainment, to same-sex marriage, immigration reform, and the best way to teach biology. Some of the most divisive and mean-spirited public debates have their roots in strongly held personal beliefs. And, as Shirien Elamawy, a student at Louisiana State University who is quoted at the beginning of this chapter, discovered (and shares in an essay on page 18), asking people to set their beliefs aside long enough to listen to other points of view can be a difficult—and painful—undertaking. Why? In large part because of the expanding reach of talk radio and TV, of online journals and blogs, and even of more traditional partisan publications such as books and newspapers. While these media have helped to democratize public discourse—by, for example, giving anyone with a laptop and a modem a voice and the means to transmit it to thousands, if not millions, of others—they also have changed the nature of our exchanges. These media and the people who dominate them have popularized the personal attack, made being right a cultural imperative, and turned not listening into a badge of honor (as Elamawy puts it in her essay, about her efforts to enlighten readers about Islam: many people "would rather hear what they *assumed* to be true…than the truth itself"). The result: These most distinctive—and dangerous—characteristics of what sociolinguist Deborah Tannen calls "the argument culture" now define the way we deal with doubt, indecision, and disagreement in much of our public discourse.

Where does that leave us? How about with the question columnist and radio host Matt Miller asks at the start of this chapter (his complete essay starts on page 16): "Is it possible in America today to convince anyone of anything he doesn't already believe?" If we take into consideration Miller's hyperbole—he's exaggerating to make a point—and consider that the answer might be "no," we could ask another question: How did we become so locked in to our positions that we can't talk about our differences constructively? Trying to answer that one might help us find a way to start a more civil and productive conversation. And who knows where that could lead.

HOW DID WE GET HERE?

"Liberals simply refuse to consider thoughts that would interfere with their lemming-like groupthink. They hold their hands over their ears like little children who don't want to listen to mother."

—Ann Coulter, *"Liberal Arguments: Still a Quagmire"*

"The members of the right-wing media are not interested in conveying the truth. That's not what they are for. They are an indispensable component of the right-wing machine that has taken over our country."

—Al Franken, *Lies and the Lying Liars Who Tell Them*

Assigning blame for our growing inability to discuss difficult issues and to work toward common goals is easy because, no matter what our political leanings, convenient scapegoats abound: the far right and the radical left; the conservative media and the liberal press; talk radio and trash TV; rock 'n' roll, pop, rap, and hip-hop; public schools, colleges, and universities; the courts, Congress, and the White House; and, finally, everybody's favorite punching bag, Hollywood. But what does all this finger-pointing get us? Nothing more, really, than a familiar list of easy targets, none of which could possibly be responsible alone. Think about it:

- Are Ann Coulter, Al Franken, and their partisan-pundit cohorts to blame for the dysfunctional way we engage over public issues? To a degree, perhaps, just as the entertainment media have a hand in popularizing trends in dress, language, and behavior, especially among teenagers and young adults.
- Are video games, movies, TV, and music responsible for teaching young people that aggression—even outright violence—is an acceptable way to settle disagreements? Again, maybe they are, to a certain extent. But wasn't the world violent long before the electronic age?
- Are our school systems and universities failing to do their jobs? The answer depends on what we think their jobs are, and we seem to have a hard time agreeing on that.
- What about our lawmakers? Can we dump our problems at their feet? We do this all the time, but that rarely brings any solutions, only the occasional election-year shakeup.

What makes these targets so convenient—so comforting, even—and ultimately so unhelpful is an odd combination of their familiarity and distance. At the very least, we're all aware of these people, industries, and institutions. We watch TV and movies, listen to the radio, and follow the news in print or online, just as we've been exposed to education, to political campaigns, and to public debates. The extent to which each of us engages in or with any of these sources of information and knowledge varies greatly, of course. But it's nearly impossible to avoid them. And when things go wrong in the public eye—when a student opens fire at a high school, when a corporation sinks under the weight of executive corruption, or when people scream at each other on TV about the best way to deal with immigration issues—we find it hard not to look immediately to these usual suspects for someone or something to blame.

Why do we do this? Not simply because government at all levels and media of various kinds are so prevalent and familiar, but also because they are so vast, so remote, that they make blame without accountability easy. Think about it this way: If you wanted to file a complaint about "the media" or "Hollywood" or "education," where could you go? Whom could you see? Whose job would be on the line if you pressed your case? There are no easy answers because public institutions and bureaucracies aren't monolithic entities with a boss of bosses at the top. We can't get "Hollywood" to do anything because there is no "Hollywood." Instead, there are thousands of people involved in the entertainment industry,

Mario Tama/Getty Images

FIGURE 1-1

In this photo from January 2007, protesters on both sides face off in New York City on the occasion of the 3,000th U.S. military death in the war in Iraq. The war remains one of the most polarizing issues in the United States—and one of the most difficult to talk about because of the strong feelings on all sides. Note how the sign in the photo—"Warning: Leftist protestors are trying to demoralize our troops"—labels those who are against the war without allowing for any kind of discussion of the issue. On the other hand, can you see how the photo itself does something similar to the woman supporting the troops? How does the image "label" the woman? Argument, in its classical sense, can offer a way out of our unproductive pattern of public discourse.

all of them making decisions every day. Trying to get just some of them to focus on an issue such as the prevalence of sexualized violence against women on TV seems like so much more trouble than just blaming "Hollywood" on a blog or in a letter to the editor and moving on. And maybe we feel comfortable implicating institutions and bureaucracies because, no matter how close they are *to* us, they are not *of* us. They are always something bigger and more powerful than we are, which means that we—individually—are never to blame. Although this kind of finger-pointing might make us feel better for a while, the root problems almost always remain for two reasons: First, those of us looking for someone to blame usually call it quits after settling on a culprit; and, second, those we blame rarely have the impetus or ability to bring about change by themselves.

So, back to our original question: How did we get here—how did we get to the point where we have trouble talking about and trying to solve even our most pressing problems? One self-described angry blogger—fed up, frustrated, and "insane with rage and grief" because of the general state of the world—put it this way: "Powerlessness. This is born of powerlessness." Maryscott O'Connor, who runs a Web site called My Left Wing, told the *Washington Post* that she "was not like this before. I was riddled with empathy for everyone suffering in the world. Classic bleeding-heart liberal." Then, according to the *Post* article:

> George W. Bush was elected. Then came 9/11, Afghanistan, Iraq, Guantanamo Bay, Abu Ghraib, the Patriot Act, secret prisons, domestic eavesdropping, the revamping of the Supreme Court, and the thought "It has come to the point where the worst people on Earth are running the Earth." And now, "I have become one of those people with all the bumper stickers on their car," [O'Connor said].

The powerlessness O'Connor speaks of, and the anger and vitriol it has produced, is hard to miss for anyone who spends time scrolling through blogs and bulletin boards online. And it isn't limited to sites that tilt left of center: There are likely just as many—if not more—frustrated conservatives out there pounding out angry articles, columns, and postings (check out www.Townhall.com for scores of examples).

Does this mean that we can add the Internet to our list of scapegoats? No. Cyberspace is just the latest setting in our long-running national melodrama (some might call it a tragicomedy instead). To try to figure out how we got into this predicament—in the hope of finding a way out—we have to start by looking at ourselves. Somewhere along the way, many of us seem to have given up and given in: given up on the idea that what we think and say and do as individuals matters, and given in to the lure of convenient, self-serving outlets for our frustration, impatience, and anger. We stopped listening and started shouting, and the resulting din seems nearly impenetrable. But it's not. And argument is one tool we can use to break through.

WHY ARGUMENT MATTERS

"The aim of argument, or of discussion, should not be victory, but progress."

—Joseph Joubert, *18th century French philosopher and essayist*

"Extremists and ideological purists on either side of the political aisle condemn compromise. But inflexibility either creates deadlock or dooms a cause to irrelevance."

—John P. Avlon, *Independent Nation*

In short, argument matters because it offers a productive alternative to the name-calling, mud-slinging, win-at-any cost approach that has come to dominate public discourse in America. But before we explore how argument can do this, we should look back at the roots of argumentation—how it was conceived of as a constructive tool for decision making—and be clear about what we mean by "argument." Think of it this way: defining is a vital early step on the way to understanding. So, to understand why argument matters—why you should care enough to learn how it works (and doesn't work) and what it can achieve—we should settle on a basic definition of the term. Keep in mind, though, that definitions evolve and that the meaning of argument outlined over the next few pages isn't necessarily universal. It is, however, a definition common to writing classes, with its roots in Classical rhetoric (more on that in Chapters 2 and 3). The definition is also particularly useful in learning how to analyze arguments presented by others and how to compose effective arguments of your own.

Before we get to our definition, however, let's take a quick look back. The study and practice of argument is nothing new: The ancient art of persuasion and argument, now called Classical rhetoric, developed alongside the birth of democracy in the fifth and fourth centuries B.C.E. in the Greek city-state of Athens. Just as we can use argument to help us reach consensus on divisive political issues and to help us make decisions about the personal questions that define our lives, Classical rhetoric helped Athenian citizens settle disputes and decide on important policy matters some 2,500 years ago.

You might have read about the invention of Athenian democracy in one of your history courses, but you may not have considered the way public discourse informed and defined the day-to-day business of Athens' democratic government. Persuasion was integral to the citizens of ancient Athens because of the *direct* nature of their democracy. Unlike our modernized form of this type of government, which relies on elected representatives to vote on policy, Athenian democracy held that every citizen had the right—indeed, the responsibility—to debate and decide on the policies of the state. All citizens were encouraged to attend meetings of the Assembly, the most important decision-making body in Athens, and they could raise and discuss with their peers any issue that concerned them. Because it was up to each citizen to define the terms of issues, to attempt to persuade his peers which courses of action were just, and finally, to vote on those issues, public speech was the single most important skill a citizen needed to gain prominence in the community. No matter what his class or economic status, any citizen who could capture the imagination of his peers had the power to influence Athenian society.

Though this was a remarkable system—indeed, unheard of in its time—it is important to remember that it was not a social utopia. Athens narrowly defined the parameters of citizenship, meaning that no woman, slave, or resident alien was allowed to participate in democratic affairs. While acknowledging the social inequities that underscored Athenian culture, we can still recognize the power of persuasion in ancient democracy, and we can look to the strategies used by Athenian citizens for crafting powerful arguments to help us in our modern rhetorical situations. And while Classical rhetoric may seem a bit dusty and old-fashioned, what it has to offer modern practitioners of argument is a set of theories and practices that teach us the capacity to respond, in any given case, with the best possible means of persuasion. You'll read more about these theories and practices—and put them to work—in later chapters. For now, what we'll take from Classical rhetoric is the root of our definition of "argument."

What Argument Is Not

As you'll read in Chapter 4, one of the most effective ways to define something—to determine what the thing *is*—is to start by establishing what it is *not*. This is especially true for terms and concepts that we feel are frequently misused or misunderstood, and argument certainly fits that criterion. With that in mind, let's explore a few characteristics that, despite their popular association with the term, don't fit the definition of argument we'll be using in this book.

Argument Is Not Simply about Winning

Bugs Bunny: Say, Doc. Are you trying to get in trouble with the law? This ain't rabbit hunting season.

Elmer Fudd: It's not?

Bugs: No, it's duck hunting season.

Daffy Duck: That, sir, is an unmitigated fabrication. It's rabbit season.

Bugs: Duck season.

Daffy: Rabbit season.

Bugs: Duck season.

Daffy: Rabbit season.

Bugs: Duck season.

Daffy: Rabbit season.

Bugs: Rabbit season.

Daffy: Duck season.

Bugs: Rabbit season.

Daffy: I say it's duck season . . . and I say fire!

If you're familiar with the classic Merry Melodies cartoon "Rabbit Fire," you know what happens next (even if you're not, you can probably guess): Elmer follows Daffy's command and blows the duck's beak to the opposite side of his face. Daffy shakes off the "wound" and starts the debate anew. Although his perseverance is admirable, and despite his unshakable desire to prove himself correct, Daffy never accomplishes much. Why? A couple of reasons stand out:

First, Daffy and Bugs are having a disagreement over what essentially is a fact: It is either duck season, rabbit season, both, or neither. Were Elmer to pursue the matter with the proper authorities—the Merry Melodies Game and Fishing Commission, for example—he could find out for sure (but that would be about as funny as a social studies film strip). In short, they are debating a question ("What season is it?") that isn't debatable because there is a definitive answer. This leads directly to Reason No. 2: Because there's no room for informed and supportable opinion in this disagreement, the goal for both sides is simply to win. This desire to prevail drives Bugs to trickery (notice how he switches his response to confuse Daffy in the fourth line from the end) and leads Daffy to one humiliation (and shotgun blast) after another. Again, despite investments of time, energy, and emotion, the participants accomplish little. *

Does that make wanting to win wrong? Of course not. But engaging in discussion, debate, or argument with nothing but winning in mind is a problem. It can lead us to do things we know to be unethical (such as trick or attack our opponents), to take positions we don't really believe in, or to ignore good ideas simply because they don't agree with our own. As essayist and commentator John P. Avlon points out in his book *Independent Nation*, this win-at-any-cost attitude also can produce a kind of inflexibility that "either creates deadlock or dooms a cause to irrelevance." Although the drive to triumph over an opponent—or to feel like we've proven ourselves right—can produce a momentary emotional rush, it also can shut down serious discussion and prevent action on issues that desperately need attention.

Abortion is a good example of this process and its consequences. Few other issues so sharply—and immediately—divide our nation, and few have proven so polarizing for so long. Because of this, and because the loudest voices representing the most entrenched positions on both sides are determined to win the debate, serious problems at the core of the issue get far less attention than they should. For more than three decades now, winning this debate has meant one of two things: banning abortion or keeping abortion legal. But what about the related issues of preventing unwanted pregnancies, of sex and health education, and of health care for women (especially those who live below the poverty line)? Unfortunately, those voices on the extremes of the abortion debate, in their unrelenting drive to win, often drown out conversations about these other important issues.

As the French philosopher Joseph Joubert writes in the quotation that opens this section, "The aim of argument, or of discussion, should not be victory, but progress." To achieve this progress, we have to see argument as more than a contest with winners and losers. Otherwise, we could end up spending all our time shouting "Duck season" and "Rabbit season" across the room at each other.

Argument Is Not an Exercise in Knee-jerk Contradiction

Man: An argument isn't just contradiction.

Mr. Vibrating: It can be.

Man: No, it can't. An argument is a connected series of statements intended to establish a proposition.

Mr. Vibrating: No, it isn't.

Man: Yes, it is! It's not just contradiction.

Mr. Vibrating: Look, if I argue with you, I must take up a contrary position.

Man: Yes, but that's not just saying "No, it isn't."

Mr. Vibrating: Yes, it is!

Man: No, it isn't! Argument is an intellectual process. Contradiction is just the automatic gainsaying of any statement the other person makes.

(short pause)

Mr. Vibrating: No, it isn't.

—Monty Python, *"The Argument Clinic"*

In this skit by the groundbreaking comedy troupe Monty Python, Michael Palin plays a man looking for a good argument. As a staff member at the Argument Clinic, John Cleese, playing Mr. Vibrating, does his best (or worst) to satisfy his client. Given the state of public discussion that dominates the airwaves today, the old saying "it's funny because it's true" feels especially apt. TV, radio, and the Internet are full of people like Mr. Vibrating who seem to think that the best (or only) way to make an argument is to contradict or disagree with someone else. While this certainly is an easy way to construct an air of opposition, and perhaps even to lead some to believe that a dialogue is taking place, little of note is rarely said and even less accomplished. Yes, argument frequently involves people who hold opposing views and divergent beliefs, but the issues at stake are often far too complex to be boiled down to a "yes, it is"/"no, it isn't" type of exchange. Constructive discussions require more nuanced thinking and more willingness to listen.

Argument Is Not a Means for Personal Attack

"I wrote a book about her [Hillary Rodham Clinton] more than four years ago. . . . What I concluded was that Mrs. Clinton was an unusually cynical leftist political operative who had no great respect for the citizens of the United States or for America itself, but who saw our country as a platform for her core ambitions: to rise and achieve historic personal and political power both with her husband and without him."

—Peggy Noonan, *"Where Are They Now?"*

In the 1972 film *The Godfather*, as Michael Corleone tries to persuade his older brother, Sonny, to allow him to retaliate for an attempted hit on their father, Michael utters what has become a classic line: "It's not personal, Sonny. It's strictly business." Of course, the business Michael speaks of couldn't be more personal: He wants to kill the men he blames for arranging the assassination attempt on his father. Whether Michael wants to admit it or not, the business and the personal are, in this case, impossible to separate.

We can often find the same kind of entanglement in the world of public discourse (though, thankfully, without all the violence). We tend to link issues and ideas with the people who espouse them—think Al Gore and global warming; James Dobson and family values; or the Dixie Chicks and the anti-Bush, anti-war movement. And when we disagree with a position, we sometimes attack the people linked to it, rather than the position itself. The business, in other words, becomes personal. The goal of these *ad hominem* (Latin for "to the man") attacks is to divert attention from the issues at hand—usually because the writers or speakers expect to have little success engaging in more civil discussion—by chipping away at the character of people linked to the issues. Natalie Maines, lead singer of the Dixie Chicks, used a mild ad hominem attack when she said in 2003, as President Bush was preparing to send troops to Iraq, that the band was "ashamed the president of the United States is from Texas." Rather than address the question of whether a U.S. invasion of Iraq was an appropriate response to the terror attack of September 11, 2001, Maines took aim at Bush personally. In response, critics of the Dixie Chicks launched a wave of their own personal attacks, questioning the band's patriotism and integrity. Even though the flap got lots of media attention, there was little constructive conversation about the core issue.

Why? Because personal attacks nearly always squelch any possibility of well-reasoned discussion and often make readers and listeners turn away in disgust. One attack brings on another, and anyone without a direct stake in the mudslinging usually tunes out. In her quotation that opens this section, for example, columnist Peggy Noonan practically precludes the possibility of a dispassionate discussion of Hillary Rodham Clinton's political career by labeling her subject a power-hungry, "cynical leftist political operative." In the space of a few words, Noonan renders her argument ineffective against anyone who doesn't already agree with her. She lets the business of presenting a case against Clinton get personal, making her piece a diatribe rather than an argument. And diatribes, because they polarize rather than build consensus, rarely help advance productive public discussions of difficult issues.

Argument Is Not All about You

"Your Business is to shine; therefore you must by all means prevent the shining of others, for their Brightness may make yours the less distinguish'd. To this End,

"If possible engross the whole Discourse; and when other Matter fails, talk much of your-self, your Education, your Knowledge, your Circumstances, your Successes in Business, your Victories in Disputes, your own wise Sayings and Observations on particular Occasions, &c. &c. &c. . . ."

—Benjamin Franklin, *"Rules for Making Oneself a Disagreeable Companion"*

Although argument isn't the subject of Benjamin Franklin's satirical "Rules for Making Oneself a Disagreeable Companion," the "advice" quoted above is relevant. Unfortunately, it's not too hard to find writers and commentators who, in addressing various issues, can't seem to stop talking about themselves. This is especially true when speakers or writers have expertise in a field (politics, for example, or sports) and feel that they have to remind the audience of that expertise frequently. Although often obnoxious and rarely informative, these cases are relatively harmless. More dangerous to the cause of productive public discourse are those who focus on themselves to, as Franklin puts it, "prevent the shining of others" or to shut down the genuine exchange of ideas. These people use their power as writers and talk-show hosts to steer discussion constantly back to themselves so that they always have the final word. What results is less a conversation than a monologue peppered with just enough "opposing viewpoints" to give the proceedings a whiff of fairness and balance.

What Argument Is

Okay, we've established a few important things that argument is *not*:

- Argument is not always a contest to be won.
- It's not an exercise in contradiction for contradiction's sake.
- It's not a means for personal attack.
- And it's not an opportunity for you, the writer, to show off or engage in self-promotion.

Now, let's consider what argument *is*. As we'll explore further in Chapters 2 and 3, our ideas about argument descend directly from the ancient Greek philosopher Aristotle's definition of rhetoric as "the faculty of observing in any given case the available means of persuasion." Notice that Aristotle didn't boil it down to a simple equation (rhetoric = persuasion). Instead, a significant element of the definition involves finding the best way to persuade, given the situation at hand. With that in mind, we'll think of argument as both a process and a product. If you're using this textbook, you're probably going to have to write a few argumentative essays before your course is over, and argument encompasses all those things you'll do as you think about and then actually produce your essays, as well as the essays themselves. In other words, you'll use argument to write arguments.

Although these two elements of our definition are tightly intertwined, it might help to think of them separately for a moment. As a process, argument involves exploration, analysis, synthesis, and composition, not always in that order and never in isolation:

- **Exploration** includes all those things we do as we think about issues and start to form (or reconsider) opinions, among them reading, talking, listening, researching, and thinking. The sources we use in this stage may vary widely, from TV and radio; to newspapers and magazines; to Web sites and blogs; to parents, friends, and classmates. The more open we are to the information we encounter—the better we listen before drawing conclusions, in other words—the richer our explorations will be.

- **Analysis**—the careful examination of a subject and its constituent elements—begins as we think critically about the information we encounter during exploration. If we come across an editorial on the use of steroids in sports, for example, we might look carefully at the source of the piece, its purpose and intended audience, the support it provides for its assertions, and its style and tone. This will help us decide what to do with the information the editorial provides.
- **Synthesis** is the process we use to pull together strands of information—data, reportage, opinion, anecdotes—from the various sources we encounter and analyze so that we can start to weave them into something new (in the classroom, this usually involves research and proper documentation). Sometimes, the result will prove so useful and exciting that we'll want to turn it into something more formal.
- **Composition**—the act of fashioning or creating—is the stage at which we transform argument as process into a product by turning our attention from accumulating information and knowledge to doing something with it. The result can be anything from a photo to a film, an advertisement to an editorial, or a campaign slogan to a song. But because our focus is written texts, we'll take composing to mean just about any step that leads toward a polished written essay—note taking, idea mapping, outlining, drafting, revising, and anything in between.

As a product, we'll define argument as a text, composed with a specific purpose and a particular audience in mind, that asserts and supports an informed position and provides ample reason for readers to, at the very least, take the position into consideration. Some writers, of course, will want to do more than that with their arguments: They'll want to challenge—even sway—the audience's beliefs or move them to action. Those who are successful will be rooted in the process of argument, having encountered an array of information and considered a range of opinions before staking out their own positions.

In short, then, argument is a process of exploring issues from many perspectives and of gathering and analyzing information and knowledge, with the goal of producing texts designed to inform or persuade. The essays you're likely to write—and many of those you'll read in this textbook—will be the products of this process.

WHAT YOU CAN DO

"Difficult questions should not be met with silence or slogans; they should be met with speech, speech and more speech."

—Anna Quindlen, *"Life Begins at Conversation"*

If you're reading this textbook, you're already on your way to doing something. At a minimum, you're trying to understand argument as a tool you can use to help change the way we talk about issues—especially controversial issues—in this country. To get there, as you work your way through the following chapters and begin composing arguments of your own, you can:

- Listen, with an open mind, especially to those with whom you disagree.
- Keep up with the world around you.
- Ask questions, especially when everyone seems to be in agreement.
- Read books, newspapers, magazines, blogs, posts, whatever.
- Write questions, answers, lists, ideas, drafts.
- Think.
- Act.

ARGUMENT IN ACTION

The texts that follow offer three perspectives on the need for public commitment to argument and persuasion in their most constructive forms—as decision-making processes that rely as much on listening as on speaking or writing. The first piece is by an Athenian teacher of rhetoric named Isocrates, who lived in the fifth century B.C.E. and who saw it as his duty to use education—specifically rhetorical education—to produce virtuous and capable citizens. The excerpt, from a text Isocrates wrote about the situation in Athens after a rebellion by some of its allies, is notable for our purposes because, in it, the great teacher instructs his audience on the importance of getting sound advice and of engaging in earnest deliberation when deciding on a course of action. Notice, too, the relevance of the topic—whether to choose war over peace—and the focus on how that choice should be made.

FROM *ON THE PEACE*

[1] All who come before you are accustomed to say that the matters they are about to advise you on are the most important and most worth the city's attention. Nonetheless, even if one might fittingly say this as a preface in some other situations, it seems right for me to begin my treatment of the present situation in just this way. For we have gathered in the Assembly to discuss war and peace; these matters have the greatest effect on human life, and people who plan well must necessarily do better than others. Such is the importance of the question about which we have come together.

[2] I see that you do not listen to speakers equally. You pay attention to some but cannot even endure the voice of others. That you do this is not surprising, for in the past you usually rejected all speakers except those who gave advice that matched your own desires. Someone could rightly fault you for this, since even though you know that many great homes have been ruined by flatterers and you hate those who practice this art in private matters, you do not feel the same way about them in public affairs, where, despite condemning those who welcome such men and enjoy their company, you yourselves clearly trust them more than the rest of the citizens. Indeed, you have made speakers practice and study not what will help the state but how they might say what pleases you. And even now, most of them have rushed to speak such words, for it is clear to everyone that you will be more pleased by those who urge you to war than those who recommend peace. Those who urge war lead you to expect that we will regain the property we had in other cities and recover the power we had before, whereas those who counsel peace offer nothing of the sort; they say rather that we must live in peace and not desire more than justice allows but be content with what we have at present, which is the most difficult thing of all for most people. We depend so much on our hopes and are so greedy for what seems advantageous that even those with the greatest wealth are not willing to be content with that, but in their desire for more they always risk what they now have. We too ought to fear getting caught up in such foolish thinking. For some seem to me to be excessively eager for war, as if they had gotten advice not from ordinary advisors but from the gods themselves that we will set everything right and will easily conquer our enemies.

³ Intelligent people should not deliberate about what they already know—that is a waste of time—but should do what they have decided; and when they deliberate about something, they should not assume that they know what will happen, but they should think about such matters aware that they are relying on their best judgment and that the future depends on chance. You are doing neither of these things but are behaving with as much confusion as possible. You came into the Assembly on the pretext that it was necessary to choose the best of all that was recommended, but as if you already know what needs to be done, you are not willing to listen to anyone except to those who say what pleases you.

Indeed, if you really want to find out what is most advantageous to the city, you should pay attention to those who oppose your views more than those who favor them, for you know that some of those who come here can easily trick you by telling you what you want to hear (for what is spoken to please you clouds your ability to see what is best), but you would have no such experience from advisors who are not seeking to please you, for there is no way they could persuade you unless they make the advantages clear. And besides this, how could anyone either judge well about the past or plan well about the future unless he sets out the arguments on both sides and then examines them both equally?

In the next essay, Matt Miller, a senior fellow at the progressive think tank Center for American Progress and the author of *The 2 Percent Solution*, picks up on some of the same themes as Isocrates, wondering about the high cost of our growing inability to engage in true argument and persuasion. Miller wrote this essay for the June 4, 2005, edition of the *New York Times*.

IS PERSUASION DEAD?

By Matt Miller

¹ Speaking just between us—between one who writes columns and those who read them—I've had this nagging question about the whole enterprise we're engaged in.

² Is persuasion dead? And if so, does it matter?

³ The significance of this query goes beyond the feelings of futility I'll suffer if it turns out I've wasted my life on work that is useless. This is bigger than one writer's insecurities. Is it possible in America today to convince anyone of anything he doesn't already believe? If so, are there enough places

where this mingling of minds occurs to sustain a democracy?

⁴ The signs are not good. Ninety percent of political conversation amounts to dueling "talking points." Best-selling books reinforce what folks thought when they bought them. Talk radio and opinion journals preach to the converted. Let's face it: the purpose of most political speech is not to persuade but to win, be it power, ratings, celebrity or even cash.

⁵ By contrast, marshaling a case to persuade those who start from a different

position is a lost art. Honoring what's right in the other side's argument seems a superfluous thing that can only cause trouble, like an appendix. Politicos huddle with like-minded souls in opinion cocoons that seem impervious to facts.

6 The politicians and the press didn't kill off persuasion intentionally, of course; it's more manslaughter than murder. Persuasion just isn't relevant to delivering elections or eyeballs. Polls have figured out that to get votes you don't need to change minds. Even when they want to, modern media make it hard. They give officials seconds to make their point, ignore their ideas in favor of their poll numbers or showcase a clash of caricatures, believing this is the only way to make "debate" entertaining. Elections may turn on emotions like hope and fear anyway, but with persuasion's passing, there's no alternative.

7 There's only one problem: governing successfully requires influencing how people actually think. Yet when the habits of persuasion have been buried, the possibilities of leadership are interred as well. That's why Bill Clinton's case on health care could be bested by savage "Harry and Louise" ads. And why, even if George Bush's Social Security plan had been well conceived, the odds were always stacked against ambitious reform.

8 I'm not the only one who amid this mess wonders if he shouldn't be looking at another line of work. A top conservative thinker called recently, dejected at the sight of Ann Coulter on the cover of *Time*. What's the point of being substantive, he cried, when all the attention goes to the shrill?

9 But the embarrassing truth is that we earnest chin-strokers often get it wrong anyway. Take me. I hadn't thought much about Iraq before I read Ken Pollack's book, *The Threatening Storm: The Case for Invading Iraq*, a platonic ideal of careful analysis meant to persuade. It worked. I was persuaded! So what should we conclude when a talent like Pollack can convince us—and then the whole thing turns out to be based on a premise (W.M.D.) that is false?

10 If serious efforts to get it right can lead to tragic errors, why care about a culture of persuasion at all? On one level, everyone needs a good rationalization at the core of his professional life; mine holds that the struggle to think things through, even when we fail, is redeeming.

11 But beyond this, the gap between the cartoon of public life that the press and political establishment often serve up and the pragmatic open-mindedness of most Americans explains why so many people tune out—and how we might get them to tune back in. Alienation is the only intelligent response to a political culture that insults our intelligence.

12 The resurrection of persuasion will not be easy. Politicians who've learned to survive in an unforgiving environment may not feel safe with a less scripted style. Mass media outlets where heat has always sold more than light may not believe that creatively engaging on substance can expand their audience. But if you believe that meeting our collective challenges requires greater collective understanding, we've got to persuade these folks to try.

13 I'm guessing Ann Coulter isn't sweating this stuff. God willing, there's something else keeping her up nights. In the meantime, like Sisyphus, those who seek a better public life have to keep rolling the rock uphill. If you've read this far, maybe you're up for the climb, too.

In this next essay, written in 2007, Shirien Elamawy, a student journalist at Louisiana State University, explores the personal risks of acting publicly and presents a compelling case for the need for listening, especially in discourse about difficult issues.

MY STRUGGLE TO SHARE THE LIGHT

By Shirien Elamawy

[1] A solar eclipse has slowly been creeping across America for almost seven years now, and the ensuing darkness is leaving some people cold and bitter.

* * *

[2] It is April 2006, and I'm walking to class at Louisiana State University; I decide pick up our campus paper, *The Daily Reveille*, just like every other day. The first section I always turn to is Op-Ed, which my high school principal justifiably called "the real estate of the paper." When I open to the section, a cartoon catches my eye: Iranian President Mahmoud Ahmadinejad is sitting in a laundromat waiting for his brain to finish being "washed." Seems like a normal political cartoon. But then I look more closely and realize that the detergent box has the word "Quran" on it.

[3] I am furious. I'll be the first to admit the Iranian president may be a little wacko, but to suggest that his views are based on some sort of brainwashing from the Quran is unacceptable. And, as I would soon discover, such thinking displays an even greater ignorance about Islam than I had imagined.

[4] I go to the newsroom demanding to speak to the cartoonist. He is unavailable so I find the editor-in-chief and complain to him. (This isn't the first time Muslims have complained to the paper for its utter disrespect and ignorance of Islam. We are, in fact, just as sick of going to complain as the staff are of seeing us in their office.) The editor-in-chief suggests that I apply to write for the paper to make sure that this type of thing doesn't happen again. I am happy to apply; after all, I am a Mass Communications major.

* * *

[5] I started writing opinion columns that fall semester, following my annual summer trip to Egypt. I've always dreamed of trying to make a difference wherever I would live, and what better way of doing this than guiding people—from the darkness of ignorance to the light of true knowledge. I wrote about Islam, trying to convince readers that what they know about Islam is most likely wrong or misunderstood. What they were seeing in the media did not represent the true teachings of Islam. I covered everything from the misconception that Muslim women are oppressed to the mistaken belief that Islam is a tyrannical and violent religion.

[6] It was the biggest jihad—or struggle—I had ever dealt with publicly. (Yes, in Arabic *jihad* means "struggle" . . . see what I mean?) I knew I would have some people who would be really prejudiced against me, but nothing prepared me for what I would encounter. It's a phase I like to call "Bring on the hate mail." I have a folder in my email inbox specifically labeled as such. And why wouldn't people be angry? I basically told them that all their predispositions about Muslims were false and that they had been lied to and manipulated for years by politicians, the media, and some religious leaders determined to further their own agendas. They would rather hear what Islam is from a news reporter who had never opened a Quran in his life than from one living her life according to the message inside the book.

They would rather hear what they *assumed* to be true about Islam than the truth itself.

7 The worst of the hate messages were spurred by anti-Islamic websites like Jihad Watch <www.jihadwatch.com>, run by Robert Spencer, and the media empire run by evangelical preacher Pat Robertson. People "inspired" by the likes of Spencer, Robertson, and others would visit the online version of *The Daily Reveille* <www.lsureveille.com> and post their hateful comments. These were the people left cold and bitter by the darkness of their ignorance. I got scores of anti-Islamic comments—up to 150 at one point—under my columns telling me to "go back to an Islamic country" (I was born and raised here in the United States). I was accused of lying to readers about certain elements of Islam by people who knew nothing of the religion, other than what they had heard or read from people like Spencer and Robertson. These comments hurt. But at least most of them came from a distance.

8 Then there was Kortnie—the one known in the newsroom as "Crazy Woman." This was someone who stalked me because she could not stand the fact that I was explaining to people that Muslim women are not oppressed, that we choose to dress according to the Islamic dress code, and that our male relatives don't and can't force us to do this. Kortnie was a feminist, and she had this special nickname for me that she used in all of her emails. She called me "Burqa," the garment some Muslim women choose to wear (most commonly in Afghanistan), and, to her, a symbol of oppression. Here is an excerpt from one of her emails:

> Hey "Mustafa," - Go back to Iran, Loser! Are you aware, Burqa, that Muslim males in Islamic countries rape girls and women ALL THE TIME AND THEY HAVE NO CONSEQUENCES TO PAY? Are you aware of that fact that EVERYONE KNOWS, Burqa? Ask your LSU Daddy - he knows. Truly, you need to leave the US and go live in an Islamic country. You're a

> traitor. You have no business being here, Burqa. You are as big a loser as your bearded bud, Mustafa. LEAVE! Go live in your beloved Egypt!

9 And it got worse. She kept harassing me to the point that I had to call the LSU police department and file a complaint. After the police tracked her down and talked to her, she stopped harassing me for a while, but started again after I resumed writing the next semester. Turns out she wasn't even a student; she was a 40-something woman who apparently loves to read our college newspaper.

10 These things had an emotional toll on me. Was anyone out there listening? Was anyone out there even going to consider my request that they read the Quran for themselves to realize the truth about Islam? Perhaps one of the hardest things to do these days is to convince people that what they have believed all their lives might be wrong. And it's just as difficult to get people to simply *listen* to anything or anyone that doesn't support their beliefs.

11 Then I received an email that gave me hope. Here is some of what this reader had to say:

> I am writing to you because I wanted to thank you for writing your articles in the Daily Reveille. You have inspired me to seek out the truth about Islam and the Qur'an. After reading your article, "The actions of a few do not represent the many," I decided to research the Islamic faith and read the Qur'an to see for myself if there was any Truth to be found in it. Partly because of your articles, I have been able to acquire a better view of the Islamic faith and have been able to throw away my previously held beliefs of Islam, beliefs that were taken from the media and biased individuals . . . Recently, I realized that I have held prejudice beliefs about Muslims and the Islamic faith; I have even possessed hatred towards them. I have judged them, and I have judged you. I hope that you will forgive me and forgive others who may have judged you or other Muslims or have hurt you or someone

you know because of prejudiced beliefs. Again, I also thank you for writing the articles. I do not know that I would have realized my own ignorance and judgments of the Islamic faith if it were not for your articles.

***

12 At the end of the day, I realize that there is a lot of work to be done. I've had many people tell me that I've changed their minds about Islam. The fact that I can get even one person to change his viewpoint on such vital issues makes my struggles all the more satisfying and worthwhile. All I hope for is that some of my efforts will bring a little sunshine when the eclipse finally starts to pass away.

from reading to writing

1. How do you define "argument"? How does your definition compare with those discussed in this chapter?
2. The French writer and philosopher Joseph Joubert wrote that "[t]he aim of argument, or of discussion, should not be victory, but progress." What do you think he means by this? Do you see any value in arguing to learn rather than to win?
3. In the excerpt from "On the Peace," Isocrates tells the members of the Athenian assembly that, "if you really want to find out what is most advantageous to the city, you should pay attention to those who oppose your views more than those who favor them." How do you think listening to opposing opinions might help someone make a better decision or construct a more persuasive argument?
4. Examine the photograph on page 7, the excerpt from Isocrates' "On the Peace" (page 15) and Matt Miller's essay "Is Persuasion Dead?"(page 16). What central problem related to public discourse do all three address? Which do you think most effectively presents this problem? Why? Which one most effectively proposes a solution to the problem?
5. How does Matt Miller define "persuasion"? In his essay, he writes, "Ninety percent of political conversation amounts to dueling 'talking points.' . . . By contrast, marshaling a case to persuade those who start from a different position is a lost art." Do you agree with him? Explain your answer.
6. Compare Miller's essay "Is Persuasion Dead?" with Kathleen Parker's "Seeking Balance in an Either-Or World" in Chapter 5 (page 152). What do Parker and Miller say about the state of public discourse in America today? Does either writer offer possible solutions to this problem? What are they?
7. In her essay "My Struggle to Share the Light," Shirien Elamawy explains her decision to use a public medium—her campus newspaper—to try to persuade readers to learn more about Islam and to counter the many misconceptions and mistruths about the religion. Describe an issue about which you feel so strongly that you might make your voice public. What would you say about the issue? What would you want your audience to know? What medium do you think would be most appropriate for your message?
8. In 400 to 500 words, describe an argument you had recently. What was the source of disagreement? What viewpoints were argued? Who, in your opinion, made the most persuasive arguments and why? Was there a "winner"? Why or why not? (See the sample student paper below.)

Sample Student Response

Greg Meuli was a first-year student at the University of South Carolina when he wrote this paper in response to Question 8 on the previous page.

Opening My Eyes to Argument

By Greg Meuli

The biggest obstacle I've had to overcome as an incoming student at such a large university has been understanding that people have diverse backgrounds and varied views on subjects that I've been brought up believing very specific things about. People have been taught certain principles and values throughout their lives at home, and it's hard understanding where other people are coming from because they've been raised in different surroundings, with different backgrounds, and influences from other cultures, religions, situations, and societies.

In my University 101 class recently, our professor put us into pairs and gave us topics to discuss. Another student and I tumbled into an argument over the death penalty. She viewed the death penalty as a horrible thing, and I think it's one of those necessary evils that bad people bring into our society.

She felt that the government has no right to play the part of God, and that it's God's, and only God's, right to sentence a man to death—whether it be in this world or the next. She tried to explain to me that taking one life never brings back the life of the lost, and that more death can't be the answer. She also brought up the fact that executed convicts have later been proven innocent, and how she felt that the government had murdered these innocent people. She demonstrated the idea that there are many inconsistencies with the enforcement of the death penalty. She questioned what crime warranted the death penalty and how old someone should be in order to be held accountable for his actions in that fashion. She questioned the fairness in the application of the death penalty, and the varied percentages of blacks, whites, other races, and even genders that received the death penalty. Although her viewpoint differed from mine, I had to admit that she had some valid points.

When it was my turn to talk, I first told her that I could understand how she felt, but I told her that I couldn't agree with what she had said. It's a touchy subject because there are so many different cases, and it's hard to make generalizations. However, I feel that if someone takes the life of another, then that person has consciously decided to forfeit his own life. Every citizen in this country knows the penalty for killing someone, but if one should choose to take life with complete disregard to the principles and laws of this country, he should then accept that he must pay the penalty. It's a double-edged sword in that the death penalty enacts justice on the committer of the crime, but does nothing to fulfill the justice for his victim. As much as our society does not want innocent people being executed for crimes they haven't committed, I feel that many in society also don't believe that guilty people have the right to continue living while the person they murdered doesn't have that chance. I agreed with her that our justice system has many flaws and inconsistencies, but I had to hold fast to my belief that the death penalty is necessary.

I told her to close her eyes and image having just buried her teenage daughter: one that was smart, beautiful, with all her life to live, and everything going for her. Then, I told her to imagine a stranger, wrapping his fingers around her throat, and squeezing all of the life out of her amazing daughter, with no regard for her life. She agreed with me that, in that case, she would've wanted the death penalty. I asked her that if it were right in that case, then should it not be right in every other murder case? It was at this point in our conversation that our professor told us that we had run out of time.

I have to admit that the discussion she and I had opened my eyes to the diverse nature of the college experience. This topic has been one that's plagued our society since the introduction of the death penalty into the American culture. Obviously, there is no right answer. She had the more persuasive argument in that she had more facts, but I think that I had the more passionate argument because I wrenched her emotions, and emotions seem always to prevail over reason. Although I got her to admit that the death penalty is sometimes necessary, I don't think that I won the argument, because her thoughts got me to question my viewpoints, and agree with some of her feelings. I left that room with a sense of accomplishment. I went into the discussion with a closed mind, but her rational views opened my mind, and made me realize that although people from different places have differing views from mine, that doesn't necessarily make them wrong.

reading for a reason

C H A P T E R 2

"Books allow me to see my feelings put into words."
—**Isabel Allende,** *"Reading the History of the World"*

"If you want to be a writer, you must do two things above all others: read
a lot and write a lot. There's no way around these two things that I'm
aware of, no shortcut."
—**Stephen King,** *On Writing: A Memoir of the Craft*

"[K]ids don't read for pleasure. And because they don't read, they are less
able to navigate the language. If words are the coin of their thought,
they're working with little more than pocket change."
—**Michael Skube,** *"Writing Off Reading"*

Let's face it: in the academic world, if you don't read, you won't learn. Oh, you might pick up a few things here and there by paying attention to class lectures, by listening to students who *are* reading talk about assignments and work their way toward understanding, or by photocopying classmates' notes and muddling through their impenetrable handwriting. This strategy for getting by is often enough to warrant a passing grade, and some students seem oddly proud about adopting it, as if they were accomplishing something by skating through college on the path of least resistance. But because these students avoid reading, they miss out on the richness of academic study that college offers. To put it another way, and to pick up on the metaphor from the Michael Skube quotation on page 23, if you don't read, you're "working with little more than pocket change" in a world that places a premium on intellectual currency.

But enough of the lecturing. In this chapter, we want to show you a few strategies that we think will make you a more effective and discerning reader—skills that will also help you improve your writing. Before we get to all of that, however, let's talk a bit more about reading in general and about the reading and writing you'll be doing in college.

If you read a lot as a child—or if you had teachers or family members who tried to get you to read—then you've probably heard a number a variations on the quotation by Isabel Allende that opens this chapter. From her essay titled "Reading the History of the World," the quotation shows how books speak to the prolific author as she thinks about the world around her and her place in it. Her sentiment is shared by many lifelong readers, people like Stephen King who fall in love with books at an early age and for whom reading comes as naturally as eating and sleeping. In his memoir, *On Writing*, King is more direct: He says unequivocally that we can't learn to write—or improve our writing—if we don't read. And he has no patience for people who say they can't find time to read: "There are all sorts of opportunities to dip in," he says, listing waiting rooms, theater lobbies, checkout lines, bathrooms, the gym, the car (with books on tape), and meals as prime places and times to get a little reading done. But what if you don't love to read? What if you find it difficult, even tedious? Well, we have some good news and some better news. The good news is, if you're in college, you're going to have to read whether you like it or not (of course, you might find this to be good in the same way that broccoli is good for you). The better news is, the more you do it—especially if you adopt some of the strategies spelled out in this chapter—the better you'll become at it. And then, maybe, you'll like it a little more.

You probably won't be surprised to hear that the reading you'll do in college will be vastly different from your pleasure reading and even from most of what you read in high school. And we're not just talking about content. Yes, your teachers will assign some books you've never encountered about topics that are new to you. But even if you're assigned a book for college that you read in high school, the reading itself will be different. It'll have to be if you're going to meet your teachers' expectations that you'll be able to do something intelligent with what you've read. And because much of that "something" will involve analytical or argumentative writing, we want to show you a few ways to approach this reading and writing that will help you succeed. All of these strategies share one important characteristic: They are grounded in an understanding of the rhetorical situation.

THE RHETORICAL SITUATION

As we mentioned briefly in Chapter 1, the most productive definitions of argument and argumentation spring from Classical rhetoric, more specifically from the teachings of Aristotle. Born in 384 B.C.E., Aristotle was a student and teacher during the height of rhetoric's development in and around Athens. He studied under Plato, the founder of Western philosophy; he tutored a young Macedonian prince named Alexander (later, Alexander the Great); he opened his own school, called the Lyceum, in Athens; and he wrote many of the most important texts we have from antiquity, covering subjects ranging from logic and philosophy to the physical and natural sciences to psychology and the arts. Aristotle's great contribution to rhetoric was to provide a governing method for the field, and to systematize the study and teaching of the subject, with the collection of writings called *Rhetoric* (the text we have was not conceived of as a full book, but instead was a collection of notes delivered to and recorded by students, probably over a period of twenty years). We can see this idea of systemization in his famous definition of rhetoric, which opens the excerpt below:

FROM *RHETORIC*, BOOK 1, CHAPTER 2

1 Rhetoric may be defined as the faculty of observing in any given case the available means of persuasion. This is not a function of any other art. Every other art can instruct or persuade about its own particular subject-matter; for instance, medicine about what is healthy and unhealthy, geometry about the properties of magnitudes, arithmetic about numbers, and the same is true of the other arts and sciences. But rhetoric we look upon as the power of observing the means of persuasion on almost any subject presented to us; and that is why we say that, in its technical character, it is not concerned with any special or definite class of subjects.

2 Of the modes of persuasion some belong strictly to the art of rhetoric and some do not. By the latter I mean such things as are not supplied by the speaker but are there at the outset—witnesses, evidence given under torture, written contracts, and so on. By the former I mean such as we can ourselves construct by means of the principles of rhetoric. The one kind has merely to be used, the other has to be invented.

3 Of the modes of persuasion furnished by the spoken word there are three kinds. The first kind depends on the personal character of the speaker; the second on putting the audience into a certain frame of mind; the third on the proof, or apparent proof, provided by the words of the speech itself. Persuasion is achieved by the speaker's personal character when the speech is so spoken as to make us think him credible. We believe good men more fully and more readily than others: this is true generally whatever the question is, and absolutely true where exact certainty is impossible and opinions are divided. This kind of persuasion, like the others, should be achieved by what the speaker says, not by what people think of his character before he begins to speak. It is not true, as some writers assume in their treatises on rhetoric, that the personal goodness revealed by the speaker contributes nothing to his power of persuasion; on the contrary, his character may almost be called the most effective means of persuasion he possesses. Secondly, persuasion may come through the

hearers, when the speech stirs their emotions. Our judgments when we are pleased and friendly are not the same as when we are pained and hostile. It is towards producing these effects, as we maintain, that present-day writers on rhetoric direct the whole of their efforts. This subject shall be treated in detail when we come to speak of the emotions. Thirdly, persuasion is effected through the speech itself when we have proved a truth or an apparent truth by means of the persuasive arguments suitable to the case in question.

Throughout the *Rhetoric*, Aristotle goes into great detail as he explains his subject, how it works, and how it should be practiced and learned. For now, we'll introduce you to two of his most important concepts about rhetoric, each of which is vital to a rhetorical approach to reading and writing:

- **The rhetorical situation.** Simply put, the rhetorical situation is all about context. One of the most important and useful things Aristotle did in the *Rhetoric* was to give us a way to think about all the conditions surrounding and influences on the speech and the speaker (or the essay and the writer). You may have encountered something like this before, called the *rhetorical* or the *communication triangle*. The idea is basically the same: Every situation in which we use or encounter rhetoric—in essence, just about every instance of communication—involves a speaker (or writer), an audience, a message, and a purpose. Understanding the rhetorical situations we encounter will make us more savvy audience members and much more effective speakers and writers.

- **Appeals based on *ethos* (character), *pathos* (emotion or imagination), and *logos* (logic or the intellect).** One of the reasons that understanding the rhetorical situation is so important is that this knowledge can help us decide how best to present our argument to the audience. Aristotle put it this way: "[S]ince rhetoric exists to affect the giving of decisions . . . the orator must not only try to make the argument of his speech demonstrative and worthy of belief; he must also make his own character look right and put his hearers, who are to decide, into the right frame of mind." What he's saying is that, to truly be persuasive, the speaker must appeal to the audience's intellect (*logos*), its sense of his character (*ethos*), and its imagination and emotions (*pathos*). As we'll see in the next chapter, this idea gives us an excellent guide for analyzing arguments and composing our own.

In this chapter and the next, you'll see how paying attention to the rhetorical situation and to the ways that texts appeal to the audience can make you a better reader and writer of arguments. Recognizing and understanding this important contextual information will help you analyze and evaluate arguments you encounter and decide when and how you want to enter the conversations—big and small—that make up your everyday life. Let's say, for example, you came across this quotation on a music blog:

> HSAN is concerned about the growing public outrage concerning the use of the words "bitch," "ho," and "nigger." We recommend that the recording and broadcast

industries voluntarily remove/bleep/delete the misogynistic words "bitch" and "ho" and the racially offensive word "nigger."

> —Russell Simmons and Dr. Benjamin Chavis,
> co-chairs of the Hip-Hop Summit Action Network,
> "Recommendation to the Recording and Broadcast
> Industries"

On first glance, there might not seem to be much noteworthy about this call for the music and radio industries to clean up their acts. After all, these kinds of statements have been made by political, religious, and civic leaders for decades. But consider how your reading of the quotation might change if you knew a little more about the rhetorical situation that produced it:

- First of all, the quotation came in the days after radio host Don Imus' firing in 2007 for using offensive language in reference to the Rutgers University women's basketball team. (This places the quotation in a larger conversation and makes it seem more relevant and timely.)
- Secondly, although Dr. Benjamin Chavis, a religious and civic leader, could be expected to express such an opinion, the call for bleeping might seem unusual coming from Russell Simmons, one of the most respected and successful rap music producers of all. (This gives the quotation a little more authority and weight, especially among younger music fans.)
- Thirdly, the Hip-Hop Summit Action Network is an advocacy group that believes hip-hop music can and should be a positive social and cultural force. (This clarifies the purpose of the quotation, showing that it comes not from someone attacking hip-hop and rap, but from an organization that celebrates its power to do good.)
- Finally, the quotation comes from a statement—"Recommendation to the Recording and Broadcast Industries"—that was released to the news media and posted on the HSAN website. (This sheds some light on the intended audiences—people in the industry, consumers of mainstream news, and visitors to HSAN's homepage).

Many writing students find it useful to think of the rhetorical situation as a confluence of elements that fall into three general categories, based on Aristotle's model:

- The writer's purpose (what she's trying to accomplish).
- The audience the writer will engage in conversation and how this audience will respond to her and the issue she presents.
- The writer or speaker herself and how she comes across as having a particular motive, attitude, and personality that bears on both the audience's reception of her and the significance of the message she hopes to present.

Because all of these elements are connected, it's also helpful to think about the rhetorical situation in terms of the rhetorical triangle (see Figure 2-1). The design—the "medium" in the middle represents the mode of delivery (for our purposes, writing)—shows how each point is always in relation and response to the others. In other words, if one element in the triangle shifts, then the entire rhetorical situation changes. (Think how a different writer might affect the rhetorical situation in the

The Rhetorical Triangle

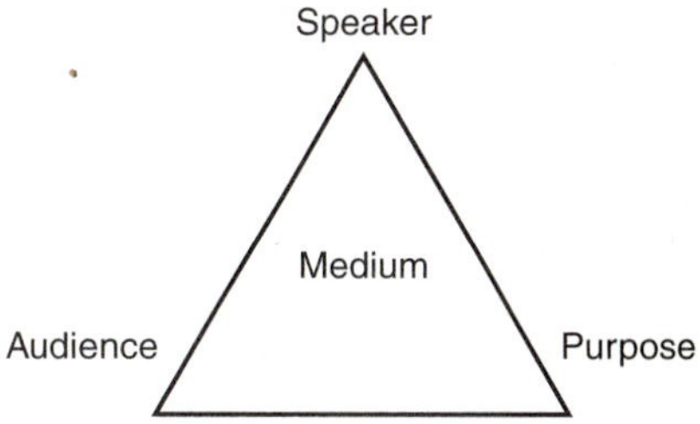

FIGURE 2-1

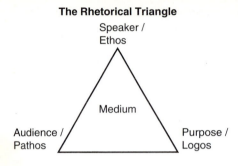

The Rhetorical Triangle

Speaker /
Ethos

Medium

Audience /
Pathos

Purpose /
Logos

FIGURE 2-2

HSAN example above; if, for instance, President Bush had written the quotation.)

The diagram is also useful for thinking about the way that the rhetorical appeals—to *ethos* (the writer's character, as perceived by the audience), *pathos* (the audience's emotions and imagination), and *logos* (the audience's intellect)—must work in conjunction with the elements of the rhetorical situation (see Figure 2-2).

When you read and write arguments, then, it's vital that you pay attention to the ways that these rhetorical appeals (Aristotle called them the "artistic proofs" because the speaker or writer has to create them) work within the rhetorical situation. Another example might make this clearer. Imagine that you and your friends are going to a movie. You want to see *Pineapple Express*, but everybody else has decided on *Tropic Thunder*. Is it worth trying to persuade them to change their minds? If so, how would you go about persuading them? Thinking in terms of the rhetorical situation can help you figure out the most appropriate and effective way to respond to this challenge.

Let's start with your ethos. Do you often try to get your friends to do what you want to do? Did you convince them to see a movie of your choosing last time? If so, you might consider keeping your feelings to yourself in this instance. Your friends might not take your suggestion seriously if you often put your own desires ahead of theirs. On the other hand, if you rarely ask your friends to do something you want to do over and against their wishes, they might consider your suggestion more strongly. These considerations will affect whether and how you proceed with your argument.

When it comes to a low-stakes decision like what movie to see, however, the ethical appeal probably will not be as powerful as it would in a situation where character matters a great deal (say, in a presidential election). So, in arguing for your movie choice, you might want to focus on a logical appeal. You might mention that *Pineapple Express* is playing at a more convenient time and that by seeing this movie you'll be able to squeeze in dinner beforehand. You might also suggest that the lines for *Pineapple Express* will be significantly shorter than those for *Tropic Thunder* and that it's really annoying to sit in a crowded, noisy theater. To augment this appeal to intellect, you might also try to move your friends' emotions and imagination. If you knew, for example, that one of your friends was a big fan of James Franco, you could use a vivid description of the actor in full slacker regalia, slumped happily on a sofa, to capture her imagination and perhaps make her more inclined to see his movie.

While this might seem like a lot of thinking in preparation for something as simple as choosing a movie, it's important to remember that, regardless of the stakes, every rhetorical situation matters. Just as importantly, you should understand that every rhetorical situation is different and requires a unique, well-planned approach that takes into account all three points on the triangle as well as the appeals associated with them. As a reader, paying attention to the rhetorical situation will help you understand not just what a text says, but also the context that produced the text, possible agendas that might be driving the author, and other important details that can influence your perception and reception of the author's message. As a writer, thinking about your rhetorical situation—an assignment for an English class, for example, or a personal statement for a scholarship—can help you craft the most appropriate and effective response possible. Over the next several pages—in this chapter and the next—we'll explore a few specific ways you can read and write with the rhetorical situation in mind.

STRATEGIES FOR READING ARGUMENTS

As teachers, we've seen this scenario play out many times: It's the first day of class, and, after a round of nervous introductions and some shop talk about expectations, assignments, and other course details, our students flip to the day-by-day schedule in the syllabus and begin calculating the amount of reading they'll have to do for each class meeting. Sometimes, the groans are audible. After talking with students about this phenomenon over the course of several semesters, and after watching them engage (or not) with the required reading, we've come to believe that this response has less to do with the number of pages assigned than with students' uncertainty about *why* we want them to read this stuff in the first place. In other words, most students seem willing to do the reading, but they're not sure what to do with it. And this is understandably frustrating.

As is the case with most questions or concerns you have about your classes, the best place to start if you don't understand what a teacher wants is with the teacher. You can save yourself a lot of time and grief by simply asking. Granted, this won't always solve your problems—you might still be unsure about what to do after talking with your teacher—but more often than not, it'll help. For those times when it doesn't—or anytime you have a reading assignment, really—we've gathered a set of approaches that we think can help you not only understand what you're reading, but also figure out why you're reading it and what you can do with it. Borrowing from other teachers and composition theorists, we call these approaches *careful reading, generous reading, skeptical reading, analytical reading,* and *rhetorical reading.* All have their roots in the rhetorical situation, and all require active participation in the reading process—most obviously in the form of annotations, or notes you make on the text.

To show you these approaches at work, we apply them, over the next several pages, to an excerpt from an essay about the television show *Ugly Betty.* One thing to remember as you read through our descriptions and examples: There are no right or wrong annotations. Your notes, comments, and questions might not look like those we've produced, and that's all right because your annotations will be based on your reading. The only wrong thing you can do is not pay attention to the text. Before moving on to our descriptions and sample annotations on the excerpts, here's the essay in full:

UGLY, THE AMERICAN

James Poniewozik

Media and television critic JAMES PONIEWOZIK wrote this column for the November 27, 2006, edition of *Time* magazine.

[1] Few prime-time TV characters are more American than Betty Suarez. On ABC's hit comedy-soap "Ugly Betty," she's a fashion-magazine assistant who is distinctly

unfashionable—chunky sweaters, frizzy hair, bear-trap braces—but succeeds through good old Yankee values like perseverance, optimism and hard work. Smart and sweet-hearted, she embodies the Puritan-Shaker-Quaker principle of valuing inner good over outer appearance. She's as Norman Rockwell as a chestnut-stuffed turkey. The actress who plays her is even named America Ferrera.

[2] And yet—if you listen to some politicians and pundits—she should have been booted out of the country years ago. Betty's father is an illegal immigrant from Mexico. To hear Lou Dobbs and Pat Buchanan tell it, our fellow citizens are boiling with resentment against people like Betty. Taking our kids' spots in college! Helping themselves to our orthodontia! Stealing low-paid magazine jobs that rightfully belong to American trust-fund babies!

[3] So why do some 14 million people a week watch and root for her? Because it's easier to hate a straw man—or a straw Mexican—than a person, even a fictional one. And because, as our pop culture shows, Americans' attitude toward foreigners is more complex than the build-a-fencers would make it.

[4] On its face, the political debate is about illegal immigration—law, security and fairness. But this immigration panic, like past ones, taps into fears not limited to illegals. Who gets to say what American culture is? Is there enough room—and prosperity—to go around? Ugly Betty's overarching story is metaphorically about the same battle. Betty is an outsider at *Mode* magazine not just because she dresses badly but also because of things that have to do directly with her ethnicity. She grosses out her skinny, preening, (mostly) Anglo co-workers by bringing empanadas for lunch. Her features are broad and unmistakably Mesoamerican. (Ferrera is strikingly pretty

in real life.) On her first day at work, she wears a hideous poncho with GUADALAJARA emblazoned on it.

[5] Betty's scheming co-workers resent her in the same way immigration demagogues do: she's an interloper. Yet she succeeds—and even wins over some of her *Mode* enemies—for exactly that reason. Like generations of immigrants, legal or not, she brings fresh eyes, a tireless work ethic and a different perspective to revitalize a tired institution. (Like Borat, she's in the tradition of the outsider who helps America see itself.) Ironic, amid the effete fashionistas, that she's the one the audience identifies with as an everyday American.

[6] It's no coincidence that "Ugly Betty" the series is itself an immigrant, a remake of a worldwide-sensation telenovela franchise. That's what makes our pop culture so vital: from TV to music to fashion, it is constantly transfused by foreigners who are able to out-American Americans.

[7] Take reality TV. It embodies everything there is to love and despise about this country—ambition and greed, free-spiritedness and vulgarity, boldness and shamelessness. But it is an American staple that was pioneered overseas, much like pizza and gunpowder. "American Idol" is British. "Big Brother," Dutch. "Survivor," Swedish and imported by Mark Burnett, a Brit. And every week on reality shows, Americans embrace foreigners with Emma Lazarene openness—Heidi Klum and Simon Cowell, East European and Latin hoofers on "Dancing with the Stars," Mexican boxers on "The Contender" and a Siberian drag queen on "America's Got Talent."

[8] Reality TV may be so hospitable to immigrants because it's a fun house mirror of the immigrant experience. You leave your

comfort zone and prove your worth with little more than gumption and (maybe) talent. Wherever you come from, you embrace a new, anything-goes culture that values chutzpah over tradition and propriety. Emigré Burnett's shows, like "The Apprentice," are full of Horatio Algerisms about industry and opportunity—not unlike "Ugly Betty."

[9] Political observers suggest that immigration law will be one of the areas where a Democratic Congress and a Republican White House may be able to reach consensus. Before they do, they should flick on a TV. They would see that you can pass laws and put up walls but it is much harder to erect a fence around your culture. (Just ask the French.) That while borders need to be protected, new blood is what makes this country the maddening, fantastic free-for-all that it is. And that what makes Betty ugly is, in the long run, what makes us America the beautiful.

Careful Reading

Simply put, *careful reading*—the basis for every approach on this list—means paying attention. What's not so simple is that this means you have to pay attention to *everything*— or at least everything you can manage. Careful reading requires active participation (some people, in fact, call this strategy "active reading"); this means that you have to do some things while you read, that you can't just let your eyes drift over the text until you reach the end of the assignment. You have to engage with the text by working with it, in it, and through it so that you become part of the conversation it presents. Doing this will help you see the text as something more than a collection of words and sentences and will increase your chances of knowing a little more about the topic the text addresses than when you began.

In particular, careful reading means:

- **Setting up.** If you're going to read a text carefully, you have to get rid of as many distractions as possible. Maybe cracking open your textbook at 1 a.m. the night before class with your iPod cranked, the television on, and your roommate fighting over the phone (again) with his girlfriend back home isn't the best setting for paying attention to anything. You have to find a place—and the time—that will allow you to concentrate on the task at hand.
- **Slowing down.** Everybody knows that being in college can be a time-management nightmare, especially when "being in college" can mean not only taking classes, but also fulfilling family, work, social, and other obligations. Still, you have to make time to read the texts you're assigned. Careful reading requires extra time because it depends on a deliberate pace that allows for thinking, note-taking, and other actions spelled out in this list. In short, skimming won't do.

- **Reading everything.** Careful reading also takes time because it requires that you read the entire text, not just the title, introduction, and conclusion. Actually, it means reading *more* than the entire text because you have to consider the rhetorical situation, too. Ideally, you'll read everything more than once (especially if you have a writing assignment connected to the reading).

- **Making notes.** Before we go any further, put the cap on that highlighter and throw it away. Dragging a lime-green, hot-pink, or electric yellow pen across the page might seem like active reading, but it's not. It's passive reading in disguise, and it's especially dangerous because it leads you to believe you're doing something that will help you remember, understand, and synthesize the material you're reading. All using a highlighter really does is slow you down for all the wrong reasons. Making notes—or annotating—is a much more effective way of engaging with the text because it forces you to think and to do something with the material you're reading. And you can use these notes to guide you through the text on subsequent readings.

- **Looking stuff up.** There's nothing wrong with not knowing the meaning of a word or a reference you come across in a text, but there's everything wrong with leaving it that way. Figuring these things out is an integral part of understanding any text—and the rhetorical situation that produced it. Having a dictionary handy whenever you read is a big help, and the Internet can make things even easier, especially when it comes to references or allusions you might not know. If you can't look something up immediately, make a note about it so you can do the necessary research later.

- **Asking questions.** As you read—and make notes and look stuff up—you should also ask questions about things in the text that puzzle or intrigue you or things you would simply like to think more about later. Asking questions is one of the most active ways you can engage with a text (and one of the best ways to explore the rhetorical situation) because it immediately makes you part of the conversation. And don't worry about responding to all the questions you ask: Some you'll answer, others you'll just think about, and still others you might discard altogether.

- **Making connections.** As you read and try to understand a text, it's often useful to think about your reading in a larger setting. Why, for example, is the text important to your course and your field of study? How does the text relate to other material in the class? Why might the instructor have chosen the text? And where might the text lead next? Making connections—to other readings, to lectures and discussions, and to other material in and out of the classroom—can help you see the big picture and better understand the text itself and its place in a larger system of discourse.

- **Drawing conclusions.** Although you should always leave open the possibility—even likelihood—that you'll change your position, don't shy away from drawing conclusions about the texts you read, and their rhetorical situations, while reading them. What is the author's main point? Why did she write the piece? What is she trying to accomplish? Does she succeed? Why (or why not)? This kind of thinking requires that you understand the text well enough to sum it up and to offer a bit of critique—two important steps toward understanding.

- **Doing it all again.** Yes, you read correctly. Reading a text carefully means sometimes having to read—and do all the things on this list—more than once. Why? Think about it this way: There aren't many people who can drive a golf ball or play a musical instrument after one lesson. It takes practice because there's a lot to learn. The same goes with reading—especially with reading the kinds of texts you're going to be assigned in college. There's going to be a lot to learn from these texts so you might have to read them—carefully—more than once.

In the excerpt below, we've made a list of comments and questions that came to us as we read Poniewozik's piece carefully. Notice that many of our annotations are questions about elements of the text that we want to think about further.

from UGLY, THE AMERICAN

By James Poniewozik

Few prime-time TV characters are more American than Betty Suarez. On ABC's hit comedy-soap "Ugly Betty," she's a fashion-magazine assistant who is distinctly unfashionable—chunky sweaters, frizzy hair, bear-trap braces—but succeeds through good old Yankee values like perseverance, optimism and hard work. Smart and sweet-hearted, she embodies the Puritan-Shaker-Quaker principle of valuing inner good over outer appearance. She's as Norman Rockwell as a chestnut-stuffed turkey. The actress who plays her is even named America Ferrera.

And yet—if you listen to some politicians and pundits—she should have been booted out of the country years ago. Betty's father is an illegal immigrant from Mexico. To hear Lou Dobbs and Pat Buchanan tell it, our fellow citizens are boiling with resentment against people like Betty. Taking our kids' spots in college! Helping themselves to our orthodontia! Stealing low-paid magazine jobs that rightfully belong to American trust-fund babies!

So why do some 14 million people a week watch and root for her? Because it's easier to hate a straw man—or a straw Mexican—than a person, even a fictional one. And because, as our pop culture shows, Americans' attitude toward foreigners is more complex than the build-a-fencers would make it.

CAREFUL READING NOTES AND QUESTIONS

1. Have I ever seen this show?

2. Look on http://abc.go.com/ for a picture of the character. Is this really how she looks? Why do her looks matter so much?

3. Why are they called "Yankee" values? Look this up! Also look up the "Puritan-Shaker-Quaker principle of valuing inner good over outer appearance."

4. What does "as Norman Rockwell as a chestnut-stuffed turkey" mean?

5. Look up "pundit."

6. Where is the author going with this? The immigration debate?

7. Who are Lou Dobbs and Pat Buchanan, and where do they stand on immigration?

8. These last three sentences sound like sarcasm. Is the author just trying to be funny? Or does the tone reflect his feelings about some anti-immigration advocates?

9. Is this number—14 million per week—accurate? How do the show's ratings compare with others on TV?

10. Look up "straw man."

11. This last sentence seems important; does the writer support/explain this claim?

Generous Reading

To be a *generous reader*, you have to try to put aside any immediate negative feelings or skepticism you might have about the issue, the author, or anything else related to the rhetorical situation while giving the text your full attention and fair consideration. Just as important, being a generous reader means you're committed to trying to find something useful, informative, or engaging in every text, even if you find it ultimately distasteful, ineffective, or otherwise irrelevant. Generous reading is vital to the spirit of argument as exploration (as discussed in Chapter 1) because it forces us to delay our almost instinctive rush to judgment, thus keeping the lines of intellectual inquiry open. In other words, it keeps our knee-jerk reactions from dictating the terms of our engagement with the text.

As you read our comments below, notice how we try to give the writer the benefit of the doubt as we respond generously to his text. We want to give the author every opportunity to make his point and to try, no matter how we feel about the argument the text makes, to take something productive from our reading.

from UGLY, THE AMERICAN

By James Poniewozik

Few prime-time TV characters are more American than Betty Suarez. On ABC's hit comedy-soap "Ugly Betty," she's a fashion-magazine assistant who is distinctly unfashionable—chunky sweaters, frizzy hair, bear-trap braces—but succeeds through good old Yankee values like perseverance, optimism and hard work. Smart and sweet-hearted, she embodies the Puritan-Shaker-Quaker principle of valuing inner good over outer appearance. She's as Norman Rockwell as a chestnut-stuffed turkey. The actress who plays her is even named America Ferrera.

And yet—if you listen to some politicians and pundits—she should have been booted out of the country years ago. Betty's father is an illegal immigrant from Mexico. To hear Lou Dobbs and Pat Buchanan tell it, our fellow citizens are boiling with resentment against people like Betty. Taking our kids' spots in college! Helping themselves to

GENEROUS READING NOTES AND QUESTIONS

- Things about which I'm going to give Poniewozik the benefit of the doubt in these three paragraphs:

1. That there aren't other characters on TV who are "more American" than Betty Suarez (I *could* argue for a bunch of others, including Veronica Mars, Tony Soprano, Bernie Mac, and just about the entire cast of *My Name Is Earl*).

2. That perseverance, optimism, and hard work are truly the keys to Betty's success (rather than the scriptwriters' whims and the audience's expectations).

3. That pop culture in general and TV characters in particular are good measures of how people really feel about important issues.

our orthodontia! Stealing low-paid magazine jobs that rightfully belong to American trust-fund babies!

So why do some 14 million people a week watch and root for her? Because it's easier to hate a straw man—or a straw Mexican—than a person, even a fictional one. And because, as our pop culture shows, Americans' attitude toward foreigners is more complex than the build-a-fencers would make it.

4. That people who oppose immigration or who want to see the government do something more to control it are driven in large part by fear and hatred of "foreigners."

Skeptical Reading

Although this approach does require that you bring a skeptic's eye to the text, it doesn't mean you should be unreasonable or unfair. As a *skeptical reader*, your task is to question the author's assertions, assumptions, and agenda, as well as the choices she makes in response to the rhetorical situation (How does she present herself in the text? Why does she present herself in that way?). Using this approach is especially useful when you encounter writers and arguments that echo your own beliefs. To be a thorough and effective reader, you have to set aside even your positive feelings about the issues at hand and approach each argument based on its merits, not simply on your willingness to agree with its claims. Skeptical reading doesn't require that you abandon your beliefs, however, only that you develop the ability to set them aside long enough to read texts thoughtfully and without judgment so that you can learn as much as possible from them.

In the excerpt that follows, notice how our comments and questions are nearly the opposite of those in the generous reading section. Rather than give the author the benefit of the doubt, as skeptical readers we ask questions that force us to focus on the argument the author makes and on how well he makes it.

from UGLY, THE AMERICAN

By James Poniewozik

Few prime-time TV characters are more American than Betty Suarez. On ABC's hit comedy-soap "Ugly Betty," she's a fashion-magazine assistant who is distinctly unfashionable—chunky sweaters, frizzy hair, bear-trap braces—but succeeds through

SKEPTICAL READING NOTES AND QUESTIONS

1. How does Poniewozik define "American"? Are "perseverance, optimism and hard work" the only defining characteristics? I think others might define the concept differently and thus be able to come up with a more suitable TV character to fit that definition.

good old Yankee values like perseverance, optimism and hard work. Smart and sweet-hearted, she embodies the Puritan-Shaker-Quaker principle of valuing inner good over outer appearance. She's as Norman Rockwell as a chestnut-stuffed turkey. The actress who plays her is even named America Ferrera.

2. Isn't much of our pop culture driven more by appearance than by "inner good"? How does Poniewozik account for this?

And yet—if you listen to some politicians and pundits—she should have been booted out of the country years ago. Betty's father is an illegal immigrant from Mexico. To hear Lou Dobbs and Pat Buchanan tell it, our fellow citizens are boiling with resentment against people like Betty. Taking our kids' spots in college! Helping themselves to our orthodontia! Stealing low-paid magazine jobs that rightfully belong to American trust-fund babies!

3. On the TV show, was Betty born in the United States? If so, *she* wouldn't be forced out, would she?

4. I realize Poniewozik is trying to be funny here, but what *are* the reasons people want to keep immigrants out of this country? Does the author consider any of these reasons to be legitimate?

So why do some 14 million people a week watch and root for her? Because it's easier to hate a straw man—or a straw Mexican—than a person, even a fictional one. And because, as our pop culture shows, Americans' attitude toward foreigners is more complex than the build-a-fencers would make it.

5. Does the show's popularity have anything at all to do with Betty's ethnicity? Or with immigration? Or do people simply find it entertaining?

6. Is our attitude about foreigners really as complex as Poniewozik says?

7. This last sentence shows how the writer contradicts himself. He accuses "build-a-fencers" of oversimplifying the immigration issue, but, in the previous paragraph, he implies that anyone who doesn't agree with him on immigration is driven by simple fear and hate.

Analytical Reading

The goal of any analysis is to ask how and why a thing—a text, a chemical process, a car engine—works. To do this, you have to examine the thing as a whole and then take it apart to see how the parts work individually and then put it back together to reexamine how the parts work together well or not so well. Thus, *analytical reading* requires two things: exceptional attention to detail and unwavering focus (the latter is important because you have to suppress—at least for a while—any feelings you might have about the topic of the text so you can examine how the text itself works as an argument). Unless your teacher explicitly asks for it, your opinion about the topic of the text doesn't matter. Your job as an analytical reader is to figure out what the author is doing and how she is doing it. To do this, you'll have to pull the text apart—figuratively speaking, of course—to see how and why it works (or doesn't work). If you let your feelings about the issue creep in, your analysis will likely get sidetracked. In the *Ugly Betty* excerpt, for example, notice how we stay away from our opinions about TV comedies and immigration and talk instead about how the author writes his argument and why he does the things he does in the text.

As analytical readers, we try to approach the excerpt below as objectively as we can. In our notes and questions, we focus on the nuts and bolts of Poniewozik's argument: the points he makes and the way he makes them. We also examine how the author tries to connect with his audience.

from UGLY, THE AMERICAN

By James Poniewozik

Few prime-time TV characters are more American than Betty Suarez. On ABC's hit comedy-soap "Ugly Betty," she's a fashion-magazine assistant who is distinctly unfashionable—chunky sweaters, frizzy hair, bear-trap braces—but succeeds through good old Yankee values like perseverance, optimism and hard work. Smart and sweet-hearted, she embodies the Puritan-Shaker-Quaker principle of valuing inner good over outer appearance. She's as Norman Rockwell as a chestnut-stuffed turkey. The actress who plays her is even named America Ferrera.

And yet—if you listen to some politicians and pundits—she should have been booted out of the country years ago. Betty's father is an illegal immigrant from Mexico. To hear Lou Dobbs and Pat Buchanan tell it, our fellow citizens are boiling with resent-ment against people like Betty. Taking our kids' spots in college! Helping themselves to our orthodontia! Stealing low-paid maga-zine jobs that rightfully belong to American trust-fund babies!

ANALYTICAL READING NOTES AND QUESTIONS

1. Why is the author using a television show as a starting point for saying something about the immigration debate? More importantly, *how* does he do this?

2. He starts by introducing something everybody is familiar—and comfortable—with, TV characters. Then he gets more specific by talking about one character in particular. And then he lets us know what his real topic is. This is an effective way of broaching a divisive subject like immigration.

3. In this paragraph, he does something similar, but this time he uses humor to make the issue he introduces in the first sentence—that a lot of people think illegal immigrants should be kicked out of the United States—a little easier to deal with. As a reader, I might not really be interested in talking about immigration, but the humor at the end of the paragraph at least keeps me reading.

So why do some 14 million people a week watch and root for her? Because it's easier to hate a straw man—or a straw Mexican—than a person, even a fictional one. And because, as our pop culture shows, Americans' attitude toward foreigners is more complex than the build-a-fencers would make it.

4. In this paragraph, he introduces a statistic—14 million people a week watch *Ugly Betty*—to add some credence to his argument.

5. Interestingly, he follows that piece of data with an opinion in the second sentence. This is an effective way to balance "fact" and opinion.

Steven Rubin/The Image Works

FIGURE 2-3

You can apply the reading strategies we present in this chapter to just about any text—whether it's composed from words, images, sound, or other elements. Take the highway sign pictured in Figure 2-3, for example. One of many placed by the state of California near San Diego after several immigrants were hit and killed by vehicles in the 1980s and '90s, the signs are meant to warn drivers that they might encounter people darting through traffic as they try to avoid border security. But a rhetorical reading of the sign can reveal it to be a text much more complicated than its original purpose would lead us to believe. Try reading the sign carefully, generously, and skeptically, using the steps outlined on the previous pages.

Rhetorical Reading

This is the easiest approach to explain and the most complicated to use—and for the same reason. We use *rhetorical reading* to mean doing all of the above—reading carefully, generously, skeptically, and analytically—if not at the same time, then at least as part of an extended engagement with the text. Even though we hope you understand the need to read every text carefully, the other approaches you focus on will often be dictated by the purpose behind your reading: If you have to write an analysis, for example, you'll spend most of your time reading analytically; for a response paper, you might choose to read generously and skeptically while developing your opinion. The thing to remember is that these approaches are designed to help you *do something* as you read and with your reading. We believe doing something with the text, rather than just letting it sit there on the page, will help you become a more effective reader and a better learner.

ARGUMENT IN ACTION

To help you practice these reading strategies, we include here *Encomium of Helen*, one of the most famous persuasive texts from the Classical period. Written by Gorgias of Leontini, a diplomat turned teacher, philosopher, and public speaker, *Encomium of Helen* presents a convincing case for the power of language over all other things, using Helen's abduction (or seduction) from Sparta by the Trojan prince Paris (this, you might remember from Homer's *Iliad*, lit the fuse for the Trojan War). Though she may well have been kidnapped, Helen was often blamed for causing the conflict, which left thousands of Greeks dead and the great city of Troy in ruins. Early in the speech, Gorgias clearly states his purpose, to "free the accused [Helen] of blame" no matter how she ended up in Troy. As you read the text, use the strategies outlined in the previous pages to examine exactly how Gorgias makes the case for Helen. When you have completed your careful reading, ask yourself if Gorgias presents a successful argument.

ENCOMIUM OF HELEN

[1] What is becoming to a city is manpower, to a body beauty, to a soul wisdom, to an action virtue, to a speech truth, and the opposites of these are unbecoming. Man and woman and speech and deed and city and object should be honored with praise if praiseworthy and incur blame if unworthy, for it is an equal error and mistake to blame the praisable and to praise the blamable. It is the duty of one and the same man both to speak the needful rightly and to refute the unrightfully spoken. Thus it is right to refute those who rebuke Helen, a woman about whom the testimony of inspired poets has become univocal and unanimous as has the ill omen of her name, which has become a reminder of misfortunes. For my part, by introducing some reasoning into my speech, I wish to free the accused of blame and, having reproved her detractors as prevaricators and proved the truth, to free her from their ignorance.

² Now it is not unclear, not even to a few, that in nature and in blood the woman who is the subject of this speech is preeminent among preeminent men and women. For it is clear that her mother was Leda, and her father was in fact a god, Zeus, but allegedly a mortal, Tyndareus, of whom the former was shown to be her father because he was and the latter was disproved because he was said to be, and the one was the most powerful of men and the other the Lord of all. Born from such stock, she had godlike beauty, which taking and not mistaking, she kept. In many did she work much desire for her love, and her one body was the cause of bringing together many bodies of men thinking great thoughts for great goals, of whom some had greatness of wealth, some the glory of ancient nobility, some the vigor of personal agility, some command of acquired knowledge. And all came because of a passion which loved to conquer and a love of honor which was unconquered. Who it was and why and how he sailed away, taking Helen as his love, I shall not say. To tell the knowing what they know shows it is right but brings no delight.

³ Having gone beyond the time once set for my speech, I shall go on to the beginning of my future speech, and I shall set forth the causes through which it is likely that Helen's voyage to Troy should take place. For either by will of Fate and decision of the gods and vote of Necessity did she do what she did, or by force reduced or by words seduced or by love possessed.

⁴ Now if through the first, it is right for the responsible one to be held responsible; for god's predetermination cannot be hindered by human premeditation. For it is the nature of things, not for the strong to be hindered by the weak, but for the weaker to be ruled and drawn by the stronger, and for the stronger to lead and the weaker to follow. God is a stronger force than man in might and in wit and in other ways. If then one must place blame on Fate and on a god, one must free Helen from disgrace.

⁵ But if she was raped by violence and illegally assaulted and unjustly insulted, it is clear that the raper, as the insulter, did the wronging, and the raped, as the insulted, did the suffering. It is right then for the barbarian who undertook a barbaric undertaking in word and law and deed to meet with blame in word, exclusion in law, and punishment in deed. And surely it is proper for a woman raped and robbed of her country and deprived of her loved ones to be pitied rather than pilloried. He did the dread deeds; she suffered them. It is just therefore to pity her but to hate him.

⁶ But if it was speech which persuaded her and deceived her heart, not even to this is it difficult to make an answer and to banish blame as follows. Speech is a powerful lord, which by means of the finest and most invisible body effects the divinest works: it can stop fear and banish grief and create joy and nurture pity. I shall show how this is the case, since it is necessary to offer proof to the opinion of my hearers: I both deem and define all poetry as speech with meter. Fearful shuddering and tearful pity and grievous longing come upon its hearers, and at the actions and physical sufferings of others in good fortunes and in evil fortunes, through the agency of words, the soul is wont to experience a suffering of its own. But come, I shall turn from one argument to another. Sacred incantations sung with words are bearers of pleasure and banishers of pain, for, merging with opinion in the soul, the power of the incantation is wont to beguile it and persuade it and alter it by witchcraft. There have been discovered two arts of witchcraft and magic: one consists of errors of soul and the other of deceptions of opinion. All who have and do persuade people of things do so by molding a false argument. For if all men on all subjects had both memory of things past

and awareness of things present and fore-knowledge of the future, speech would not be similarly similar, since as things are now it is not easy for them to recall the past nor to consider the present nor to predict the future. So that on most subjects most men take opinion as counselor to their soul, but since opinion is slippery and insecure it casts those employing it into slippery and insecure successes. What cause then prevents the conclusion that Helen similarly, against her will, might have come under the influence of speech, just as if ravished by the force of the mighty? For it was possible to see how the force of persuasion prevails; persuasion has the form of necessity, but it does not have the same power. For speech constrained the soul, persuading it which it persuaded, both to believe the things said and to approve the things done. The persuader, like a constrainer, does the wrong and the persuaded, like the constrained, in speech is wrongly charged. To understand that persuasion, when added to speech, is wont also to impress the soul as it wishes, one must study: first, the words of Astronomers who, substituting opinion for opinion, taking away one but creating another, make what is incredible and unclear seem true to the eyes of opinion; then, second, logically necessary debates in which a single speech, written with art but not spoken with truth, bends a great crowd and persuades; and, third, the verbal disputes of philosophers in which the swiftness of thought is also shown making the belief in an opinion subject to easy change. The effect of speech upon the condition of the soul is comparable to the power of drugs over the nature of bodies. For just as different drugs dispel different secretions from the body, and some bring an end to disease and others to life, so also in the case of speeches, some distress, others delight, some cause fear, others make the hearers bold, and some drug and bewitch the soul with a kind of evil persuasion.

[7] It has been explained that if she was persuaded by speech she did not do wrong but was unfortunate. I shall discuss the fourth cause in a fourth passage. For if it was love which did all these things, there will be no difficulty in escaping the charge of the sin which is alleged to have taken place. For the things we see do not have the nature which we wish them to have, but the nature which each actually has. Through sight the soul receives an impression even in its inner features. When belligerents in war buckle on their warlike accouterments of bronze and steel, some designed for defense, others for offense, if the sight sees this, immediately it is alarmed and it alarms the soul, so that often men flee, panic stricken from future danger as though it were present. For strong as is the habit of obedience to the law, it is ejected by fear resulting from sight, which coming to a man causes him to be indifferent both to what is judged honorable because of the law and to the advantage to be derived from victory. It has happened that people, after having seen frightening sights, have also lost presence of mind for the present moment; in this way fear extinguishes and excludes thought. And many have fallen victim to useless labor and dread diseases and hardly curable madnesses. In this way the sight engraves upon the mind images of things which have been seen. And many frightening impressions linger, and what lingers is exactly analogous to what is spoken. Moreover, whenever pictures perfectly create a single figure and form from many colors and figures, they delight the sight, while the creation of statues and the production of works of art furnish a pleasant sight to the eyes. Thus it is natural for the sight to grieve for some things and to long for others, and much love and desire for many objects and figures is engraved in many men. If, therefore, the eye of Helen, pleased by the figure of Alexander, presented to her soul eager desire and contest of love, what wonder?

If, being a god, Love has the divine power of the gods, how could a lesser being reject and refuse it? But if it is a disease of human origin and a fault of the soul, it should not be blamed as a sin, but regarded as an affliction. For she came, as she did come, caught in the net of Fate, not by the plans of the mind, and by the constraints of love, not by the devices of art.

[8] How then can one regard blame of Helen as unjust, since she is utterly acquitted of all charge, whether she did what she did through falling in love or persuaded by speech or ravished by force or constrained by divine constraint?

[9] I have by means of speech removed disgrace from a woman; I have observed the procedure which I set up at the beginning of the speech; I have tried to end the injustice of blame and the ignorance of opinion; I wished to write a speech which would be a praise of Helen and a diversion to myself.

from reading to writing

1. Put together a "reading profile" by doing the following (be prepared to share your profile with the class):
   a. Start with *what* you read. Make a list of the kinds of texts you read during an average week (for pleasure, for school, and for work). Include actual titles where you can (for example, names of books or newspapers).
   b. Now, characterize *how* you read by writing one or more of the following words next to each item on the list:
      i. skim (for things you read quickly)
      ii. study (for things you read carefully)
      iii. annotate (when you take notes while you read)
      iv. reread (for things you read more than once)
   c. Based on steps a and b, write a paragraph characterizing yourself as a reader and your reading habits.
2. Read Michael Skube's "Writing Off Reading" (page 120) and Howard Gardner's "The End of Literacy? Don't Stop Reading" (page 125). What are their central arguments? What evidence do they provide to support their claims? Which author's argument do you find more convincing? Why?
3. Choose an article or opinion piece from a newspaper (or the video equivalent from an online news source) and answer the following questions related to the rhetorical situation surrounding the text:
   a. Who is the author of the text? Based on the text, what do you know about the author?
   b. What is the author's purpose? Does the author succeed in accomplishing this purpose?
   c. Who is the targeted audience? Explain why you think this.
   d. How does thinking about the rhetorical situation affect the way you read the text?

4. Examine the highway sign pictured in Figure 2-3 (page 38). How would you characterize the rhetorical situation of the sign? Who is the "author"? Who is the intended audience? What is the sign's purpose? Do you see any other ways the sign can be read—ways that might conflict with the sign's original purpose? Explain your answer.

5. In his *Encomium of Helen*, what evidence does Gorgias provide to support his claim that "[s]peech is a powerful lord"? Do you agree with his position? Why or why not?

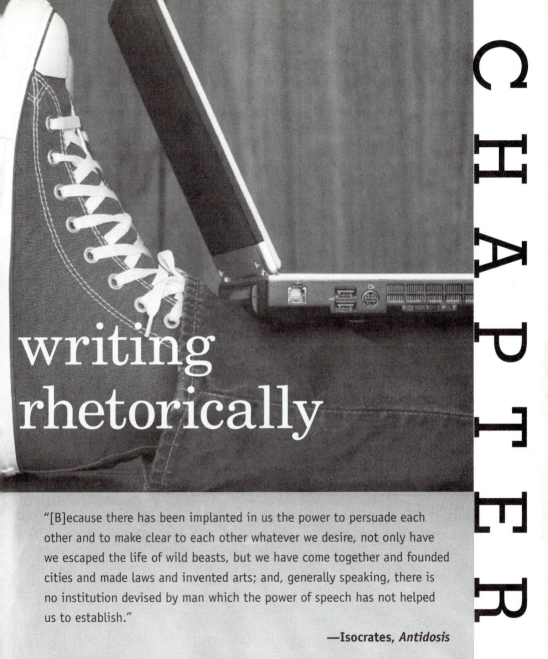

writing
rhetorically

"[B]ecause there has been implanted in us the power to persuade each other and to make clear to each other whatever we desire, not only have we escaped the life of wild beasts, but we have come together and founded cities and made laws and invented arts; and, generally speaking, there is no institution devised by man which the power of speech has not helped us to establish."

—Isocrates, *Antidosis*

In Chapter 1 you read about the vitriolic state of public discourse in the United States, and you learned how argument—as both a process (something you do) and a product (something you write or analyze)—can help you break through the conversational impasse that defines the way we talk. You also learned that the study and practice of argument have been going on for more than two millennia and that Classical rhetoric, the ancient art of persuasion and argument, is inextricably linked with the development of democracy in ancient Athens. From there, our goal has been to walk you through a few strategies for reading—in Chapter 2, where we discussed reading with a clear purpose in mind—and for writing. In this chapter and the next, we'll explore the latter.

WRITING ABOUT YOUR READING

You'll learn quickly—if you haven't already—that your teachers often will give you something to do with your reading: They'll frequently want you to write about what you've read. This is a common practice because writing and learning are inextricably linked. Writing helps us understand and absorb important content, organize concepts into patterns that are easier for us to remember, and synthesize ideas from different sources. Of course, it also helps us learn how to write more gracefully and effectively. As we tried to make clear in the last chapter, one way to become a better reader is to get in the habit of writing—making notes, asking questions, drawing conclusions—while you read. Now, we want to talk about two more formal kinds of writing projects that can help you understand and think more critically about your reading—the summary-and-response paper and the rhetorical analysis.

Summary and Response

One of the most useful things you can learn in college is how to summarize and respond to a text fairly and accurately. Being able to summarize means that you've read a text carefully and that you truly understand what's going on in it. Teachers in many subjects frequently assign summary and response papers to test their students' reading and comprehension skills. Summarizing is a vital element in the writing of any kind of research paper, in which you might have to convey in a sentence or two the most important features of sources that could be dozens of pages long. This leads us to the cardinal rule of summary writing: You have to be accurate. Next to plagiarizing them, just about the worst thing you can do to another person's words or ideas is misrepresent them. How do you ensure accuracy? By practicing and paying attention (or paying attention and practicing). Here are a few more specific tips:

- Make sure you understand the assignment. Does your teacher want a summary only? Or a summary and response? How long? Should the response be based on your opinion? Or on your analysis of the text? If you're not sure, ask.
- Accept that you're going to have to read the text more than once to do this well.
- Read and annotate the text carefully. If you have to write a response in addition to a summary, make sure you jot down your reaction to specific elements in the piece.
- Read the text again, this time focusing on the writer's central idea or argument. Identify this idea or argument and write it in your own words in the margins.
- Look for the evidence the author provides to support the central idea or argument. If there doesn't seem to be any, make a note of it.
- Examine the conclusion. What does the author do to bring closure to the piece?

- Read over your notes and prepare to write your summary.
- Start by writing a one-sentence summary (and, if it's required, a one-sentence response). No matter how long the assignment is supposed to be, boiling the main idea down into one sentence will help you decide if you're on the right track—if you're being accurate.
- Draft your summary to the required length. Ask yourself if it's accurate and if it fairly represents what the author says.
- If you have to include a response, make sure it's specific and justified.

To show you how this works, we've annotated an essay and written two summaries of different lengths and one summary-response. As you read each of them, check to make sure that all of the essential elements are there (title of the piece and publication information, the author's name, a clear statement of the central idea or argument, and an accounting of the support the author provides for her claim or position). Then, determine the accuracy of the summaries—if they fairly convey what it is the author is saying—and if the response seems justified.

A DESIRED EPIDEMIC: OBESITY AND THE FOOD INDUSTRY

Deborah Cohen

DEBORAH COHEN is a physician and a senior natural scientist at the RAND Corporation, a nonprofit research organization. She is the co-author of the book *Prescription for a Healthy Nation, a New Approach to Improving Our Lives by Fixing Our Everyday World* (Beacon Press). This piece was published on February 20, 2007, at www.washingtonpost.com.

In the Middle Ages, alchemists sought to turn common metals into gold. Today some doctors and scientists seeking to prevent and treat obesity in the United States are attempting an equally difficult transformation. They want to change people, their willpower, their lifestyles, their metabolism, even their DNA to make it harder to gain weight and easier to lose it.

However, transforming people with drugs, weight-loss surgery, genetic engineering,

SUMMARY AND RESPONSE NOTES AND QUESTIONS

1 Cohen is a doctor and works for the RAND Corporation, a public policy think tank.

2 This was published on the *Washington Post's* website (think about audience).

3 Cohen opens by comparing some medical treatments for obesity to alchemy. Her point? Maybe that these treatments are just as unlikely as alchemy to work—and just as much a waste of time.

hypnosis and other extreme steps is not the answer to obesity, because people are not the problem.

The problem is the food industry, which provides us with the calories we consume but washes its hands of responsibility for causing the worldwide obesity epidemic. Food industry marketers say they are only offering people what they want and that individuals choose what they put in their mouths.

Is it plausible that two out of three Americans have an eating disorder? And if we really believe that people are choosing to eat foods that are making them fat, does that mean we think that two-thirds of Americans are foolish, stupid, and lazy? Or that overweight and obese people have weaker characters and are morally inferior to people who have a normal weight?

The food industry spends billions of dollars each year to develop products, packaging, advertising and marketing techniques that entice us to buy more food because selling more food means making more profits. And businesses exist to make profits.

Food marketers test whether the color, the font size of words and the images used to market food will grab our attention by studies of eye movement. They conduct focus groups to come up with catchy names and symbols that recall positive memories and thoughts to condition a response that may lead us to purchase their products. And food marketers work to increase the frequency with which we see their products and their presence in stores, wanting to make their products always available.

The food industry also alters the nutritional content of foods to make them longer lasting on store shelves by increasing fats, sugars, and salt, making it less healthy for the average person to consume them.

Much evidence shows that individuals are not the cause of America's obesity epidemic.

4 Important point: "people are not the problem" with obesity. So, what is?...

5 ... the food industry! Why? Because they provide us with bad choices(?) Not sure about this.

6 Cohen gives the food industry a (very) brief chance to defend itself.

7 Here she challenges the food industry defense and supports her claim that "people are not the problem." But are these questions oversimplified?

8 Is this news to anyone? That businesses do things to make people buy their products?

9 Interesting list of some of the things that go into marketing food. But what's her point?

10 This seems a little more serious ...

11 Okay, she's making her case that people aren't the problem.

A wealth of research on marketing and decision-making reveals that people are easily manipulated, biased and influenced to make decisions that are not in their own best interests by how choices are presented to them.

Daniel Kahneman and Amos Tversky won a Nobel Prize by proving that rational decision-making is limited. Another school of research indicates that people typically make decisions about what and how much to eat unconsciously and can be manipulated to eat excessively without their awareness, simply by altering factors such as portion size, variety, ambience and packaging.

Just as a bell became a cue for Pavlov's dog to salivate, the current environment has ubiquitous cues that condition people to eat, even when they know they shouldn't. It is very difficult for people to resist the largely reflexive and automatic nature of our response to available food.

We can throw up our hands and say that's the way it is, and let the marketing that is leading more Americans to become obese and ill go unchecked.

A wiser choice would be to demand that government bring more regulation to the food environment, making sure that what is available is healthy, and that the contents of foods are transparent and easily understandable, even to those who are illiterate. Such regulation could reduce the magnitude of flawed decision-making by individuals by presenting us with healthier choices. And such regulation is literally a matter of life and death.

Food marketing efforts are the modern Sirens, leading us inexorably to chronic diseases and sometimes to early deaths. Just as Ulysses was able to defeat the Sirens by having his men plug their ears and tie him to the mast, today we need active protection from an aggressive food industry that is luring us to obesity and illness.

12 But she says we're easily manipulated into making bad decisions. Isn't that kind of like saying we're "foolish, stupid, and lazy"? (See paragraph 4.)

13 And maybe we're weak, too, at least when we make decisions unconsciously.

14 Again, Cohen seems to be arguing that we *are* weak.

15 Transition to her proposal.

16 Her idea: more government regulation of the packaging and marketing of food.

17 Question: Just because we have healthier options, will we choose them?

18 Cohen uses an allusion to the *Odyssey* to support her argument.

19 She wants "active protection" for consumers.

People who are overweight and obese are unknowing victims of a food environment created for corporate profits rather than health. When people suffer from an unhealthy environment that is cutting years from their lives, they need help from government to assure healthy conditions through regulation and enforcement.

As a society, regulation has served us well. We regulate building construction as a means of assuring quality and value. If contractors use substandard materials or techniques, good inspectors will require the work to be done right before approval is granted.

We regulate the car industry. Seat belts and air bags have saved tens of thousands of lives. We regulate the alcohol industry, only allowing sales in licensed establishments to people 21 and over, and have found fewer alcohol-related traffic fatalities in localities with more controls. We regulate water quality, air quality and tobacco.

Today we view clean air and water as a right to which we are entitled. Regulation is an assertion of, and not an infringement to, our rights. Regulation of the food environment is the next right we need to claim.

An estimated 150 million Americans are overweight or obese. Too many will die before their time due to heart disease, diabetes and other ailments. While the nation remains focused on waging war on terrorism, which has claimed thousands of lives, millions are dying prematurely because they aren't getting the government protection they need from the Sirens of the food industry.

20 By calling obese people "victims," Cohen seems to again support the idea that people are weak and foolish.

21 Over these next three paragraphs, she introduces other areas where government regulation works. She does this to support her plan.

22 She closes by comparing the toll that obesity takes to the toll from the war on terror. Is this a good strategy?

Sample Summaries and Responses

One-sentence (fifty-word) summary

In her essay "A Desired Epidemic: Obesity and the Food Industry," posted on www.washingtonpost. com in 2007, Deborah Cohen, a physician, argues that the government should more closely regulate food marketing because consumers are being misled into making bad choices that often lead to obesity and other serious health problems.

One-hundred-word summary

In her essay "A Desired Epidemic: Obesity and the Food Industry," posted on www. washingtonpost.com in 2007, Deborah Cohen argues that the food industry is to blame for America's obesity problem and, therefore, should be more closely regulated by the federal government. Cohen, a physician, dismisses the common belief that obese people themselves are to blame for their problem by showing how the food industry manipulates consumers into making bad choices that often lead to serious health issues, including obesity. She supports her call for more regulation by showing how the government has made other industries safer over the past century.

Summary and response

Summary: *In her essay "A Desired Epidemic: Obesity and the Food Industry," posted on www. washingtonpost.com in 2007, Deborah Cohen argues that the food industry is to blame for America's obesity problem and, therefore, should be more closely regulated by the federal government. Cohen, a physician, dismisses the common belief that obese people themselves are to blame for their problem by showing how the food industry manipulates consumers into making bad choices that often lead to serious health issues, including obesity. She supports her call for more regulation by showing how the government has made other industries—including building construction, auto manufacturing, and alcohol sales—safer over the past century. Finally, she emphasizes the need for action by citing the massive toll obesity and its related illnesses will continue to take on Americans.*

Response: *Although I agree with Cohen that obesity is a major health issue in this country and that food marketing can lead people to make unhealthy choices in their diets, I can't completely accept her claim that "people are not the problem." I feel this way partly because I believe we're always responsible, at least to a degree, for the choices we make and partly because Cohen seems to undermine her own position. In the fourth paragraph, for example, in defending her contention that people aren't the problem, she adopts an almost sarcastic tone when she asks if, in holding the overweight responsible for their choices, we "think that two-thirds of Americans are foolish, stupid, and lazy" or are weaker and "morally inferior" to everybody else. In other words, she equates holding people responsible with thinking they're lazy and stupid. Then, however, she introduces scientific evidence that shows how easily people can be manipulated, compares consumers to Pavlov's dog, and refers to obese people as "victims." This seems to support the argument that, sometimes, people are weak. Despite this flaw in Cohen's reasoning, I think she makes a valid point about the need for more oversight of the food industry by showing how devastating obesity can be and how the government has intervened in the past to regulate other industries to protect consumers.*

Rhetorical Analysis

Like analytical reading (discussed in Chapter 2), rhetorical analysis demands attention to detail and a focus on how—and how well—texts work. More specifically, this kind of assignment asks you to think about how the author uses the rhetorical appeals—ethos, pathos, and logos—to produce his argument and reach his readers. And just as the text you're analyzing should make an argument about an issue, your rhetorical analysis should present a claim about the text itself and the argument it makes. Remember, though, that the focus should not be on your opinion about the topic being discussed in the text, but on explaining how the author has put together an argument that appeals (or fails to appeal) to the audience.

What follows are a few tips for writing a rhetorical analysis and then a sample set of notes and questions about an essay titled "A Christian View of War" that appeared in *USA Today*. The annotations are coded to help you understand how to think and write about an argument in terms of the rhetorical appeals. Comments that deal with ethos are marked with an (E), those about pathos with (P), and those focusing on logos (L). You'll notice some annotations have more than one label; that's because the appeals often spill over into one another. (If you need a reminder about what the appeals are and how they work, turn to page 26 in Chapter 2). But first, the tips:

- Start by carefully reading and annotating the text under analysis.
- Based on this reading (and rereading), try to develop an interesting, specific claim about the text itself. But remember that you're not entering into this conversation via your opinion about the writer or her topic. Instead, you're thinking about how the text is working; what types of appeals it relies on; what types of vocabulary it uses; how it establishes logos, ethos, and pathos; and the ways it engages with the issues at hand. (See "Formulating a Claim," on page 56.)
- Next, identify those places in the text that speak directly to your thesis. What parts of the essay support the points you're making about the text? How and why did these elements make you come to your claim or conclusion? At this point you might also want to think about organization. How might you best incorporate these points into your rhetorical analysis? How should they be ordered?
- Now, start drafting. In a formal essay, you'll probably begin with an engaging introduction that also includes your very specific thesis statement. (For example, "Oliver 'Buzz' Thomas uses several different kinds of appeals in his essay 'A Christian View of War'" is vague and uninformative. Here's a better thesis: "In 'A Christian View of War,' Oliver 'Buzz' Thomas uses his position as a minister, his knowledge of the Bible, and clear understanding of how Americans feel about their faith and about the war on terror to argue for a more Christian approach our thinking about the conflict.")
- Early in your paper, you should identify the rhetorical situation for the essay you're analyzing. In other words, explain who you think the target audience is and why you think the author wrote the piece. This discussion will provide important background information for your readers.
- As you move into the body of your paper, you'll need to analyze the elements of the text you have identified in your thesis. Do this by first summarizing or even quoting each portion of the text you want to deal with (you must be accurate in your summaries and provide context for your quotations). Next, show how each of these sections is working rhetorically—what appeals it makes, how it works independently and with the rest of the text, and how it is (or isn't) effective. This is your analysis, so make sure you're clear and provide plenty of specific details from the text.
- Finally, close your essay. This is often easier said than done because you might feel like you have nothing left to write about. At the very least, you can always recap your analysis and tell your readers why you think the text was effective (or not).

A CHRISTIAN VIEW OF WAR

Oliver "Buzz" Thomas

OLIVER "BUZZ" THOMAS is a minister in Tennessee and author of *10 Things Your Minister Wants to Tell You (But Can't Because He Needs the Job)*. He wrote this column for the September 18, 2006, edition of *USA Today*.

"Pray for our troops." Millions of signs and bumper stickers carry the message, and part of me likes it. But part of me keeps waiting for another bumper sticker—the one I still haven't seen. Whether Jesus would drive an SUV, I'm still not sure. Truth is he'd probably ride the bus. Or the subway. But if he had money for a car and didn't give it all away to the hookers and the homeless before he got to the used-car lot, I'm pretty sure that his bumper sticker would say "pray for our enemies."

Before you write me off as a left-wing crackpot, consider what we know. During his famous Sermon on the Mount, Jesus said three things relevant to the subject of war:

- Blessed are the peacemakers.
- Turn the other cheek.
- Pray for your enemies.

Here's something else we know. Three-quarters of the U.S. population consider themselves Christian. That translates into about 224 million Americans. So why are so few of us taking the teachings of Jesus seriously when it comes to this latest war?

RHETORICAL ANALYSIS NOTES

1 The title—with "Christian" and "War" in the same phrase—might appeal to readers' emotions or imaginations. **(P)**

2 Thomas is a minister, which gives him some authority and expertise since he's writing about Christianity and the Bible. **(E)**

3 The title of Thomas' book is interesting; he doesn't seem like a politically conservative minister. **(E)**

4 This was published in *USA Today*, popular mainstream newspaper. What does this say about his target audience? **(E,L,P)**

5 The first sentence is a strong emotional appeal, especially among the religious. **(P)**

6 He uses first person, which can place him closer to his audience. Also, his tone is friendly (he uses a little humor in the this paragraph). **(E, P)**

7 The last sentence might really push the emotional buttons of some Christians by making them rethink their assumptions about how Jesus would respond—with compassion, according to the author—to our enemies. **(P)**

8 Thomas directly addresses his ethos by proving what he is not: a "left-wing crackpot." **(E)**

9 He shows his knowledge of the Bible by introducing a specific sermon to bolster his position. **(E, L)**

10 These three points also support Thomas' claim about how Jesus would feel about war and our enemies. **(L)**

11 Thomas sets up a logical question by introducing these numbers. His suggestion is that since there are so many self-identified Christians, more people should be taking the teachings of Jesus seriously. **(L)**

12 His question challenges readers—especially those who are Christian. **(P, L)**

Out here in the heartland, only a handful of churches are even talking about it.

Christian obligations

The most plausible explanation is that we're scared. Some things, it seems, may trump religion. Fear is one of them. If Christians are afraid (and who could blame them after 9/11?), it's not surprising that they're listening to other voices besides Jesus' when it comes to the war in Iraq. So what should the three-fourths of Americans who identify themselves as "Christian" make of the Iraq war?

We could spend a lot of time debating whether St. Augustine's "Just War Theory" can be stretched to accommodate our invasion of Iraq, but at this late date it really doesn't matter. We invaded. And, if the Just War Theory means anything, it means that we shouldn't leave Iraq in a bigger mess than we found it. Americans of faith, it would seem, are obligated to do at least the following:

• Express concern for all suffering, including that of our enemies. That means more than paying lip service. As James, the brother of Jesus, said, it does not suffice to tell a hungry man "God bless you!" or "We will pray for you!" We must address his hunger. The same can be said for the additional food, health care, police and countless other things the Iraqi people need. And, though an immediate withdrawal would be precipitous, we must work diligently to respond to the Iraqis' desire that our troops leave as quickly as possible.

• Recommit ourselves to the fundamental principles of justice and human rights that have been a hallmark of our faith, as well as of our nation. That means no more secret prisons, no more secret trials and no more torture. America cannot resort to the worst practices of the Gulag (where citizens were

13 "Out here in the heartland" is a phrase that helps Thomas seem like a regular guy, not a "left-wing crackpot." **(E, P)**

14 Thomas offers one possible answer to his question (this is a logical appeal because his answer makes sense). **(L)**

15 He shows empathy with this parenthetical, saying it's understandable that people are afraid. **(E, P)**

16 Thomas uses this question to set up his proposal. **(L)**

17 But first tries to establish some common ground with those who might not agree with him by saying, basically, "Let's agree that there's no reason to debate the justification of the war; what's important is deciding what to do now." **(E, L)**

18 He uses the word "obligated," an appeal to Christians' sense of morals and duty (he continues this throughout his proposal), and evidence of his authority. **(E, P)**

19 He presents his proposal in a clear list. **(L)**

20 Thomas continues his authoritative tone throughout his proposal, opening each point in his list with a strong verb ("express," "recommit," "repudiate," "force") and using the word *must* several times. **(E)**

21 Introducing the story of James further shows Thomas' knowledge of the Bible while also setting up an analogy between the needs of the "hungry man" and those of the Iraqi people. **(E, L)** Comparing what's going on in Iraq to a story from the Bible might anger some people, however. **(P)**

22 He acknowledges that leaving Iraq immediately isn't a good idea, another attempt to establish common ground with those who disagree with him. **(E)**

23 This is another strong emotional appeal. Thomas links specific principles that are important to both Christianity and the United States and says we have to "recommit" to them, which means we *aren't* committed to them now. Such suggestions play on feelings of sympathy and even guilt. **(P)**

declared "enemies of the state" and whisked away to Siberian work camps without the benefit of a fair trial or the assistance of counsel) and expect to be an accepted member of the world community, much less a leader of it.

• Repudiate the statements of any religious or political leader who suggests that America has a special claim on God. He may have a special claim on us, but we do not have a special claim on him. Our beloved nation is a civil state, not a religious one. There are no references to God in our Constitution. The only reference to religion—other than in the First Amendment—is found in Article VI, which proclaims that there will be no religious test for public office in the USA. The Founding Fathers gave us a secular state in which all religions are free to flourish or flounder on their own initiative without interference by the government. Those running around claiming we are "in the army of God" or slapping up copies of the Ten Commandments on government buildings threaten to turn us into the very sort of society we are fighting against in this new war.

• Force our elected officials to address the conditions that have given rise to global terrorism in the first place. Terrorism exists for a reason. One of those reasons is that our society has been far too unconcerned about the plight of Muslim people around the world. Why, for example, have we not instituted a mini-Marshall Plan for the millions of Palestinians who have often gone without adequate land, roads, hospitals and schools since the 1967 war with Israel? Corruption among Palestinian leaders has squandered billions in the past, but responsible partners on the ground can and must be found. Private foundations with a long history of engagement might be a good place to start.

24 This is also an emotional appeal because he's comparing us to the Soviet Union (and its Gulag prison system). Here, too, he seems to play on our feelings of guilt, fear, and maybe even pride. (P)

25 He uses an analogy here: We can't act like the bad guys and hope to be seen as the good guys. (L)

26 If Thomas' target audience is Christians—and it seems to be, based on his tone and approach—then this is probably his strongest emotional appeal, and the thing that could really anger some readers. He's asking Christians to abandon the idea that the United States is a religious state and has a "special claim on God." (P)

27 He supports his position by making intellectual appeals—pointing out what is and isn't in the Constitution and explaining why the Founding Fathers did what they did. This is also another example of his expertise and authority. (L, E)

28 Here, Thomas changes his tone a little as he takes a jab at specific Christians—those who he says are trying to turn America into a religious state. He compares these people to the Muslim fundamentalists we're fighting in Iraq and Afghanistan. (P, E)

29 In this paragraph, he makes his strongest and most sustained logical appeal—trying to get his audience to understand the causal relationship between the dire living conditions of many Palestinians and the spread of terrorism. (L)

30 He makes an analogy to the Marshall Plan, the U.S.-led and -financed effort to rebuild Europe after World War II. (L)

31 Here, he makes a concession, acknowledging that there have been problems with corruption in the past. (E)

32 But, he says, past problems are no reason to give up completely. (L, P)

Tackling terrorism's roots

We need not and should not repudiate our long-standing alliance with Israel to accomplish this. It's simply that our religious traditions teach us that to whom much is given, much is required. The irony, of course, is that it's in our best interest to relieve Palestinian suffering. True, some terrorist leaders come from affluent families and cite Western worldliness and decadence as their motivation for jihad, but the economic factor cannot be ignored. There is no better recruiting ground for the troops of terror than the maddening monotony and grinding poverty of a refugee camp.

In ancient times, particular gods were associated with particular nations. "Tribal deities," we call them. Today we know better. God is not the mascot of Republicans, Democrats or, for that matter, Americans. God transcends all national and political affiliations. His precinct is the universe.

America is in the deep woods. Never have we been less popular in the eyes of the world. Never have we faced so unsettling an enemy. But before we circle the wagons, Christians should get serious about following the teachings of the one by whose name we are called. He might just know the way out.

33 In this first sentence, Thomas anticipates a possible objection to his argument by offering reassurance about Israel. **(L, P)**

34 Again, he appeals to Christian obligations ("our religious traditions teach us …") **(P)**

35 Then he shows why this stance also makes logical sense. **(L)**

36 As he moves toward his conclusion, Thomas reasserts his claim that God has no particular political alignment. **(P)**

37 He closes with one last, powerful emotional appeal: that, by truly following the teachings of Jesus, Christians might get a better sense of how to move forward in the war against terrorism. **(P)**

Formulating a Claim

Next, we want to show you a few steps to help you move from your reading notes to a claim that you can use to write a rhetorical analysis essay (along with an example of these steps in action, using the essay "A Christian View of War," above).

Step 1: Identify the Argument

a. Underline the author's thesis statement.

b. Write down what you think the author is trying to argue (the main argument she is trying to make in the essay). This may

Step 1

What is Thomas' thesis? See the second paragraph after the "Christian obligations" subhead (especially the last sentence).

be more than one sentence and may be found in a few places in the text.

Note: If you can't do this, go back to the text and read it again. Ask yourself: What is the point? What is the author trying to do in the essay?

We think the main argument is this: Christians should reexamine their thinking about the war in Iraq by revisiting and more closely following Jesus' teachings.

Step 2: Look at Your Notes

a. Have you analyzed the parts of the essay thoroughly?

- Have you looked for each rhetorical appeal at work?
  - o Which appeal(s) seem strongest? Most effective? Why?
  - o Which seem weakest? Why?
  - o If you don't see evidence of one of the appeals, make sure you note that. Sometimes, rhetorical analysis is as much about what's *not* there as what is. Think about why an author might want to emphasize one appeal while avoiding another.

b. Have you thought about how the parts of the essay work as a whole, to give the essay meaning?

- How do the appeals overlap?
- How do they work together?
- What is the overall effect of the appeals on the reader?
- Does the argument work? (Is it effective or ineffective?)

Step 3: Decide What You Want to Say

a. Based on Steps 1 and 2, develop an analytical claim that includes a statement of your position on the text (the argument you want to make about the text, based on your analysis) and a summary of the reasons you'll use to support your claim.

b. Fashion this into a thesis statement. Keep in mind that you'll probably have to do this a few times before you settle on your actual thesis.

Step 2

The strongest appeals seem to be based on ethos and pathos.

Thomas' appeals to intellect (logos) aren't necessarily weak, but they seem to be there to help establish his ethical position as the author (his authority and credibility) and thus are the least prominent.

Pathos and logos often overlap with ethos—and vice versa. In other words, his ethos pervades the whole argument.

The appeals combine to make Thomas seem like a reasonable, authoritative, and intelligent critic of how Christians are thinking about the war. He may say some things that some people don't like, but it's hard to question his credibility and sincerity.

The appeals make the text interesting and make Thomas seem like a guy worth hearing out.

Yes, we think the argument is effective. It probably makes some people stop and think about how their faith influences their thinking about the war.

Step 3

Thomas has written an effective argument by establishing himself as an authoritative and credible source and by piquing the audience's interest with emotion and reason. He does this by using all three rhetorical appeals.

Our thesis statement: Oliver "Buzz" Thomas uses his position as a minister and his knowledge of the Bible to press all of the right emotional and intellectual buttons to get his audience to listen to his message: that many Christians need to rethink their position on the war in Iraq.

Sample Rhetorical Analysis

The following essay is based on the notes above, although you'll notice that it doesn't use every item listed in the notes. Part of making the transition from annotations to more formal notes to a draft involves deciding what to use and what to leave out in order to make a claim and support it. The rhetorical analysis was written in response to Exercise 3 at the end of this chapter.

WHAT WOULD JESUS DO? USE RHETORIC WISELY

1 With the war in Iraq well into its fifth year, with the U.S. death toll moving past 4,000, and with no end to the conflict in sight, many Americans seem to have stopped paying attention to the fighting. While those with family and friends in the military no doubt are fully aware that the war is still raging, many others are consumed by more immediate concerns like rising gas prices and a falling economy. But the war drags on, and many Americans—and even more Iraqis—will continue to die because of it. For this reason, according to an opinion piece by Oliver "Buzz" Thomas, Americans need to keep the war in their minds. And, Thomas argues, if they identify themselves as Christians, they also should change the way they think about the war so that they can figure out how to bring it to an end. Writing in *USA Today*, the nation's largest circulation newspaper, Thomas speaks directly to Christians in the column, titled "A Christian View of War." He uses his position as a minister and his knowledge of the Bible to press all of the right emotional and intellectual buttons to get his audience to listen to his message: that Christians need to rethink their position on the war by trying to think and act in a more Christ-like manner.

2 In rhetorical terms, Thomas' strongest and most consistent appeal is his ethos. Writing to a large and broad audience—*USA Today* claimed 2,259,329 daily readers in 2006, the year "A Christian View of War" was published ("Timeline")—he specifically reaches out to the "[t]hree-quarters of the U.S. population [who] consider themselves Christian" (Thomas). The fact that he is a minister is explained in a biographical note, and Thomas shows his expertise on the subject of Christianity with specific examples from the Bible and an authoritative tone. In the third paragraph, for example, he brings up Jesus' Sermon on the Mount; in the seventh, he discusses a relevant quote from James, the brother of Jesus; and in the ninth, he explains why Americas don't, in fact, have a special claim on God. Thomas seems to know that, because he is trying to connect with Christian readers, he needs to establish his credentials if he wants them to listen. What makes his argument especially effective, however, is that Thomas doesn't stake his ethical appeal entirely on his credentials as a minister. Early in his column, he uses humor and self-awareness of the task before him to help readers see him as more than a know-it-all who is trying to tell them what to do. In the second

paragraph, he establishes a friendly and slightly humorous tone when he talks about the kind of car Jesus might drive, and he starts the third paragraph with, "Before you write me off as a left-wing crackpot..." (Thomas). By doing these things, Thomas lets readers know that he is a reasonable person worth hearing out, even though he might say some things they don't agree with.

3 As strong and consistent as his ethos is, Thomas doesn't rely on that appeal alone. He also weaves in effective pathetic and logical appeals to reach out to his readers and persuade them to listen to his argument. Because the implications of a drawn-out war are grave, Thomas' appeals to his audience's emotions are especially evocative. He calls our attention to the plight of the Iraqi people in paragraph seven when he makes an analogy between them and the "hungry man" of James' parable. By bringing the Iraqi civilians into the position of the hungry man for whom Christians should feel compassion, Thomas vividly illustrates the necessity of caring for our enemies. His decision to appeal to his audience's emotions at this particular moment in the column is especially shrewd because just following his analogy of the Iraqi civilians to the sympathetic hungry man, Thomas puts forth what might be a divisive claim: that "we must work diligently to respond to the Iraqis' desire that our troops leave as quickly as possible" (Thomas). By evoking sympathy from his readers for the Iraqi people, Thomas makes it more likely that his readers (perhaps even those who disagree with his position) will soften towards the idea that the U.S. troops should withdraw from Iraq. Thus, his no-nonsense policy claim is cushioned by his attempts to soften the audience's emotions.

4 While Thomas appeals to his audience's sense of compassion and concern for humanity, he also, on occasion, makes rhetorical moves to stoke its sense of guilt. In paragraph eight, in which Thomas suggests that Christians should "[r]ecommit [themselves] to the fundamental principles of justice and human rights," he implies that they are *not* committed to them at present. This lack of commitment amounts to the abandonment of a central tenet of the Christian faith, an abandonment that no serious Christian should abide. In addition to subtly pointing out what qualities his Christian audience is lacking, Thomas intensifies his appeal to his audience's sense of guilt by appealing to some common fears. He writes that "America cannot resort to the worst practices of the Gulag (where citizens were declared 'enemies of the state' and whisked away to Siberian work camps without the benefit of a fair trial or the assistance of counsel) [...]" (Thomas). The phrase "whisked away to Siberian work camps" is full of vivid imagery that conjures up mental pictures of cold, barren, and unforgiving landscapes where innocents are pushed well beyond their physical and mental limits in the service of a state that is not their own. This violent and cruel picture works in two ways. First, it encourages readers to imagine themselves in this situation—to imagine themselves as cold, frightened, stripped of free will, and forced into painful and burdensome manual labor. Second, it encourages readers to transfer this emotional terror from themselves to the prisoners and the victims of our current War in Iraq. After all, it is our country that has been exposed for torturing prisoners of war at Abu Ghraib. It is our country that has been widely criticized for holding large numbers of individuals at Guantanamo Bay without lodging any official charges against them. Though Thomas does not list these incidents by name, he is no doubt playing on this knowledge of his audience in order to help them feel empathy for the enemy. This single passage causes the audience to feel the victims' pain, and

then it forces them to imagine themselves as complicit with the ones causing it.

5 In the hands of another, less sensitive writer, these appeals might seem like ham-fisted, emotional manipulation. Indeed, if they were not handled with just the right balance, they would undoubtedly turn readers off instead of predisposing them to listen to the author's claims. Thomas, however, is able to make successful use of this kind of rhetorical force because he positions himself as a knowledgeable, lighthearted, and reasonable person throughout the column. Even when he hits on the most emotionally incendiary issues, his humor and compassion come through. When he concludes his column, for example, Thomas makes the claim that "God is not the mascot of the Republicans, the Democrats or, for that matter, Americans" (Thomas). Though this is an important element of Thomas's claim that America is a secular nation that does not possess God's will to impose itself on another country, it still has a sense of humor. The very notion of God as a mascot—as if he were rallying a college football team—lightens the mood even as it conveys this serious point. It is this light touch that allows Thomas's gravity to work so effectively on the audience.

6 What makes Thomas truly successful is not the effectiveness of any single rhetorical appeal—in fact, more often than not the appeals overlap. Much of Thomas' ethos, for example, is built on appeals to the audience's emotion, imagination, and intellect. He often cites specific incidents from the Bible, simultaneously reinforcing his ethos as an expert on the subject and reassuring his audience that it makes sense for them to listen to his argument. In the fourth paragraph, he again embeds one appeal in another when he posits the question: if three-quarters of the U.S. population—224 million people—identify themselves as Christians, "why are so few of us taking the teachings of Jesus seriously when it comes to this latest war" (Thomas)? Here, and in the fifth paragraph, where he provides one possible answer to the question (the understandable fear that lingers after 9/11), Thomas blends logic and emotion into a single, powerful appeal. His logical claim is that because so many Americans identify themselves as Christians, it seems that more of them should share his view on the war. Beyond making a logical point, however, this claim also provokes the audience—perhaps to shame, guilt, or even anger—into considering the possibility that it is not behaving in a truly Christian manner. As he does elsewhere his column, Thomas tempers his provocations with his compassion and affability. In this instance he sympathetically refers to the emotional aftermath of 9/11, and he goes so far to lump himself in—"why are so few of *us*?" —with those he addresses (Thomas). Here again, Thomas's ethos helps make palatable claims that might otherwise turn an audience off.

7 In the end, this artful use of rhetoric is the key to the difficult task Thomas has undertaken: to ask Christians to reexamine the application of their faith in their thinking about the war. And rather than preach to them, he persuades, allowing his knowledgeable, humorous, and cordial ethos to usher through his sometimes serious and cutting claims.

Works Cited

Thomas, Oliver "Buzz." "A Christian View of War." *USA Today* (Sept. 18, 2006): 13A.

"Timeline." *USA Today* online. (May 2008). http://www.usatoday.com/media_kit/pressroom/pr_timeline.htm (accessed May 30, 2008).

CLASSICAL RHETORIC AND WRITING ARGUMENTS

One of the things we want to stress in this chapter and the next is that, for persuasion to be effective, it must respond appropriately to specific situations. If, for example, you are trying to make an argument in a paper for an English assignment, you will have to take a different approach than the one you would adopt if you were trying to convince your friend to attend yoga class with you. Although the latter can take place over a few informal conversations and might entail your listing the myriad benefits of holding downward facing dog, the former will require a sustained line of thinking and, very likely, a formal tone that suggests you have done some research. Knowing a thing or two about rhetoric can help you identify and think critically about the situations to which you must respond and can help you decide just how you want to approach each of your attempts at persuasion. Thus, we'll use the rest of this chapter to tell you a bit more about Classical rhetoric so you can better understand why it is still so vital, and then we'll show you how to use some of these Classical approaches to compose your own arguments. We'll spend most of our time preparing you for the in-depth instruction on writing arguments that comes in Chapter 4.

As we've mentioned in previous chapters, the study and practice of rhetoric rose in response to the demands of Athens' burgeoning democracy, and the composition of the decision-making bodies determined what types of arguments citizens needed to make in order to govern themselves. The most prominent realms for such public discourse were the Athenian Assembly, where citizens voted on the city-state's political policies, and the legal courts, where citizens could bring prosecutions against one another and where they might have to defend themselves against such cases.

Unlike our own legislative branch, which relies on a relatively small group of elected representatives who can conceivably maintain power for their entire lives, the Athenian Assembly required that all citizens participate directly, debating and ultimately voting on the issues that came before its very large audience (the quorum, or majority vote, was about 6,000 citizens). The Athenians resisted a representative election system precisely because they feared it would grant too much power to too few individuals. Instead of such elections, the Assembly's officials were selected by lot, and those who did win lotteries generally held their positions for only one year. In addition to these short terms, the officials had limited power: they could set meeting agendas, prepare informational materials, and make recommendations to those in attendance. Because this format allowed individual citizens to weigh in on issues that included strategies for war, the allocation of taxes, and relations with neighboring city-states, having the capacity to persuade an audience was of the utmost importance.

One famous example of this power of persuasion comes from the Athenian general Themistocles, who once made a speech in the Assembly that is said to have saved the fate of Athens when it could have been destroyed by a powerful enemy. Around 480 B.C.E, the Athenians discovered a previously unknown silver mine, and the normal response to such a boon was to divide this newfound wealth among all the citizens. Themistocles, however, had a greater vision, realizing that Athens was threatened by the larger and more powerful Persian army. Alone in stressing the long-term danger to his fellow citizens, Themistocles is said to have delivered a dazzling speech in which he successfully argued that, instead of dividing the silver among the citizens, Athens should use it to build a large naval fleet that could protect the city from invasions.

The Athenians voted according to Themistocles' charge and used their newfound wealth to build ships. With their powerful fleet, Athens was later able to defeat the invading Persian army even though their soldiers were far outnumbered. Themistocles' speech didn't rely on reason alone: In order to persuade his large audience to give up their shares of silver, the general suggested that the citizens faced imminent danger from a neighboring city-state, making the threat seem immediate and personal. Recognizing what ideals were most important to his audience (immediacy above long-term planning), Themistocles delivered a speech that made the most effective appeals to their beliefs and persuaded them to vote in his favor.

Like the Assembly, Athenian legal courts required that citizens speak for themselves; indeed, they had to try their own cases. There were no lawyers or experts who could speak persuasively for them, and the juries they had to sway were large—usually composed of about 200 people. This meant that Athenian citizens had to be skilled enough in argument to be able to sway large numbers of citizens to vote in their favor. Artful persuasion was especially important because ancient juries took no time for deliberation in the way that modern juries do. Immediately after the speeches ended, jurors cast their votes and the issues were decided. Whether or not a man was found guilty of murder could rest almost entirely on how he had affected the jury with his speech.

While the mechanics of the jury system certainly have evolved over the past two millennia, the crimes and complaints that led Athenians to court are strikingly similar to those that fill our dockets today. From adultery and murder to inheritance disputes and fraud, the list sounds like a programming guide for Court TV. One such trial, in the early fourth century B.C.E., involved an Athenian citizen named Euphiletus, a farmer of humble means who murdered a man named Eratosthenes for committing adultery with his wife. The facts of the case were not in question: The defendant Euphiletus admitted killing Eratosthenes, and the letter of Athenian law allowed a man who had caught another committing adultery with his wife to kill the offender (although most outraged husbands in his position would have demanded remuneration rather than exacting the penalty of death). Furthermore, no one prosecuting on behalf of the slain Eratosthenes denied that he had slept with the farmer's wife. But Eratosthenes' family did claim that the killing was premeditated and thus not allowable under Athenian law. So, Euphiletus found himself in court trying to show the jury that the killing was both legal and understandable. Not practiced in the art of rhetoric, he presented a defense speech prepared for him by the famous logographer Lysias. It begins as follows:

FROM *ON THE MURDER OF ERATOSTHENES*

[1] I would be very grateful, gentlemen, if you, the jurymen in this case, judged me as you would judge yourselves, were you to go through the same sort of experience. For I am well aware that if you employed the same standards for others as you do for your own behavior, there is not a single one of you who would not be furious at what has happened. In fact, all of you would consider the penalties light for those who practice such things.

² And these feelings would be acknowledged not just by you but by the whole of Greece. For in the case of this crime alone both democracy and oligarchy offer the same redress to their weakest members as to their most powerful. The result is that the least individual has the same opportunity as the greatest. In the same way, gentlemen, all humanity considers this kind of violation to be the most outrageous of acts.

³ I believe, then, that all of you have the same opinion about the severity of the punishment, and that no one considers the matter to be so frivolous that he supposes that those guilty of such acts should be pardoned or deserve light penalties.

⁴ I believe, gentlemen, that what I have to demonstrate is this: that Eratosthenes seduced my wife and corrupted her, that he brought shame on my children and insulted me by entering my house, that there was no cause for enmity between him and me apart from this, and that I did not commit this deed for money, to make myself rich instead of poor, nor for any other advantage except revenge, as the law allows.

⁵ I shall, then, reveal the whole story to you from the beginning, omitting nothing, but telling the truth. For I believe my only chance of survival lies in my telling you everything that has taken place.

While we have no record of the verdict, the speech itself clearly shows how important the ability to persuade was, even for ordinary Athenians. The man who wrote the piece, Lysias, made his living by selling speeches to litigants in ancient Athens and was famous for his ability to dramatically articulate unique human characteristics for each of his customers. According to the classical rhetoric scholar George A. Kennedy, this "technique of conveying the character of the speaker"—called *ethopoeia*—was one of Lysias' great gifts to oratory. "A speech appeared more genuine and less rehearsed if it seemed to be the work of the speaker himself," rather than the speechwriter, Kennedy says in *A New History of Classical Rhetoric*. Lysias often would establish rapport with an audience by revealing some trivial weakness in his client that also worked to convey the client's credibility. In the excerpt above, for example, Euphiletus, the defendant, comes off as overly blunt. Although the jury might not like him, this bluntness could make it harder for them to believe that he had set a sly trap for his wife's lover in order to kill him.

Though these examples from antiquity may seem distant—even a bit dusty—what they demonstrate is the enduring power of rhetoric to help individuals respond to real-life situations. The training and techniques devised and practiced by these Classical rhetoricians are as useful and adaptable today as they were 2,500 years ago. What Classical rhetoric teaches us is that whatever rhetorical situation we face—whether it be asking a professor for an extension or composing a public persona on Facebook—our rhetorical skills can help us determine how best to proceed in the face of uncertainty. It was precisely this need for persuasive savvy that made rhetoric such an integral part of Athenian culture and in turn gave rise to an expert group of writers, teachers, and speakers called the Sophists whose influence is still evident today.

Ancient Rhetoric Teachers
and What We Can Learn from Them

Given that argument and persuasion figured so prominently in the most pressing policy and legal decisions in Athens, it's no surprise that the study and practice of persuasion flourished during this time. In response to these practical demands of democracy, and because people needed to know how to argue well, a group of roaming teachers called the Sophists (from the Greek word *sophos*, or wise one) began to flourish in the fifth century B.C.E. These teachers, many of whom traveled to Athens (and elsewhere) from other parts of the Mediterranean, developed rhetoric as a system of study and sold their services, often for large sums of money. Unlike Plato and other philosophers whose primary concern was the discovery of truth, the Sophists were more pragmatic. Some believed that if truth were to be found, it would be only through argument; others were more interested in practical matters, seeing rhetoric as a useful means for making decisions and for producing persuasive public speech. Plato famously condemned the Sophists—and rhetoric—in some of his dialogues, giving voice to feelings that many in Athens had: that these men—many of them foreigners—were making a living by teaching people how to flatter and deceive with words. This reputation has dogged the Sophists since, though in recent years scholars have begun to reassess their contributions to Western culture.

The Sophists taught by example, preparing and delivering speeches that their students would memorize and developing training practices that helped students compose their own orations. They believed in the power of *kairos* or timeliness—the idea that each instance of persuasion must respond appropriately to its moment. In other words, their belief was that speaking was always situational and that successful orators had the capacity to judge when and how they should attempt to persuade; they could identify the right moment to intervene. And although they were the first to offer systematic and intensive instruction in rhetoric—some of their stylistic and pedagogical practices are still in use—their work was never consolidated into a single source that set forth their thinking about the subject. Indeed, most of their individual work has been lost or is known only through its mention in texts written by others. Still, what we do have from these teachers of rhetoric such as Gorgias, Isocrates, and others is invaluable. Their extant speeches and fragments show us the power of language and the importance of persuasion in social discourse, and their approaches to teaching—often reproduced in texts by later writers—help us understand and appreciate the value of intensive study and training in rhetoric.

One of the most famous and influential of the Sophists was Gorgias of Leontini, a diplomat turned teacher, philosopher, and public speaker who reportedly lived to be more than a hundred years old (you'll find his most famous speech, *Encomium of Helen*, starting on page 39). Citing an ancient historian named Didorus Siculus, George A. Kennedy says Gorgias was sent to Athens as a diplomat from his hometown in Sicily in 427 B.C.E. and made an immediate impression with his oratorical skill. Quoting Siculus, Kennedy writes that Gorgias "addressed the Athenians on the subject of an alliance, and by the novelty of his style he amazed" them. Not surprisingly, his specialty was ceremonial rhetoric, and he often spoke at festivals and on other special occasions, a rare honor for a foreigner in Athens.

Though Gorgias was a dazzling entertainer and a sought-after teacher, it is his enduring claim about the power of language that interests us most. As he suggests in his *Encomium of Helen,* Gorgias taught that speech was no less important than action. Instead he argues that language had concrete effects—that it could "stop fear, banish grief, create joy, nurture pity, and cause shuddering." Much like a drug, it had the capacity to both help and harm its recipient, and beyond this power, he argued that language was our only means of perceiving the world and interacting with it.

If Gorgias was the celebrity orator of his time, able by his own accounts to speak extemporaneously on just about any topic, it was a master teacher of rhetoric named Isocrates who makes the most compelling case for the continued relevance of rhetorical study. Born in 436 B.C.E.—about 50 years after Gorgias—Isocrates was, unlike most of the earlier rhetoric teachers, a citizen of Athens. He spent a period as a speechwriter, like his contemporary Lysias, and later opened the first school of rhetoric in the city. It was there, as a teacher and writer, that Isocrates made his great reputation.

One of the lessons we have taken from Isocrates involves his belief in intensive rhetorical training; another is his focus on developing in students the capacity to respond. In his speech called *Antidosis,* a lengthy defense of his life and work, Isocrates outlines a philosophy of education that compares "physical training for the body" with "philosophy for the soul." In other words, for Isocrates, the study of rhetoric isn't just about learning how to give a single speech, and it isn't even about memorizing a set of general precepts you can follow blindly. Instead, rhetoric is useful because it helps you develop the ability to deliver the most appropriate speech based on whatever rhetorical circumstances face you. His goal for rhetorical training was to condition students so that they could respond appropriately to any situation, especially to those that no one could predict. To this end, Isocrates' students took up subjects that weren't immediately useful to their day-to-day lives, but their learning processes conditioned their minds so that they were fit to undertake any intellectual task that might come up in the future.

Isocrates also argued that his students—whether they were famous leaders or private citizens—made Athens a better democracy and claimed that no student ever left his school an immoral scoundrel. Thus, Isocrates argued that rhetorical education was a kind of training in citizenship, and he claimed that the more ardently a student wanted to become a good speaker, the more he would strive to be a good person, too, because those who commanded the most respect and had the best motives were the most persuasive to their audiences. With its emphasis on civic response, Isocrates' work is a testament to the enduring power of rhetorical study, even in a modern-day context. The more you write, and the more practice you get in fashioning different arguments for different audiences, the better prepared you will be to respond to the rhetorical situations that face you in the future.

USING CLASSICAL APPROACHES: ARISTOTLE AND HERMAGORAS

Aristotle and the Art of Rhetoric

Because so little of the Sophists' work survives—and because these teachers and orators apparently were disinclined toward formalizing and writing down their thinking about the subject—most of our foundational knowledge about rhetoric comes from Aristotle. His position as a student of Plato's and a contemporary of many of the great Sophists gave him a unique perspective on the use and teaching of rhetoric, and in his classic text called *Rhetoric* (written in part while he was teaching rhetoric courses at Plato's Academy), he responds both to Plato's vocal objections to the subject and its most famous teachers as well as to the Sophists themselves and their pedagogical practices.

Aristotle saw rhetoric as more than a simple bag of tricks, as critics often referred to it, but he didn't agree with the methods used by some of the Sophists in their teaching, either. Gorgias, for one, taught by example: He delivered dazzling model speeches and then required his students to memorize them. What bothered Aristotle about this approach was that it was not governed by a *techne* (an art or method). Contrary to that Sophistic approach, Aristotle (as you read in Chapter 2) defined rhetoric as "the faculty of observing in any given case the available means of persuasion." This idea of rhetoric as a faculty (or an ability) is what makes his rhetorical definition just as useful in the realm of writing as it does in the realm of critical reading. Indeed, his interest here is in placing invention, or the discovery of lines of argument, at the center of the rhetorical enterprise. Aristotle also linked his work to the Sophists' focus on successful persuasive speaking while simultaneously setting his system apart by emphasizing the process of "observing" or exploring. This idea was at the heart of Aristotle's *techne*, or method, for rhetoric. And this is important to us for a couple of reasons:

- First, by presenting rhetoric as a process ("the faculty of observing") rather than simply a product (like a great speech), he gave us a model for using argument to do more than win a debate. He showed us how to use the process to think about, explore, and consider many courses of action before making a decision.
- Second, in declaring that rhetoric has no specific subject matter ("in any given case"), Aristotle stressed the ability to attend to whatever issue was at hand (an idea similar to Isocrates' desire to teach students to be able to respond to any situation they might encounter). We'll take this to mean that we can apply rhetoric to just about any subject and that we encounter rhetoric in a variety of genres, from the written word to food presentation and everything in between.

As you read in Chapter 2, understanding the rhetorical situation can be incredibly useful for analyzing texts and responding to them critically. What Aristotle's definition of rhetoric tells us, however, is that they have incredible generative power as well. Indeed, the rhetorical situation can guide you in every writing task you undertake by forcing you to consider—in every given case—your purpose and your audience. Think back for a moment to our analytical reading of the Oliver "Buzz" Thomas essay "A Christian View of War" on page 53. Our task there was to be thorough and critical readers, to figure out how he was using ethos, pathos, and logos to connect with and persuade his audience. Now, we want you to approach elements of the rhetorical situation from the other direction—as writers rather than as readers. We want you to understand how consideration of audience and purpose can help you figure out not only *how* to argue, but also *what* exactly you want to say. In other words, thinking about a topic for a particular audience in a particular moment can transform what it is you think you want to say. To help in understanding how this might work, let's go back to the Thomas essay again and think about the rhetorical situation from the perspective of the writer. (Of course, this is hypothetical since we can't know what he was thinking while producing his essay; our point is to show you how thinking about elements of the rhetorical situation can transform content. With practice, you'll be able to use this process in your own writing projects.)

A minister and a regular contributor to *USA Today*, Thomas frequently writes about issues of faith. Though the topics of his columns vary widely, he often considers how people can transform their faith and their religious values into action. He wrote this column in September of 2006, and was likely thinking about his general purpose—to write about issues of faith—in the context of the war in Iraq, which was beginning to take its toll on the minds of many Americans. In fact, it was during September of 2006 that the number of U.S. military deaths in Iraq surpassed the number of deaths in the 9/11 attacks. With this timing in mind (remember here the significance of *kairos* or timeliness in our discussions of rhetoric), Thomas may have been better able to locate and specify his interest in faith. Indeed, his article attempts to answer the question: What can people of faith do when their nation is engaged in a questionable war?

So, let's put ourselves in Thomas' shoes for a moment. Broadly speaking, our task is to write a column about faith for the readership of *USA Today*. The rhetorical moment of the war's toll on the cultural imagination leads us to narrow our purpose—we want to say something about religion and the war—and our audience—we want to target practicing Christians. This thinking about audience and purpose helps us refine our topic: We decide to argue that Christians should take a more Christ-like approach in their thinking about the war in Iraq.

What this speculation about Thomas' approach demonstrates is how thinking about elements of the rhetorical situation can serve you as a writer as well as a reader: It can help you develop every part of your argument, from topic, to claim and support, to organization. And, as we discussed in Chapter 2, the appeals associated with the rhetorical situation—based on ethos, pathos, and logos—are critical to composing strong arguments because they allow you to connect with, and ultimately persuade, your audience.

Like so many other tasks associated with writing, effective use of the rhetorical appeals starts with consideration of your audience. Who are they? What do they know? What do they believe? What do they care about? What do they like and dislike? What will make them angry? What will make them laugh or cry? What do they expect from you as the author? Thinking about and answering questions like these should become a routine part of the writing process if you want to effectively respond to the writing situations you encounter. To help you get into the habit of giving the rhetorical situation thorough consideration, we've put together a checklist of ways to think about and use appeals in your writing. One important thing to notice about this checklist and the discussion that accompanies it is how the appeals often work together or overlap.

- **Ethos, or appeals based on your character**

One way to think about ethos is to ask the question: How do you want your audience to perceive you? Many students have a difficult time understanding how ethical appeals work because they see character as innate and unchangeable. But it's not. Try thinking about character in the sense of a role an actor plays. Every writing task will require you to take on the role of an author, and, because each task will come with its own unique rhetorical situation, that role will change. For example, in one case (such as an essay exam) you might need to take on the role of an expert on a subject; in another (such as an exploratory review of local coffee shops), you might want to demonstrate your newness to the subject and your willingness to let an array of customers lead the way.

In your writing, you'll use ethical appeals to:

- Connect with the audience, to make them want to listen to you.
- Claim authority, to convince them that you're in a position to legitimately address the subject at hand.
- Establish credibility, to show them that they can trust and believe you.

How can you do this?

- With your language: Think about the differences between formal, informal, and casual language. There isn't necessarily a right or wrong approach here, but you do have to consider your purpose and how one of these choices (informal instead of formal, for example) might affect your audience. Your level of formality should depend on your audience's expectations and what you hope these readers will take from your writing.

FIGURE 3-1

Whether we realize it or not, we make appeals based on character every time we communicate. In other words, the messages we send—and how we send them—say something about us to our audiences. In Figure 3-1, the "author"—a graffiti artist called Banksy—sends a definite message about art. But what can we say, based on the image and its presentation, about the author himself? How might the author want us to think about him? What has he done to make us think about his character in a particular way?

- With your tone: How do you want to "sound" to your audience? Knowledgeable? Disinterested? Angry? Bossy? Funny? Stodgy? Fair? In some cases, it can be incredibly persuasive to use a humorous tone, whereas in others, only the most serious approach will work. You can successfully determine which way to proceed by taking into consideration the elements of the rhetorical situation. If you are writing a letter to your state legislator to protest the increasing cost of in-state tuition, your audience will likely respond more favorably to a knowledgeable tone than to a humorous one. If you are trying to call your fellow students' attention to this problem on the op-ed pages of your school newspaper, however, a humorous tone might be the perfect way to go.
- With pertinent biographical information and expertise: In some cases, including personal experience can be a strong component of your argument. For example, your work and observations as a lifeguard at a public pool can be compelling in a proposal to your former teachers to require swimming classes as part of the grade school curriculum. If you were writing a grant proposal seeking funding for such a program, however, you might decide to forego your personal experience in favor of statistical data. In short, when crafting your ethos, consider if there are things about you that the audience should know and that would help you connect with them.

- **Pathos, or appeals based on the audience's emotions and imagination**

When you think about how to (or even if you should) construct pathetic appeals in your writing, consider this question: How do you want to make your audience feel? In some cases, you may want to rely solely on your logical and reasoned claims and so may try to avoid evoking the audience's emotions at all. In other instances, you'll want to make your argument more interesting, powerful, and compelling by getting the audience to respond emotionally to your subject. Not surprisingly, appeals to pathos are ubiquitous in advertising, which depends on making audiences feel the need to do and buy certain things. Unfortunately, they have become almost as common in public debate, where many pundits and talking heads prefer to pull on the audience's heartstrings or play on its fears at the expense of making well-reasoned arguments. Although it might seem tempting to marshal pathetic appeals haphazardly because of their power over the audience, responsible rhetoricians know two things: First, they must balance pathetic appeals with well-reasoned claims, and second, they must avoid too great a reliance on them because the audience will recognize this as simple manipulation. Thus your task is to strike just the right chord with your audience, evoking their emotions at the right time and in the right manner to best bring them around to your claim.

In your writing, you can use pathetic appeals to:

- Make the audience care about your subject.
- Pique the audience's interest.
- Build bridges with the audience by finding common ground based on shared beliefs or values.
- Stoke your audience's imagination.
- Make your audience laugh.
- Shock or anger your audience.
- Make your argument more memorable.

FIGURE 3-2

Pathos at work: Pathetic appeals seek to tap the audience's emotions and imaginations to make them more inclined to consider and accept the author's argument. What emotions do you think the graffiti artist who created Figure 3-2 seeks to provoke in his audience? What message do you think the artist is trying to convey (in other words, what do you think he is trying to argue)?

How can you do this?

- With your language and tone: Just as with ethical appeals, the language you choose will determine your voice and set the tone of your work. For example, you might choose certain words and phrases to shock or anger your audience and thus will draw them more fully into the problem you're trying to address. Vivid diction, images, and description can have a similar effect: they can make an audience envision the scene you're trying to set and, again, draw them in. Consider how this passage from Wendy Shanker's *The Fat Girl's Guide to Life* in Chapter 8 uses concrete language to appeal to the audience's imagination: "Enough of punishing myself and my body by reading Danielle Steel in the shade while everyone else was swimming in the pool. Enough of looking up at mirrored ceilings in elevators to assure myself that I was pretty. Enough of squeezing into nylon undergarments that cut off my circulation and left red welts in my skin." Just as Shanker does here, you can use language to get your audience emotionally invested in the issue you've taken up.
- By sharing relevant personal details and anecdotes: Often you can help your audience become more open to your argument by sharing relevant personal experiences from your life. For example, in "A Prince Charming for the Prom" (found in Chapter 9),

Frank Paiva recounts his role as an openly gay high school student and go-to date for his female friends in order to articulate how he longed to go to the prom with a real date. Paiva uses details from his own life to evoke an emotional reaction and to make his piece more real and more urgent to his readers.

- By talking about issues and problems in concrete terms of the people they affect, rather than in the abstract: Journalists call this "putting a face on" an issue, and it's an effective way of turning problems-as-theory into problems that audiences actually care about. Most readers will find a generalized discussion of health care reform far less compelling than the story of a working single mother who cannot afford to buy her son the hearing aid he needs. Putting a human face on an issue of policy, in other words, can help you more easily move your audience to a new, perhaps more compassionate position.

- By using narratives, or telling stories, to get your audience involved: Everybody loves a good story, right? Good rhetoricians can take advantage of their audiences' natural affinity for narrative structure (we like to think about things in terms of a beginning, a middle, and an end) by allowing stories to make arguments for them. You can find one particularly compelling example of this in Travis Kavulla's "Death on Facebook: A Different Kind of Funeral" in Chapter 9. Although his larger argument is about how social networking sites are redefining friendships at every stage, it's the story of his reaction to the death of an acquaintance—and his fascination with the Facebook "funeral"—that gets his readers emotionally involved.

- **Logos, or appeals based on the audience's intellect**

The most basic and effective way to make an appeal to logos is to present an argument that makes sense. If your audience can't follow what you're trying to say or doesn't understand how you're making your claim or building support, none of your other appeals will matter. Beyond the basics of logical development and presentation, there are plenty of other reasons to try to satisfy your readers' intellectual demands. Some audiences, for example, will care little about ethos and pathos—they will want instead to be persuaded by data and sound reasoning. Others will need to have their intellectual curiosity piqued in order to take an interest in your subject. And still others will simply insist that, whatever your claim, you "prove it" with strong, factual evidence and informed opinion.

In your writing, you can use logical appeals to:

- Provoke—and satisfy—your audience's curiosity.
- Support your claim with solid reasoning (including data, facts, and expert opinion).
- Help your audience understand your position by providing details and examples.

How can you do this?

- By thinking about the intellectual needs and expectations of your audience and adjusting your argument accordingly: What does your audience know about your subject? What kind of evidence will it need in order to be persuaded? Although you won't be able to answer these questions about every member of every audience you encounter, you should try to learn a few basic things about your readers. Think of how your approach to a writing task would change, for example, if you learned you were writing an essay on global warming for a gathering of climatologists rather than for your classmates.

FIGURE 3-3

Logos at work: Logical appeals are meant to stimulate the audience's intellect. The graffiti artist who created Figure 3-3 deftly combines pathos (by using Paddington Bear, an image familiar to many people from childhood) and logos to challenge his audience to rethink their positions on immigration. How, for example, does the artist's use of the word *migration* rather than *immigration* force the audience to reconsider the terms of the debate? (What are the differences between the two words' denotations and connotations?) What are your emotional and intellectual responses to this image?

- By presenting your ideas clearly and coherently: Again, none of your work will matter—not the appeals, the claim, or the evidence—if your audience can't understand what you're trying to say. In this sense, how you present your work—the organization and development—is just as important as, and inseparable from, what you have to say. Consider what information you must include early in your writing in order for your argument to build naturally and make sense.
- By using and correctly documenting sources to bolster your argument: Even if you're an expert on a subject, your argument can be made stronger with the judicious use of good source material. This can include data, statistics, narratives and anecdotes, and opinion—from people who agree with your position and from those who disagree. The more controversial your claim—and the more skeptical or hostile your audience—the more you'll likely need to use sources to support your position.

Hermagoras and Stasis Theory

Although there are scores of other notable people in the history and development of rhetoric, the final figure from ancient Greece we'll introduce is the teacher and scholar named Hermagoras of Temnos, who lived about two hundred years after Aristotle. As is the case with many of the

Sophists, what we know of Hermagoras' work comes from other, later sources because none of his own writing survives. His influence is clear, however, because the system he refined for determining which questions needed to be answered in legal speeches has been adapted over thousands of years and remains useful today. Hermagoras' primary concern in developing his approach—called stasis theory—was on the needs of forensic, or legal, oratory—the kinds of speeches that citizens had to make in court when they were bringing cases or defending themselves from prosecution. His theory develops from Aristotle's mention in the *Rhetoric* of four issues that must be considered in legal oratory: "(1) If you maintain that the act was not committed, your main task in court is to prove this. (2) If you maintain that the act did no harm, prove this. If you maintain that (3) the act was less than is alleged, or (4) justified, prove these facts, just as you would prove the act not to have been committed if you were maintaining that." From these issues, Hermagoras put together a set of questions that speakers could use to determine the stasis point—the place where disputants in a case stood in agreement about what was at issue (the word *stasis* comes from a Greek term meaning "stand"). In other words, they could find the place where they agreed that they disagreed.

Though tightly focused on legal oratory, Hermagoras' stasis questions, when adapted, give us a way to explore "the available means of persuasion" on almost any issue so that we can figure out the best way to enter and present an argument (you'll read more about this in Chapter 4). The idea behind this approach is that, before starting to argue an issue, we should thoroughly examine it by asking and answering a series of questions that build on one another. Because many different rhetoricians used the stasis questions, there are a number of variations in what they are and how they should be applied. We'll focus on five basic categories of questions (and in Chapter 4, we'll discuss how to develop arguments based on four of these):

- **Questions of fact:** Is there a thing to be considered?
- **Questions of definition:** How can the thing be defined or classified?
- **Questions of quality or evaluation:** What is the quality of the thing? Is it good or bad? Right or wrong? Fair or unfair?
- **Questions of cause and effect:** What caused the thing? What are the consequences of the thing?
- **Questions of policy:** What should we do about the thing?

Exploring an issue by working through the stasis questions can help you do several important things: It can help you understand how others—including your audience—think about the issue and clarify your own thinking about the points in dispute; it can help you figure out where exactly you want to enter the discourse and make your argument and decide which kinds of rhetorical appeals might work best; and it can help ensure that you cover all the bases in your argument, leaving no important questions unanswered.

How to Apply Classical Rhetoric to a Modern Issue

Just as Hermagoras presented his stasis questions in a particular order, so, too, are modern adaptations most effective when approached in the same pattern. To understand why the order is important—and to see how stasis theory can help you discover and develop ideas—we'll first look at the questions as applied to a few public issues (global warming, smoking bans, and abstinence-based sex education). Then, we'll take a more detailed look at one issue in particular—the use of anabolic steroids in sports—and how stasis theory can help us formulate arguments about it.

- **Questions of fact:** In the legal cases for which Hermagoras developed the stases, the key question—Did a crime occur?—was often in dispute and had to be fully argued. Sometimes, however, as in Euphiletus' killing of Eratosthenes (see page 62), both sides agreed that the act occurred so there was no need to argue that fact. This is frequently the case in arguments about public issues, too (sometimes, the questions of fact seem so obvious that asking them feels kind of silly, but you should always ask anyway). Some examples:
  - **Global warming.** Does it exist? No matter what they think about causes or consequences or what to do about it, most people agree that the earth's atmosphere is getting warmer.
  - **Public smoking bans.** Do people smoke in public? Does secondhand smoke reach other people? Yes and yes.
  - **Abstinence-based sex-education programs.** Do young people have sex? Research shows many of them do. Does abstaining prevent all the consequences that come from having sex? Yes.

In each of these cases, if we decided that the questions of fact seem settled for most people, especially our audience, there wouldn't be much point in making an argument here. So, we would move on to examine the ...

- **Questions of definition:** These questions arise when we disagree about how something is categorized or named. Although some arguments deal only with definitional issues— for example, "Is the conflict in Iraq a civil war or an insurgency?"—many others have these issues embedded in them (we've all heard the phrase "defining your terms"). Let's look at our issues again:
  - **Global warming.** What exactly do we mean when we use this phrase? Does everyone use it in the same way? In researching the issue, we might find room for an argument about what "global warming" means. Or, we might find general agreement here, just as with the question of fact. In either case, what would be important is making sure our audience understands—and has reason to accept—the definition we use.
  - **Public smoking bans.** Here, there's probably less room to argue over definitional issues. But we would still have to be clear about how we used key terms. What, for example, do we mean by "public"? Do we mean in public buildings? On sidewalks and streets? In parks? So, here, we might engage more in clarification than argument.
  - **Abstinence-based sex-education programs.** The definitional question that jumps out here is, "How do we define 'abstinence'?" Some people might want to know, too, whether telling children to not have sex is a form of (or can be defined as) sex education at all.

As you can see, the opportunities for argument grow as we move down the list of stasis questions. And as we keep going, the links between the questions and the reason they're ordered in this way become even clearer. Now that we've considered the first two categories, we'll look at ...

- **Questions of quality or evaluation:** Sometimes, these questions deal with practical value—whether a movie is good or bad, for example, or whether a policy is effective or ineffective. In other cases, they focus on ethical or moral quality—whether a decision is fair or an action is right, based on a certain set of beliefs. We can find both kinds of questions in our examples:

- Global warming. There probably aren't many people who would argue that global warming is a good thing, so that question seems settled. Other evaluative questions would likely come up, however, in the discussion of what to do about global warming ("What's the best way to deal with the problem?" "Do we have a moral obligation to protect the environment?").
- Public smoking bans. Because this debate touches on issues and health and of individual freedoms, we could ask both kinds of questions, the practical ("Is a public ban an effective way of reducing the effects of smoking?") and the ethical ("Is banning smoking fair?").
- Abstinence-based sex-education programs. This issue, too, lends itself to arguments based on both kinds of evaluative questions. There's a lot of public debate not only about the effectiveness of such programs but also about whether schools have an obligation to teach students more about sexual health than abstention.

As you might have guessed, any policy or course of action designed to respond to a problem is open to evaluation (we should always ask if a plan is working, right?). And this makes arguments based on evaluative questions common. Sometimes, however, when there is general agreement on evaluative issues, or when we don't see those as the issues that most need our attention, we could turn to the ...

- **Questions of cause and effect:** As their name indicates, these questions ask about the forces behind and consequences of actions, events, trends, and the like. Many arguments focus entirely on causal issues; just as often, however, causal arguments are part of larger policy discussions (more on that in a moment). In either case, these questions deal with causal relationships. Let's look again at our examples:
  - Global warming. Look at just about any news source, and you're likely to encounter disagreement about the causes of global warming. This most basic question—"What is causing the earth's atmosphere to heat up?"—is hotly debated in part because we can't hope to fix the problem until we understand what's behind it. Nearly as common—and contentious—are questions about the consequences of global warming. Even though science can provide some answers to both kinds of questions, the absence of certainty makes this a powerful place to present an argument.
  - Public smoking bans. Although there are important and interesting causal questions about why people smoke and why they don't stop, when the issue of smoking bans comes up, much of the public debate focuses on consequences. Restaurant and bar owners might worry about the effects on their businesses, smokers and libertarians might be concerned about an erosion of individual rights, and public health experts might tout the benefits of smoke-free workplaces and other public spaces.
  - Abstinence-based sex-education programs. As with smoking bans, the questions most people are likely to have about abstinence-based sex education deal with consequences. Perhaps the most common of these questions is also the most basic: "Do these programs work?" or, "What effects do these programs have?" But there are also important questions about causes that we could consider, among them, "Why do teenagers have sex?"

Notice that, with each step along way, the stasis questions can grow more complicated. This happens because, as we work through all of the different issues raised by the questions, we tend to start thinking in a more sophisticated and layered way about the issues at hand. And this process often culminates when we turn to ...

- **Questions of policy:** Like causal questions, these usually begin with a problem. But our purpose in asking policy questions is different: We ask because we're trying to figure out the best course of action to take to address the problem. And because they fall at the end of the stasis line, meaning we should consider them only after all the other questions have been addressed, these often include factual, definitional, evaluative, and causal elements—everything we need to think about as we go through the decision-making process. Finally, it's useful to think of policy questions in two parts, the first dealing with what we should do and the second with how we can persuade people to do it. Let's take one last look at our examples:

  ○ **Global warming.** The most obvious question here is, of course, "What should we do about global warming?" And just as there are many opinions about the causes and effects of the problem, so, too, are there lots of ideas about how to "fix" it.

  ○ **Public smoking bans.** If we consider smoking to be a problem, then a ban on lighting up in public is itself one answer to the question, "What should we do about smoking?" The question that comes next—"How do we enact a ban on public smoking?"—would likely prove more challenging.

  ○ **Abstinence-based sex-education programs.** If we believe that abstinence is an effective way of teaching students about sex, one policy question we might ask is, "How can we persuade teenagers to abstain?" And again, selling the idea would probably be the toughest part of the proposal.

Clearly, using stasis theory can take some time. But it will be time well spent because considering each set of questions can help you focus and organize your thinking about an issue and, ultimately, compose more logical and effective arguments. It's important to keep a few things in mind, however. First, the stasis questions are hierarchical—they build on one another—which means you have to take the time to work through them in order (this is how they help prevent gaps in your arguments). Second, the questions can be recursive; in other words, answering a later question might force you to loop back around and deal with an earlier one in a slightly different way. And, finally, stasis theory is an invention tool—a method for thinking about an issue as you prepare to write—not a guide for organizing an argument. Although the questions, asked and answered in order, might look or feel like an outline, they don't work very well in that way, mainly because they lead to mechanical—or, worse—clunky writing. To see how we can use the questions effectively, let's examine one more issue—the use of steroids in sports. First, some background, adapted from the National Institute on Drug Abuse website <http://www.nida.nih.gov/>:

What are anabolic steroids?

[1] "Anabolic steroids" is the familiar name for synthetic substances related to the male sex hormones (e.g., testosterone). They promote the growth of skeletal muscle (anabolic effects) and the development of male sexual characteristics (androgenic effects) in both males and females. . . . Anabolic steroids were developed in the late 1930s primarily to treat hypogonadism, a condition in which the testes do not produce sufficient testosterone for normal growth, development, and sexual functioning. The primary medical uses of these compounds are to treat delayed puberty, some types of impotence, and wasting of the body caused by HIV infection or other diseases. During the 1930s, scientists discovered that anabolic steroids could facilitate the growth of skeletal muscle in laboratory animals, which led to abuse of the compounds first by bodybuilders and weightlifters and then by athletes in other sports. Steroid abuse has become so widespread in athletics that it can affect the outcome of sports contests.

What are steroidal supplements?

[2] In the United States, supplements such as tetrahydrogestrinone (THG) and androstenedione (street name "Andro") previously could be purchased legally without a prescription through many commercial sources, including health food stores. Steroidal supplements can be converted into testosterone or a similar compound in the body. Less is known about the side effects of steroidal supplements, but if large quantities of these compounds substantially increase testosterone levels in the body, then they also are likely to produce the same side effects as anabolic steroids themselves. The purchase of these supplements, with the notable exception of dehydroepiandrosterone (DHEA), became illegal after the passage in 2004 of amendments to the Controlled Substances Act.

What is the scope of steroid use in the United States?

[3] Steroid abuse affects individuals of various ages. However, it is difficult to estimate the true prevalence of steroid abuse in the United States because many data sources that measure drug abuse do not include steroids. Scientific evidence indicates that anabolic steroid abuse among athletes may range between one and six percent.

Why do people abuse anabolic steroids?

[4] One of the main reasons people give for abusing steroids is to improve their athletic performance. Among athletes, steroid abuse has been estimated to be less that 6 percent, according to surveys, but anecdotal information suggests more widespread abuse. Although testing procedures are now in place to deter steroid abuse among professional and Olympic athletes, new designer drugs constantly become available that can escape detection and put athletes willing to cheat one step ahead of testing efforts. . . . Another reason people give for taking steroids is to increase their muscle size or to reduce their body fat. This group includes people suffering from the behavioral syndrome called muscle dysmorphia, which causes them to have a distorted image of their bodies.

What are the health consequences of steroid abuse?

[5] Anabolic steroid abuse has been associated with a wide range of adverse side effects ranging from some that are physically unattractive, such as acne and breast development in men, to others that are life threatening, such as heart attacks and liver cancer. Most are reversible if the abuser stops taking the drugs, but some are permanent, such as voice deepening in females.

What effects do anabolic steroids have on behavior?

[6] Case reports and small studies indicate that anabolic steroids, when used in high doses, increase irritability and aggression. Some steroid abusers report that they have committed aggressive acts, such as physical fighting or armed robbery, theft, vandalism, or burglary. Abusers who have committed aggressive acts or property crimes generally report that they engage in these behaviors more often when they take steroids than when they are drug free. A recent study suggests that the mood and behavioral effects seen during anabolic-androgenic steroid abuse may result from secondary hormonal changes.

What can be done to prevent steroid abuse?

[7] Most prevention efforts in the United States today focus on athletes involved with the Olympics and professional sports; few school districts test for abuse of illicit drugs. It has been estimated that close to 9 percent of secondary schools conduct some sort of drug testing program, presumably focused on athletes, and that less than 4 percent of the nation's high schools test their athletes for steroids. Studies are currently under way to determine whether such testing reduces drug abuse. Research on steroid educational programs has shown that simply teaching students about steroids' adverse effects does not convince adolescents that they can be adversely affected. Nor does such instruction discourage young people from taking steroids in the future. Presenting both the risks and benefits of anabolic steroid use is more effective in convincing adolescents about steroids' negative effects, apparently because the students find a balanced approach more credible, according to the researchers.

Now, let's suppose that we're interested in writing about this issue, but we're not sure where to start. That's where stasis theory comes in. Let's run the topic through the questions and identify some arguments we could make:

- **Questions of fact:** Are steroids used in athletic training and competition? The background information above and a quick scroll through the results of a Google search show the answer to be an unequivocal yes. So there's no reason to make our stand here.
- **Questions of definition:** What are anabolic steroids? Are they only performance enhancing drugs or do they have other uses? Does their use in sports constitute cheating? Science provides definitive answers to the first two questions, and since steroids are banned in most sports, there's not much room for argument on the third. So we would be best served by moving to the next category of questions.
- **Questions of quality or evaluation:** Is the use of steroids bad for sports? Do steroids make sporting events more exciting to watch by improving performance and increasing competition? Is using steroids fair? The first two questions are practical evaluations—we're asking if steroids have positive or negative effects on sports (notice the causal element in this argument). The third is an ethical evaluation that involves personal and cultural beliefs about what is right and wrong.

- **Questions of cause and effect:** Why do athletes use steroids? What are the effects of steroids on those who take them? What are the effects on the sporting events themselves? These are all interesting questions involving causes or effects. Science might provide some answers—especially about the physical and emotional effects on athletes who use steroids—but there is certainly room for argument here.
- **Questions of policy:** Should sports leagues and governing bodies do more to enforce the ban on steroids and increase penalties for their use? Should more high schools test for them? Should the use of steroids in sports be legalized? In answering these questions, we could find ourselves arguing for a specific policy to deal with the problems created by the use of steroids in sports. And in proposing and justifying our policy, we might incorporate elements from each of the stasis questions.

Without a doubt, we have several interesting questions to consider as we think about the issue. We know that there are no questions of fact or definition to argue. Even though we're not going to argue these, we'll make sure our audience understands the definitions we're using. Which leads us to the evaluative questions. And, again, although these are certainly interesting and arguable, we're not interested in challenging the accepted position that steroids are bad for sports because they have more negative consequences than positive for athletes and the games they play. What we decide to do, after working our way through the first three stasis levels, is explore a causal question: Why do athletes use steroids? In researching the issue, we'll look for studies that ask that question, interviews with sports psychologists and other experts on behavior who might provide some insight, and stories about athletes who have used steroids or know others have. With this information, we'll craft a causal claim (we'll talk more about how to do that in Chapter 4). And, who knows, after that, we might decide to follow up with a policy argument that spells out a plan for dealing with the problem.

from reading to writing

1. Select one of the readings from Part 2 (or use one assigned by your teacher). Read the piece and write a 100-word summary and a one-sentence summary (about 25 to 50 words), following the models on pages 50–51. Besides the length, what are the key differences between the two summaries? Which do you think is more accurate? Why? Does having more space to write ensure a more accurate summary?
2. Seek out a compelling visual argument. This can be a sleek ad from a fashion magazine, a poster from your local Starbucks that encourages you to try a new seasonal beverage, or just about anything you can find that uses images to persuade (you might consider Image 4-1 on page 86). Based on the rhetorical artifact you've chosen, develop an audience analysis (or a written description of the audience you imagine the argument to be targeting). To what values, characteristics, and tastes do the creators of the argument seem to be appealing? What can you guess about the audience based on the images found in the text?

3. Using the Rhetorical Analysis Notes on "A Christian View of War" (page 53) and the Sample Rhetorical Analysis as a guide, select one of the readings from Part 2 ("Why We Hate Fat People" or "The Case for Reality TV: What the Snobs Don't Understand" are good options for this) and write a rhetorical analysis of the text. Your argument should take into account the author's purpose and analyze how capably the writer uses the rhetorical appeals to persuade the audience.

4. To help you understand how your ethos can and must change according to the rhetorical situations you encounter, we're going to list three hypothetical writing tasks on the same general issue—smoking in the movies. For each task, discuss how you would want your audience to perceive you and why.

    - **Task 1:** You must write a letter to the Directors Guild of America, an organization representing thousands of motion picture and TV directors, arguing for a ban on the portrayal of smoking in all moves rated G, PG, and PG-13.

    - **Task 2:** You must write a speech for a film studies class in which you explain the importance of allowing directors to portray life realistically and argue against any kind of ban on showing characters who smoke.

    - **Task 3:** You must write an exploratory essay for your English classmates and teacher that informs them of the current debates over the representation of smoking in film and, based on the research you've done on these claims, ultimately posits your own position on the issue.

genres of argument

"In today's food-fight environment, where extremes dominate debate and choice is defined by either-or, finding a comfortable place to land is increasingly difficult."
— **Kathleen Parker,** *"Seeking Balance in an Either-Or World"*

FINDING A WAY IN

T his chapter is all about finding a place to land, as columnist Kathleen Parker puts it in her essay at the end of Chapter 5. Much like this textbook, Parker is worried about the state of argument in America because the political extremes have stretched the fabric of public discourse so thin that the middle has begun to fray. She identifies herself as a centrist—like many Americans—and she writes that she's tired of feeling squeezed out of public discussion and decision making by the far right and the far left. She advocates for a middle ground, a place where passion and commitment are still strong, but where ideas are more important than agendas, where listening is as common as talking, and where, working together, we can find realistic solutions to complicated problems. The metaphor Parker uses to describe her frustration works on another level, as well: Once we decide that we have something to say on an issue, we have to find "a comfortable place to land"—we have to decide how and where to enter the argument.

Let's say, for example, that you're interested in global warming. You feel strongly about the issue, you've read about it in newspapers and online and talked about it in class and among your friends. Perhaps you've even seen Al Gore's documentary *An Inconvenient Truth*. Now, you want to write a letter to your college newspaper or post a thoughtful comment on a blog. What are you going to say? Global warming is a huge and complicated issue that reaches into nearly every facet of our lives:

- from economics (think about corporate objections to pollution controls and about what alternative fuel sources might add to the cost of your next car);
- to politics (think about the prevalence of campaign promises to protect the environment vs. the difficulty of getting the appropriate legislation passed);
- to pop culture (think about the debate over "fast fashion"—cheap knock-offs of high-priced designer clothes made to be worn and tossed away—and the toll it takes on the environment);
- and even to religion (think about the growing number of religious organizations that have joined the call for action to protect the environment).

And while the debate over its existence is all but over—just about everyone with an opinion acknowledges that Earth's atmosphere is getting warmer—global warming remains a divisive issue because there is less agreement about its causes and less still about how to deal with the problem.

So, again, if you wanted to write about global warming, how would you decide where to start—how would you figure out what you wanted to argue and how you wanted to argue it? Or, to use Kathleen Parker's words, how would you go about finding "a comfortable place to land" in the midst of the ongoing debate? This chapter, by building on what you've read, thought about, and practiced in the previous pages, and by focusing in particular on the stasis questions as an invention tool, will help you answer that question so that you have the best possible chance of contributing to whatever public conversations or debates you wish to enter.

A QUICK LOOK BACK

Before we look specifically at how to use the stasis questions to figure how and where to enter an argument, let's quickly review the major points we've covered thus far in this book:

- In Chapter 1, you read about the state of argument in our nation today and about the many things that argument is not—especially compared with the Classical Greek tradition of rhetoric and persuasion—and we settled on a definition of the term for this textbook: Argument is a process and a product. The process part asks you to explore issues from many perspectives and to gather and analyze information and knowledge. It requires that you keep an open mind and that you listen and consider other perspectives during this exploration. The product part asks you to create texts designed to inform or persuade; this is where the writing you'll do for your course comes in.

- In Chapter 2, you learned a few strategies—all rooted in Classical rhetoric—for being an active reader and for reading with a larger purpose in mind. You explored the meaning of "rhetorical reading" and encountered some examples of this and other strategies at work.
- Finally, in Chapter 3, you read about the transition from reading to writing and about using the rhetorical appeals and the stasis questions to craft effective arguments.

Now it's time to pull together everything you've learned to help you prepare to compose your own effective and engaging arguments. And, again, to do that, we'll focus on the stasis questions, the system devised by the ancient Greek rhetor Hermagoras to set the progression of questions that needed to be answered as speakers prepared to present their cases in courts of law (see page 73). Although Hermagoras was concerned primarily with legal oratory, the stasis questions have been adapted over the centuries for use in just about any case where a speaker or writer is trying to present an argument. Because, as we have seen, individual arguments involving public issues never exist in a vacuum—they are almost always part of a much larger system of discourse—and because there can be many places to enter these ongoing conversations, it might help to think of the stasis questions as a framework for finding the most effective place to present your position. The idea is to ask those important questions that were introduced in Chapter 3—dealing with issues of fact, definition, quality or evaluation, cause and effect, and policy—to find the stasis, or the point where people with different opinions come together about what is at issue (in other words, the point where "we agree that we disagree"). Once you've figured out that point, you'll better understand exactly what you want to argue, how you want to argue it, and why.

With that in mind, you might want to use the stasis questions as a checklist to help you figure out where you want to jump into the conversation and to make sure you've answered any questions your readers might have as you build your argument. (Remember that the five stasis questions build upon one another; in other words, questions of fact must be answered before those of definition, definitions must be decided before evaluations, and so forth.)

THE STASIS QUESTIONS AT WORK

To put the stasis questions to work—and to make this whole process a little easier to understand—let's go back to the global warming example mentioned previously. Remember, you're interested in the issue, but you're not sure exactly what you want to say or how you want to say it. Remember, too, that global warming is a broad issue that can be approached from many different perspectives. To help decide how you want to come at the issue and what kind of argument you want to make, you can turn to the stasis questions as a guide. And here's where a stasis checklist can be helpful. You can list the stasis categories and apply them to global warming to decide what kind of questions you're most interested in pursuing:

- **Questions of fact:** This first rung on the stasis ladder asks simply whether global warming exists. You decide that this might have been a good place to start a decade ago, when there was less agreement that Earth's atmosphere was heating up. But now the question of global warming's existence seems settled. So, you move on to . . .

- **Questions of definition:** Here again, you decide that most people seem to agree on the general definition of "global warming" (something along the lines of "a gradual increase in the temperature of Earth's atmosphere"). So, unless you want to introduce and argue for a new definition of the term, you turn to . . .
- **Questions of quality or evaluation:** The most basic question this category asks is whether global warming is a good thing or a bad thing. You decide that's a no-brainer. Other questions of evaluation might come up, however, especially within the categories that follow (e.g., What is the best explanation for global warming? Or the most effective policy for combating it?). But, for now, you consider . . .
- **Questions of cause and effect:** Although the questions of definition and evaluation surrounding global warming may seem all but settled, you find that there's plenty of disagreement over what is causing our planet to heat up. This, then, is one interesting place where you could enter the discussion, by presenting a case for a particular set of causes of, or consequences resulting from, global warming. You might, however, find yourself agreeing with one of the many public positions on causes and/or effects. In that case, you would want to consider . . .
- **Questions of policy:** The category at the top of the stasis ladder starts with a simple question: What should we do? Here, after making sure you've accounted for the questions of fact, definition, evaluation, and cause and effect surrounding the issue, you might decide to present an argument for a particular course of action that you believe would help slow the rate of global warming.

In this example, then, because the questions dealing with fact, definition, and evaluation have been answered, it seems that the best place to enter the conversation about global warming is in the discussion over causes and effects or the discussion about what should be done to deal with the problem. In both cases, there's a lot to talk about because so many important questions have yet to be definitively answered. Exactly what kind of argument you decided to make—or where you decided to land—would depend on your interests, your research, and your feelings about the issue.

What follows in the rest of this chapter is a detailed discussion of four kinds of argumentative essays based on the stasis questions that are most useful to public discourse and decision making based on logical—though not necessarily scientifically provable—reasoning: arguments of definition, of evaluation, of cause and effect, and of policy. We're leaving out arguments of fact for a few reasons: first, because of this focus on public rather than private or personal issues. Second, because many arguments of fact are based on measurable data (Did Iraq have weapons of mass destruction before the U.S. invasion?) or legal evidence (Did a particular crime occur?) to which student writers are unlikely to have access. And third, because many other arguments of fact are based on personal beliefs (Does God exist?) that those who hold them are unwilling to question.

To help explain these different kinds of arguments and how to compose them, we'll begin each of the remaining sections with questions and responses about an organization called the Animal Liberation Front. This group generates a range of responses based on its words and deeds and is thus a useful subject for consideration using the stasis questions that are our focus. Each section will conclude with an example or two of the kind of argument that has just been discussed, so you can see how professional writers make these arguments.

We'll start with an excerpt from an animal liberation movement website that lays out the philosophy that drives groups like ALF:

"The Animal Liberation movement is a loosely-associated collection of cells of people who intentionally violate the law in order to free animals from captivity and the horrors of exploitation. As activists in one cell do not know activists in another cell, their non-hierarchical structure and anonymity prevent legal authorities from breaking up the organization. Animal Liberation activists break into any building or compound—be it a fur farm or university laboratory—in order to release and/or rescue animals. They also destroy property in order to prevent further harm done to animals and to weaken exploitation industries economically. Their actions have damaged many operations, shut down others, and prevented still others from ever forming for fear of attack. They may also utilize intimidation to prevent further animal abuse and murder."

> —*"Philosophy of the Animal Liberation Movement"*
> *http://www.animalliberationpressoffice.org/history.htm*
> *(accessed November 10, 2008)*

QUESTIONS OF DEFINITION

Question: *Can members of the Animal Liberation Front be considered heroes?*
Response: *Members of the Animal Liberation Front who engage in direct actions regularly risk their own well-being for a cause to which they are entirely dedicated—saving threatened and abused animals. The actions they undertake are in many cases extraordinary—though sometimes illegal—as is the character they show in continuing to fight for their cause. For these reasons, ALF members are as much heroes as police officers, firefighters, and soldiers who risk their own well-being to help others.*

Defining "Definitional Arguments": What is the Nature of the Thing?

The question and response above are parts of an argument of definition, the kind you'll find on the opinion pages of newspapers, on talk radio and TV, and, most commonly these days, on blogs. The writer is trying to convince her audience that members of the Animal Liberation Front, who endorse trespassing and the destruction of property to save the lives of animals, are heroes by comparing them to other people who fit a generally accepted definition of that term. Although the argument is incomplete as it stands, it does help us define definitional arguments. In the language of the stasis issues discussed on the previous pages and in Chapter 3, these arguments spring from the question, "What is the nature of the thing?" and usually come in one of two forms:

- Formal definitions, sometimes called genus definitions (think back to your intro biology class), which seek to determine the essential qualities or meaning of a term or concept. Sometimes, writers will use formal definitions to challenge or expand accepted meanings. (You might write a formal definition, for example, to clarify the meaning of the word *hero*.)

- Categorical definitions, also known as species definitions, which try to show that particular concepts or terms belong (or don't belong) in specific, larger classes. (After establishing your definition of *hero*, for example, you might want to show that members of the Animal Liberation Front should [or should not] be considered heroes).

Because they are the starting point for many other kinds of arguments, questions of definition pop up frequently in the news:

- Is making a person stand naked for 20 consecutive hours in a cold room torture or effective interrogation?
- Is cheerleading a sport? Are cheerleaders athletes?
- What is date rape?
- Are illegal immigrants criminals, refugees, or something else?

More often than not, however, questions of definition are imbedded in other kinds of arguments. You might encounter a brief opinion column or blog entry devoted entirely to a definitional issue, but most public arguments focus on questions further down the stasis list

Images courtesy of the Animal Liberation Front

FIGURE 4-1

In this poster from its website, the Animal Liberation Front presents a definitional argument: What is a terrorist? By presenting a simple definition in the poster and linking it with two contrasting images of a small monkey, the group hopes that those who see the poster will question the common depiction of ALF members who rescue animals and destroy property as domestic terrorists. See page 79 (Exercise 2) for a writing prompt related to this poster.

(policy arguments—dealing with things we should or shouldn't do—are perhaps the most common). Let's look at that list above again, this time placing the definitional issues in the context of broader arguments:

- The U.S. government denies that it has—or would ever—use torture against suspected terrorists. But the government does allow what it calls "coercive interrogation" techniques that include forcing prisoners to stand naked for long periods of time in cold rooms. This definitional issue has been a key element in the U.S. anti-terrorism policy.
- In proposing to offer scholarships to cheerleaders, a university athletics director would have to show other administrators that cheerleading is indeed a sport and that cheerleaders are athletes who deserve the same benefits as students who participate in other sports. Again, the definitional element would serve the larger policy argument.
- A student organization trying to decide which of two proposals to support as part of a campus-wide effort to prevent date rape must, before completing its evaluation, reach a consensus on the definition of the term. An unclear or unconvincing definition of date rape would likely doom the proposals.
- Before adopting a position in the debate over illegal immigration and deciding how best to help those in need, a community church would have to determine if it believed illegal immigrants were defined by the laws they broke to reach this country or by their desire to live here. The nature of the definition would affect the subsequent policy decisions made by the church.

You can see how making an argument of definition isn't mere semantics. The way we define things can have concrete—indeed, even life and death—effects on the communities involved.

Whether they stand alone or operate as elements of broader, more complicated debates, definitional arguments occur when people can't agree about the meaning of a term or concept ("What is an enemy combatant?") or about whether one thing belongs in a particular category with other, similar things ("Are enemy combatants the same as POWs?"). At the root of these arguments are definitional criteria.

Criteria

Effective definitions depend on clearly established criteria. Remember those papers you wrote that started, "According to Webster's . . ."? Well, according to Webster's, a hero is "a man admired for his achievements and noble qualities" or "one that shows great courage." Even a definition as simple—and in many ways incomplete—as this has clear criteria: To be considered a hero, the person (we'll go ahead and broaden the gender restriction) in question must possess achievements and noble qualities worthy of admiration or must show great courage. There's still a lot of room for interpretation, though, isn't there? What, for example, counts as a "noble" quality? And what exactly is courage? Questions like these should serve as a reminder about audience. Criteria have to be clear and acceptable not only to the person arguing for the definition (the writer or speaker), but also to the audience (readers or listeners). Let's take up the Animal Liberation Front example again:

Members of the Animal Liberation Front who engage in direct actions regularly risk their own well-being for a cause to which they are entirely dedicated—saving threatened and abused animals. The actions they undertake are in many cases extraordinary—though sometimes illegal—as is the character they show in continuing to fight for their cause. For these reasons, ALF members are as much heroes as police officers, firefighters, and soldiers who risk their own well-being to help others.

In short, the writer is arguing, like Webster's, that heroes do admirable, sometimes courageous, things and show noble character, and that ALF members who rescue animals fit these criteria and, therefore, are heroes. Now, imagine two different publications and audiences for this argument, the first a Humane Society of America newsletter and the second a magazine for police and firefighters. There's little reason to believe that the Humane Society members would immediately reject the writer's basic definition of hero or the comparison between ALF members and police officers or firefighters. But firefighters and police might bristle at the suggestion that breaking the law to save lab rats is the same thing as pulling children from a burning building or taking a bullet to protect a hostage. The point is, audience members must agree to the nature of the criteria in a definitional argument before they can consider the argument as a whole. And a hostile audience might require more convincing, even about the most basic criteria of the definition in question.

Another, related, note about criteria: There are often many ways to define things; many criteria we can choose from to establish the meaning of a term. In writing an argument of definition, part of your task will be to separate the criteria that have to be present from those that don't. Take the word sport, for example. Among the possible criteria that spring to mind when trying to explain what a "sport" is include athletic skill, competition, the keeping of score, standardized rules, uniforms and equipment, physical exertion, practice or training, and some kind of playing area. That's a pretty long list. But do all of those criteria have to be met for an activity to be called a sport? Probably not. In putting together a formal definition of the term, you might decide that the only essential criteria are physical skill, practice, and competition; these, and all of these, must be present for an activity to be considered a sport. Some of the other criteria, like uniforms and equipment, might be present, but they aren't required (nor does their absence prevent the activity from being called a sport). You could call these incidental criteria. Knowing the difference between essential and incidental criteria, and how to use them effectively, will help you keep your definitional arguments precise and the audience focused on the heart of your claims, or thesis statements.

In general, then, establishing acceptable criteria is critical to crafting an effective definitional argument. Exactly what kind of criteria the argument needs and the best way to present and support them depend on the kind of definition in question.

Criteria and Formal Definitions

If you're writing a formal definition, your job is to walk your readers step by step toward a clear understanding of your criteria. One good way to do this is to place the term or concept in question in a group of similar things and then distinguish it from the other members of the group. Let's consider the question of whether cheerleading is a sport. Before arguing whether cheerleading is or isn't, you would have to tell your readers just what you mean by *sport* (you would have to present a formal definition of the term). So, back to Webster's: According to the dictionary, a sport is a kind of activity. But what distinguishes it from other activities, such as reading, writing, gardening, and watching grass grow? As in the previous example, you might argue that a sport is an activity that involves athletic skill, practice or training, and competition. Then, you would have to show why your criteria are essential to the definition of the term.

Because you would be writing an argument, not just a dictionary entry, your starting point in the drafting stage would be a clear statement of the main point you were trying to make in your definition, along with a summary of the criteria you would use to craft your definition. Here's an example:

> Many activities, from archery to the X-Games, are considered to be sports. But what is it that earns them this designation? Simply put, any competitive activity that demands practice and athletic skill for success is a sport.

Here, the criteria involve competition (and a desire for success), practice, and athletic skill. In the body of this paper, you would have to offer evidence—examples of what is and is not a sport, anecdotes, and other support—to show why your criteria are valid and essential and, therefore, why your argument is worthy of the audience's attention and consideration.

Criteria and Categorical Definitions

This type of argument begins much like the formal definition, with clearly established criteria and evidence showing why those criteria are valid and essential. But a categorical definition doesn't end there: Its purpose is to show that some specific thing or concept fits the stated criteria (and, therefore, the definition) of a broader group or class. To make this clearer, let's continue with the cheerleading example and argue that it is a sport. Here's a thesis statement made up of a claim (a statement of your central argument) and reasons (a summary of the reasoning you'll use to support your argument):

> Cheerleading is as much a sport as any of the "big three" in the United States—football, basketball, and baseball—because it requires athleticism, practice, dedication, and skill. And, in many ways, it is more competitive than other sports.

Actually, this thesis statement makes two related claims. The first is a formal definition (a sport is an activity that involves athletic skill, competition, practice, and dedication). The second applies those criteria to cheerleading to show that it is indeed a sport. So, in this kind of argument, the criteria serve two purposes: They define the broader term (in this example, sport) and include—or exclude—the term in question (cheerleading).

Definition in Action

The following essays examine definitional issues that have been in the news recently. The first, from *Washington Post* writer Shankar Vedantam's weekly series "Dispatch from the Department of Human Behavior," looks at the debate over stripping Pluto of its designation as a planet and at our fascination with and dependence on defining things in general. In the second essay, archaeologist Neil Asher Silberman offers a definition of his profession as he explains his objections to the Indiana Jones series of movies.

WHAT ONE FEWER PLANET MEANS TO OUR WORLDVIEW

Shankar Vedantam

SHANKAR VEDANTAM is a reporter for the *Washington Post*, where this article was first published on August 28, 2006.

[1] Is Pluto a planet?

[2] The world's astronomers met in Prague last week to vote on this question, and in a sort of cosmic game of "Survivor," they voted Pluto off the solar system.

[3] Many people were anguished. One colleague asked, "Don't you think it's at least possible that somewhere we're being voted off the solar system?"

[4] This space is designed to explore human behavior, and the topic today is why people care so intensely about whether Pluto is a planet. As Johns Hopkins astronomer William P. Blair put it, "Pluto hasn't changed just because of our nomenclature. It is the same today as it was yesterday and as it has been for thousands of years."

[5] Blair is basically asking whether it is rational to care about definitions and categories, which always involve a degree of arbitrariness. (The astronomers, after all, had to take a vote. It could have gone another way, and we would now have 12 planets instead of eight.)

[6] While Blair makes perfect sense, he also misses the point entirely: Whether or not it is rational, human beings do care intensely about definitions. Some of our most contentious public debates are about definitions. Is the conflict raging in Iraq a civil war? In the abortion debate over when life begins, what exactly do we mean by life?

[7] Definitions and categories are the handles by which we grasp the world. If we change the handles, we change how we see the world.

[8] Peter Lipton, a University of Cambridge philosopher of science, argues that science itself is a composite of external reality and human interpretation of that reality. This is why, after a paradigm shift such as the redefinition of a planet, reality itself can feel different. Whether we say the solar system has eight planets or nine or 12 makes no difference to the solar system, but it makes an enormous difference to us.

[9] Much of the business of science, in fact, has to do with the construction and demolition of categories. No sooner had the astronomers devised their new definition of a planet—the idea that planets need to be large enough to "clear out their neighborhoods" of smaller bodies—than others began testing the solidity of the definition.

[10] "You have the Trojan asteroids that arch 60 degrees in front of and behind Jupiter, so what in the world they mean by 'clearing out' I don't know," said Owen Gingerich, a Harvard astronomer and historian.

[11] If Pluto cannot be a planet because its orbit intersects with Neptune's, how is it that Neptune—which definitely is a planet—can have an orbit that intersects with Pluto's? "Clearly Neptune has not cleared its orbit," declared Karl Glazebrook, an astronomer at Johns Hopkins.

[12] Defenders of the new definition, including outgoing International Astronomical Union President Ronald D. Ekers and Caltech astronomer Mike Brown, dismissed such criticism as lawyerly nitpicking, a sure sign that a debate over definitions will rage for some time.

[13] The reason people care so much about one definition rather than another is because definitions are markers for group identity, said Barbara King, a biological anthropologist at the College of William and Mary who studies social behavior in primates. Wanting to see the world a particular way is an extension of our innate tendency to form groups, coalitions and tribes.

[14] For a Democrat who thinks the war in Iraq is a mistake, for example, it makes sense to define the ongoing carnage as a civil war. For a Republican who thinks the war is justified, it makes sense to define the internal conflict as a hurdle that can be overcome. Arguing about the definition of a civil war, therefore, is an effective (and ostensibly high-minded) shortcut to arguing about politics.

[15] But what in the world does eight planets or nine have to do with group identity and social behavior? Knowledge, King said, is also wrapped up in social experience. King's 12-year-old daughter, for example, is upset that Pluto is no longer a planet, partly because one of her cherished memories is of a trip to Flagstaff, Ariz., where the family went to see the place where an astronomer discovered Pluto. Questioning the importance of Pluto implicitly undermines the importance of that family trip.

[16] People often find it threatening when the categories with which they are familiar are challenged, agreed New York psychiatrist Jack Drescher, who has studied how boundaries of gender and sexuality are constructed. Drescher recently wrote a paper exploring the issue, and cited a 1948 comment in a book by sex researcher Alfred Kinsey:

[17] "The world is not to be divided into sheep and goats. Not all things are black nor all things white. It is a fundamental of taxonomy that nature rarely deals with discrete categories. Only the human mind invents categories and tries to force facts into separated pigeon-holes. The living world is a continuum in each and every one of its aspects."

REAL ARCHAEOLOGISTS DON'T WEAR FEDORAS

Neil Asher Silberman

NEIL ASHER SILBERMAN, former director of the Ename Center for Public Archaeology and Heritage Presentation in Belgium, is the author of *Digging for God and Country* and co-author of *The Bible Unearthed*. He wrote this piece for the May 25, 2008, edition of the *Washington Post*.

[1] After 17 years, Hollywood's most famous archaeologist is back in action. Now grayer and a bit creakier, Indiana Jones is again hacking his way through thick jungles, careering wildly in car chases and scrambling through dark tunnels to snatch a precious artifact from the clutches of an evil empire (Soviet, this time).

[2] And I'm thinking, oh no. Here we go again. Get ready for another long, twisting jump off the cliff of respectability for the image of archaeology.

[3] Don't get me wrong. I'm a fan of pop culture. But I have a problem with the entertainment tail wagging the archaeological

dog. As someone who's been involved in archaeology for the past 35 years, I can tell you that Indiana Jones is not the world's most famous fictional archaeologist; he's the world's most famous archaeologist, period. How many people can name another? Whether I'm sitting on a plane, waiting in an office or milling around at a cocktail party, the casual mention that I'm an archaeologist inevitably brings up Indiana Jones. People conjure up images of gold, adventure and narrow escapes from hostile natives. And while "Indiana Jones and the Kingdom of the Crystal Skull" will almost certainly break worldwide box office records, it will also spread another wave of viral disinformation about what archaeologists actually do.

4 I know that the Indiana Jones series is just a campy tribute to the Saturday afternoon serials of the 1930s and the B-movies of the 1950s, but believe me, it totally misrepresents who archaeologists are and what goals we pursue. It's filled with exaggerated and inaccurate nonsense. Even the centerpiece of the new movie—the "crystal skull"—is a phony. Archaeologists have long known about this class of rare and bizarre artifacts, purportedly from the pre-Columbian cultures of Central and South America. But in the current issue of *Archaeology* magazine, Jane McLaren Walsh of the Smithsonian Institution reveals how she and her colleagues discovered the telltale marks of modern drills and sanders on their surface—and recognized that these supposedly mystical ancient relics were made by profit-hungry forgers to feed the modern black market in antiquities.

5 Even worse, the picture of the vine-swinging, revolver-toting archaeological treasure hunter is all wrong. Gone are the days when all that mattered was museum-quality treasure, and the "natives" didn't matter at all. Certainly in the age of the great colonial empires, archaeologists were often solitary adventurers who could count on the prestige and power of their nations to claim the ruins and relics of ancient empires for themselves. Even without a fedora and a bullwhip, Lord Elgin shipped the famous Parthenon marbles home to England, Heinrich Schliemann smuggled away Troy's golden treasures, and Howard Carter managed to spirit away precious artifacts from King Tutankhamen's tomb in Egypt.

6 But today, the rules are different, and the professional attitude of archaeologists has changed. In place of loners acting on hunches have come teams of specialists in anthropology and the natural sciences who work closely with local scholars and administrators to excavate and painstakingly document their sites centimeter by centimeter. Individual objects are now less important than contexts; the goal is not to collect exotic or mystical artworks but to fit pieces together to form new ideas about history.

7 In my own work in Israel, I've traced the early archaeologists' attempts to discover relics that would provide proof of the historical reliability of the Scriptures—not too different from Indy's search for the biblical Ark of the Covenant. But in the last generation, archaeological teams at sites throughout the Middle East—working to analyze everything from ancient plant remains to distributions of animal bones to ancient metallurgy and environmental data gathered from satellite imagery—have begun to understand the social and cultural background to the rise of the biblical tradition. In the process, they've revealed that many of the taken-for-granteds of biblical history, such as the exodus from Egypt, the conquest of the Promised Land by Joshua and even the vast kingdom of David and Solomon, were mostly literary tall tales and exaggerations of the historical reality.

8 Today, the typical archaeological site is a combination laboratory, field school, campground and open-air classroom, inhabited

by professional archaeologists, their students and eager volunteers from all over the world. The dust still rises and the landscapes are often still exotic, but the problems of research, rather than threatening natives and enemy agents, are the main obstacles to archaeological success.

[9] That's why I cringe when I see how the fedora, leather jacket and bullwhip have become recognizable international promotional symbols of archaeology. Many archaeologists have enthusiastically embraced the Hollywood fantasy, borrowing a bit of Indiana Jones's mystique for themselves. Zahi Hawass, secretary general of Egypt's Supreme Council of Antiquities and archaeological czar of the relics and tombs of ancient Egypt, recently raised funds for charity on a U.S. tour by selling autographed copies of his trademark Indiana Jones hat. The National Science Foundation has just put up an Indiana Jones–themed home page, complete with bullwhip and fedora, and the Archaeological Institute of America, a venerable academic organization of classical archaeologists and art historians, has elected Harrison Ford to its board of directors, in tribute to his "significant role in stimulating the public's interest in archaeological exploration." And professor Cornelius Holtorf of the University of Kalmar in Sweden has offered the opinion that "Indiana Jones is no bad thing for science," suggesting that the film series has attracted many students and supporters to real-life archaeological work.

[10] Of course, archaeologists have to reach out to the public to raise funds and gain attention for their efforts, but I'm convinced that there's something misguided and destructive in this academic love affair with Indiana Jones. It's not just that the films are harmlessly caricatured visions of old-fashioned archaeology; they are filled with destructive and dangerous stereotypes that undermine American archaeology's changing identity and goals. At a time when our national political debates are centered on our relationships with other cultures, when the question of talking to rather than attacking perceived enemies has become a contentious presidential campaign issue and when claims for the repatriation of looted relics are being seriously addressed by courts and professional archaeological organizations, the thrill-a-minute adventures of Indiana Jones are potentially dangerous and dysfunctional models for both modern archaeology and American behavior in the world.

[11] So let the show go on and watch Indy snatch the crystal skull from the grasp of the evil Soviet agents and return to the jungles of South America to rescue the world from an ancient curse. Fantasy can be a guilty pleasure. But don't confuse it with archaeology. And please don't ever ask me about my fedora and bullwhip again.

QUESTIONS OF EVALUATION

Question: *Are the Animal Liberation Front's tactics, which advocate breaking the law to help save other species, right? Are they the best way to deal with the problem of animal cruelty?*

Response: *Because the corporate abuse of animals is so widespread, and because American consumers are blinded by their addiction to cheap and convenient products, the Animal Liberation Front's strategy of direct—if sometimes illegal—action is the best way to end the cruelty perpetrated against other species.*

Defining "Evaluative Arguments": What is the Quality of the Thing?

We make dozens of informal evaluations every day—from what to wear and eat, to which radio station to tune in, to how to spend our free time. And we encounter lots of other evaluations—such as movie, music, and restaurant reviews—online, in newspapers, and on television. We also love lists—rankings, ratings, tallies of winners and losers—and these, too, are types of evaluative arguments in that they make claims about the value of one thing over another. These evaluations make arguments about how well specific things fit into larger categories or how they measure up against other, similar things in those categories—how *American Idol* ranks among the best television shows of all time, for example. (You might have noticed that these kinds of evaluations sound a lot like categorical definitions in their reliance on specific criteria; we'll talk more about that in a moment.) Of course, not all evaluative arguments are as mundane as the ranking of TV shows: We also engage in evaluation when we make major life decisions, both private and public. Voters make evaluations on Election Day, for example, as they ponder how to cast their ballots; doctors and nurses evaluate treatment options before deciding how to proceed with patients; and we all make ethical evaluations when we try to decide what are the right, just, and fair things to do in our lives.

In both cases—when engaging in categorical and ethical evaluations—we make decisions by examining our options and measuring them against criteria, in much the same way we make categorical definitions. Although definitional criteria are usually value-neutral, however, evaluative criteria should, as their name implies, help us measure worth or quality. Think about the difference between these questions:

- "What is a 'leader'?"
- "Who is the most effective national leader in the United States today?"

The first question (one of definition) invites a descriptive response, probably a list of characteristics, whereas the second (a question of evaluation) requires criteria that measure and evaluate effective leadership. The excerpts about the Animal Liberation Front's goals and tactics that open this section provide another useful example. In the claim that responds to the questions, the writer has examined the group's primary goal (saving animals) and methods (direct action that includes breaking the law) and measured them against criteria governing ethical human behavior (think of these as standards for deciding what is right and wrong, moral and immoral, fair and unfair). In her claim, the writer finds that, based on her sense of what is right and moral, the Animal Liberation Front's methods are the best way to bring an end to animal cruelty. In short, she has evaluated ALF's actions and found them to be acceptable and effective, based on a set of ethical criteria that she will have to explain and support elsewhere in her essay (see "Criteria and Ethical Evaluations" below).

Other evaluative arguments, such as reviews and rankings, are often far less weighty. Consider, for example, this summary from dvdjournal.com's list of the 10 worst DVDs ever released (this is from the entry for the 1998 movie called *The Avengers*):

> "The Avengers: *Plot? Incomprehensible. Characters? Thin. Sean Connery? Terrible.*"

The first problem facing the editors at dvdjournal.com would have been to figure out how to decide which of all the terrible DVDs out there to include on their list; in other words, they would have had to establish criteria they could use to evaluate the awfulness of some truly awful DVDs. The blurb about *The Avengers* gives us a glimpse of these criteria—some bad movies have serious problems with plot, characterization, and acting. Although these were not the only criteria listed on the website, and they certainly don't constitute a complete evaluative argument, they do show that the editors were being driven by something more complicated than, "We just hated *The Avengers*." In an more fully developed evaluative argument, the editors would indicate why the criteria they selected matter—why plotting, acting, and characterization are important in movies—and how *The Avengers* failed to meet their standards for each criterion (see "Criteria and Categorical Evaluations" below).

For our purposes, then, we will focus on two types of evaluative arguments, categorical and ethical, and the kinds of criteria and support that make them effective.

Criteria and Categorical Evaluations

As in definitional arguments, clear, well-justified criteria lie at the heart of effective categorical evaluations. Generally speaking, you need to do three things involving criteria in a categorical evaluation: You need to list what your criteria are, why your criteria are a good and fair way to measure your subject, and how your subject does or does not fit your criteria. You don't necessarily have to do these things in this order, but you do need to cover them at some point. Let's take a closer look:

- **Listing your criteria.** Think about it: Your readers will have a hard time following and accepting your evaluation if they don't know what exactly you're evaluating. Let's say you write in your campus newspaper that, "The Toby Keith concert last night was the best live show I've ever seen. I give it five stars out of five," and then you spend the rest of your review talking about what a good time you had. This wouldn't be of much use to your readers; for all they know, you might be a die-hard Toby Keith fan who loves anything and everything he does. Your readers might want to know what specifically was so good about the concert before they accept your argument. On the other hand, if you explain in your review that you're judging the concert on vocal and instrumental performances, sound quality, atmosphere (lighting and stage effects), song selection, and audience involvement, your readers will have a much clearer understanding of how you made your evaluation and will be much more likely to take your review seriously.
- **Explaining (and possibly defending) your criteria.** Letting your readers know what the criteria are is just the first step. You also need to do your best to ensure that your readers believe, as you do, that the criteria you select are a reasonable way to measure the quality or value of the subject at hand. Sticking with the concert review example, you would have to provide reasons why readers should accept your criteria—vocal and instrumental performances, sound quality, atmosphere, song selection, and audience involvement—as good measures of a concert's quality. In some cases, like these concert criteria, this might not require much work because the criteria are commonly accepted. In other cases—if you listed costuming among your criteria for reviewing a Toby Keith concert, for example—you might have to spend some time getting your readers to accept the criteria. Whatever the case, you should ask yourself, "Have I given my audience enough reason to accept my criteria as valid?"
- **Making the criteria match.** After establishing what your criteria are and why they matter, you have to show how your subject does or does not fit the criteria. This may

sound a lot like what goes on in a criteria-match definitional argument, and that's because the basic idea is the same: you're defining a broader category and trying to show how a specific subject fits (or doesn't fit). So, once you've told your readers how you're going to judge the Toby Keith concert—by listing your criteria and proving them to be valid—you'll explain, by using details from the concert itself, how the show met or surpassed those criteria. You might, for example, write about Keith's singing on one song and the band's accompaniment on another. And you might point to specific ways the audience interacted with the singer and his band.

If you read a lot of reviews, one thing you might have noticed is that professional writers often imply—rather than spell out—their criteria. This is a common feature of book, film, music, and other arts reviews in newspapers and magazines (and their online counterparts) in part because the people who write these pieces seem to think that the standards in their fields are well established and universally understood. Often, of course, they are right. We can all probably guess the basic criteria for most movie or book reviews based on our own viewing and reading experiences. Still, the best reviewers, even when they don't explicitly state their criteria, make it easy for their readers to figure them out (see the A. O. Scott review on p. 99, for example). As you think about writing your categorical evaluations, don't feel like you have to emulate examples you see in the media. For one thing, most of these are poor examples of evaluative arguments; they're more like dressed-up opinion columns with little, if any, support. Remember that your obligations are to the audience. You want your readers to be able to understand your arguments so that they will give them fair consideration.

And that consideration will come not just from your explanation of the criteria you're using to make your evaluation, but also from the kind of evidence you provide to show that your criteria are valid and that your subject fits—or doesn't fit—those criteria. In general, there are two categories of evaluative evidence, the objective (or measurable) and the subjective (or non-measurable).

- **Evaluations using objective evidence:** In short, these kinds of arguments rely on criteria that can be measured, counted, or demonstrated. If, as a parent, you were trying to decide which school district in your city was better at preparing students for college, many of your criteria would likely be objective (or quantitative)—test scores, numbers of students who get into college, rankings of student performance at college, and other data. Although this kind of evidence can provide solid support for evaluative claims, it isn't irrefutable. The numbers themselves may not be subject to debate, but *how* those numbers are presented—and which numbers are left out—almost always is. What if, for example, one school district reported that its average SAT score was 1,350. That's an impressive number, and there may be no reason to challenge it. But what if that same district failed to report that only 50 percent of eligible students had taken the test? You would be correct in wanting to know why the other students were not tested or, if they were, what tests they took and what those results were. This is not to say that you should discount quantitative evidence; on the contrary, it can be extremely effective. But you should approach the presentation of statistics, measurements, and numbers with a critical eye.
- **Evaluations using subjective evidence:** Much of what we like to argue about and evaluate cannot be quantified. What statistics, for example, could the editors at dvdjournal.com cite in their selection of awful DVDs? Some might argue for the inclusion of box office receipts. But that really only measures popularity, not artistic merit (or lack thereof).

Because subjective criteria are not measurable, you have to spend some time persuading your readers to accept the criteria and the evidence presented to support them. Think back to the Toby Keith concert review example above. If you thought that one of the things that made the concert so good was the quality of Keith's voice—in other words, if you wanted to use vocal quality as one of your criteria—you would have to show in your review how Keith's voice met or exceeded the standard. And because there are no objective measures for this, no data you could marshal to support your claim, you would have to provide convincing and authoritative subjective evidence to win your readers over (you might, for example, compare Keith's voice to those of other excellent singers you've seen). Subjective evidence can also make strong appeals to values and beliefs and, as a consequence, can depend heavily on the character of the writer, which means you should think carefully about how you will present yourself and how you will argue your position (we'll discuss this further in "Criteria and Ethical Evaluations," below).

As you may have guessed by now, some of the most effective arguments of evaluation are those that use both objective and subjective criteria. If you can use both types of criteria, do so. But don't worry if you're dealing with a subject that simply cannot be quantified. Many excellent evaluations are based solely on subjective criteria. One kind of especially powerful argument—the ethical evaluation—often depends heavily, if not entirely, on criteria that cannot be measured.

Criteria and Ethical Evaluations

Although categorical evaluations bear a strong resemblance to definitional arguments in their content and structure, ethical evaluations are often linked to policy arguments because they make judgments about things we do. Ethical evaluations frequently begin with a question such as, "What is the right thing to do?" (And *right* can be swapped out with words like *fair* or *moral* or *best*.) Some begin by questioning the actions of others, often governmental agencies or businesses ("Is teaching abstinence the best way to prevent the spread of AIDS?" "Do automakers have an obligation to produce more fuel-efficient vehicles?") Others, as you'll read later in this chapter, play an integral role in policy arguments by providing justification for adopting a particular course of action ("Banning smoking from college campuses is the right thing to do because administrators have an obligation to protect the health of their students"). These arguments, embedded in larger proposals, usually must make a special kind of appeal to the audience to be successful. And this is where they are very different from categorical evaluations that rely primarily on objective or measurable evidence: In most ethical evaluations you write, you will build support for your criteria by appealing to your audience's values, its beliefs, or its basic sense of right and wrong.

Let's look at the Animal Liberation Front example again to see how this works. Here's the claim that opens this section on evaluative arguments:

> Because the corporate abuse of animals is so widespread, and because American consumers are blinded by their addiction to cheap and convenient products, the Animal Liberation Front's strategy of direct—if sometimes illegal—action is the best way to end the cruelty perpetrated against other species.

Although this claim doesn't propose a policy of its own, it does present an argument in favor of the actions taken by the Animal Liberation Front. And the argument the writer makes is in no way a categorical evaluation. The author is not trying to measure her subject—ALF's strategy of engagement—against a broader category of good or bad strategies; rather, she's arguing that the group's actions are ethically justifiable as the best way to deal with the problem of animal cruelty. The two reasons she mentions in her claim—the prevalence of animal abuse and Americans' desire for low prices and convenience above all else—will form the basis of her attempt to get readers to accept her position. Her challenge will be to show readers that, even though they may not share her beliefs on this subject, those beliefs are nevertheless valid and worthy of their consideration. She doesn't have to change her readers' beliefs or values; that's probably an unrealistic expectation for a piece of writing. But she can do her best to convince the audience that her beliefs aren't unreasonable and to show them how those beliefs led her to her conclusions about the Animal Liberation Front.

How can she do this—and how can you do the same in your own ethical evaluations? There's no easy formula when it comes to arguments that appeal to morals and values, in large part because these are often rooted in religious faith or other spiritual beliefs. But there are some things you can think about and do to make your ethical arguments more persuasive (these are all related to the rhetorical situation discussed in Chapters 2 and 3):

- **Know your audience.** Although this piece of advice applies to just about every writing situation, it is especially important when you're invoking a system of beliefs to support a claim. And the trick is to not stop once you know who your readers are; you need to also understand, as best you can, what they believe about your topic and why they believe these things. Arguing in favor of the Animal Liberation Front's tactics on a blog sponsored by People for the Ethical Treatment of Animals is one thing. Making the same case on the *Wall Street Journal*'s editorial page—one of the most conservative in the country—is quite another. Learning about your audience might require a little research, but it will be time well spent.
- **Explain your beliefs thoroughly.** Again, you shouldn't expect to be able to change your readers' minds about their values or other beliefs. Your goal should be to help them understand what you believe and why you believe it. And to do this, you might have to articulate some values that you've held so closely for so long that they've become second nature to you. Just remember that your audience doesn't necessarily know what you know or believe what you believe. The more clearly and thoroughly you explain your beliefs, the more likely your readers will be to give you the benefit of the doubt.
- **Treat others' beliefs fairly.** The quickest way to lose an audience is to insult it. And one of the quickest ways to insult audience members is to make light of or otherwise disparage the things they believe in. Touting one set of values as unquestionably superior to all others rarely leads to productive public discourse. Such a strategy might seem work with a like-minded audience. But if you want to reach out to a broader audience, you'll find readers with different beliefs far more likely to see your argument as worthy of consideration if they see you as fair minded and knowledgeable.

Evaluation in Action

The two texts that follow present two kinds of evaluative arguments. In the first, reviewer A. O. Scott, writing for the *New York Times*, argues that *Iron Man* is an "unusually good superhero picture" and "a superhero movie that's good in unusual ways." Like most professional critics, Scott doesn't make the criteria he uses to judge the film explicit, but the criteria are there nonetheless. He writes about the importance of a good script, a solid cast not prone to posing, and a director who asserts himself judiciously. In the second piece, an ethical argument, writer Ariel Dorfman presents a case against the United States' use of torture. His argument is based entirely on the principle that torture is morally wrong and always unacceptable.

HEAVY SUIT, LIGHT TOUCHES

A. O. Scott

A. O. SCOTT, a film critic for the *New York Times*, wrote this review for the May 2, 2008, edition of the newspaper.

[1] The world at the moment does not suffer from a shortage of superheroes. And yet in some ways the glut of anti-evil crusaders with cool costumes and troubled souls takes the pressure off of "Iron Man," which clanks into theaters today ahead of Hellboy, Batman and the Incredible Hulk. This summer those guys are all in sequels or redos, so Iron Man (a Marvel property not to be confused with the Man of Steel, who belongs to DC and who's taking a break this year) has the advantage of novelty in addition to a seasonal head start.

[2] And "Iron Man," directed by Jon Favreau ("Elf," "Zathura"), has the advantage of being an unusually good superhero picture. Or at least—since it certainly has its problems—a superhero movie that's good in unusual ways. The film benefits from a script (credited to Mark Fergus, Hawk Ostby, Art Marcum and Matt Holloway) that generally chooses clever dialogue over manufactured catchphrases and lumbering exposition, and also from a crackerjack cast that accepts the filmmakers' invitation to do some real acting rather than just flex and glower and shriek for a paycheck.

[3] There's some of that too, of course. The hero must flex and furrow his brow; the bad guy must glower and scheme; the girl must shriek and fret. There should also be a skeptical but supportive friend. Those are the rules of the genre, as unbreakable as the pseudoscientific principles that explain everything (An arc reactor! Of course!) and the Law of the Bald Villain. In "Iron Man" it all plays out more or less as expected, from the trial-and-error building of the costume to the climactic showdown, with lots of flying, chasing and noisemaking in between. (I note that there is one sharp, subversive surprise right at the very end.)

[4] What is less expected is that Mr. Favreau, somewhat in the manner of those sly studio-era craftsmen who kept their artistry close to the vest so the bosses wouldn't confiscate it, wears the genre paradigm as a light cloak rather than a suit of iron. Instead of the tedious, moralizing, pop-Freudian origin story we often get in the first installments of comic-book-franchise movies—childhood trauma; identity crisis; longing for justice versus thirst for revenge; wake me up when the explosions start—"Iron

Man" plunges us immediately into a world that crackles with character and incident.

5 It is not quite the real world, but it's a bit closer than Gotham or Metropolis. We catch up with Tony Stark in dusty Afghanistan, where he is enjoying a Scotch on the rocks in the back of an armored American military vehicle. Tony is a media celebrity, a former M.I.T. whiz kid and the scion of a family whose company makes and sells high-tech weaponry. He's also a bon vivant and an incorrigible playboy. On paper the character is completely preposterous, but since Tony is played by Robert Downey Jr., he's almost immediately as authentic and familiar—as much fun, as much trouble—as your ex-boyfriend or your old college roommate. Yeah, that guy.

6 Tony's skeptical friend (see above) is Rhodey, an Air Force officer played with good-humored sidekick weariness by Terrence Howard. The girl is one Pepper Potts (Gwyneth Paltrow, also in evident good humor), Tony's smitten, ultracompetent assistant. His partner and sort-of mentor in Stark Enterprises is Obadiah Stane, played by Jeff Bridges with wit and exuberance and—spoiler alert!—a shaved head.

7 These are all first-rate actors, and Mr. Downey's antic energy and emotional unpredictability bring out their agility and resourcefulness. Within the big, crowded movements of this pop symphony is a series of brilliant duets that sometimes seem to have the swing and spontaneity of jazz improvisation: Mr. Downey and Ms. Paltrow on the dance floor; Mr. Downey and Mr. Howard drinking sake on an airplane; Mr. Downey and Shaun Toub working on blueprints in a cave; Mr. Downey and Mr. Bridges sparring over a box of pizza.

8 Those moments are what you are likely to remember. The plot is serviceable, which is to say that it's placed at the service of the actors (and the special-effects artists), who deftly toss it around and sometimes forget it's there. One important twist seems glaringly arbitrary and unmotivated, but this lapse may represent an act of carefree sabotage rather than carelessness. You know this ostensibly shocking revelation is coming, and the writers know you know it's coming, so why worry too much about whether it makes sense? Similarly, the patina of geopolitical relevance is worn thin and eventually discarded, and Tony's crisis of conscience when he discovers what his weapons are being used for is more of a narrative convenience than a real moral theme.

9 All of which is to say that "Iron Man," in spite of the heavy encumbrances Tony must wear when he turns into the title character, is distinguished by light touches and grace notes. The hardware is impressive, don't get me wrong, but at these prices it had better be. If you're throwing around a hundred million dollars and you have Batman and the Hulk on your tail, you had better be sure that the arc reactors are in good working order and that the gold-titanium alloy suit gleams like new and flies like a bird.

10 And everything works pretty well. But even dazzling, computer-aided visual effects, these days, are not so special. And who doesn't have superpowers? Actually, Iron Man doesn't; his heroism is all handicraft, elbow grease and applied intelligence. Those things account for the best parts of "Iron Man" as well.

ARE WE REALLY SO FEARFUL?

Ariel Dorfman

ARIEL DORFMAN, a Chilean American writer and professor at Duke University, is author of "Death and the Maiden." He wrote this piece for the September 24, 2006, edition of the *Washington Post*.

[1] It still haunts me, the first time—it was in Chile, in October of 1973—that I met someone who had been tortured. To save my life, I had sought refuge in the Argentine Embassy some weeks after the coup that had toppled the democratically elected government of Salvador Allende, a government for which I had worked. And then, suddenly, one afternoon, there he was. A large-boned man, gaunt and yet strangely flabby, with eyes like a child, eyes that could not stop blinking and a body that could not stop shivering.

[2] That is what stays with me—that he was cold under the balmy afternoon sun of Santiago de Chile, trembling as though he would never be warm again, as though the electric current was still coursing through him. Still possessed, somehow still inhabited by his captors, still imprisoned in that cell in the National Stadium, his hands disobeying the orders from his brain to quell the shuddering, his body unable to forget what had been done to it just as, nearly 33 years later, I, too, cannot banish that devastated life from my memory.

[3] It was his image, in fact, that swirled up from the past as I pondered the current political debate in the United States about the practicality of torture. Something in me must have needed to resurrect that victim, force my fellow citizens here to spend a few minutes with the eternal iciness that had settled into that man's heart and flesh, and demand that they take a good hard look at him before anyone dare maintain that, to save lives, it might be necessary to inflict unbearable pain on a fellow human being. Perhaps the optimist in me hoped that this damaged Argentine man could, all these decades later, help shatter the perverse innocence of contemporary Americans, just as he had burst the bubble of ignorance protecting the young Chilean I used to be, someone who back then had encountered torture mainly through books and movies and newspaper reports.

[4] That is not, however, the only lesson that today's ruthless world can learn from that distant man condemned to shiver forever.

[5] All those years ago, that torture victim kept moving his lips, trying to articulate an explanation, muttering the same words over and over. "It was a mistake," he repeated, and in the next few days I pieced together his sad and foolish tale. He was an Argentine revolutionary who had fled his homeland and, as soon as he had crossed the mountains into Chile, had begun to boast about what he would do to the military there if it staged a coup, about his expertise with arms of every sort, about his colossal stash of weapons. Bluster and braggadocio—and every word of it false.

[6] But how could he convince those men who were beating him, hooking his penis to electric wires and waterboarding him? How could he prove to them that he had been lying, prancing in front of his Chilean comrades, just trying to impress the ladies with his fraudulent insurgent persona?

[7] Of course, he couldn't. He confessed to anything and everything they wanted to drag from his hoarse, howling throat; he invented accomplices and addresses and culprits; and then, when it became apparent that all this was imaginary, he was subjected to further ordeals.

[8] There was no escape.

[9] That is the hideous predicament of the torture victim. It was always the same story, what I discovered in the ensuing years, as I became an unwilling expert on all manner of torments and degradations, my life and my writing overflowing with grief from every continent. Each of those mutilated spines and fractured lives—Chinese, Guatemalan, Egyptian, Indonesian, Iranian, Uzbek, need I go on?—all of them, men and women alike, surrendered the same story of essential asymmetry, where one man has all the power in the world and the other has nothing but pain, where one man can decree death at the flick of a wrist and the other can only pray that the wrist will be flicked soon.

[10] It is a story that our species has listened to with mounting revulsion, a horror that has led almost every nation to sign treaties over the past decades declaring these abominations as crimes against humanity, transgressions interdicted all across the earth. That is the wisdom, national and international, that has taken us thousands of years of tribulation and shame to achieve. That is the wisdom we are being asked to throw away when we formulate the question—Does torture work?—when we allow ourselves to ask whether we can afford to outlaw torture if we want to defeat terrorism.

[11] I will leave others to claim that torture, in fact, does not work, that confessions obtained under duress—such as that extracted from the heaving body of that poor Argentine braggart in some Santiago cesspool in 1973—are useless. Or to contend that the United States had better not do that to anyone in our custody lest someday another nation or entity or group decides to treat our prisoners the same way.

[12] I find these arguments—and there are many more—to be irrefutable. But I cannot bring myself to use them, for fear of honoring the debate by participating in it.

[13] Can't the United States see that when we allow someone to be tortured by our agents, it is not only the victim and the perpetrator who are corrupted, not only the "intelligence" that is contaminated, but also everyone who looked away and said they did not know, everyone who consented tacitly to that outrage so they could sleep a little safer at night, all the citizens who did not march in the streets by the millions to demand the resignation of whoever suggested, even whispered, that torture is inevitable in our day and age, that we must embrace its darkness?

[14] Are we so morally sick, so deaf and dumb and blind, that we do not understand this? Are we so fearful, so in love with our own security and steeped in our own pain, that we are really willing to let people be tortured in the name of America? Have we so lost our bearings that we do not realize that each of us could be that hapless Argentine who sat under the Santiago sun, so possessed by the evil done to him that he could not stop shivering?

QUESTIONS OF CAUSE AND EFFECT

Question: *Why does the Animal Liberation Front believe that it is acceptable—even necessary— to break the law in order to protect animals?*

Response: *Organizations such as the Animal Liberation Front may feel driven to extreme measures to protect animals from abuse because they believe that such abuse is engrained in our consumer-oriented culture and that most Americans don't care enough about the problem to do anything about it. These organizations thus see themselves as the animals' last hope.*

Defining "Causal Arguments":
What Are the Causes (or Effects) of the Thing?

Causal arguments investigate the forces behind and/or the consequences of particular actions, events, trends, or phenomena. We encounter them in their most familiar form in business and public life, often when someone or some organization (like a government agency or Major League Baseball) is trying to figure out how to solve a problem. Think about it: Policy-makers can't effectively find solutions to problems if they don't understand what causes the problems in the first place, and it would be shortsighted for any business or government leader to institute a policy without considering its potential consequences. Causal arguments are also common in the sciences and in private life. And they aren't always part of larger policy arguments. Some seek only to answer questions of cause and effect. A few examples include:

- Why has church attendance in Great Britain declined recently?
- What would be the consequences of requiring all young adults to perform some kind of public or military service?
- Why has the number of autism cases risen so dramatically in the United States over the past decade?
- What effect is technology—in the form of iPods, cell phones, and other handheld devices—having on academic cheating?

None of these questions has an irrefutable answer, meaning that anyone who tries to respond will have to make claims based on probable causes and effects using reasonable evidence. In fact, while scientists and other researchers who deal in hard data often prove causal relationships definitively, few of the causal questions that dominate public policy debates are clearly definable. Let's have another look at those four questions and some starting points for trying to answer them:

- Why is church attendance falling in Great Britain? Even though there are statistics that prove the trend—the *New York Times*, citing an organization called Christian Research, reports that regular church attendance has fallen to about 6 percent—no one can say for sure what is causing the trend. Why? In part because the trend involves human behavior, which can be unpredictable and difficult to analyze, as well as a large number of subjects who may have hundreds of different reasons for their actions.
- What would happen if the United States required young adults to perform public or military service? This question, too, involves human behavior. And, to make a definitive answer even more unlikely, it requires speculation about the consequences of an action (the service requirement) that hasn't even been taken yet.
- Why has the number of autism cases in the United States risen so much in recent years? Again, as with the church attendance question, there is data to prove the trend (the Centers for Disease Control and Prevention reports that the rate is up from four or five cases per 10,000 children in the 1990s to more than six per 1,000 now). And researchers are working to find a definitive cause. In the meantime, however, answers about the cause of autism and its growing prevalence remain speculative—and the subject of intense public argument.
- How is technology affecting academic cheating? This question, although again dealing with human behavior, offers the possibility of a well-documented—if still not definitive—answer. Because some of the effects—cases where text messaging is used to cheat on exams, for example—may be measurable, we could draw conclusions based on this kind of data.

The point here is that, as you think about questions of cause and effect and about how to compose a causal argument, you should remember that you won't be able to prove your case beyond all doubt—you might, for example, be dealing with a trend (such as a decline in church attendance) that doesn't have a single, provable cause, or a proposed action (such as a community service requirement for young adults) about whose consequences you can only speculate. In other cases, you might have to make an argument about causes that are entirely subjective. The Animal Liberation Front question that opens this section—What motivates ALF members to do the things they do?—is a good example. After researching the organization and responses to its actions, the writer presents a causal claim saying essentially that ALF resorts to extreme measures to protect animals because its members see themselves as the animals' last hope in a culture that values consumerism and convenience over the lives of other species. This is an interesting claim, but can the writer prove it irrefutably? No, she can't; this isn't mathematics or chemistry, where causal relations are often provable. But she can present a thoughtful and informed argument for the causal relationship she proposes (more on how she might do that in a moment).

A Word about Causality and Correlation

Before moving ahead to examine some different types of causal arguments and strategies for writing them, we should make sure we're all on the same page about one of the most common mistakes people make when thinking about causal relationships—the difference between causality and correlation. To understand how the two get confused—and how they are different—think about the relationship between television viewing and obesity. More specifically, think about this often-cited research finding: The more television children watch, the more likely they are to be overweight. There are many sources of data that support this statement, and just as many organizations that want to do something about the situation. So it seems clear that there is a relationship—a correlation—between children's TV viewing habits and their weight. But what do we *really* know about that relationship? Does watching TV cause obesity? Does obesity lead to more hours staring at the tube? Or is there no direct causal link between the two? Although we might accept that the two are correlated (that they have a relationship), we might not have enough evidence to establish causality (to say whether one causes the other). Still, it's easy to find arguments that mistake correlation for a cause.

In their popular book *Freakonomics*, which urges readers to reexamine their assumptions about causal relationships, economist Steven D. Leavitt and journalist Stephen J. Dubner explain the two terms this way: "A correlation simply means that a relationship exists between two factors—let's call them *X* and *Y*—but it tells you nothing about the direction of that relationship. It's possible that *X* causes *Y*; it's also possible that *Y* causes *X*; and it may be that *X* and *Y* are both being caused by some other factor, *Z*." The authors then present a correlation that could easily—and has been—misinterpreted as a causal relationship. Here's what they have to say:

> "Think about this correlation: cities with a lot of murders also tend to have a lot of police officers. . . . Denver and Washington, D.C., have about the same population—but Washington has nearly three times as many police as Denver, and it also has eight times the number of murders. Unless you have more information, however, it's hard to say what's causing what. Someone who didn't know better might contemplate these figures and conclude that it is all those extra police in Washington who are causing the extra murders."

Again, this kind of confusion is common. But it's also easy to avoid if you remember that the purpose of causal argument is not simply to show that a relationship exists between two things; it is also to investigate the nature of that relationship and to make a claim based on that investigation.

Categories of Causal Arguments

Even though they have similar purposes, causal arguments come in many forms and, like definitions and evaluations, often appear as parts of other arguments. For our purposes, we'll separate causal arguments into three categories:

- **Arguments that make claims about the causes of particular events, trends, or phenomena.** In this case, you might start with a trend such as the massive popularity of inspirational and self-help books like *The Purpose Driven Life* and *The Secret* and ask, "Why are so many people buying so many of these books?" To explore the topic, you might research publishing trends; read interviews with authors, booksellers, and cultural critics; and talk to some people you know who like to read these kinds of books. Then, you might settle on a claim along these lines: "Self-help books are perennially popular because they offer hope in a convenient package that readers can use or discard without having to openly acknowledge their shortcomings." The key to making your argument work would be showing your readers that the link from the trend back to the causes you present in your claim is valid and compelling.
- **Arguments that make claims about consequences of actions that have already occurred.** Here, your concern would be the effects of some action, event, or trend that has already occurred (or continues to occur). You might begin, for example, with a trend such as the rapid increase in tuition at public colleges and universities in the United States and then investigate the consequences of that trend. In this case, because tuition has been rising for years, you should be able to find data on the subject that you could use to form and support your claim. Because you would likely find many different consequences related to rising tuitions, you would probably be best served by limiting your argument to one or two that you find especially compelling. For example, your claim might be, "Rising tuition in the United States is having two profound effects on college-age students: It is either pricing them out of higher education or driving them deeply into debt even before they begin their careers." To argue your position effectively, you would have to show clearly how the cause was leading to the consequences.
- **Arguments that make claims about consequences that might occur.** These kinds of arguments usually spring from discussions of policy. In other words, when we're trying to decide whether to do something—like ban smoking on a college campus—our deliberations usually include some thinking about the consequences of that action. Thus, the major difference between this category and the one discussed previously is the speculative nature of the argument. Because the action hasn't even been taken, we can't comment on the effects. However, we can still make informed claims and support them with convincing evidence based on similar cases and on well-reasoned speculation. You could, for example, base an argument about how the ban on smoking at your campus affects the bans at other colleges or similar large institutions. The biggest challenge in this type of argument is convincing your audience that the described effects could occur.

Showing Causal Relationships

Once you've decided on the causal argument, you'll have to figure out how you're going to convince your readers to accept as valid the causal relationship presented in your claim. The evidence and support you offer should help your readers understand and accept the causal links you're trying to establish. In some cases, you might be able to do this directly, by introducing specific evidence about the nature of the relationship in question. In others, you might have to rely on more speculative evidence. And in still others, you might do both. Let's look at some examples, using the three claims from our discussion about the categories of causal arguments:

- **Showing evidence of causes.** Here, again, is the sample claim about what drives the popularity of self-help books: "Self-help books are perennially popular because they offer hope in a convenient package that readers can use or discard without having to openly acknowledge their shortcomings." In effect, this claim argues that these books are popular because they're encouraging, convenient, and private. So, how might you support this claim? You could use direct evidence in the form of surveys or interviews in which readers cited these as reasons for their book purchases. You could also use statements by experts in publishing and psychology who made similar claims. Also, you could explain your logic by walking readers, step by step, through your thinking process to show them how you reached your conclusions.

- **Showing evidence of consequences when the cause is established.** Our claim in this category was, "Rising tuition in the United States is having two profound effects on college-age students: It is either pricing them out of higher education or driving them deeply into debt even before they begin their careers." Here again, because you're dealing with something that has happened or is happening, you should have plenty of convincing direct evidence at your disposal. From your research, you could cite data on enrollment trends among different socioeconomic groups, for example, or statistics on the growing number of student loans and on rising levels of student debt. Another effective form of support for this kind of claim would be anecdotal evidence—stories about how tuition increases have affected actual students.

- **Showing evidence of speculative consequences.** Supporting these kinds of claims can prove a bit more difficult because, as we noted previously, they require informed speculation. Let's say you wanted to present an argument with the following claim, "If our university banned smoking on all its property—even outdoors—we would have a cleaner campus, healthier students and faculty, and an enhanced reputation as a progressive thinking institution." Because the university has not in fact banned smoking, you would have no direct evidence about the school to use in your argument. However, you could certainly do more than just guess about the consequences of such a ban. You could, first, research smoking bans at other colleges or similar institutions and use the findings on the effects of the bans to support your claim. You could also show how the generally accepted health benefits of a smoke-free environment would logically apply to your campus. And you could use expert commentary about the possible public relations benefits of a smoking ban to show how a ban could enhance your school's reputation. All of this would constitute informed speculation.

When thinking about the type of argument you want to present and the kinds of evidence you'll use to support your claim, keep in mind that your primary goal is to help your readers see and accept the causal relationships you're trying to make. The more specific and well-supported reasons you give readers to accept your claims, the better your argument will be.

Causal Argument in Action

In the first essay below, writer Nora Ephron takes a tongue-in-cheek look at our tendency to make hasty causal connections between things that happen in temporal proximity. Though Ephron chooses absurd examples for comedic effect, her point is serious, especially when it comes to reading and writing causal arguments: Just because two things happen in a particular order doesn't mean that they have any kind of causal relationship. In the second essay, "A Bargain at 77 Cents to a Dollar," policy analyst and author Carrie Lukas briefly examines a trend—the wage gap between men and women in some jobs—and then presents a case for the causes of that trend. As you read her argument, notice that she doesn't simply list what she sees as the causes; she also explains how these causes have led directly to the trend.

THE CHICKEN SOUP CHRONICLES

Nora Ephron

NORA EPHRON, the author, most recently, of *I Feel Bad About My Neck: And Other Thoughts on Being a Woman*, is a contributing columnist for the *New York Times*, where this piece was published on January 13, 2008.

[1] The other day I felt a cold coming on. So I decided to have chicken soup to ward off the cold. Nonetheless I got the cold. This happens all the time: you think you're getting a cold; you have chicken soup; you get the cold anyway. So: is it possible that chicken soup gives you a cold?

[2] I will confess a bias: I've never understood the religious fervor that surrounds breast-feeding. There are fanatics out there who believe you should breast-feed your child until he or she is old enough to unbutton your blouse. Their success in conning a huge number of women into believing this is one of the truly grim things about modern life. Anyway, one of the main reasons given for breast-feeding is that breast-fed children are less prone to allergies. But children today are far more allergic than they were when I was growing up, when far fewer women breast-fed their children. I mean, what is it with all these children dropping dead from sniffing a peanut? This is new, friends, it's brand-new new, and don't believe anyone who says otherwise. So: is it possible that breast-feeding causes allergies?

[3] It's much easier to write a screenplay on a computer than on a typewriter. Years ago, when you wrote a screenplay on a typewriter, you had to retype the entire page just to make the smallest change; now, on the computer, you can make large and small changes effortlessly, you can fiddle with dialogue, you can change names and places with a keystroke. And yet movies are nowhere near as good as they used to be. In 1939, when screenwriters were practically still using quill pens, the following movies were among those nominated for best picture: "Gone With the Wind," "The Wizard of Oz," "Mr. Smith Goes to Washington," "Wuthering Heights" and "Stagecoach," and that's not even the whole list. So: is it possible that computers are responsible for the decline of movies?

4 There is way too much hand-washing going on. Someone told me the other day that the act of washing your hands is supposed to last as long as it takes to sing the song "Happy Birthday." I'm not big on hand-washing to begin with; I don't even like to wash fruit, if you must know. But my own prejudices aside, all this washing-of-hands and use of Purell before picking up infants cannot be good. (By the way, I'm not talking about hand-washing in hospitals, I'm talking about everyday, run-of-the-mill hand-washing.) It can't possibly make sense to keep babies so removed from germs that they never develop an immunity to them. Of course, this isn't my original theory—I read it somewhere a few weeks ago, although I can't remember where. *The New York Times*? *The Wall Street Journal*? Who knows? Not me, that's for sure. So: is it possible that reading about hand-washing leads to memory loss?

5 I love Google. I love everything about it. I love the verb Google and I love the noun and sometimes I can even use the word as an adjective. For a long time, I liked to think there would some day be a person called the Google, a mixture of a researcher, an assistant and a butler, who would stand by ready to ride to the rescue at all Google moments. No more desperately trying to come up with the name of that movie Jeremy Irons was in, which lurks like a hologram while everyone makes stabs at figuring out what on earth it was called. We can never remember the name of that movie, the one about Claus von Bulow, but never mind—the Google is here. The Google will find the answer. But as it turns out, no Google is necessary. Somebody has a BlackBerry. The answer is seconds away! It's here! The movie was called "Reversal of Fortune!" What a fantastic relief! On the other hand, I have to say, there was something romantic about the desperate search for an answer. On the road to trying to remember the name of Ethel Rosenberg's brother, for instance, you might find yourself having a brief but diverting chat about Alger Hiss's wife, which might in turn get you to a story about Whittaker Chambers's teeth, which might in turn get you to *Time* magazine, which might in turn get you to Friday nights at *Time* magazine back in the old days, which might in turn get you to sex. This meandering had its charms. It was, in fact, what used to be known as conversation. But no more. Instead, we have the answer. Ethel Rosenberg's brother was named David Greenglass. And that's that. So: is it possible that Google will mean the end of conversation as we know it?

A BARGAIN AT 77 CENTS TO A DOLLAR

Carrie Lukas

CARRIE LUKAS is vice president for policy and economics at the Independent Women's Forum and the author of *The Politically Incorrect Guide to Women, Sex, and Feminism*. This column was first published in the April 3, 2007, edition of the *Washington Post*.

1 Why are politicians again championing the Equal Rights Amendment—newly minted as the Women's Equality Amendment—when the speaker of the House, secretary of state and the Democratic presidential front-runner are women, and when women are

making gains in education and the workforce? One reason is that many claim women are systematically discriminated against at work, as the existence of the so-called wage gap proves.

2 Talking about wage discrimination against women is a political mainstay. Last month, Sen. Hillary Clinton expressed consternation that women continue to make "just 77 cents for every dollar that a man makes" and reintroduced legislation, the Paycheck Fairness Act, that would give the government more power to make "an equal paycheck for equal work" a reality.

3 This statistic—probably the most frequently cited of the Labor Department's data—is also its most misused.

4 Yes, the Labor Department regularly issues new data comparing the median wage of women who work full time with the median wage of men who work full time, and women's earnings bob at around three-quarters those of men. But this statistic says little about women's compensation and the influence of discrimination on men's and women's earnings. All the relevant factors that affect pay—occupation, experience, seniority, education and hours worked—are ignored. This sound-bite statistic fails to take into account the different roles that work tends to play in men's and women's lives.

5 In truth, I'm the cause of the wage gap—I and hundreds of thousands of women like me. I have a good education and have worked full time for 10 years. Yet throughout my career, I've made things other than money a priority. I chose to work in the nonprofit world because I find it fulfilling. I sought out a specialty and employer that seemed best suited to balancing my work and family life. When I had my daughter, I took time off and then opted to stay home full time and telecommute. I'm not making as much money as I could, but I'm compensated by having the best working arrangement I could hope for.

6 Women make similar trade-offs all the time. Surveys have shown for years that women tend to place a higher priority on flexibility and personal fulfillment than do men, who focus more on pay. Women tend to avoid jobs that require travel or relocation, and they take more time off and spend fewer hours in the office than men do. Men disproportionately take on the dirtiest, most dangerous and depressing jobs.

7 When these kinds of differences are taken into account and the comparison is truly between men and women in equivalent roles, the wage gap shrinks. In his book "Why Men Earn More," Warren Farrell—a former board member of the National Organization for Women in New York—identifies more than three dozen professions in which women outearn men (including engineering management, aerospace engineering, radiation therapy and speech-language pathology). Farrell seeks to empower women with this information. Discrimination certainly plays a role in some workplaces, but individual preferences are the real root of the wage gap.

8 When women realize that it isn't systemic bias but the choices they make that determine their earnings, they can make better-informed decisions. Many women may not want to follow the path toward higher pay—which often requires more time on the road, more hours in the office or less comfortable and less interesting work—but they're better off not feeling like victims.

9 Government attempts to "solve" the problem of the wage gap may in fact exacerbate some of the challenges women face, particularly in balancing work and family. Clinton's legislation would give Washington bureaucrats more power to oversee how

wages are determined, which might prompt businesses to make employment options more rigid. Flexible job structures such as the one I enjoy today would probably become scarcer. Why would companies offer employees a variety of work situations and compensation packages if doing so puts them at risk of being sued?

10 Women hearing Clinton's pledge to solve their problems and increase their pay should think hard about the choices they have made. They should think about the women they know and about their career paths. I bet they'll find that maximizing pay hasn't always been the top priority. Eliminating the wage gap may sound like a good campaign promise, but since the wage gap mostly reflects individual differences in priorities, it's a promise that we should hope a President Hillary Clinton wouldn't try to keep.

QUESTIONS OF POLICY

Question: *How should the American public treat the Animal Liberation Front?*
Response: *Even though the Animal Liberation Front openly admits to breaking the law, we should not treat its members as criminals. Rather, we should try to learn from ALF's commitment to protecting animals so that we can change our way of thinking about the rights of other species. This would make us better people and more responsible inhabitants of our planet.*

Defining "Policy Arguments": What Should We Do about the Thing?

Policy arguments—sometimes called proposal arguments—call for action. We engage in them when we're trying to decide what to do about particular problems or issues. Sometimes we might use the argument process to consider several different courses of action; other times, we might advocate for one course in particular. However we use them, policy arguments routinely include definitional, evaluative, and causal claims—they are, in fact, the culmination of the stasis question process. An effective policy argument, as it urges the audience to action, will leave no matters of definition, evaluation, or causality in question. For our purposes, we'll consider two kinds of policy arguments:

- The policy proposal, which generally offers a broad plan of action to solve major social, economic, or political problems that affect large numbers of people (improving voter turnout, for example). These kinds of arguments dominate editorial pages and political discourse in the media. The claim about the Animal Liberation Front that opens this section is a policy proposal in that it argues for acceptance of ALF's principles as a way to make us all better people.
- The practical proposal, which offers a specific and detailed course of action to solve a smaller-scale problem (reducing the incidence of date rape on campus, for example).

Practical proposals show up often in letters to the editor and on blogs, and are common in the business world, as companies seek real solutions to their problems.

Because they usually ask people to do something—sometimes the requested action may be nothing more than thinking about the issue at hand—policy arguments must do three things: first, they must convince readers of the need for action; second, they must explain exactly what should be done; and, third, they must be clear about why the proposed action is the right thing to do. Let's take a closer look:

- **The problem.** No one's going to listen to you if no one believes that your issue is a problem that requires action. So, your first step is to persuade the audience that you're dealing with a genuine problem that needs to be addressed. One of the most effective ways to do this is to make the issue matter to your audience (some teachers call this giving the problem presence). If you were arguing the Animal Liberation Front claim, for example, you would have to make your audience care enough about animal cruelty to consider finding ALF's methods for addressing the problem acceptable.
- **The solution.** Next, you have to be sure that your readers understand the action you want them to take. How you do this will depend on the type of argument you're making. A policy proposal, like the ALF example, might not require much explanation; what you want the audience to do (accept and learn from ALF's mission) is pretty simple. In this case, you would likely have to spend much more time justifying your proposal (see below) than explaining it. On the other hand, a practical proposal—such as a plan to reduce the number of date rapes on your campus—might require a much more detailed explanation of the steps involved and how they would be implemented.
- **The justification.** Finally, no matter what kind of argument you're making, you must show your readers why your course of action is the one they should follow. This sometimes difficult process often starts with overcoming apathy: It is much easier for us to do nothing about problems that we don't think directly affect us than it is to get involved (the ALF proposal is a good example). In addition, you should identify and deal with alternative proposals for addressing the issue, measuring your own plan against these and proving it to be the better choice. One effective way of doing this is to appeal to your audience's logic and emotions. Logical appeals might include an examination of consequences (of your plan, other plans, and of doing nothing) or of the successes of proposals similar to yours. Emotional appeals, on the other hand, might involve a call to readers' ethics, morals, or spiritual beliefs.

Policy Argument in Action

In the essay that follows, former Senator Alan K. Simpson, once an ardent opponent of allowing gays and lesbians to serve openly in the military, proposes that the Pentagon's "don't ask, don't tell" policy be dropped and that sexual orientation no longer play a role in deciding whom the armed services accept and reject. Though his essay is brief, notice that Simpson includes all three key components of an effective policy argument: He calls our attention to the issue and makes it matter; he clearly explains what he wants us to do; and he spells out why we should listen to him.

BIGOTRY THAT HURTS OUR MILITARY

Alan K. Simpson

ALAN K. SIMPSON, a Republican senator from Wyoming from 1979 to 1997, wrote this piece for the March 14, 2007, edition of the *Washington Post*.

[1] As a lifelong Republican who served in the Army in Germany, I believe it is critical that we review—and overturn—the ban on gay service in the military. I voted for "don't ask, don't tell." But much has changed since 1993.

[2] My thinking shifted when I read that the military was firing translators because they are gay. According to the Government Accountability Office, more than 300 language experts have been fired under "don't ask, don't tell," including more than 50 who are fluent in Arabic. This when even Secretary of State Condoleezza Rice recently acknowledged the nation's "foreign language deficit" and how much our government needs Farsi and Arabic speakers. Is there a "straight" way to translate Arabic? Is there a "gay" Farsi? My God, we'd better start talking sense before it is too late. We need every able-bodied, smart patriot to help us win this war.

[3] In today's perilous global security situation, the real question is whether allowing homosexuals to serve openly would enhance or degrade our readiness. The best way to answer this is to reconsider the original points of opposition to open service.

[4] First, America's views on homosexuals serving openly in the military have changed dramatically. The percentage of Americans in favor has grown from 57 percent in 1993 to a whopping 91 percent of 18- to 29-year-olds surveyed in a Gallup poll in 2003.

[5] Military attitudes have also shifted. Fully three-quarters of 500 vets returning from Iraq and Afghanistan said in a December Zogby poll that they were comfortable interacting with gay people. Also last year, a Zogby poll showed that a majority of service members who knew a gay member in their unit said the person's presence had no negative impact on the unit or personal morale. Senior leaders such as retired Gen. John Shalikashvili and Lt. Gen. Daniel Christman, a former West Point superintendent, are calling for a second look.

[6] Second, 24 nations, including 12 in Operation Enduring Freedom and nine in Operation Iraqi Freedom, permit open service. Despite controversy surrounding the policy change, it has had no negative impact on morale, cohesion, readiness or recruitment. Our allies did not display such acceptance back when we voted on "don't ask, don't tell," but we should consider their common-sense example.

[7] Third, there are not enough troops to perform the required mission. The Army is "about broken," in the words of Colin Powell. The Army's chief of staff, Gen. Peter Schoomaker, told the House Armed Services Committee in December that "the active-duty Army of 507,000 will break unless the force is expanded by 7,000 more soldiers a year." To fill its needs, the Army is granting a record number of "moral waivers," allowing even felons to enlist. Yet we turn away patriotic gay and lesbian citizens.

[8] The Urban Institute estimates that 65,000 gays are serving and that there are 1 million gay veterans. These gay vets include Capt. Cholene Espinoza, a former U-2 pilot who logged more than 200 combat hours over

Iraq, and Marine Staff Sgt. Eric Alva, who lost his right leg to an Iraqi land mine. Since 2005, more than 800 personnel have been discharged from "critical fields"—jobs considered essential but difficult in terms of training or retraining, such as linguists, medical personnel and combat engineers. Aside from allowing us to recruit and retain more personnel, permitting gays to serve openly would enhance the quality of the armed forces.

9 In World War II, a British mathematician named Alan Turing led the effort to crack the Nazis' communication code. He mastered the complex German enciphering machine, helping to save the world, and his work laid the basis for modern computer science. Does it matter that Turing was gay? This week, Gen. Peter Pace, chairman of the Joint Chiefs, said that homosexuality is "immoral" and that the ban on open service should therefore not be changed. Would Pace call Turing "immoral"?

10 Since 1993, I have had the rich satisfaction of knowing and working with many openly gay and lesbian Americans, and I have come to realize that "gay" is an artificial category when it comes to measuring a man or woman's on-the-job performance or commitment to shared goals. It says little about the person. Our differences and prejudices pale next to our historic challenge. Gen. Pace is entitled, like anyone, to his personal opinion, even if it is completely out of the mainstream of American thinking. But he should know better than to assert this opinion as the basis for policy of a military that represents and serves an entire nation. Let us end "don't ask, don't tell." This policy has become a serious detriment to the readiness of America's forces as they attempt to accomplish what is arguably the most challenging mission in our long and cherished history.

from reading to writing

1. Crafting a Definition

   Working with a partner or in a small group, identify an issue of definition that is of interest to you, your community, or to college students in general. Some possibilities:
   - What is the American Dream?
   - What is hazing?
   - What is a compassionate conservative?
   - What is an adult?

   As we have discussed elsewhere in this chapter, issues of definition are often embedded in other types of arguments. For this exercise, however, you should focus solely on the definitional issue at hand.

   After you settle on a subject, work with your partner or group members to develop essential criteria for your definition and to find examples of cases that fit the criteria and cases that don't. Keep in mind that borderline cases—those that fit some of the criteria but not others—are often the most useful in helping readers fully understand a definition.

   Write your criteria and your examples down. Now, fashion what you have into a one- to two-paragraph definition of your term. Be prepared to share this with your classmates.

2. Writing an Evaluative Argument

Write a 750-word evaluative essay on one of the following topics:
- Which five books should all students read before going to college?
- What is the best film adaptation of a Shakespearean play?
- Who is the most effective public leader in the United States today?
- What is the most effective way to prevent crime on your college campus?
- What is the most effective way to reduce underage drinking on your college campus?
- Is alternative medicine an effective form of health care?
- Are organic foods worth the extra cost?
- Are hybrid vehicles worth the extra cost?
- Is the U.S. war on terror working?
- What is the best way to learn how to write well?

After choosing your topic, you should start thinking about the criteria upon which you will base your evaluation (what, for example, makes a great public leader?). Then, as with criteria-match arguments of definition, think about how you will show that your subject fits those criteria. Also, think about how you will address those who have opposing views. How can you convince readers that they should listen to you?

3. Writing an Evaluation for a Skeptical Audience

Write a 300- to 500-word essay in which you persuade a skeptical audience that _____ is a great movie (you fill in the blank). For example, you might try to persuade readers who have no interest in fantasy books and movies that the *Lord of the Rings* series is the best movie trilogy ever made. (You may substitute a TV show if you are more comfortable writing about television.)

Keep in mind that this is not simply a movie (or TV) review. Most reviews provide only unsupported opinion and summary. You are writing a categorical evaluation—an argument—that must include a clear claim and enough support to persuade an audience that will not be inclined to accept your position.

Because this is a short assignment, don't spend too much time introducing the issue (a couple of sentences will do). You should get to your thesis quickly so you can spend most of the paper establishing the evaluative criteria for "a good X" (a great movie or TV show) and showing how "Y" (the movie or TV show you chose) fits those criteria.

4. Exploring Causal Relationships

Part 1: Working with a partner or small group, select one of the problems from the list below and then discuss and explore possible causes of that problem. Remember that for each cause you propose, you must be able to show how it is linked to the problem, either directly or indirectly. Once you have settled on at least three or four possible causes, write a paragraph or two explaining each and how it is linked to the problem.

Part 2: After you have completed your explanation of possible causes, discuss with your partner or group mates what the consequences of not dealing with the problem might be. In other words, think about—and jot down—what you think might happen if the problem is not solved (and why you think these consequences are possible).
- Drunken driving
- Rising college costs (tuition, housing, textbooks, and supplies)
- Gang violence

- Record high turnout among young voters in the 2008 presidential election
- The rising popularity of methamphetamine (crystal meth), especially in rural areas
- High rates of obesity among children in the United States

5. Writing a Policy Argument

Good policy arguments call for action and give readers good reason to take action. Your task in this essay is to try to move your audience to action by calling attention to a problem, proposing a solution to that problem, and presenting a justification for your solution.

You have a choice for your rhetorical context: you may write a letter to a member of Congress or your state legislature or you may write an essay to be submitted for publication to your campus or local newspaper. In making your choice, think carefully about your audience and purpose. You must decide which option is the more appropriate place for your topic, as well as how you will present your essay (and yourself as the writer). Your instructor may require that you include research in your essay.

To get started, answer the following questions and be prepared to discuss them in class or with your instructor:

a. Which audience option are you choosing? Explain why you chose that option.
b. What problem will you address? Why is this a problem?
c. Who has the power to solve the problem? Why hasn't it been solved yet?
d. Summarize your proposed solution to the problem.
e. What are some other possible solutions?
f. Why should your solution be enacted rather than some other proposal?
g. What are the consequences of doing nothing?

readings for writing

reading and writing

C H A P T E R 5

"I don't worry for a nanosecond that reading and writing will disappear.
Even in the new digital media, it's essential to be able to read and write
fluently and, if you want to capture people's attention, to write well."
—Howard Gardner, *"The End of Literacy? Don't Stop Reading"*

What does it mean to be able to read and write? For some of the authors in this chapter, literacy depends on reading the right kinds of books—and lots of them. "[K]ids don't read for pleasure," Michael Skube complains in "Writing Off Reading" (and by "read" he means "read great works of literature"). If you don't know which books to read, he'll be happy to tell you. Others see reading and writing undergoing an evolution, driven by changes in technology and the habits of children and young adults. "'Books aren't out of the picture,'" Motoko Rich quotes one researcher as saying in her article, "'but they're only one way of experiencing information in the world today.'" Howard Gardner, whose words open this chapter, sees this evolution as inevitable and even exciting. But others are less optimistic. Whatever their positions, these writers present some interesting ideas about literacy and how it is changing. And although what they have to say by no means exhausts the subject, they may offer a point of reference as you think about your own reading and writing.

Michael Skube, who teaches journalism at Elon University in Elon, NC, wrote this piece for the August 20, 2006, edition of the Washington Post. *As you read, note not only Skube's central argument, but also the way he presents his case. How would you describe the ethos he presents in the essay?*

WRITING OFF READING

Michael Skube

[1] We were talking informally in class not long ago, 17 college sophomores and I, and on a whim I asked who some of their favorite writers are. The question hung in uneasy silence. At length, a voice in the rear hesitantly volunteered the name of . . . Dan Brown.

[2] No other names were offered.

[3] The author of "The DaVinci Code" was not just the best writer they could think of; he was the *only* writer they could think of.

[4] In our better private universities and flagship state schools today, it's hard to find a student who graduated from high school with much lower than a 3.5 GPA, and not uncommon to find students whose GPAs were 4.0 or higher. They somehow got these suspect grades without having read much. Or if they did read, they've given it up. And it shows—in their writing and even in their conversation.

[5] A few years ago, I began keeping a list of everyday words that may as well have been potholes in exchanges with college students. It began with a fellow who was two months away from graduating from a well-respected Midwestern university.

[6] "And what was the impetus for that?" I asked as he finished a presentation.

[7] At the word "impetus" his head snapped sideways, as if by reflex. "The what?" he asked.

[8] "The impetus. What gave rise to it? What prompted it?"

[9] I wouldn't have guessed that impetus was a 25-cent word. But I also wouldn't have guessed that "ramshackle" and "lucid" were exactly recondite, either. I've had to explain both. You can be dead certain that today's college students carry a weekly planner. But

they may or may not own a dictionary, and if they do own one, it doesn't get much use. ("Why do you need a dictionary when you can just go online?" more than one student has asked me.)

10 You may be surprised—and dismayed—by some of the words on my list.

11 "Advocate," for example. Neither the verb nor the noun was immediately clear to students who had graduated from high school with GPAs above 3.5. A few others:

12 "Derelict," as in neglectful.

13 "Satire," as in a literary form.

14 "Pith," as in the heart of the matter.

15 "Brevity," as in the quality of being succinct.

16 And my favorite: "Novel," as in new and as a literary form. College students nowadays call any book, fact or fiction, a novel. I have no idea why this is, but I first became acquainted with the peculiarity when a senior at one of the country's better state universities wrote a paper in which she referred to "The Prince" as "Machiavelli's novel."

17 As freshmen start showing up for classes this month, colleges will have a new influx of high school graduates with gilded GPAs, and it won't be long before one professor whispers to another: Did no one teach these kids basic English? The unhappy truth is that many students are hard-pressed to string together coherent sentences, to tell a pronoun from a preposition, even to distinguish between "then" and "than." Yet they got A's.

18 How does one explain the inability of college students to read or write at even a high school level? One explanation, which owes as much to the culture as to the schools, is that kids don't read for pleasure. And because they don't read, they are less able to navigate the language. If words are the coin of their thought, they're working with little more than pocket change.

19 Say this—but no more—for the Bush administration's No Child Left Behind Act: It at least recognizes the problem. What we're graduating from our high schools isn't college material. Sometimes it isn't even good high school material.

20 When students with A averages can't write simple English, it shouldn't be surprising that people ask what a high school diploma is really worth. In California this year, hundreds of high school students, many with good grades, faced the prospect of not graduating because they could not pass a state-mandated exit exam. Although a judge overturned the effort, legislators (not always so literate themselves) in other states have also called for exit exams. It's hardly unreasonable to ask that students demonstrate a minimum competency in basic subjects, especially English.

21 Exit exams have become almost a necessity because the GPA is not to be trusted. In my experience, a high SAT score is far more reliable than a high GPA—more indicative of quickness and acuity, and more reflective of familiarity with language and ideas. College admissions specialists are of a different view and are apt to label the student with high SAT scores but mediocre grades unmotivated, even lazy.

22 I'll take that student any day. I've known such students. They may have been bored in high school but they read widely and without prodding from a parent. And they could have nominated a few favorite writers besides Dan Brown—even if they thoroughly enjoyed "The DaVinci Code."

23 I suspect they would have understood the point I tried unsuccessfully to make once when I quoted Joseph Pulitzer to my students. It is journalism's job, he said, to comfort the afflicted and afflict the comfortable. Too obvious, you think? I might have thought so myself—if the words "afflicted" and "afflict" hadn't stumped the whole class.

Write a 50- to 100-word summary of this essay, followed by a 100-word response. In your summary, make sure you accurately and fairly convey the author's central idea or argument. In your response, focus on what the essay does (its effectiveness, given what you know about the author's audience and purpose) or how the essay does it (the author's style of presentation or argumentation). Unless your teacher instructs you otherwise, stay away from a response based on what you liked or disliked about the piece.

ANALYZE

Choose one of the rhetorical appeals (to ethos, pathos, or logos) and briefly analyze how the author uses this appeal in the essay. Ask yourself, for example, how the appeal affects the audience and why the author might have chosen to do this. Make sure you point to specific examples of the appeal at work in the text to support your analysis.

ARGUE

If you were in Michael Skube's position, how would you try to get students to read more? Or to at least invest more time and energy in the reading they have to do for school?

Don Campbell, who teaches journalism at Emory University in Atlanta and is a member of USA Today's *board of contributors, expresses some of the same concerns as Michael Skube. In this column, published September 10, 2008, in* USA Today, *he examines the influence that the Internet has on reading and learning and offers a few ideas about how to address what he and many others see as a threat to traditional literacy.*

PLUGGING IN, TUNING OUT

The digital culture has changed the way kids learn, but at the expense of literacy and cultural awareness

Don Campbell

[1] I ask students on the first day of my journalism classes to fill out a questionnaire. Most questions inquire about their interest in journalism and any experience they have that is journalism-related. One question is: "What do you read, at least fairly regularly?"

[2] Used to be, they would say *The New York Times* or *Newsweek* or *Sports Illustrated*. A few would list the local newspaper, or *The New Yorker* or *The Economist* to impress me. In recent years, the answers more often have been CNN.com, ESPN.com, blogs and other Internet offerings.

3 And then, at the beginning of the last semester, a student who claimed to be interested in journalism wrote this about what she reads: "Nothing."

4 Her answer astonished me but shouldn't have, because it epitomized the lack of intellectual curiosity in students that I have noticed in recent years, along with a decline in such basic skills as grammar, spelling and simple math. A sense of history? History is what happened since they left middle school.

5 As both a teacher and a father of two multi-tasking teenage daughters, I had long suspected that something was going on. While some students seem just as smart or smarter than they did 15 years ago, I'm also confronted with college sophomores who can't identify Henry Kissinger or perform simple percentage exercises; who argue, as one did, that misspelling someone's name was no big deal because I knew who she meant; students who begin sentences with lowercase letters and embellish news stories by adding their own facts.

6 I thought I was just a closet curmudgeon. After all, every young generation is associated with some kind of negative stereotype. But then I read two publications over the summer, one that validated my every suspicion, and one that gave me a glimmer of hope.

A narrowing horizon

7 The first is a book by Emory University English professor Mark Bauerlein, called *The Dumbest Generation: How the Digital Age Stupefies Young Americans and Jeopardizes our Future*. As Bauerlein admits, the title is "a little over the top," but don't let that put you off. If you're the parent of someone under 20 and read only one non-fiction book this fall, make it this one.

8 Bauerlein's simple but jarring thesis is that technology and the digital culture it has created are not broadening the horizon of the younger generation; they are narrowing it to a self-absorbed social universe that blocks out virtually everything else.

9 "The Internet doesn't impart adult information; it crowds it out," Bauerlein writes. "Video games, cell phones and blogs don't foster rightful citizenship. They hamper it."

10 Bauerlein, who served as a director of research and analysis at the National Endowment for the Arts, makes his case not with anecdotes, but with numerous studies that examined the knowledge, skills and intellectual habits of teenagers. He concludes that the "screen time" occupying so many youngsters on the Internet, cell phones and video games is depriving them of the cultural experiences and learning traditionally associated with liberal arts and civic awareness.

11 My own interpretation is that, for the younger generation, the Internet has moved knowledge from the brain to the fingertips: Who needs to know about Impressionism or Charles Dickens or George Washington Carver or—hell—even George Washington? Why carry such information around in your head when Google will deliver it in seconds?

Technology's ill effects

12 The second publication is a study by the Pew Internet and American Life Project based on interviews with 700 teens and their parents, as well as a series of focus groups. The youngsters acknowledge that the dumbed-down writing style they use in instant messaging, texting and other social networking sometimes seeps into their schoolwork, with negative effects. But they also say they understand the need to be more formal in composing homework assignments than they are in text-messaging friends. In fact, they are hungry for the kind of mentoring and feedback that inspires and rewards good writing, and a majority of them still believe that good writing is the ticket to success in life.

13 The alarm bell sounds, however, when you read what some students had to say about how social networking has become such an important part of their lives, devouring hours each day in a way that is much more pervasive than even television.

14 So what can we—parents and teachers—do? We can't fight technology, nor should we. The Internet is the greatest research tool ever invented. But we must fight the dark side. One way, starting with this school year, is to insist that kids spend less "screen time" communicating with their friends, and more time reading and being exposed to the kinds of cultural and civic activities that will make them well-rounded citizens. This fall's presidential campaign would be a good place to start.

15 Otherwise, the future is going to be populated by adults who sound like the high school student in a Midwestern city who gave this response in the Pew survey when asked why social networking held such an attraction for her:

16 "It sounds stupid and everything but like once you like get into it it's really like addicting—just like everything. Like you have your song and like you write like all this stuff about yourself and like all my friends basically have it. So like we always like read each other's pages and like call each other and like kind of, and like you put like 300 pictures up so . . . people's pictures and stuff and comments."

17 Sounds stupid? Why in the world would she think that?

RESPOND

Campbell says he asks his students, on the first day of class: "What do you read, at least fairly regularly?" Make a list of the things you read. How does your response compare with what your classmates said? How does it compare with the answers Campbell's students gave?

DISCUSS

In his essay, Campbell writes: "My own interpretation is that, for the younger generation, the Internet has moved knowledge from the brain to the fingertips." What does he mean by this? Do you agree with his point? Do you see a problem with not knowing things, as long as you know how to look them up?

ARGUE

In Paragraph 4, Campbell writes of a "lack of intellectual curiosity in students" and "a decline in such basic skills as grammar, spelling and simple math." Write an brief argument in which you respond to Campbell's statements. You might, for example, use evidence from your own experiences in school to disagree with Campbell, or you might offer a causal argument to explain the declines Campbell points out.

Howard Gardner, who teaches cognitive psychology at the Harvard Graduate School of Education, understands the concerns that Michael Skube and Todd Hagstette express in their essays. But, as you'll see in the piece that follows, Gardner takes a broader view of the evolution of reading and writing. Gardner, who is directing a study of the ethical dimensions of the new digital media, wrote this piece for the February 17, 2008, edition of the Washington Post.

THE END OF LITERACY?
DON'T STOP READING

Howard Gardner

1 What will happen to reading and writing in our time?

2 Could the doomsayers be right? Computers, they maintain, are destroying literacy. The signs—students' declining reading scores, the drop in leisure reading to just minutes a week, the fact that half the adult population reads no books in a year—are all pointing to the day when a literate American culture becomes a distant memory. By contrast, optimists foresee the Internet ushering in a new, vibrant participatory culture of words. Will they carry the day?

3 Maybe neither. Let me suggest a third possibility: Literacy—or an ensemble of literacies—will continue to thrive, but in forms and formats we can't yet envision.

4 That's what has always happened as writing and reading have evolved over the ages. It was less than 100,000 years ago that our human predecessors first made meaningful marks on surfaces, notating the phases of the moon or drawing animals on cave walls. Within the past 5,000 years, societies across the Near East's Fertile Crescent began to use systems of marks to record important trade exchanges as well as pivotal events in the present and the past. These marks gradually became less pictorial, and a decisive leap occurred when they began to capture certain sounds reliably: U kn red ths sntnz cuz Inglsh feechurs "graphic-phoneme correspondences."

5 A master of written Greek, Plato feared that written language would undermine human memory capacities (much in the same way that we now worry about similar side effects of "Googling"). But libraries made the world's knowledge available to anyone who could read. The 15th-century printing press disturbed those who wanted to protect and interpret the word of God, but the availability of Bibles in the vernacular allowed laypeople to take control of their spiritual lives and, if historians are correct, encouraged entrepreneurship in commerce and innovation in science.

6 In the past 150 years, each new medium of communication—telegraph, telephone, movies, radio, television, the digital computer, the World Wide Web—has introduced its own peculiar mix of written, spoken and graphic languages and evoked a chaotic chorus of criticism and celebration.

7 But of the changes in the media landscape over the past few centuries, those featuring digital media are potentially the most far-reaching. Those of us who grew up in the 1950s, at a time when there were just a few computers in the world, could never have anticipated the ubiquity of personal computers (back then, IBM's Thomas Watson famously declared that there'd

FIGURE 5-1

In his essay, Howard Gardner writes, "U kn red ths sntnz cuz Inglsh feechurs 'graphic-phoneme correspondences.'" This feature is also what allows us to make sense of the ubiquitous abbreviations used in texting. One of Gardner's points is that, although they will certainly evolve, reading and writing will never disappear. Others, however, fear that technology is driving literacy down by turning people away from books and traditional forms of writing. How do you define literacy? What kinds of reading and writing does your definition value? Why? Compare your definition with those written by your classmates. What similarities and differences do you see? Is there a consensus in your class about what it means to be literate?

be a market for perhaps five computers in the world!). A mere half-century later, more than a billion people can communicate via e-mail, chat rooms and instant messaging; post their views on a blog; play games with millions of others worldwide; create their own works of art or theater and post them on YouTube; join political movements; and even inhabit, buy, sell and organize in a virtual reality called Second Life. No wonder the chattering classes can't agree about what this all means.

[8] Here's my take.

[9] Once we ensured our basic survival, humans were freed to pursue other needs and desires, including the pleasures of communicating, forming friendships, convincing others of our point of view, exercising our imagination, enjoying a measure of privacy. Initially, we pursued these needs with our senses, our hands and our individual minds. Human and mechanical technologies to help us were at a premium. It's easy to see how

the emergence of written languages represented a boon. The invention of the printing press and the emergence of readily available books, magazines and newspapers allowed untold millions to extend their circle, expand their minds and expound their pet ideas.

10 For those of us of a 19th- or 20th-century frame of mind, books play a special, perhaps even spiritual, role. Works of fiction—the writings of Jane Austen, Leo Tolstoy, Toni Morrison, William Faulkner—allow us to inhabit fascinating worlds we couldn't have envisioned. Works of scholarship—the economic analyses of Karl Marx and John Maynard Keynes, the histories of Thucydides and Edward Gibbon—provide frameworks for making sense of the past and the present.

11 But now, at the start of the 21st century, there's a dizzying set of literacies available—written languages, graphic displays and notations. And there's an even broader array of media—analog, digital, electronic, hand-held, tangible and virtual—from which to pick and choose. There will inevitably be a sorting-out process. Few media are likely to disappear completely; rather, the idiosyncratic genius and peculiar limitations of each medium will become increasingly clear. Fewer people will write notes or letters by hand, but the elegant handwritten note to mark a special occasion will endure.

12 I don't worry for a nanosecond that reading and writing will disappear. Even in the new digital media, it's essential to be able to read and write fluently and, if you want to capture people's attention, to write well. Of course, what it means to "write well" changes: Virginia Woolf didn't write the same way that Jane Austen did, and Arianna Huffington's blog won't be confused with Walter Lippmann's columns. But the imaginative spheres and real-world needs that all those written words address remain.

13 I also question the predicted disappearance of the material book. When they wanted to influence opinions, both the computer giant Bill Gates and the media visionary Nicholas Negroponte wrote books (the latter in spite of his assertion that the material book was becoming anachronistic). The convenience and portability of the book aren't easily replaced, though under certain circumstances—a month-long business trip, say—the advantages of Amazon's hand-held electronic Kindle reading device trumps a suitcase full of dog-eared paperbacks.

14 Two aspects of the traditional book may be in jeopardy, however. One is the author's capacity to lay out a complex argument, which requires the reader to study and reread, following a circuitous course of reasoning. The Web's speedy browsing may make it difficult for digital natives to master Kant's "Critique of Pure Reason" (not that it was ever easy).

15 The other is the book's special genius for allowing readers to enter a private world for hours or even days at a time. Many of us enjoyed long summer days or solitary train rides when we first discovered an author who spoke directly to us. Nowadays, as clinical psychologist Sherry Turkle has pointed out, young people seem to have a compulsion to stay in touch with one another all the time; periods of lonely silence or privacy seem toxic. If this lust for 24/7 online networking continues, one of the dividends of book reading may fade away. The wealth of different literacies and the ease of moving among them—on an iPhone, for example—may undermine the once-hallowed status of books.

16 But whatever our digital future brings, we need to overcome the perils of dualistic thinking, the notion that what lies ahead is either a utopia or a dystopia. If we're going to make sense of what's happening with literacy in our culture, we need to be able to triangulate: to bear in mind our needs and desires, the media as they once were and currently are, and the media as they're continually transforming.

17 It's not easy to do. But maybe there's a technology, just waiting to be invented, that will help us acquire this invaluable cognitive power.

How, according to Gardner, has technology changed literacy through history? Be specific in your response.

Compare the ethos Gardner presents with that in Michael Skube's "Writing Off Reading" or Susan Jacoby's "The Dumbing of America." How do you think each author wants to be perceived by his or her target audience? Why do you think this? Which author more effectively appeals to you? Why?

Near the end of his essay, Gardner writes that "[t]wo aspects of the traditional book may be in jeopardy." What are they? Do you agree with Gardner's contention? Explain your answer.

Reporter Motoko Rich wrote this article for the July 27, 2008, edition of the New York Times. *In it, she uses the question in her title—Is online reading really* reading?—*to explore the ways in which digital technologies are affecting traditional views of literacy. She also examines reactions, from several perspectives, to these effects.*

LITERACY DEBATE: ONLINE, R U REALLY READING?

Motoko Rich

1 BEREA, Ohio—Books are not Nadia Konyk's thing. Her mother, hoping to entice her, brings them home from the library, but Nadia rarely shows an interest.

2 Instead, like so many other teenagers, Nadia, 15, is addicted to the Internet. She regularly spends at least six hours a day in front of the computer here in this suburb southwest of Cleveland.

3 A slender, chatty blonde who wears black-framed plastic glasses, Nadia checks her e-mail and peruses myyearbook.com, a social networking site, reading messages or posting updates on her mood. She searches for music videos on YouTube and logs onto Gaia Online, a role-playing site where members fashion alternate identities as cutesy cartoon characters. But she spends most of her time on quizilla. com or fanfiction.net, reading and commenting on stories written by other users and based on books, television shows or movies.

[4] Her mother, Deborah Konyk, would prefer that Nadia, who gets A's and B's at school, read books for a change. But at this point, Ms. Konyk said, "I'm just pleased that she reads something anymore."

[5] Children like Nadia lie at the heart of a passionate debate about just what it means to read in the digital age. The discussion is playing out among educational policy makers and reading experts around the world, and within groups like the National Council of Teachers of English and the International Reading Association.

[6] As teenagers' scores on standardized reading tests have declined or stagnated, some argue that the hours spent prowling the Internet are the enemy of reading—diminishing literacy, wrecking attention spans and destroying a precious common culture that exists only through the reading of books.

[7] But others say the Internet has created a new kind of reading, one that schools and society should not discount. The Web inspires a teenager like Nadia, who might otherwise spend most of her leisure time watching television, to read and write.

[8] Even accomplished book readers like Zachary Sims, 18, of Old Greenwich, Conn., crave the ability to quickly find different points of view on a subject and converse with others online. Some children with dyslexia or other learning difficulties, like Hunter Gaudet, 16, of Somers, Conn., have found it far more comfortable to search and read online.

[9] At least since the invention of television, critics have warned that electronic media would destroy reading. What is different now, some literacy experts say, is that spending time on the Web, whether it is looking up something on Google or even britneyspears.org, entails some engagement with text.

Setting Expectations

[10] Few who believe in the potential of the Web deny the value of books. But they argue that it is unrealistic to expect all children to read "To Kill a Mockingbird" or "Pride and Prejudice" for fun. And those who prefer staring at a television or mashing buttons on a game console, they say, can still benefit from reading on the Internet. In fact, some literacy experts say that online reading skills will help children fare better when they begin looking for digital-age jobs.

[11] Some Web evangelists say children should be evaluated for their proficiency on the Internet just as they are tested on their print reading comprehension. Starting next year, some countries will participate in new international assessments of digital literacy, but the United States, for now, will not.

[12] Clearly, reading in print and on the Internet are different. On paper, text has a predetermined beginning, middle and end, where readers focus for a sustained period on one author's vision. On the Internet, readers skate through cyberspace at will and, in effect, compose their own beginnings, middles and ends.

[13] Young people "aren't as troubled as some of us older folks are by reading that doesn't go in a line," said Rand J. Spiro, a professor of educational psychology at Michigan State University who is studying reading practices on the Internet. "That's a good thing because the world doesn't go in a line, and the world isn't organized into separate compartments or chapters."

[14] Some traditionalists warn that digital reading is the intellectual equivalent of empty calories. Often, they argue, writers on the Internet employ a cryptic argot that vexes teachers and parents. Zigzagging through a cornucopia of words, pictures, video and sounds, they say, distracts more than strengthens readers. And many youths spend most of their time on the Internet playing games or sending instant messages, activities that involve minimal reading at best.

[15] Last fall the National Endowment for the Arts issued a sobering report linking flat or declining national reading test scores among teenagers with the slump in the proportion of adolescents who said they read for fun.

[16] According to Department of Education data cited in the report, just over a fifth of 17-year-olds said they read almost every day for fun in 2004, down from nearly a third in 1984. Nineteen percent of 17-year-olds said they never or hardly ever read for fun in 2004, up from 9 percent in 1984. (It was unclear whether they thought of what they did on the Internet as "reading.")

[17] "Whatever the benefits of newer electronic media," Dana Gioia, the chairman of the N.E.A., wrote in the report's introduction, "they provide no measurable substitute for the intellectual and personal development initiated and sustained by frequent reading."

[18] Children are clearly spending more time on the Internet. In a study of 2,032 representative 8- to 18-year-olds, the Kaiser Family Foundation found that nearly half used the Internet on a typical day in 2004, up from just under a quarter in 1999. The average time these children spent online on a typical day rose to one hour and 41 minutes in 2004, from 46 minutes in 1999.

[19] The question of how to value different kinds of reading is complicated because people read for many reasons. There is the level required of daily life—to follow the instructions in a manual or to analyze a mortgage contract. Then there is a more sophisticated level that opens the doors to elite education and professions. And, of course, people read for entertainment, as well as for intellectual or emotional rewards.

[20] It is perhaps that final purpose that book champions emphasize the most.

[21] "Learning is not to be found on a printout," David McCullough, the Pulitzer Prize-winning biographer, said in a commencement address at Boston College in May. "It's not on call at the touch of the finger. Learning is acquired mainly from books, and most readily from great books."

What's Best for Nadia?

[22] Deborah Konyk always believed it was essential for Nadia and her 8-year-old sister, Yashca, to read books. She regularly read aloud to the girls and took them to library story hours.

[23] "Reading opens up doors to places that you probably will never get to visit in your lifetime, to cultures, to worlds, to people," Ms. Konyk said.

[24] Ms. Konyk, who took a part-time job at a dollar store chain a year and a half ago, said she did not have much time to read books herself. There are few books in the house. But after Yashca was born, Ms. Konyk spent the baby's nap time reading the Harry Potter novels to Nadia, and she regularly brought home new titles from the library.

[25] Despite these efforts, Nadia never became a big reader. Instead, she became obsessed with Japanese anime cartoons on television and comics like "Sailor Moon." Then, when she was in the sixth grade, the family bought its first computer. When a friend introduced Nadia to fanfiction.net, she turned off the television and started reading online.

[26] Now she regularly reads stories that run as long as 45 Web pages. Many of them have elliptical plots and are sprinkled with spelling and grammatical errors. One of her recent favorites was "My absolutely, perfect normal life? ARE YOU CRAZY? NOT!," a story based on the anime series "Beyblade."

[27] In one scene the narrator, Aries, hitches a ride with some masked men and one of them pulls a knife on her. "Just then I notice (Like finally) something sharp right in front of me," Aries writes. "I gladly took it just like that until something terrible happen. . . ."

28 Nadia said she preferred reading stories online because "you could add your own character and twist it the way you want it to be."

29 "So like in the book somebody could die," she continued, "but you could make it so that person doesn't die or make it so like somebody else dies who you don't like."

30 Nadia also writes her own stories. She posted "Dieing Isn't Always Bad," about a girl who comes back to life as half cat, half human, on both fanfiction.net and quizilla.com.

31 Nadia said she wanted to major in English at college and someday hopes to be published. She does not see a problem with reading few books. "No one's ever said you should read more books to get into college," she said.

32 The simplest argument for why children should read in their leisure time is that it makes them better readers. According to federal statistics, students who say they read for fun once a day score significantly higher on reading tests than those who say they never do.

33 Reading skills are also valued by employers. A 2006 survey by the Conference Board, which conducts research for business leaders, found that nearly 90 percent of employers rated "reading comprehension" as "very important" for workers with bachelor's degrees. Department of Education statistics also show that those who score higher on reading tests tend to earn higher incomes.

34 Critics of reading on the Internet say they see no evidence that increased Web activity improves reading achievement. "What we are losing in this country and presumably around the world is the sustained, focused, linear attention developed by reading," said Mr. Gioia of the N.E.A. "I would believe people who tell me that the Internet develops reading if I did not see such a universal decline in reading ability and reading comprehension on virtually all tests."

35 Nicholas Carr sounded a similar note in "Is Google Making Us Stupid?" in the current issue of the Atlantic magazine. Warning that the Web was changing the way he—and others—think, he suggested that the effects of Internet reading extended beyond the falling test scores of adolescence. "What the Net seems to be doing is chipping away my capacity for concentration and contemplation," he wrote, confessing that he now found it difficult to read long books.

36 Literacy specialists are just beginning to investigate how reading on the Internet affects reading skills. A recent study of more than 700 low-income, mostly Hispanic and black sixth through 10th graders in Detroit found that those students read more on the Web than in any other medium, though they also read books. The only kind of reading that related to higher academic performance was frequent novel reading, which predicted better grades in English class and higher overall grade point averages.

37 Elizabeth Birr Moje, a professor at the University of Michigan who led the study, said novel reading was similar to what schools demand already. But on the Internet, she said, students are developing new reading skills that are neither taught nor evaluated in school.

38 One early study showed that giving home Internet access to low-income students appeared to improve standardized reading test scores and school grades. "These were kids who would typically not be reading in their free time," said Linda A. Jackson, a psychology professor at Michigan State who led the research. "Once they're on the Internet, they're reading."

39 Neurological studies show that learning to read changes the brain's circuitry. Scientists speculate that reading on the Internet may also affect the brain's hard wiring in a way that is different from book reading.

40 "The question is, does it change your brain in some beneficial way?" said Guinevere F. Eden, director of the Center for the Study of Learning at Georgetown University. "The brain is malleable and adapts to its environment. Whatever the pressures are on us to succeed, our brain will try and deal with it."

41 Some scientists worry that the fractured experience typical of the Internet could rob developing readers of crucial skills. "Reading a book, and taking the time to ruminate and make inferences and engage the imaginational processing, is more cognitively enriching, without doubt, than the short little bits that you might get if you're into the 30-second digital mode," said Ken Pugh, a cognitive neuroscientist at Yale who has studied brain scans of children reading.

But This Is Reading Too

42 Web proponents believe that strong readers on the Web may eventually surpass those who rely on books. Reading five Web sites, an op-ed article and a blog post or two, experts say, can be more enriching than reading one book.

43 "It takes a long time to read a 400-page book," said Mr. Spiro of Michigan State. "In a tenth of the time," he said, the Internet allows a reader to "cover a lot more of the topic from different points of view."

44 Zachary Sims, the Old Greenwich, Conn., teenager, often stays awake until 2 or 3 in the morning reading articles about technology or politics—his current passions—on up to 100 Web sites.

45 "On the Internet, you can hear from a bunch of people," said Zachary, who will attend Columbia University this fall. "They may not be pedigreed academics. They may be someone in their shed with a conspiracy theory. But you would weigh that."

46 Though he also likes to read books (earlier this year he finished, and loved, "The Fountainhead" by Ayn Rand), Zachary craves interaction with fellow readers on the Internet.

"The Web is more about a conversation," he said. "Books are more one-way."

47 The kinds of skills Zachary has developed—locating information quickly and accurately, corroborating findings on multiple sites—may seem obvious to heavy Web users. But the skills can be cognitively demanding.

48 Web readers are persistently weak at judging whether information is trustworthy. In one study, Donald J. Leu, who researches literacy and technology at the University of Connecticut, asked 48 students to look at a spoof Web site (http://zapatopi.net/treeoctopus/) about a mythical species known as the "Pacific Northwest tree octopus." Nearly 90 percent of them missed the joke and deemed the site a reliable source.

49 Some literacy experts say that reading itself should be redefined. Interpreting videos or pictures, they say, may be as important a skill as analyzing a novel or a poem.

50 "Kids are using sound and images so they have a world of ideas to put together that aren't necessarily language oriented," said Donna E. Alvermann, a professor of language and literacy education at the University of Georgia. "Books aren't out of the picture, but they're only one way of experiencing information in the world today."

A Lifelong Struggle

51 In the case of Hunter Gaudet, the Internet has helped him feel more comfortable with a new kind of reading. A varsity lacrosse player in Somers, Conn., Hunter has struggled most of his life to read. After learning he was dyslexic in the second grade, he was placed in special education classes and a tutor came to his home three hours a week. When he entered high school, he dropped the special education classes, but he still reads books only when forced, he said.

52 In a book, "they go through a lot of details that aren't really needed," Hunter said. "Online just gives you what you need, nothing more or less."

53 When researching the 19th-century Chief Justice Roger B. Taney for one class, he typed Taney's name into Google and scanned the Wikipedia entry and other biographical sites. Instead of reading an entire page, he would type in a search word like "college" to find Taney's alma mater, assembling his information nugget by nugget.

54 Experts on reading difficulties suggest that for struggling readers, the Web may be a better way to glean information. "When you read online there are always graphics," said Sally Shaywitz, the author of "Overcoming Dyslexia" and a Yale professor. "I think it's just more comfortable and—I hate to say easier—but it more meets the needs of somebody who might not be a fluent reader."

55 Karen Gaudet, Hunter's mother, a regional manager for a retail chain who said she read two or three business books a week, hopes Hunter will eventually discover a love for books. But she is confident that he has the reading skills he needs to succeed.

56 "Based on where technology is going and the world is going," she said, "he's going to be able to leverage it."

57 When he was in seventh grade, Hunter was one of 89 students who participated in a study comparing performance on traditional state reading tests with a specially designed Internet reading test. Hunter, who scored in the lowest 10 percent on the traditional test, spent 12 weeks learning how to use the Web for a science class before taking the Internet test. It was composed of three sets of directions asking the students to search for information online, determine which sites were reliable and explain their reasoning.

58 Hunter scored in the top quartile. In fact, about a third of the students in the study, led by Professor Leu, scored below average on traditional reading tests but did well on the Internet assessment.

The Testing Debate

59 To date, there have been few large-scale appraisals of Web skills. The Educational Testing Service, which administers the SAT, has developed a digital literacy test known as iSkills that requires students to solve informational problems by searching for answers on the Web. About 80 colleges and a handful of high schools have administered the test so far.

60 But according to Stephen Denis, product manager at ETS, of the more than 20,000 students who have taken the iSkills test since 2006, only 39 percent of four-year college freshmen achieved a score that represented "core functional levels" in Internet literacy.

61 Now some literacy experts want the federal tests known as the nation's report card to include a digital reading component. So far, the traditionalists have held sway: The next round, to be administered to fourth and eighth graders in 2009, will test only print reading comprehension.

62 Mary Crovo of the National Assessment Governing Board, which creates policies for the national tests, said several members of a committee that sets guidelines for the reading tests believed large numbers of low-income and rural students might not have regular Internet access, rendering measurements of their online skills unfair.

63 Some simply argue that reading on the Internet is not something that needs to be tested—or taught.

64 "Nobody has taught a single kid to text message," said Carol Jago of the National Council of Teachers of English and a member of the testing guidelines committee. "Kids are smart. When they want to do something, schools don't have to get involved."

65 Michael L. Kamil, a professor of education at Stanford who lobbied for an Internet component as chairman of the reading test guidelines committee, disagreed. Students

"are going to grow up having to be highly competent on the Internet," he said. "There's no reason to make them discover how to be highly competent if we can teach them."

66 The United States is diverging from the policies of some other countries. Next year, for the first time, the Organization for Economic Cooperation and Development, which administers reading, math and science tests to a sample of 15-year-old students in more than 50 countries, will add an electronic reading component. The United States, among other countries, will not participate. A spokeswoman for the Institute of Education Sciences, the research arm of the Department of Education, said an additional test would overburden schools.

67 Even those who are most concerned about the preservation of books acknowledge that children need a range of reading experiences.

"Some of it is the informal reading they get in e-mails or on Web sites," said Gay Ivey, a professor at James Madison University who focuses on adolescent literacy. "I think they need it all."

68 Web junkies can occasionally be swept up in a book. After Nadia read Elie Wiesel's Holocaust memoir "Night" in her freshman English class, Ms. Konyk brought home another Holocaust memoir, "I Have Lived a Thousand Years," by Livia Bitton-Jackson.

69 Nadia was riveted by heartbreaking details of life in the concentration camps. "I was trying to imagine this and I was like, I can't do this," she said. "It was just so—wow."

70 Hoping to keep up the momentum, Ms. Konyk brought home another book, "Silverboy," a fantasy novel. Nadia made it through one chapter before she got engrossed in the Internet fan fiction again.

SUMMARIZE

Summarize the various positions on literacy and online reading that Rich presents in her article. How many can you identify? Which of these seems most reasonable to you? Why?

ANALYZE

Rich opens and closes her article with the story of Nadia Konyk, a teenager who spends much more time reading online than she does reading books. How does Nadia's narrative serve to help Rich connect with her audience? What kinds of rhetorical appeals do you see at work in Nadia's story?

DISCUSS

Compare the reading you do online vs. off-line. How do these reading tasks differ? How are they similar? How much time to you spend doing each during a typical day? Which kind of reading do you prefer? Why?

As a nation, we're dumb and getting dumber, according to writer Susan Jacoby, whose latest book is The Age of American Unreason. *In this essay from the February 17, 2008, edition of the* Washington Post, *she warns about a "flood" of anti-intellectualism fostered by pop culture and the technologies that spread it.*

THE DUMBING OF AMERICA

Call Me a Snob, but Really, We're a Nation of Dunces

Susan Jacoby

[1] "The mind of this country, taught to aim at low objects, eats upon itself." Ralph Waldo Emerson offered that observation in 1837, but his words echo with painful prescience in today's very different United States. Americans are in serious intellectual trouble—in danger of losing our hard-won cultural capital to a virulent mixture of anti-intellectualism, anti-rationalism and low expectations.

[2] This is the last subject that any candidate would dare raise on the long and winding road to the White House. It is almost impossible to talk about the manner in which public ignorance contributes to grave national problems without being labeled an "elitist," one of the most powerful pejoratives that can be applied to anyone aspiring to high office. Instead, our politicians repeatedly assure Americans that they are just "folks," a patronizing term that you will search for in vain in important presidential speeches before 1980. (Just imagine: "We here highly resolve that these dead shall not have died in vain. . . and that government of the folks, by the folks, for the folks, shall not perish from the earth.") Such exaltations of ordinariness are among the distinguishing traits of anti-intellectualism in any era.

[3] The classic work on this subject by Columbia University historian Richard Hofstadter, "Anti-Intellectualism in American Life," was published in early 1963, between the anti-communist crusades of the McCarthy era and the social convulsions of the late 1960s. Hofstadter saw American anti-intellectualism as a basically cyclical phenomenon that often manifested itself as the dark side of the country's democratic impulses in religion and education. But today's brand of anti-intellectualism is less a cycle than a flood. If Hofstadter (who died of leukemia in 1970 at age 54) had lived long enough to write a modern-day sequel, he would have found that our era of 24/7 infotainment has outstripped his most apocalyptic predictions about the future of American culture.

[4] Dumbness, to paraphrase the late senator Daniel Patrick Moynihan, has been steadily defined downward for several decades, by a combination of heretofore irresistible forces. These include the triumph of video culture over print culture (and by video, I mean every form of digital media, as well as older electronic ones); a disjunction between Americans' rising level of formal education and their shaky grasp of basic geography, science and history; and the fusion of anti-rationalism with anti-intellectualism.

[5] First and foremost among the vectors of the new anti-intellectualism is video. The decline of book, newspaper and magazine reading is by now an old story. The drop-off

is most pronounced among the young, but it continues to accelerate and afflict Americans of all ages and education levels.

[6] Reading has declined not only among the poorly educated, according to a report last year by the National Endowment for the Arts. In 1982, 82 percent of college graduates read novels or poems for pleasure; two decades later, only 67 percent did. And more than 40 percent of Americans under 44 did not read a single book—fiction or nonfiction—over the course of a year. The proportion of 17-year-olds who read nothing (unless required to do so for school) more than doubled between 1984 and 2004. This time period, of course, encompasses the rise of personal computers, Web surfing and video games.

[7] Does all this matter? Technophiles pooh-pooh jeremiads about the end of print culture as the navel-gazing of (what else?) elitists. In his book "Everything Bad Is Good for You: How Today's Popular Culture Is Actually Making Us Smarter," the science writer Steven Johnson assures us that we have nothing to worry about. Sure, parents may see their "vibrant and active children gazing silently, mouths agape, at the screen." But these zombie-like characteristics "are not signs of mental atrophy. They're signs of focus." Balderdash. The real question is what toddlers are screening out, not what they are focusing on, while they sit mesmerized by videos they have seen dozens of times.

[8] Despite an aggressive marketing campaign aimed at encouraging babies as young as 6 months to watch videos, there is no evidence that focusing on a screen is anything but bad for infants and toddlers. In a study released last August, University of Washington researchers found that babies between 8 and 16 months recognized an average of six to eight fewer words for every hour spent watching videos.

[9] I cannot prove that reading for hours in a treehouse (which is what I was doing when I was 13) creates more informed citizens than hammering away at a Microsoft Xbox or obsessing about Facebook profiles. But the inability to concentrate for long periods of time—as distinct from brief reading hits for information on the Web—seems to me intimately related to the inability of the public to remember even recent news events. It is not surprising, for example, that less has been heard from the presidential candidates about the Iraq war in the later stages of the primary campaign than in the earlier ones, simply because there have been fewer video reports of violence in Iraq. Candidates, like voters, emphasize the latest news, not necessarily the most important news.

[10] No wonder negative political ads work. "With text, it is even easy to keep track of differing levels of authority behind different pieces of information," the cultural critic Caleb Crain noted recently in the New Yorker. "A comparison of two video reports, on the other hand, is cumbersome. Forced to choose between conflicting stories on television, the viewer falls back on hunches, or on what he believed before he started watching."

[11] As video consumers become progressively more impatient with the process of acquiring information through written language, all politicians find themselves under great pressure to deliver their messages as quickly as possible—and quickness today is much quicker than it used to be. Harvard University's Kiku Adatto found that between 1968 and 1988, the average sound bite on the news for a presidential candidate—featuring the candidate's own voice—dropped from 42.3 seconds to 9.8 seconds. By 2000, according to another Harvard study, the daily candidate bite was down to just 7.8 seconds.

[12] The shrinking public attention span fostered by video is closely tied to the second important anti-intellectual force in American culture: the erosion of general knowledge.

13 People accustomed to hearing their president explain complicated policy choices by snapping "I'm the decider" may find it almost impossible to imagine the pains that Franklin D. Roosevelt took, in the grim months after Pearl Harbor, to explain why U.S. armed forces were suffering one defeat after another in the Pacific. In February 1942, Roosevelt urged Americans to spread out a map during his radio "fireside chat" so that they might better understand the geography of battle. In stores throughout the country, maps sold out; about 80 percent of American adults tuned in to hear the president. FDR had told his speechwriters that he was certain that if Americans understood the immensity of the distances over which supplies had to travel to the armed forces, "they can take any kind of bad news right on the chin."

14 This is a portrait not only of a different presidency and president but also of a different country and citizenry, one that lacked access to satellite-enhanced Google maps but was far more receptive to learning and complexity than today's public. According to a 2006 survey by National Geographic-Roper, nearly half of Americans between ages 18 and 24 do not think it necessary to know the location of other countries in which important news is being made. More than a third consider it "not at all important" to know a foreign language, and only 14 percent consider it "very important."

15 That leads us to the third and final factor behind the new American dumbness: not lack of knowledge per se but arrogance about that lack of knowledge. The problem is not just the things we do not know (consider the one in five American adults who, according to the National Science Foundation, thinks the sun revolves around the Earth); it's the alarming number of Americans who have smugly concluded that they do not need to know such things in the first place. Call this anti-rationalism—a syndrome that is particularly dangerous to our public institutions and discourse. Not knowing a foreign language or the location of an important country is a manifestation of ignorance; denying that such knowledge matters is pure anti-rationalism. The toxic brew of anti-rationalism and ignorance hurts discussions of U.S. public policy on topics from health care to taxation.

16 There is no quick cure for this epidemic of arrogant anti-rationalism and anti-intellectualism; rote efforts to raise standardized test scores by stuffing students with specific answers to specific questions on specific tests will not do the job. Moreover, the people who exemplify the problem are usually oblivious to it. ("Hardly anyone believes himself to be against thought and culture," Hofstadter noted.) It is past time for a serious national discussion about whether, as a nation, we truly value intellect and rationality. If this indeed turns out to be a "change election," the low level of discourse in a country with a mind taught to aim at low objects ought to be the first item on the change agenda.

SUMMARIZE AND RESPOND

How does Jacoby define *anti-intellectualism*? What does she argue are the dangers of this trend? Do you agree with her position?

ANALYZE

Analyze the links Jacoby presents between "digital culture," short attention spans, and negative political ads. Does she make a convincing causal argument? Explain your response.

Jacoby presents three factors "behind the new American dumbness." What are they? How are they related? Which does she find most dangerous? Why?

Nicholas Carr, whose most recent book is The Big Switch: Rewiring the World, From Edison to Google, *studies and writes about technology, business, and culture. He uses his own experience as a starting point in this examination of how digital technologies such as Google's search engines affect intelligence. He wrote this essay for the July/August 2008 issue of* Atlantic Monthly.

IS GOOGLE MAKING US STUPID?

Nicholas Carr

1 "Dave, stop. Stop, will you? Stop, Dave. Will you stop, Dave?" So the supercomputer HAL pleads with the implacable astronaut Dave Bowman in a famous and weirdly poignant scene toward the end of Stanley Kubrick's *2001: A Space Odyssey*. Bowman, having nearly been sent to a deep-space death by the malfunctioning machine, is calmly, coldly disconnecting the memory circuits that control its artificial "brain." "Dave, my mind is going," HAL says, forlornly. "I can feel it. I can feel it."

2 I can feel it, too. Over the past few years I've had an uncomfortable sense that someone, or something, has been tinkering with my brain, remapping the neural circuitry, reprogramming the memory. My mind isn't going—so far as I can tell—but it's changing. I'm not thinking the way I used to think. I can feel it most strongly when I'm reading. Immersing myself in a book or a lengthy article used to be easy. My mind would get caught up in the narrative or the turns of the argument, and I'd spend hours strolling through long stretches of prose. That's rarely the case anymore. Now my concentration often starts to drift after two or three pages. I get fidgety, lose the thread, begin looking for something else to do. I feel as if I'm always dragging my wayward brain back to the text. The deep reading that used to come naturally has become a struggle.

3 I think I know what's going on. For more than a decade now, I've been spending a lot of time online, searching and surfing and sometimes adding to the great databases of the Internet. The Web has been a godsend to me as a writer. Research that once required days in the stacks or periodical rooms of libraries can now be done in minutes. A few Google searches, some quick clicks on hyperlinks, and I've got the telltale fact or pithy quote I was after. Even when I'm not working, I'm as likely as not to be foraging in the Web's info-thickets reading and writing emails, scanning headlines and blog posts, watching videos and listening to podcasts, or just tripping from link to link. (Unlike footnotes, to which they're sometimes likened, hyperlinks don't merely point to related works; they propel you toward them.)

4 For me, as for others, the Net is becoming a universal medium, the conduit for most of the information that flows through my eyes and ears and into my mind. The

advantages of having immediate access to such an incredibly rich store of information are many, and they've been widely described and duly applauded. "The perfect recall of silicon memory," *Wired*'s Clive Thompson has written, "can be an enormous boon to thinking." But that boon comes at a price. As the media theorist Marshall McLuhan pointed out in the 1960s, media are not just passive channels of information. They supply the stuff of thought, but they also shape the process of thought. And what the Net seems to be doing is chipping away my capacity for concentration and contemplation. My mind now expects to take in information the way the Net distributes it: in a swiftly moving stream of particles. Once I was a scuba diver in the sea of words. Now I zip along the surface like a guy on a Jet Ski.

5 I'm not the only one. When I mention my troubles with reading to friends and acquaintances—literary types, most of them—many say they're having similar experiences. The more they use the Web, the more they have to fight to stay focused on long pieces of writing. Some of the bloggers I follow have also begun mentioning the phenomenon. Scott Karp, who writes a blog about online media, recently confessed that he has stopped reading books altogether. "I was a lit major in college, and used to be [a] voracious book reader," he wrote. "What happened?" He speculates on the answer: "What if I do all my reading on the web not so much because the way I read has changed, i.e. I'm just seeking convenience, but because the way I THINK has changed?"

6 Bruce Friedman, who blogs regularly about the use of computers in medicine, also has described how the Internet has altered his mental habits. "I now have almost totally lost the ability to read and absorb a long-ish article on the web or in print," he wrote earlier this year. A pathologist who has long been on the faculty of the University of Michigan Medical School, Friedman elaborated

on his comment in a telephone conversation with me. His thinking, he said, has taken on a "staccato" quality, reflecting the way he quickly scans short passages of text from many sources online. "I can't read *War and Peace* anymore," he admitted. "I've lost the ability to do that. Even a blog post of more than three or four paragraphs is too much to absorb. I skim it."

7 Anecdotes alone don't prove much. And we still await the long-term neurological and psychological experiments that will provide a definitive picture of how Internet use affects cognition. But a recently published study of online research habits, conducted by scholars from University College London, suggests that we may well be in the midst of a sea change in the way we read and think. As part of the five-year research program, the scholars examined computer logs documenting the behavior of visitors to two popular research sites, one operated by the British Library and one by a U.K. educational consortium, that provide access to journal articles, e-books, and other sources of written information. They found that people using the sites exhibited "a form of skimming activity," hopping from one source to another and rarely returning to any source they'd already visited. They typically read no more than one or two pages of an article or book before they would "bounce" out to another site. Sometimes they'd save a long article, but there's no evidence that they ever went back and actually read it. The authors of the study report:

> It is clear that users are not reading online in the traditional sense; indeed there are signs that new forms of "reading" are emerging as users "power browse" horizontally through titles, contents pages and abstracts going for quick wins. It almost seems that they go online to avoid reading in the traditional sense.

8 Thanks to the ubiquity of text on the Internet, not to mention the popularity

of text-messaging on cell phones, we may well be reading more today than we did in the 1970s or 1980s, when television was our medium of choice. But it's a different kind of reading, and behind it lies a different kind of thinking—perhaps even a new sense of the self. "We are not only what we read," says Maryanne Wolf, a developmental psychologist at Tufts University and the author of *Proust and the Squid: The Story and Science of the Reading Brain*. "We are how we read." Wolf worries that the style of reading promoted by the Net, a style that puts "efficiency" and "immediacy" above all else, may be weakening our capacity for the kind of deep reading that emerged when an earlier technology, the printing press, made long and complex works of prose commonplace. When we read online, she says, we tend to become "mere decoders of information." Our ability to interpret text, to make the rich mental connections that form when we read deeply and without distraction, remains largely disengaged.

9 Reading, explains Wolf, is not an instinctive skill for human beings. It's not etched into our genes the way speech is. We have to teach our minds how to translate the symbolic characters we see into the language we understand. And the media or other technologies we use in learning and practicing the craft of reading play an important part in shaping the neural circuits inside our brains. Experiments demonstrate that readers of ideograms, such as the Chinese, develop a mental circuitry for reading that is very different from the circuitry found in those of us whose written language employs an alphabet. The variations extend across many regions of the brain, including those that govern such essential cognitive functions as memory and the interpretation of visual and auditory stimuli. We can expect as well that the circuits woven by our use of the Net will be different from those woven by our reading of books and other printed works.

10 Sometime in 1882, Friedrich Nietzsche bought a typewriter—a Malling-Hansen Writing Ball, to be precise. His vision was failing, and keeping his eyes focused on a page had become exhausting and painful, often bringing on crushing headaches. He had been forced to curtail his writing, and he feared that he would soon have to give it up. The typewriter rescued him, at least for a time. Once he had mastered touch-typing, he was able to write with his eyes closed, using only the tips of his fingers. Words could once again flow from his mind to the page.

11 But the machine had a subtler effect on his work. One of Nietzsche's friends, a composer, noticed a change in the style of his writing. His already terse prose had become even tighter, more telegraphic. "Perhaps you will through this instrument even take to a new idiom," the friend wrote in a letter, noting that, in his own work, his "'thoughts' in music and language often depend on the quality of pen and paper."

12 "You are right," Nietzsche replied, "our writing equipment takes part in the forming of our thoughts." Under the sway of the machine, writes the German media scholar Friedrich A. Kittler, Nietzsche's prose "changed from arguments to aphorisms, from thoughts to puns, from rhetoric to telegram style."

13 The human brain is almost infinitely malleable. People used to think that our mental meshwork, the dense connections formed among the 100 billion or so neurons inside our skulls, was largely fixed by the time we reached adulthood. But brain researchers have discovered that that's not the case. James Olds, a professor of neuroscience who directs the Krasnow Institute for Advanced Study at George Mason University, says that even the adult mind "is very plastic." Nerve cells routinely break old connections and form new ones. "The brain," according to Olds, "has the ability

to reprogram itself on the fly, altering the way it functions."

14 As we use what the sociologist Daniel Bell has called our "intellectual technologies"—the tools that extend our mental rather than our physical capacities—we inevitably begin to take on the qualities of those technologies. The mechanical clock, which came into common use in the 14th century, provides a compelling example. In *Technics and Civilization*, the historian and cultural critic Lewis Mumford described how the clock "disassociated time from human events and helped create the belief in an independent world of mathematically measurable sequences." The "abstract framework of divided time" became "the point of reference for both action and thought."

15 The clock's methodical ticking helped bring into being the scientific mind and the scientific man. But it also took something away. As the late MIT computer scientist Joseph Weizenbaum observed in his 1976 book, *Computer Power and Human Reason: From Judgment to Calculation*, the conception of the world that emerged from the widespread use of timekeeping instruments "remains an impoverished version of the older one, for it rests on a rejection of those direct experiences that formed the basis for, and indeed constituted, the old reality." In deciding when to eat, to work, to sleep, to rise, we stopped listening to our senses and started obeying the clock.

16 The process of adapting to new intellectual technologies is reflected in the changing metaphors we use to explain ourselves to ourselves. When the mechanical clock arrived, people began thinking of their brains as operating "like clockwork." Today, in the age of software, we have come to think of them as operating "like computers." But the changes, neuroscience tells us, go much deeper than metaphor. Thanks to our brain's plasticity, the adaptation occurs also at a biological level.

17 The Internet promises to have particularly far-reaching effects on cognition. In a paper published in 1936, the British mathematician Alan Turing proved that a digital computer, which at the time existed only as a theoretical machine, could be programmed to perform the function of any other information-processing device. And that's what we're seeing today. The Internet, an immeasurably powerful computing system, is subsuming most of our other intellectual technologies. It's becoming our map and our clock, our printing press and our typewriter, our calculator and our telephone, and our radio and TV.

18 When the Net absorbs a medium, that medium is re-created in the Net's image. It injects the medium's content with hyperlinks, blinking ads, and other digital gewgaws, and it surrounds the content with the content of all the other media it has absorbed. A new e-mail message, for instance, may announce its arrival as we're glancing over the latest headlines at a newspaper's site. The result is to scatter our attention and diffuse our concentration.

19 The Net's influence doesn't end at the edges of a computer screen, either. As people's minds become attuned to the crazy quilt of Internet media, traditional media have to adapt to the audience's new expectations. Television programs add text crawls and pop-up ads, and magazines and newspapers shorten their articles, introduce capsule summaries, and crowd their pages with easy-to-browse info-snippets. When, in March of this year, *The New York Times* decided to devote the second and third pages of every edition to article abstracts, its design director, Tom Bodkin, explained that the "shortcuts" would give harried readers a quick "taste" of the day's news, sparing them the "less efficient" method of actually turning the pages and reading the articles. Old media have little choice but to play by the new-media rules.

20 Never has a communications system played so many roles in our lives—or exerted such broad influence over our thoughts—as the Internet does today. Yet, for all that's been written about the Net, there's been little consideration of how, exactly, it's reprogramming us. The Net's intellectual ethic remains obscure.

21 About the same time that Nietzsche started using his typewriter, an earnest young man named Frederick Winslow Taylor carried a stopwatch into the Midvale Steel plant in Philadelphia and began a historic series of experiments aimed at improving the efficiency of the plant's machinists. With the approval of Midvale's owners, he recruited a group of factory hands, set them to work on various metal-working machines, and recorded and timed their every movement as well as the operations of the machines. By breaking down every job into a sequence of small, discrete steps and then testing different ways of performing each one, Taylor created a set of precise instructions—an "algorithm," we might say today—for how each worker should work. Midvale's employees grumbled about the strict new regime, claiming that it turned them into little more than automatons, but the factory's productivity soared.

22 More than a hundred years after the invention of the steam engine, the Industrial Revolution had at last found its philosophy and its philosopher. Taylor's tight industrial choreography—his "system," as he liked to call it—was embraced by manufacturers throughout the country and, in time, around the world. Seeking maximum speed, maximum efficiency, and maximum output, factory owners used time-and-motion studies to organize their work and configure the jobs of their workers. The goal, as Taylor defined it in his celebrated 1911 treatise, *The Principles of Scientific Management*, was to identify and adopt, for every job, the "one best method" of work and thereby to effect "the gradual substitution of science for rule of thumb throughout the mechanic arts." Once his system was applied to all acts of manual labor, Taylor assured his followers, it would bring about a restructuring not only of industry but of society, creating a utopia of perfect efficiency. "In the past the man has been first," he declared, "in the future the system must be first."

23 Taylor's system is still very much with us; it remains the ethic of industrial manufacturing. And now, thanks to the growing power that computer engineers and software coders wield over our intellectual lives, Taylor's ethic is beginning to govern the realm of the mind as well. The Internet is a machine designed for the efficient and automated collection, transmission, and manipulation of information, and its legions of programmers are intent on finding the "one best method"—the perfect algorithm—to carry out every mental movement of what we've come to describe as "knowledge work."

24 Google's headquarters, in Mountain View, California—the Googleplex—is the Internet's high church, and the religion practiced inside its walls is Taylorism. Google, says its chief executive, Eric Schmidt, is "a company that's founded around the science of measurement," and it is striving to "systematize everything" it does. Drawing on the terabytes of behavioral data it collects through its search engine and other sites, it carries out thousands of experiments a day, according to the *Harvard Business Review*, and it uses the results to refine the algorithms that increasingly control how people find information and extract meaning from it. What Taylor did for the work of the hand, Google is doing for the work of the mind.

25 The company has declared that its mission is "to organize the world's information and make it universally accessible and useful." It seeks to develop "the perfect search engine," which it defines as something that "understands exactly what you mean and gives you back exactly what you want."

In Google's view, information is a kind of commodity, a utilitarian resource that can be mined and processed with industrial efficiency. The more pieces of information we can "access" and the faster we can extract their gist, the more productive we become as thinkers.

26 Where does it end? Sergey Brin and Larry Page, the gifted young men who founded Google while pursuing doctoral degrees in computer science at Stanford, speak frequently of their desire to turn their search engine into an artificial intelligence, a HAL-like machine that might be connected directly to our brains. "The ultimate search engine is something as smart as people—or smarter," Page said in a speech a few years back. "For us, working on search is a way to work on artificial intelligence." In a 2004 interview with *Newsweek*, Brin said, "Certainly if you had all the world's information directly attached to your brain, or an artificial brain that was smarter than your brain, you'd be better off." Last year, Page told a convention of scientists that Google is "really trying to build artificial intelligence and to do it on a large scale."

27 Such an ambition is a natural one, even an admirable one, for a pair of math whizzes with vast quantities of cash at their disposal and a small army of computer scientists in their employ. A fundamentally scientific enterprise, Google is motivated by a desire to use technology, in Eric Schmidt's words, "to solve problems that have never been solved before," and artificial intelligence is the hardest problem out there. Why wouldn't Brin and Page want to be the ones to crack it?

28 Still, their easy assumption that we'd all "be better off" if our brains were supplemented, or even replaced, by an artificial intelligence is unsettling. It suggests a belief that intelligence is the output of a mechanical process, a series of discrete steps that can be isolated, measured, and optimized. In Google's world, the world we enter when we go online, there's little place for the fuzziness of contemplation. Ambiguity is not an opening for insight but a bug to be fixed. The human brain is just an outdated computer that needs a faster processor and a bigger hard drive.

29 The idea that our minds should operate as high-speed data-processing machines is not only built into the workings of the Internet, it is the network's reigning business model as well. The faster we surf across the Web—the more links we click and pages we view—the more opportunities Google and other companies gain to collect information about us and to feed us advertisements. Most of the proprietors of the commercial Internet have a financial stake in collecting the crumbs of data we leave behind as we flit from link to link—the more crumbs, the better. The last thing these companies want is to encourage leisurely reading or slow, concentrated thought. It's in their economic interest to drive us to distraction.

30 Maybe I'm just a worrywart. Just as there's a tendency to glorify technological progress, there's a countertendency to expect the worst of every new tool or machine. In Plato's *Phaedrus*, Socrates bemoaned the development of writing. He feared that, as people came to rely on the written word as a substitute for the knowledge they used to carry inside their heads, they would, in the words of one of the dialogue's characters, "cease to exercise their memory and become forgetful." And because they would be able to "receive a quantity of information without proper instruction," they would "be thought very knowledgeable when they are for the most part quite ignorant." They would be "filled with the conceit of wisdom instead of real wisdom." Socrates wasn't wrong—the new technology did often have the effects he feared—but he was shortsighted. He couldn't foresee the many ways that writing and reading would serve to spread information, spur fresh

ideas, and expand human knowledge (if not wisdom).

[31] The arrival of Gutenberg's printing press, in the 15th century, set off another round of teeth gnashing. The Italian humanist Hieronimo Squarciafico worried that the easy availability of books would lead to intellectual laziness, making men "less studious" and weakening their minds. Others argued that cheaply printed books and broadsheets would undermine religious authority, demean the work of scholars and scribes, and spread sedition and debauchery. As New York University professor Clay Shirky notes, "Most of the arguments made against the printing press were correct, even prescient." But, again, the doomsayers were unable to imagine the myriad blessings that the printed word would deliver.

[32] So, yes, you should be skeptical of my skepticism. Perhaps those who dismiss critics of the Internet as Luddites or nostalgists will be proved correct, and from our hyperactive, data-stoked minds will spring a golden age of intellectual discovery and universal wisdom. Then again, the Net isn't the alphabet, and although it may replace the printing press, it produces something altogether different. The kind of deep reading that a sequence of printed pages promotes is valuable not just for the knowledge we acquire from the author's words but for the intellectual vibrations those words set off within our own minds. In the quiet spaces opened up by the sustained, undistracted reading of a book, or by any other act of contemplation, for that matter, we make our own associations, draw our own inferences and analogies, foster our own ideas. Deep reading, as Maryanne Wolf argues, is indistinguishable from deep thinking.

[33] If we lose those quiet spaces, or fill them up with "content," we will sacrifice something important not only in ourselves but in our culture. In a recent essay, the playwright Richard Foreman eloquently described what's at stake:

> I come from a tradition of Western culture, in which the ideal (my ideal) was the complex, dense and "cathedral-like" structure of the highly educated and articulate personality—a man or woman who carried inside themselves a personally constructed and unique version of the entire heritage of the West. [But now] I see within us all (myself included) the replacement of complex inner density with a new kind of self—evolving under the pressure of information overload and the technology of the "instantly available."

[34] As we are drained of our "inner repertory of dense cultural inheritance," Foreman concluded, we risk turning into "'pancake people'—spread wide and thin as we connect with that vast network of information accessed by the mere touch of a button."

[35] I'm haunted by that scene in *2001*. What makes it so poignant, and so weird, is the computer's emotional response to the disassembly of its mind: its despair as one circuit after another goes dark, its childlike pleading with the astronaut—"I can feel it. I can feel it. I'm afraid"—and its final reversion to what can only be called a state of innocence. HAL's outpouring of feeling contrasts with the emotionlessness that characterizes the human figures in the film, who go about their business with an almost robotic efficiency. Their thoughts and actions feel scripted, as if they're following the steps of an algorithm. In the world of *2001*, people have become so machinelike that the most human character turns out to be a machine. That's the essence of Kubrick's dark prophecy: as we come to rely on computers to mediate our understanding of the world, it is our own intelligence that flattens into artificial intelligence.

Carr writes that the "Web has been a godsend to me as a writer" but also that this "boon comes at a price." Summarize the advantages that Carr says the Internet offers as well as the drawbacks that he worries might accompany long-term use.

Although he expresses many of the same concerns that Michael Skube, Don Campbell, and Susan Jacoby write about in their essays, Carr uses different rhetorical approaches to make his point. How, for example, does Carr present himself in his essay? Compare his ethos with that presented by Skube, Campbell, and/or Jacoby. Which do you find more effective? Why?

In paragraphs 24–30, Carr uses Google's desire to develop the "perfect search engine" to discuss two kinds of intelligence. How would you describe these? Do you see any reason for concern about the influence technology might be having on intelligence?

Todd Hagstette is a Ph.D. candidate in English at the University of South Carolina, where he teaches introductory composition classes and other courses in writing and literature. His 2007 essay offers one solution to a problem common in many college literature classes and serves as an interesting counterpart to the Michael Skube piece that opens this chapter.

AGGRESSIVE READING WON'T KILL YOU

(NO MATTER WHAT MARK TWAIN SAYS)

Todd Hagstette

1 At the beginning of his masterpiece, *Adventures of Huckleberry Finn*, Mark Twain offers the following warning to the reader:

NOTICE

Persons attempting to find a motive in this narrative will be prosecuted; persons attempting to find a moral in it will be banished; persons attempting to find a plot in it will be shot.

2 This comic, false-modest proclamation urges readers to glance at his text lightly, with no attempt at subsurface penetration. It urges the reader, in other words, to read passively. Though Twain is obviously being

facetious, many contemporary students unfortunately seem to take this satirical injunction seriously when it comes to their own reading. They follow Twain's advice to the letter by failing to consider the overriding theme or meaning of a text (the moral), the author's intentions (the motive), or even the basics of the language itself (the plot). In short, they fail to recognize that good writing begins with aggressive reading. It is the most overlooked and disregarded step in the writing process, but without aggressive reading at the launch, papers drift as aimlessly as rafts on a river. The good news is that with a few simple (and obvious) techniques, any student can learn to read more carefully, engage with the text more thoroughly, and thus write more successfully.

The Value of Discomfort

[3] The first thing you need to do to begin the aggressive reading process is to get uncomfortable. That's right, *UN-comfortable*. One of the major problems that many students encounter in their studies is that they attempt to deal with their school reading the same way that they read for pleasure. Taking a book to bed with you to help you fall asleep or curling up in your comfy leather chair with Oprah on in the background may be great ways to enjoy the latest Nicholas Sparks novel or the new issue of *People* magazine. But, when it comes to active, retentive reading, you need to set the scene a bit more seriously. Think about it in terms of baseball: The difference between reading for pleasure and aggressive reading is like the difference between playing catch in the backyard and practicing as part of major league spring training. Playing catch can be fun, but it does nothing to improve your skills. Even the best of the best pro ball players must drill and work relentlessly to be successful in the game. And so must you in your academic reading. Play catch on your own time. Get out of the backyard hammock, and sit down at a desk or a table in a quiet room. That way you will be ready to really focus on the task at hand.

Beating Your Promiscuous Mind

[4] Better focus is exactly what most inexperienced readers need. It is easy to get distracted while reading; in fact, it is a natural, understandable consequence of the reading process. We all have had the experience of drifting off into a daydream over a text and then snapping out of it to discover that we have no idea what the last several pages were about. Reading gets your mind working. It stimulates your thinking. And often it sends your mind spinning off into tangential directions. Think of it this way: reading is like Viagra® for the imagination. The problem is that being that mentally, um, erect leads directly to intellectual promiscuity. Aggressive reading is about learning to be monogamous. Just as it takes discipline for a married man to stay home at night, you must develop the discipline to keep your brain faithful to the text at hand. And that simply takes practice. Crank up the aggressive reading by not letting your daydreams control your comprehension of the text. As soon as you wake up, go back to the last thing you remember reading and start over. Stop believing in the virtue of plowing through a story or essay, and divest yourself of the idea that the end of the text is the finish line of the assignment. Rather, come to think of comprehension as the end point. Also, make peace with reading slowly. We are trained to believe that reading quickly is a sign of proficiency and intelligence, but speed-reading is not aggressive reading. Slow down, go back when necessary, and focus on truly absorbing the material.

Texts Are Read Too Passively by You

[5] Overall, this kind of absorption is about confirming to yourself that you understand everything you have read, that you have followed along with the author every step of the way and internalized his or her arguments and themes. The best way to accomplish that assurance is to take ample notes while you read and take the time to research

anything unfamiliar to you. Vocabulary is a tricky thing, and because we are all trained to be very good at interpreting so-called context clues, most of us can glean a fairly good idea of what a word means just by noting how it is used. All words, though, have different nuances that are more complicated than what a simple deduction allows us to discern. In the previous section, for instance, I used the word "tangential." Now, you probably could figure out that I meant something like "inappropriate" or "irrelevant" based on the context of the sentence. But, why did I choose that particular word instead of some other pseudo-synonyms like "digressive," "peripheral," or "divergent"? You must know the subtleties of definition to fully grasp the specific type of wandering mind that it suggests.

[6] You must also master allusions. If you do not know the reference, then no matter how effectively you read context clues, you will not fully grasp a writer's point. For example, in a recent political article, the author suggests that vocal anti-war liberals should spend an evening with Damocles' sword before they criticize President Bush. Though you may be able to get the general idea that this author is condemning the former and supporting the latter, without knowing the Greek story of that Sicilian blowhard you will miss the specific nature of the writer's criticism. The point is: Never simply read right past elements you do not fully understand. Everything in a text is there for a conscious reason. Your job as an aggressive reader is to decode the vocabulary and allusions you encounter. So be prepared to do all of your reading with a dictionary (or Dictionary.com) and an encyclopedia (or Wikipedia) close at hand.

Breaking the Fourth Wall

[7] There is more to engaging with a text than simply eliminating your physical passivity, though. Besides being diligent in incorporating writing into your reading, you must also accept the mental challenges that a text presents. Do not simply accept everything you read—question the material. Challenge an essay writer's argument, doubt a character's motivation, criticize a poem's theme. Only by bringing your own perspective into a text will you fully internalize it. Consider the theatrical world where there is an imaginary wall that separates the performers from the audience. This fourth wall (as distinct from the three actual walls that form a play's set) maintains the distance between the real world of the audience and the imaginary world of the drama. But, some playwrights opt to violate this separation by having the actors "break the fourth wall" and speak directly to the audience. Shakespeare famously does this in *A Midsummer Night's Dream*, and so do many children's plays. The purpose of breaking the wall is to get the audience members more involved in the action, to wrest them out of their passive enjoyment of the work and make them active participants. You must do the same thing in your reading. It is not enough to simply read a text. You must interact with it and thereby become an aggressive contributor to it.

Redundancy, Repetition, Re-Reading

[8] The final step in the aggressive reading process is to simply do it all over again. No matter how accomplished a reader you are, you are unlikely to fully understand a text after reading it only once. In fact, I believe that you must read most short stories *three* times before you have a solid grasp of them; argumentative essays must be read *five* times; and, poems require *ten* readings before you can feel confident in your understanding. It sounds superfluous and painful, I know, but nobody ever said that aggressive reading was easy. Only through repeated immersion in the text will you gain the kind of focus you need, ensure that your notes and research are complete, and guarantee that you have completely

questioned the material in full. If you don't believe me, try it. You are almost at the long-anticipated end of this essay. Read it again. See if there isn't something you missed the first time or that you don't grasp better the second time. Go ahead—read it again. I dare you.

Dodging the Mark Twain Bullet

[9] This how we must come to think of Mark Twain's warning at the beginning of *Huck Finn*: not as a restriction but as a dare. He is not encouraging readers to approach his work passively, but rather challenging them to read it aggressively. Anyone who has read even a few pages of Twain's book can readily discern the author's mastery of language (plot), deep thematic import (moral), and socio-political ambition (motive). He is imploring you not to haphazardly miss those things in the text, and so am I. Because, ultimately, aggressive reading leads to proficient writing. So get uncomfortable, stay focused, take notes, look up unfamiliars, question the material, and re-read the text. Put your pole in the water and guide your raft confidently down the treacherous waters of the aggressive reading process. It won't kill you.

SUMMARIZE AND RESPOND

Write a 50- to 100-word summary of this piece, followed by a 100-word response. In your summary, make sure you accurately and fairly convey the gist of Hagstette's proposal. In your response, focus on how Hagstette appeals directly to his audience (students who might not like to read).

ANALYZE

Which of the rhetorical appeals is strongest in Hagstette's essay? Which is weakest?

DISCUSS

Comment on how Hagstette's "aggressive reading" might be of some help to the students described in Michael Skube's and Don Campbell's essays.

ARGUE

Skube, Campbell, and Hagstette are addressing the same central problem. Write a brief argument in which you identify that problem and present a case for its causes.

Eme Crawford is a Ph.D. candidate in composition and rhetoric at the University of South Carolina, where she also teaches in the First-Year English Program. As she makes clear in this 2007 essay, the question of literacy for most college students still boils down to graded writing assignments.

NOTHING BUT THE FACTS?

Eme Crawford

[1] Sitting at the front desk of Doug Jones's Auto Sales I closed David Brinkley's autobiography and imagined the splash I would make in college. As the editor of my high school newspaper, I had taken a recent interest in the daring young newspaper reporters who had broken the Watergate scandal, Woodward and Bernstein. Unfortunately, since the local library held nothing on those *enfants terrible* of the early '70s, I had to settle for the aging, dignified old man of ABC news. It didn't matter much. After all, what interested me most was *journalism*. I imagined the clean, clipped prose of a hard-boiled news story, written by pure-hearted newspapermen and women, notepad in hand, ever striving for the noble dream of objectivity.

[2] As I waited on the dozen customers who came in to make car payments throughout the day, I pondered how my past had prepared me for a life of writing. For the past four years in high school I had worked on my school newspaper climbing my way up from grunt staff writer to worldly editor. I thought about how this would be great material for my own biography. *She was ready to write. She was ready to become the next Pulitzer Prize-winning journalist. It was the summer of 1998 and Eme Crawford was ready for the world, but was the world ready for her brilliant prose?*

[3] "Eme, would you put the book down and refill the coke machine?"

[4] The monotony of a small-town summer job eventually gave way to the limitless possibility of the first week of college, and soon I found myself in my first composition course. Our assignment was on a subject I thought I knew backwards and forwards—Moses. We were to read a passage from Exodus and make an argument about his character. I had attended the requisite Sunday school classes. I knew about the miracles—the first Passover, the parting of the water, the Ten Commandments. I got it. What more was there to write about?

[5] But I wanted to be a good student. I would utilize the writing skills of those noble journalists who populated my imagination, reporting nothing but the facts of the story. I worked all weekend on that essay. I called and consulted my mother, consulted my roommate, and consulted my Bible. By Sunday I had written an essay I felt proud of. My biographer, shuffling through the papers from my college years, would pause a moment when she reached this essay. *From her earliest days as a college freshman, Crawford's writing bore the markings of future greatness.*

[6] But when our essays were returned, I was floored. I got a "C"! I had never gotten a "C" in my life! I knew this story! How could I have gotten a "C"?! I was more hurt than angry. And I felt more like a mournful Old Testament character than a brash young

reporter. I wanted to cry right there in the classroom, tear my clothes and dump ashes on my head. Instead, I went against my prophetic instincts, slinking back to my dorm room to eat a bag of double-stuffed Oreos. I imagined my biographer scrapping the first paragraph of chapter two and starting over. *Despite the success of her high school years, Crawford's first essay for English 101 turned out to be a major setback.*

7 The next day I was furious. I scheduled a meeting with my professor to get to the bottom of her crazy notions of what good writing should be and do. I explained to her that writing should be about the facts. It should honestly represent an event. In this case, I felt like I told the whole Moses story accurately.

8 "But," she pressed me, "what specifically do you find interesting about Moses as a character?"

9 "Why would you consider Moses heroic?"

10 "What characteristics constitute heroism?"

11 "What are some of his faults?"

12 I was pelted with hard questions I had no idea how to answer, or if I did answer them, I didn't know how to explain why I thought the way I thought.

13 "The facts," my professor told me, "are still up for debate. Knowledge isn't simply there to be discovered, but has to be created."

14 "Perhaps good writing," she told me, "has more to do with creatively engaging with texts and asking questions rather than summarizing the safe facts. Sure we sometimes write to accurately convey an event, but I'm asking you to write to push your thinking on what you think you know. Go back to your dorm room and think about Moses' story again. Make an argument about his character that's from you—not what someone has told you."

15 This, of course was heresy. The facts are still up for debate? My professor was nuts. She would have me cast aside objectivity and

make up facts whole cloth. I imagined David Brinkley shaking his gray head in disgust.

16 I went back to my room, my head swimming from the questions and ideas fired at me. How was I going to do this? How to un-learn the things I thought I had known all my life? If I start questioning what kind of man Moses was, how can I stop from thinking about what kind of man Jesus was? By extension what do I think about God? If God were a human and did the things attributed to him in the Old Testament, what would I think about that person? For the time being I had to stop myself. I had to limit myself to only Moses.

17 Contemplating Moses' lot in life and my own, I began to envy Moses and his trusty burning bush. How could Moses have it so easy? My mind started to wander. I wondered what really happened during the composition of the Ten Commandments. Who was doing the actual writing? Moses or God? Was this a collaborative process? Were there drafts? Did God come up with the content and Moses help with the grammar? Did they fight over word choice? Did they spend hours arguing over "Thou shall not murder" versus "Thou shall not kill"? Moses was on Mount Sinai for forty days and forty nights, but there were no first-hand witnesses as to what happened. This was bad material for a news story.

18 Then again, they had to be discussing something. Why did Moses *really* break the first tablet? After walking down the mountain, away from the eye of God the Father, God the Editor, did Moses find himself unhappy with the work? It seemed a little strange that Moses would lose his cool after seeing the Israelites sinning it up. I mean, didn't he know what they were like before? Moses must have been a big believer in the collaborative and re-writing process. He just *had* to go back for another draft.

19 As I furiously typed away at my second draft, I realized I was straying far from my

ideal of objective writing. But I also felt a rush of freedom by creating new knowledge. To be sure, Brinkley would not be pleased. I imagined my biographer in solidarity with him, trying to accommodate the stylistic shift. *Crawford's second essay, with its self-indulgence and wild speculation, bore little resemblance to the first. She was teetering on the edge.*

[20] I don't know exactly when it happened, but eventually my metaphor-hungry subconscious grasped the Moses story as its dominant trope, leaving behind those sacred cows of my high school years. Moses patiently wandered through the desert for forty years searching for the Promised Land. For four years in college I patiently searched my writing, finding out what worked and what didn't. Unlike what I had expected when I first started college, instead of turning outward and observing and summarizing the world around me, the greatest reward of writing was turning my journalistic eye inward, observing and evaluating my own beliefs and knowledge.

[21] Of course, Moses never actually reached the Promised Land. Would he have embarked on the journey, knowing that the land of milk and honey would forever elude him? Maybe not, but I'd like to think he eventually came to embrace his role in the process. If I ever make it there, I think I'll start my autobiography this way: *Sitting at the front desk of Doug Jones's Auto Sales I closed the book of Exodus and imagined the journey ahead of me in college.*

SUMMARIZE AND RESPOND

Write a 50- to 100-word summary of this piece, followed by a 100-word response. In your summary, make sure you accurately and fairly convey Crawford's central idea. In your response, focus on what the essay does (its effectiveness, given what you know about the Crawford's audience and purpose) or how the essay does it (Crawford's style of presentation or argumentation). Unless your teacher instructs you otherwise, stay away from a response based on what you liked or disliked about the piece.

ANALYZE

Crawford poses more than two dozen questions in her essay. How many of these does she answer? What is the rhetorical effect of all of these questions? How do they involve the reader in the text?

DISCUSS

Do you agree with Crawford's claim about the value of "turning [her] journalistic eye inward, observing and evaluating [her] own beliefs and knowledge"? Do you think that kind of introspection is a worthy learning tool? Why?

As the following piece shows, syndicated columnist Kathleen Parker resists easy political labels. A regular contributor to Townhall.com <www.townhall.com>, a conservative website where this column was published on April 20, 2005, Parker seeks constructive public dialogue based on issues rather than ideology. As you read this essay, think about how it addresses yet another kind of literacy—the ability to read and write responsible and effective public discourse.

SEEKING BALANCE IN AN EITHER-OR WORLD

Kathleen Parker

"Blessed are the peacemakers for they shall
catch hell from both sides."

—Sign on the wall of Justice Department attorney Burke Marshall, 1964

1 In today's food-fight environment, where extremes dominate debate and choice is defined by either-or, finding a comfortable place to land is increasingly difficult.

2 Like most people I know, I tend to run screaming from both ends of the spectrum. Too conservative for the left wing and too liberal for the right wing, I find myself scrambling for the center aisle.

3 Yet, people in the middle often are held in contempt as fence-straddlers. If you're an opinion columnist, you're forced to pick a side. People want to know: Are you conservative or liberal? "It depends" is considered a weak answer, morally relativistic, lacking in backbone.

4 Abortion provides a convenient if unpalatable example. I've written dozens of columns through the years, more or less urging a pro-life position—having a baby forces a review of one's assumptions—while clinging to a pro-choice conclusion. Abortion is a terrible thing, I say, the violent termination of a life and a decision many women (and men) regret with time and perspective.

5 Nevertheless, I can find no way to justify government-enforced maternity. Under penalty of what? By whom? Under what circumstances? The practical applications of the moral ideal become nightmarish as we extrapolate to the real. Thus, one might hope to seek compromise. Can't a female who's old enough to samba deduce that she's pregnant and decide within, oh, 6–8 weeks? This is, after all, not a "Gee whiz, I dunno" question.

6 In the spirit of compromise, I also can argue passionately in favor of tougher education standards when it comes to abortion. If we can demonstrate how to use condoms to high school students, surely we can make vivid the pros and cons of abortion as birth control. In time, given what can't be ignored when abortion is studied up close, we'd accomplish the goal supported by most Americans (64 percent, according to Luntz Research Companies, August 2003) and articulated by President Bill Clinton: to make abortion safe, legal and rare.

7 My middle road, of course, makes me equally contemptible to those who dwell in the peripheries—both to the pro-lifers who view all abortion as murder, and to

FIGURE 5-2

In arguing for an approach to public discourse that is not driven by the extremes, Kathleen Parker uses the abortion issue as an example. How does this photograph of pro-life and pro-choice protesters in Washington, D.C., illustrate Parker's point that the voices on the extremes often leave no room for discussion in the middle?

the slippery-slopers who consider objecting to "partial-birth abortion" tantamount to embracing the Vatican's view of The Pill. Caught between extremes of community morality and individual choice—amid near-hysterical ideological partisanship from parties that have been hijacked by radicals—people like me are adrift.

[8] Apparently, I'm not alone. Indeed, given current trends, we may declare that we have reached a perfect storm of political backlash. Americans who cleave to neither extreme—some 50 percent of whom identify themselves as "moderate"—are fed up with the Ann Coulter/Michael Moore school of debate and are looking for someone to articulate a commonsense, middle path. They may have found their voice in John P. Avlon, chief speechwriter for former New York Mayor Rudy Giuliani and a *New York Sun* columnist, whose 2004 book *Independent Nation* has just been released in paperback.

[9] Avlon insists that centrism is the more patriotic political position because it adheres more strictly to American values and founding principles than to ideology. A balance between idealism and realism, centrism is a yin-yang proposition that rejects shrill extremes and embraces reason, decency and a practical perspective. To those who insist that centrism is the death of dissent, Avlon argues that centrism is dissent—from outdated political orthodoxies.

[10] "Extremists and ideological purists on either side of the political aisle condemn compromise," he writes. "But inflexibility either creates deadlock or dooms a cause to irrelevance."

[11] That's from the introduction to *Independent Nation*. The balance of the book is a compendium of short biographies of several U.S. presidents, senators and governors and their personal journeys as they illuminate the theme of centrism. Avlon says his purpose in writing the book was to give today's centrists a framework for understanding their frustration with extreme politics and a place for the politically homeless to hang their iPods. Or their heart monitors, as the case may be.

[12] Extremists won't agree with Avlon that centrism is a patriotic position, but who cares? They've held the nation hostage long enough. Meanwhile, Independents are the fastest-growing group of voters across the country, especially among the young, hundreds of whom have e-mailed Avlon since his appearance last week on *The Daily Show* with Comedy Central's Jon Stewart. A Pew Poll published last week in *The Economist* broke down voters as 39 percent Independent, 31 percent Democrat and 30 percent Republican.

[13] Socially liberal and fiscally conservative, Independents could be a powerful reckoning force by 2008. Politicians better wise up and tone it down.

SUMMARIZE AND RESPOND

Write a 50-word summary of Parker's piece, followed by a 100-word response. In your response, focus on how Parker characterizes the state of public debate today. Do you agree with her position?

ANALYZE

Who is Parker's target audience? How does she appeal to these people? Use specific examples from the text in your response.

DISCUSS

Parker claims that "Americans who cleave to neither extreme—some 50 percent of whom identify themselves as 'moderate'—are fed up with the Ann Coulter/Michael Moore school of debate and are looking for someone to articulate a commonsense, middle path." What do you think can be done to help find this middle path? Do you see any leader who might be that "someone" Parker is talking about?

ARGUE

Parker suggests that centrism is a much-needed alternative to extremist politics. Write a brief essay in which you define the terms *centrism* and *extremism* in terms of public discourse. Make sure you provide examples of people, groups, or actions that fit and that don't fit your definitions.

from reading to writing

1. What is it about today's college students that concerns Michael Skube and Don Campbell? Based on your own experience in the classroom and online, do you think their claims are accurate?

2. What kind of reader are you? In your response, use the essays in this chapter that deal specifically with reading as a point of comparison with your own habits and experiences.

3. Compare the arguments presented in Skube's and Campbell's essays with Howard Gardner's position in "The End of Literacy? Don't Stop Reading." Whose position do you find more persuasive? Why?

4. Working with a partner or in a small group, describe how you think the following writers would define the word literacy: Michael Skube, Don Campbell, Howard Gardner, Susan Jacoby. Would you be considered a literate person using the criteria set forth by any of these writers? Explain your response.

5. In her article, Motoko Rich quotes David McCullough, the Pulitzer Prize-winning biographer, as saying: "Learning is not to be found on a printout. It's not on call at the touch of the finger. Learning is acquired mainly from books, and most readily from great books." Do you agree with McCullough's sentiment? Explain your answer.

6. Describe your best writing experience. What made it so good? Now, describe your most frustrating writing experience. What made it so bad? Which of these experiences affected you the most? Why?

7. In his essay, Don Campbell draws from a book by Emory University English professor Mark Bauerlein called *The Dumbest Generation: How the Digital Age Stupefies Young Americans and Jeopardizes Our Future*. In the book, as Campbell puts it, "Bauerlein's simple but jarring thesis is that technology and the digital culture it has created are not broadening the horizon of the younger generation; they are narrowing it to a self-absorbed social universe that blocks out virtually everything else." Write a brief essay in which you respond to these criticisms of social networking technologies and their effects on those who use them.

8. Do you think Google and similar technologies are making us stupid? Explain your response, using evidence from the readings in this chapter to support your position.

defining a
generation

"Much of the stuff floating around in cyberspace is tame, mundane even. But there also is plenty that's racy, embarrassing or squeamishly intimate. Bad or good, Generation Next is living out loud and doing it online, before a global audience, in a medium where digital archives may linger for a long, long time."

—Melissa Ludwig, *"LOOK@Me: Generation Next Is Living Out Loud and Online"*

W ho are the Millennials (or Generation Next or Generation Me)? Are they mutant narcissists born of the self-esteem rush of the 1990s; nurtured on Facebook, MySpace, and YouTube; and unable or unwilling to care about anything beyond themselves? Or are they self-confident, technologically savvy citizens who have as much passion about the world around them—and more ability to get things done—than any generation before them? As with most complicated questions, the answer lies somewhere in between, as you'll see when you read the pieces in this chapter. And as you read, ask yourself why we invest so much time in labeling and defining groups of people. What purpose does this serve?

Michiko Kakutani, a book critic and reporter, wrote this article for the New York Times *in March 2002. As soon as it was published, the piece became a popular source for those interested in defining the generation born after 1985. Although Kakutani's article is not an argument in the traditional sense, it does present a point of view as it explores various issues of identity and labeling.*

DEBATE? DISSENT? DISCUSSION? OH, DON'T GO THERE!

Michiko Kakutani

[1] That familiar interjection "whatever" says a lot about the state of mind of college students today. So do the catch phrases "no problem," "not even" and "don't go there."

[2] Noisy dorm and dining room debates are no longer de rigueur as they were during earlier decades; quiet acceptance of differing views—be they political or aesthetic—is increasingly the rule.

[3] Neil Howe and William Strauss's book *Millennials Rising*—a survey of the post–Gen X generation—suggests that the young people born in the early 1980's and afterward are, as a group, less rebellious than their predecessors, more practical-minded, less individualistic and more inclined to value "team over self, duties over rights, honor over feeling, action over words."

[4] "Much the opposite of boomers at the same age," the authors write, "millennials feel more of an urge to homogenize, to celebrate ties that bind rather than differences that splinter."

[5] These are gross generalizations, of course, but a student's article titled "The Silent Classroom," which appeared in the Fall 2001 issue of *Amherst* magazine, suggested that upperclassmen at that college tend to be guarded and private about their intellectual beliefs. And in this writer's own completely unscientific survey, professors and administrators observed that students today tend to be more respectful of authority—parental and professorial—than they used to be, and more reticent about public disputation.

[6] "My sense from talking to students and other faculty is that out of class, students are interested in hearing another person's point of view, but not interested in engaging it, in challenging it or being challenged," Joseph W. Gordon, dean of undergraduate education at Yale, said. "So they'll be very

accepting of other points of view very different from their own. They live in a world that's very diverse, but it's a diversity that's more parallel than cross-stitched."

7 The students' reticence about debate stems, in part, from the fact that the great issues of the day—the Sept. 11 terrorist attacks and the war in Afghanistan—do not engender the sort of dissent that the Vietnam War did in an earlier era. It also has roots in a disillusionment with the vitriolic partisanship that held sway in Washington in the 1990's: the often petty haggling between right and left, Republicans and Democrats, during President Bill Clinton's impeachment hearings and the disputed presidential election of 2000, and the spectacle of liberals and conservatives screaming at each other on television programs like *Crossfire*.

8 "Debate has gotten a very bad name in our culture," Jeff Nunokawa, a professor of English at Princeton University, said. "It's become synonymous with some of the most nonintellectual forms of bullying, rather than as an opportunity for deliberative democracy." He added that while the events of Sept. 11 may well serve as a kind of wake-up call, many of his students say that "it's not politic or polite to seem to care too much about abstract issues."

9 "Many of them are intensely socially conscientious, caring and committed," he said. "It's just not clear precisely what they wish to commit themselves to."

10 In a much talked-about article in *The Atlantic Monthly* a year ago, the writer David Brooks argued that elite college students today "don't shout out their differences or declare them in political or social movements" because they do not belong to a generation that is "fighting to emancipate itself from the past," because most of them are "not trying to buck the system; they're trying to climb it." And yet to suggest that the archetypal student today is "the Organization Kid," as

Mr. Brooks did, seems too simplistic, ignoring the powerful effect that certain academic modes of thinking—from multiculturalism to deconstruction—have had in shaping contemporary college discourse.

11 Indeed, the reluctance of today's students to engage in impassioned debate can be seen as a byproduct of a philosophical relativism, fostered by theories that gained ascendance in academia in the last two decades and that have seeped into the broader culture. While deconstruction promoted the indeterminacy of texts, the broader principle of subjectivity has been embraced by everyone from biographers (like Edmund Morris, whose biography of President Ronald Reagan mixed fact and fiction) to scholars (who have inserted personal testimony in their work to underscore their own biases). Because subjectivity enshrines ideas that are partial and fragmentary by definition, it tends to preclude searches for larger, overarching truths, thereby undermining a strong culture of contestation.

12 At the same time, multiculturalism and identity politics were questioning the very existence of objective truths and a single historical reality. As the historians Joyce Appleby, Lynn Hunt and Margaret Jacob observed in their book, *Telling the Truth About History*, radical multiculturalists celebrated "the virtues of fragmentation," arguing that "since all history has a political—often a propaganda—function, it is time for each group to rewrite history from its own perspective and thereby reaffirm its own past."

13 During the height of the culture wars of the early 90's, such views led to vociferous showdowns between academic radicals and traditionalists. It also led to the politicization of subjects like history and literature, and ideological posturing that could be reductive and doctrinaire in the extreme. Thankfully, these excesses have

begun to die down, as bipolar dogmatism has started to give way to a scholarly eclecticism—less concerned with large paradigms, and more focused on narrower issues—but the legacy of multiculturalism and identity politics remains potent on college campuses.

[14] On one hand, it has made students more accepting of individuals different from themselves, more tolerant of other races, religions and sexual orientations. But this tolerance of other people also seems to have resulted in a reluctance to engage in the sort of impassioned argumentation that many baby boomers remember from their college days.

[15] "It's as though there's no distinction between the person and the argument, as though to criticize an argument would be injurious to the person," said Amanda Anderson, an English professor at Johns Hopkins University and the author of a forthcoming book, *The Way We Argue Now*. "Because so many forms of scholarly inquiry today foreground people's lived experience, there's this kind of odd overtactfulness. In many ways, it's emanating from a good thing, but it's turned into a disabling thing."

[16] "A lot of professors complain about the way students make appeals to relativism today," Professor Anderson added. "It's difficult because it's coming out of genuinely pluralistic orientation and a desire to get along, but it makes argument and rigorous analysis very difficult, because people will stop and say, 'I guess I just disagree.'"

[17] Outside the classroom, it's a mind-set ratified by the PLUR ("Peace, Love, Unity and Respect") T-shirts worn by ravers (whose drug of choice is Ecstasy, which induces warm, fuzzy feelings of communion). It is also a mindset reinforced by television shows like *Oprah* that preach self-esteem and the accommodation of others, and by the Internet, which instead of leading to a global village, has created a multitude of self-contained tribes—niche cultures in which like-minded people can talk to like-minded people and filter out information that might undermine their views.

[18] At the same time, the diminished debate syndrome mirrors the irony-suffused sensibility of many millennial-era students. Irony, after all, represents a form of detachment; like the knee-jerk acceptance of the positions of others, it's a defensive mode that enables one to avoid commitment and stand above the fray.

[19] What are the consequences of students' growing reluctance to debate? Though it represents a welcome departure from the polarized mudslinging of the 90's culture wars, it also represents a failure to fully engage with the world, a failure to test one's convictions against the logic and passions of others. It suggests a closing off of the possibilities of growth and transformation and a repudiation of the process of consensus building. "It doesn't bode well for democratic practice in this country," Professor Anderson said. "To keep democracy vital, it's important that students learn to integrate debate into their lives and see it modeled for them, in a productive way, when they're in school."

SUMMARIZE

Write a 50- to 100-word summary of this piece that accurately conveys the perspectives Kakutani presents in her article.

What kinds of sources does Kakutani use in her article? How do these sources contribute to her piece? Can you think of other sources she might have consulted and cited to make her article more complete?

In the last paragraph of her article, Kakutani poses the following question: "What are the consequences of students' growing reluctance to debate?" Although she provides a few answers of her own, what do you think the consequences are? Explain your answer.

Mike Theiler/Getty Images

FIGURE 6-1

As several writers in this chapter point out, it's difficult to accurately characterize an entire generation—and yet we try. Members of the generation called the Millennials, Generation Y, or Generation Next are said, for example, to be less engaged with the world around them because they are so absorbed with themselves. But this photograph, of Georgetown University students protesting Immigration and Naturalization Service registration requirements for foreign students, makes the case that rebelliousness and a passion for justice are alive and well among young people. Using your own experiences as a starting point, how would you characterize the social and political awareness and engagement of college students today?

philanthropist
practice of
performing
charitable actions
love of mankind

altruistic
unselfish
concern for
others   generous

REALISTIC IDE...

Alex Williams

1 Lynn Grossman, a writer in Manhattan who is married to the actor Bob Balaban, comes from a long line of social activists. Her mother joined the civil rights movement, and she herself marched in protest of the Vietnam War. But she said that things had changed by the time her eldest daughter, Mariah, now 27, came of age.

2 For many in Mariah's generation, community service was little more than a requirement that private schools imposed for graduation. Some took brief working vacations in places like Costa Rica, or the Caribbean island of Dominica, where they helped build roads and houses. "These kids had never seen a hammer before," Ms. Grossman said with a laugh. "I don't know what they did aside from get suntans."

3 Now, she said, "things are completely different."

4 As an eighth grader, her youngest daughter, Hazel, transformed a basement storage room in a Brooklyn homeless shelter into a library stocked with 5,000 volumes. At 13, she mobilized her fellow students to paint walls, hire librarians and design a functioning library-card system linked to a computer database. "We were floored," Ms. Grossman said. "And it's not just Hazel. A lot of kids out there are like this. They are like C.E.O.'s of community service."

5 Hazel Balaban, now a freshman at Connecticut College in New London, spent her first days on campus last week trying to organize a bake sale for victims of Hurricane Katrina. "It's almost expected," she said. "With the Internet and 24-hour TV, you just see all these problems. They're everywhere."

6 Hazel is at the leading edge of a generation whose sense of community involvement was born four years ago on Sept. 11, 2001. The attacks spurred an unprecedented outpouring of donations and volunteerism from Americans. Since then teenagers have witnessed the deadly Florida hurricane season of 2004, the more than 150,000 killed by the tsunami in Asia last December, and now Katrina. Encouraged by an increasing number of high schools with community service requirements and further motivated by college admissions offices looking for reasons to choose one honor student over another, teenagers are embracing social activism with the zeal of missionaries and the executive skills of seasoned philanthropists. Not only are more students participating, educators say, the scale of ambition seems to be continually increasing.

7 "We've seen a shift in the zeitgeist away from what you would call 'community service' and

more into social action," said Tom Krattenmaker, a spokesman for Swarthmore College near Philadelphia. "It's not just about working in a soup kitchen," he said, but about "creating new programs, shooting higher."

[8] Gregory Pyke, the senior associate dean of admission at Wesleyan University in Middletown, Conn., said that one recent applicant had started a Web-based initiative to collect eyeglasses—thousands of pairs—to be passed along to the needy in underprivileged countries. Another created a large-scale program to collect and refurbish discarded computers before passing them along to the poor. "The number of discussions where a dean is pulling us aside and saying, 'You have to hear about what this kid has done' has also gone up," he said.

[9] While cynics—and not a few colleges—may question whether the young people initiating such grand projects are looking to impress admissions officers, Mr. Pyke said he thought that most of the motivation was altruistic. "These are kids who are aware of many ways in which the world is a pretty lousy place," he said. "They want to exercise more authority in the world than adults give them credit for."

[10] Educators, sociologists and parents explain the outpouring of youthful philanthropy by noting that this generation has been bombarded not only by bad news, all of which seems to demand an immediate response, but by calls to action from political leaders and celebrities. Disaster relief, unlike opposition to the Vietnam War, which stirred many in their parents' generation, is uncontroversial and encourages wide-scale participation. And once roused, young people have greater tools at their disposal, particularly the Internet, to expand projects.

[11] More than 82 percent of high school seniors performed volunteer work, according to the 2004 American Freshman survey, a nationwide poll conducted by a graduate division of the University of California, Los Angeles, compared with just over 74 percent a decade earlier, and 66 percent in 1989.

[12] The Collegiate Challenge program run by Habitat for Humanity in which students spend a week of their summer building housing for the poor in cities throughout the nation, has grown twelve-fold since it started in 1989, said Alynn Woodson, the manager. It has seen a 30 percent growth in participation by high school students in the last two years. "In some ways service has gotten to be kind of a trendy thing to do," Ms. Woodson said.

[13] Katrina is the cause of the moment, and students across the country have responded like seasoned aid workers. By Sept. 2, four days after the storm came ashore in Alabama, Louisiana and Mississippi, students at Westside High School in Houston had raised more than $16,000 for the American Red Cross.

[14] "We have 2,870 students," said Noralea Jordan, the senior class president, who helped organize the drive. "If we made $16,000 in a day, I'm sure in another week we could triple that."

[15] That same day, students at Boiling Springs High School in South Carolina collected 6,000 gallons of bottled water. "We're not very good at our football, but it's been said by rival football teams, 'Whenever it comes to things that matter, Boiling Springs always gets the job done,'" said Jessica Gregg, 17, the student body president.

[16] At many schools students were ready to mobilize because they have had so much practice. Cloydia Garrette, 17, the student council president at Jack Yates High School in Houston and a veteran of drives to raise money for tsunami victims, leukemia research and Ronald McDonald House, collected clothes and other essentials when evacuees from New Orleans began to

reach the Astrodome. Charity is infectious, she said, "A lot of kids see us doing it, and they're following along."

[17] Once rare, community service is now mandatory for an increasing number of schools in all 50 states, said Jennifer Piscatelli, a policy analyst at the Education Commission of the States. Maryland requires every high school student to perform 75 hours of public service to graduate, and similar requirements exist at school districts in Chicago, Los Angeles and Philadelphia. College officials have taken such activity into account when making admission decisions. Bruce Walker, the vice provost and director of admissions for the University of Texas in Austin, said the university, which is faced with an increasing number of qualified candidates, is paying more attention to applicants' public service, or as he said, "what kind of citizen they were, and are."

[18] But even increased basic requirements do not seem to account for the grandiosity of initiatives on the part of many teenagers, educators say. "It's kind of intimidating to see what some kids have done," Mr. Walker said. In Owings Mills, Md., two high school freshmen, Greg Becker and Michael Swirnow, exceeded the McDonogh School's 40-hour community service requirement by doing 500 hours. Starting when they were 14, the boys set out to raise money to build a house for a struggling family in Baltimore through Habitat for Humanity.

[19] "Sometimes, doing everything you can isn't enough," said Greg, who initiated the effort. Through meetings with executives at various foundations and a raffle that raised $42,000 (a Mini Cooper was the top prize), the students collected $88,000.

[20] "At first, I never really thought about it as something for college," said Michael, now 15. "As it went on, though, it suddenly hit me: this is going to be huge on my college application."

[21] Such examples of over-the-top public service can put a competitive pressure on other families who believe colleges are watching. For those who have yet to fall into line with the trend, the anxieties can be great. "I've had three families come in today saying, 'What is this community service thing?'" said Howard Greene, a private college admissions consultant in Manhattan.

[22] But some college admissions counselors have already grown skeptical about what's known in the trade as the "How I Saved the World" essay, as well as about projects that just happen to commence early in a student's junior year. "There are two sides, to me," said Jim Bock, dean of admissions and financial aid at Swarthmore, which this past year received 300 more freshman applications than the previous year. "One is the jaded side—is it a strategy? The other side is, is it part of a new generation of students who really are committed to making a better world?"

[23] Mr. Bock noted that his college put a high premium on public service: it highlights Swarthmore students' antigenocide initiatives in Sudan alongside its main features on its Web home page. Two weeks ago Mr. Bock watched a colleague ask nearly 400 freshman at an orientation seminar how many had done community service projects in high school.

[24] "I'll have to admit I was moved," Mr. Bock said. "Ninety-five percent of the freshmen stood up."

[25] Katherine Cohen, a college admissions consultant who has discussed community service with many high school students in Manhattan, noted that admitting such candidates was in the colleges' self-interest. "Colleges love to see fund-raisers, of course," Ms. Cohen said. "Ding-ding-ding, the bell goes off, because they want to see money raised in the future" for their own endowments.

[26] Teenagers who pull off outsize projects shrug off suspicions that their aims were

other than altruistic. Michael Swirnow, the Maryland youth who helped raise $88,000 for Habitat for Humanity, said the motivating factor was to "give back" to the less fortunate. "I think the most important thing is I learned I'm capable of doing something this big," he said. "It's about confidence."

27 Several educators said that it didn't really matter in the end whether teenagers were expending effort out of self-interest or altruism so long as good deeds were done. Some level of self-interest, after all, is why kids read books and do homework.

28 "This is a generation that was born after the consciousness revolution" of the 1960's and 70's, said William Strauss, the co-author with Neil Howe of *Millennials Rising: The Next Great Generation*, a portrait of Americans born after 1982. "A lot of them are now children of baby boomers, and they look at them as a generation that looked at the self instead of the community. Now they've turned that around. Generations set themselves apart by correcting the mistakes they perceive their parents to have made."

SUMMARIZE AND RESPOND

Write a 100-word summary of Williams' article and a 100-word response. Use your response to comment on the tone of the article. Do you feel like the article takes a side on the issue it addresses? Should it? Why or why not?

ANALYZE

Who do you think is Williams' target audience for this article? Point to specific elements of the article to support your response.

DISCUSS

Late in his article, Williams writes: "Several educators said that it didn't really matter in the end whether teenagers were expending effort out of self-interest or altruism so long as good deeds were done." Do you agree with this statement? Why or why not?

ARGUE

Using the Williams article as a starting point, write a brief argument in which you define "community service." As you compose your definition, make sure you present clear criteria for the term and include examples of actions that fit those criteria, as well as actions that don't.

Reporters Larry Gordon and Louis Sahagun wrote this piece for the February 27, 2007, edition the Los Angeles Times *to shed light on research about self-esteem and self-image among teens and young adults. The three pieces that follow this one deal with similar issues.*

GEN Y'S EGO TRIP TAKES A BAD TURN

A new report suggests that an overdose of self-esteem in college students could mean a rough road ahead.

Larry Gordon and Louis Sahagun

[1] No wonder YouTube is so popular.

[2] All the effort to boost children's self-esteem may have backfired and produced a generation of college students who are more narcissistic than their Gen X predecessors, according to a new study led by a San Diego State University psychologist.

[3] And the Internet, with all its MySpace and YouTube braggadocio, is letting that self-regard blossom even more, said the analysis, titled "Egos Inflating Over Time."

[4] In the study being released today, researchers warn that a rising ego rush could cause personal and social problems for the Millennial Generation, also called Gen Y. People with an inflated sense of self tend to have less interest in emotionally intimate bonds and can lash out when rejected or insulted.

[5] "That makes me very, very worried," said Jean Twenge, a San Diego State associate professor and lead author of the report. "I'm concerned we are heading to a society where people are going to treat each other badly, either on the street or in relationships."

[6] She and four other researchers from the University of Michigan, University of Georgia and University of South Alabama looked at the results of psychological surveys taken by more than 16,000 college students across the country over more than 25 years.

[7] The Narcissistic Personality Inventory asks students to react to such statements as: "If I ruled the world, it would be a better place," "I think I am a special person" and "I like to be the center of attention."

[8] The study found that almost two-thirds of recent college students had narcissism scores that were above the average 1982 score. Thirty percent more college students showed elevated narcissism in 2006 than in 1982.

[9] Twenge said she and her coauthors are not suggesting that more students today have a pathological narcissistic personality disorder that needs psychiatric treatment. Still, traits of narcissism have increased by moderate but significant amounts, said Twenge, who last year published a book titled "Generation Me: Why Today's Young Americans Are More Confident, Assertive, Entitled—and More Miserable Than Ever Before."

[10] The narcissism report is under review for publication in a scholarly journal, which

would give it the stamp of academic recognition it now lacks.

[11] It was released, Twenge said, in connection with the upcoming paperback edition of her book and with a student affairs workshop today at the University of San Diego at which she and another speaker will discuss how today's college students approach education.

[12] Some of the increase in narcissistic attitudes was probably caused by the self-esteem programs that many elementary schools adopted 20 years ago, the study suggests. It notes that nursery schools began to have children sing songs that proclaim: "I am special, I am special. Look at me."

[13] Those youngsters are now adolescents obsessed with websites, such as MySpace and YouTube, that "permit self-promotion far beyond that allowed by traditional media," the report says.

[14] Other trends in American culture, including permissive parenting, increased materialism and the fascination with celebrities and reality TV shows, may also heighten self-regard, said study coauthor W. Keith Campbell, psychology professor at the University of Georgia. "It's part of a whole cultural system," he said.

[15] The researchers seek to counter theories that current college students are more civic-minded and involved in volunteer activities than their predecessors. Because many high schools require community work, increases in volunteering "may not indicate a return to civic orientation but may instead be the means toward the more self-focused goal of educational attainment," the report says.

[16] An annual survey of U.S. college freshmen by the Higher Education Research Institute at UCLA has found growing interest in public service and social responsibility, presumably in response to Hurricane Katrina and other disasters around the world.

[17] But that survey also showed that current freshmen are much more interested in financial success and less in "a meaningful philosophy of life" than students were in the 1970s.

[18] At Cal State Long Beach on Monday, an informal survey produced divided opinions about Gen Y personality traits.

[19] Students and teachers said they often see examples of inflated egos on campus: students who converse in the computer center while others are trying to concentrate, preen in front of the reflecting windows of the economics building or expect good grades simply for showing up at class.

[20] Laura Rantala, 26, a sociology major, said the phenomenon got in the way of a survey she conducted last semester on the attitudes of men and women about jury duty.

[21] "It took about three minutes to complete the survey," she recalled. "But many students were so self-absorbed they didn't want to participate.

[22] "I think it's because we all have our own cell phone and iPod with which we're doing our own thing in our own little world," she mused.

[23] Some students seeking degrees in finance and management said, however, that they had good reason to stress confidence and esteem.

[24] James Coari, a lecturer in the College of Business Administration, agreed, to a point. In an interview in his office, Coari said, people looking for jobs "have to be concerned about image because competition is fierce."

[25] Marc Flacks, an assistant professor of sociology, said that he believed that narcissism was too harsh a description for current students and that it was more important to discuss why "we have a society in which narcissistic behavior is a good quality to have."

[26] "This is a bottom-line society, so students are smart to seek the most direct route to the bottom line," he added. "If you don't have a me-first attitude, you won't succeed."

[27] Flacks summed up the attitudes he often encounters in students, who expect a tangible payoff from their education:

[28] "The old model was a collegial one in which students and professors alike sought knowledge for knowledge's sake. The new model is 'I paid my money, give me my grade and degree.' It makes me want to ask [students], 'Want fries with that order?'"

SUMMARIZE AND RESPOND

Write a 50-word summary of this article. In your summary, make sure you accurately and fairly convey the authors' central idea.

ANALYZE

As a news report, this article isn't necessarily supposed to present an outright argument. Reread the piece carefully. Do you think it presents a position on the issue? If so, why do you think this? If not, how do the authors avoid doing this? Point to specific elements in the text to support your response.

DISCUSS

The article reports that "[p]eople with an inflated sense of self tend to have less interest in emotionally intimate bonds and can lash out when rejected or insulted." How might this affect someone's ability to develop personal and professional relationships?

While Larry Gordon and Louis Sahagun, in the preceding article, focus on a particular research study, Melissa Ludwig takes a broader look at "Generation Next" and its propensity for self-expression via the Internet. Ludwig wrote this piece for the March 25, 2007, edition of the San Antonio Express-News.

LOOK@ME: GENERATION NEXT IS LIVING OUT LOUD AND ONLINE

Melissa Ludwig

[1] Jackie Davis knows people talk trash about her.

[2] On her MySpace.com page, the self-described party girl, club promoter and 22-year-old student at the University of Texas at San Antonio has photos of herself dressed to the nines out on the town and on the beach clad in an orange bikini.

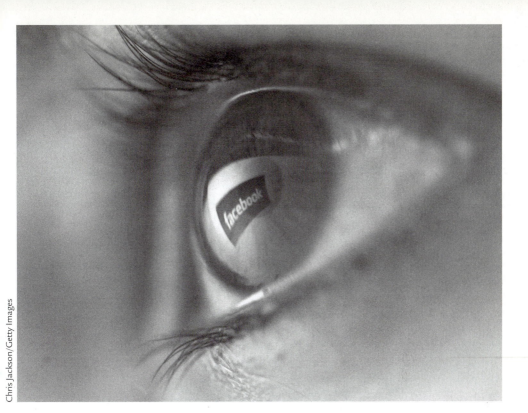

Chris Jackson/Getty Images

FIGURE 6-2

To hear some critics describe them, social networking sites such as Facebook, MySpace, and YouTube have a mesmerizing effect on their users, leading to everything from a decline in reading and writing skills to the end of modesty and discretion. Those who use the sites, however, see them in a far different light, saying they offer unprecedented opportunities for creativity and networking. Where do you fall on this continuum? Do you see these sites as having more positive or negative effects? Why?

In one photo, Jackie is wearing a skin-tight black leather Catwoman costume, two triangles of vinyl struggling to cover her silicone-enhanced breasts.

3 "People have said stuff about it," Davis said of the Web page. "I think in part it is because I have fake boobs. It doesn't mean I'm like a porn star. I mean, give me a break. In 10 years, I am not going to look like this. I want to remember that I used to be hot."

4 Her message to the trash talkers?

5 "I just am who I am. I am not going to apologize for it," Davis said. "Everyone who really knows me knows I am a good person. Other than that, why do I care?"

6 That could be an anthem for Davis' generation, a group of 18- to 25-year-olds who have been dubbed Millennials, Generation Next or the "Look at me" generation.

7 In these kids, a combination of self-confidence and technological savvy has led to the explosion of Web sites such as YouTube, which allows users to upload homemade

videos, and social networking sites such as MySpace and Facebook, where anyone can create a personalized Web site to message friends and post pictures, blogs, videos and music.

8 Much of the stuff floating around in cyberspace is tame, mundane even. But there also is plenty that's racy, embarrassing or squeamishly intimate. Bad or good, Generation Next is living out loud and doing it online, before a global audience, in a medium where digital archives may linger for a long, long time.

9 Young and old alike tout the positive aspects of the communication revolution: It empowers regular folks to create, innovate or mobilize around a cause. But there's also fear, especially among parents, that Nexters just now crossing over into "real life" still are too young to fully grasp the permanence of their online actions, and the possible consequences down the road.

10 "It is scary," said Jeanne Culver, a mother from Dallas whose daughter Katy is a freshman at Trinity University. "It is uncharted waters for the parents and the children. We are all experiencing it for the first time together."

11 Already, there are famous examples of how the Internet can come back to bite you: the Paris Hilton sex tape; Miss Nevada USA, Katie Rees, who lost her crown over risqué pictures that showed up on MySpace; Frenchie Davis, an "American Idol" contestant booted off the show after posing topless for an adult Web site.

12 In their own lives, college students say they know people who have been stalked, had their identities stolen or had relationships go sour after a revealing picture or message surfaced online.

13 So why do they do it?

14 Because it's part of life, Davis said.

15 "I have to be aware that those pictures will be there forever. People can copy that, it can be on Google someday. I can be married to a senator and that stuff will come up," she said.

16 "And like, I know that, but at the same time, I don't feel like not living life because of the chances of something happening."

17 Brooke Johnson, a 20-year-old UTSA student who blogs on her own Web site, agreed.

18 "I think it's pretty neat that people can know things about me," Johnson said. "Technology is allowing us to do amazing things and communicate in totally different ways. People abuse it, but people abuse anything."

Generation Me

19 Wednesday, 11:30 a.m., Starbucks.

20 Davis' reddish-brown hair is stuffed into a corduroy pageboy cap and her lightly freckled cheek still bears the indent of her pillow. She sits down with an iced coffee and later digs into a gold quilted bebe bag for her cigarettes.

21 Davis says she got on MySpace about a year ago, when she started doing club promotions. Before that, she thought it was a bunch of "punk rock kids and creeper guys," people who found it easier to talk online than in person.

22 Now, she checks her MySpace page every day. She has upward of 800 friends, an array of photos and ads for sexy-sounding clubs like Bliss Ultra Lounge.

23 She doesn't disown the popular party girl portrayed on the site. As a club promoter, she gets paid to be that person. But the inner Jackie stays offline, she said.

24 "I don't want people to feel like they intimately know me," she said.

25 She never would blog about her personal life under her own name, isn't interested in

meeting men online and never would pose nude.

26 Other college students do: At Boston University, an edgy sex magazine called Boink employs fellow students as models to exemplify the publication's tagline: "College Sex by the People Having It."

27 The closest thing at UTSA is Study Breaks, a lightweight entertainment magazine where the student models often are scantily clad, but not nude.

28 For Davis, the Internet is about marketing.

29 "This is the information age. They had industrialism where it's like, 'What can you build?' Now, it's like, 'Who do you know and what do you know?' It's the world we live in and MySpace is free marketing."

30 Brooke Johnson also is marketing herself online, but in a totally different way.

31 Johnson writes poetry and blogs about her life on a Web site she created. Many of the posts are abstract, but some get specific about her upbringing, her struggles moving to San Antonio from a small town and inner conflicts over character flaws like bossiness.

32 Johnson wouldn't be caught dead online in a Catwoman suit, but her blog has the kind of soul searching that would make Davis squirm.

33 Granted, her audience isn't wide. It's mostly for parents and friends to understand how she feels without "getting out a bongo drum and turning down the lights," Johnson said.

34 But she wouldn't mind a larger readership.

35 "We all do it for attention, I guess," Johnson said. "In the least vain way possible, I think I have valid things to say and I want people to know."

36 That attitude is more common among college students these days, said Jean Twenge, a psychology professor at San Diego State University in California.

37 Twenge, the author of "Generation Me," said her research shows about one-third more college kids today are narcissistic than college kids were in the 1980s, a trend she believes grew out of the self-esteem movement of the 1970s and '80s.

38 "Since birth, their generation has heard you need to put yourself first, that loving yourself is the most important thing, you shouldn't care what anyone thinks about you," Twenge said. "This is not something the baby boomers heard in the '50s."

39 Facebook, MySpace and YouTube provide an outlet to a generation of voices competing to be heard, she said. The sites have gone beyond touching base with friends to an arena where people vie for the most digital friends, the best videos, the coolest sites, and biggest audience.

40 "Now it all becomes a competition, seeking attention and seeking status rather than a true connection between people, or a meaningful connection," Twenge said.

41 In addition, many young people believe MySpace will launch them to stardom. In a recent poll conducted by the Pew Research Center, half of all 18- to 25-year-olds listed being famous as an important goal for their generation.

42 "I know some girls who are modeling or actresses and think they are going to get on Maxim and all that off of their MySpace," said Liz Bernardo, a 20-year-old student at UTSA and 2004 Miss Austin Teen USA.

43 Bernardo, who grew out of her own teenage modeling dreams, laughs at the notion.

44 "I never thought by having a profile I would become famous."

Get Used to It

45 For every self-promoter, however, there is someone like Charity Pierce or Samantha Schoenfeld, two UTSA students who use social networking sites strictly for communication with friends and family.

46 Both have profiles on MySpace and Facebook, but they are closed to any user who hasn't been accepted as a friend. Because they are in a sorority, they are required to keep their sites clean: no sloppy drunk photos.

47 Yet they spend hours on the sites.

48 "If you don't want to do homework, just get on Facebook. It's addicting," Pierce said.

49 Pierce is pretty typical. According to the Pew poll, 54 percent of Generation Nexters said their peers spent too much time on social networking sites, and 72 percent feel others post too much personal information on the Internet.

50 Pierce freaked out when a friend told her—after the fact—that she met someone online and gave him her address to come pick her up for a date.

51 "And that's just creepy," Pierce said. "It's so. . . ."

52 "Scary," Schoenfeld finished.

53 "Bizarre," Pierce added.

54 In addition to her sorority, Pierce believes employers and college officials are keeping tabs on these sites.

55 There are stories like that of a New York journalist who, after discovering her 26-year-old nanny was blogging about life in their household, fired her. Or three students at the University of Mississippi who were investigated for creating a Facebook group composed of students who wanted to have sex with a particular professor.

56 "I am graduating soon and I can't risk anyone getting a misconception about me," Pierce said.

57 But spying on social networking sites isn't yet widespread among employers.

58 "I have not heard of employers actively using it," said Becky Woods, vice president of human resources at the Doherty Employment Group, a Minneapolis company that does staffing and human resources outsourcing. "The buzz is about, should we or should we not?"

59 Woods said trying to judge applicants' work performance by what they put on a Web site is tricky.

60 "It is like putting on a stage show, and I am not sure that stage show is what employers should look for," Woods said.

61 Matthew Williams, a student at San Antonio College, agreed.

62 "A lot of stuff you put on there is not what you would say or do in real life. It is more extreme or more dopey than normal stuff," Williams said.

63 Still, once you hit go, you lose control of information, said Alan Weinkrantz, the 53-year-old owner of a high tech public relations firm and an avid blogger.

64 "It is like giving a car to a 16-year-old kid," Weinkrantz said. "Hey, it's freedom, it's neat, but you can also run over and kill someone."

65 Time and space shrink very fast in cyberspace, he said.

66 "With all the goodness of speed, you have to teach the kids to say: 'Stop. Do you really want to say this?' If you don't care, then you don't care. But realize there are consequences of not caring. You are putting an imprint of yourself that could linger for years on end that you could not take down."

67 For instance, Williams, the SAC student, blogs on MySpace about his view that Sept. 11, 2001, attacks may have been the work of the U.S. government. He wants to run for public office some day, and isn't sure whether those views may hurt or help him.

68 "If it's true, someone might pull up my MySpace and say, 'Look at this guy, he

knew the truth,'" Williams said. "If it is before the government acknowledges they took part in it, it could very well hurt my run for president."

69 Despite the cautionary tales, it's likely trial and error that will shape how people behave in this new social media.

70 "Lots of the rules that I grew up with are not rules anymore," said Cyndi Taylor Krier, a regent for the University of Texas System. "Lots of new ways of communicating have taken their place. (Young people) view (the Internet) the way we viewed picking up a phone and calling somebody when we were their age."

71 Old notions of privacy also have changed. In an age where you can Google people and find their address and phone number, where the government can drop in on your calls and where every carton of ice cream you buy is logged into a database, what does privacy mean anymore, many kids ask.

72 "The government and everyone else knows everything about you anyway," Davis said. "It's done, the Internet is here, the Internet broadcasts everything, what can you do about it? Get used to it."

SUMMARIZE AND RESPOND

Write a 50- to 100-word summary of this piece, followed by a 100-word response.

DISCUSS

Ludwig reports that "54 percent of Generation Nexters said their peers spent too much time on social networking sites" and that "72 percent feel others post too much personal information on the Internet." How much time do you spend on social networking sites each day? How do you use these sites? Do you see any reasons to be cautious about what you post on them?

ANALYZE

What kinds of pathetic appeals does Ludwig use in her article? How does she use them? Are they effective?

ARGUE

Ludwig quotes psychologist Jean Twenge as saying that social networking sites, rather than being a means to "a true connection between people, or a meaningful connection," often turn into attention-seeking competitions. Write a brief essay in which you agree or disagree with Twenge's position, using material from this article or others in the chapter to support your argument.

Jonah Goldberg, editor-at-large of National Review Online, *presents in the following essay another perspective on the supposed runaway narcissism of Generation Y. He also examines some possible causes of the self-esteem surge in young people over the past two decades. His essay was first published on August 8, 2007, on the* National Review Online *website.*

ISN'T THAT SPECIAL?

Jonah Goldberg

[1] A horrendous national shortage gripped America in the 1970s. The forces of progress rallied the American people to, in a spirit of shared purpose, combat our collective need. The leader of this movement donned a sweater and went on TV to lift the nation from its malaise.

[2] Jimmy Carter and the energy crisis? Feh. That was nothing compared to the more acute scarcity that plagued America in those dark days. I'm referring, of course, to the '70s self-esteem famine, during which cardigan-sporting Fred Rogers heroically served as a Jimmy Carter for the preschool set.

[3] These investments in self-esteem paid off royally, according to a report, "Egos Inflating Over Time." Jean Twenge of San Diego State University and a team of psychologists combed through the answers of 16,475 college students nationwide who took the Narcissistic Personality Inventory survey between 1982 and 2006. Their conclusion: Today's American youth are the most self-absorbed since we've studied the subject. "We need to stop endlessly repeating, 'You're special,' and having children repeat that back," Twenge told the Associated Press. "Kids are self-centered enough already."

[4] It seems to be a distinctly American problem. Immigrant kids are less likely, for instance, to see good grades and high compliments as a birthright.

[5] Don Chance, a finance professor at Louisiana State University, recently told the *Wall Street Journal* that Asian-born students don't argue about every bad grade. They respond to such esteem-deflating feedback by working harder.

[6] I suspect that Twenge and Chance are largely right, but the hand-wringing about youth's sense of entitlement can go overboard. Volunteerism is on the rise, not something you would necessarily expect even after discounting for the desire to pad transcripts and resumes. The best of our supposedly pampered young men seem more than able to adjust to the culture of self-sacrifice animating our armed forces.

[7] Nonetheless, what I find fascinating is how our narcissism surplus, to some extent, is the unintended consequence of trying to use psychology as just another branch of public health. Saturday-morning cartoons during my youth were peppered with public-service announcements informing kids that, "The most important person in the whole wide world is you." The long-running TV show *Wonderama* became *Kids Are People Too* to reflect a new seriousness of childhood. The burgeoning "children's rights" movement—to which a young Hillary Clinton was connected—saw treating kids as peers to be of a piece with the new egalitarianism. Movies as diverse as *Taxi Driver*, *Bugsy Malone*, and *Irreconcilable Differences* fixated on treating kids like adults in one way or another.

[8] The result? Large numbers of kids raised to be like adults have concluded that they

want to stay kids, or at least teens. People my age hate being called "Mr." or "Mrs." by kids. Grown women read idiotic magazines, obsess over maintaining a teenager's body, and follow the exploits of Lindsay Lohan. Grown men have been following professional wrestling and playing video games for 25 years.

9 I'm part of these trends. Not only do I still enjoy *The Simpsons*, but I'm addicted to shows like *House* and *Grey's Anatomy*.

10 Consider that in the old days, Marcus Welby and Ben Casey were the ideal: selfless father figures in surgical garb, dispensing not just medical advice but authoritative life counseling. Modern-day *House*, by contrast, is about a defiantly drug-addicted doctor who admits week after week that he doesn't care about his patients, but merely about the personal satisfaction of solving a medical mystery. In *Grey's Anatomy*, horribly wounded patients are wheeled through each episode to serve as metaphors for the relationship problems of the residents. Impaled by a steel rod? That reminds me,

my boyfriend hasn't told me he loves me today! The patients often die, but at least the doctors learn important life lessons about dating.

11 Another result is that the generation taught to share and care beyond all precedent has become the most singularly concerned in history with making a buck. A recent UCLA study found that nearly 75 percent of college freshmen think that it's important to be rich, compared with 62.5 percent in 1980 and 42 percent in 1966.

12 Americans, young and old, are better than these surveys and TV shows would suggest. (Just as you might say they were "worse" than *Marcus Welby, M.D.* and *I Love Lucy* suggested.) Even the most arrogant kids learn that they aren't the most important people in the whole wide world and that there's more to life than money. They usually learn these lessons when they have kids of their own. Indeed, one could say we're learning nationally what parents have been learning personally for millenniums. You can't live your kids' lives for them.

SUMMARIZE

Write a 50-word summary of Goldberg's central argument. Do you agree with his position? Explain your response.

ANALYZE

Write a brief analysis of the ethos Goldberg presents in his essay. How does he want his audience to think of him? What does he do to achieve this effect?

ARGUE

Goldberg contends that an overabundance of self-esteem in young people "seems to be a distinctly American problem." Write a one-page response in which you agree or disagree with this statement.

Although not responding specifically to the articles that precede it, Nicholas Handler does send a message to those who label his generation selfish and shallow: "We are writing a revolution. We are just putting it in our own words." Handler was a junior at Yale University, majoring in history, when he wrote this essay for the September 30, 2007, edition of the New York Times.

THE POSTEVERYTHING GENERATION

Nicholas Handler

1 I never expected to gain any new insight into the nature of my generation, or the changing landscape of American colleges, in lit theory. Lit theory is supposed to be the class where you sit at the back of the room with every other jaded sophomore wearing skinny jeans, thick-framed glasses, an ironic T-shirt and oversize retro headphones, just waiting for the lecture to be over so you can light up a Turkish Gold and walk to lunch while listening to Wilco. That's pretty much the way I spent the course, too; through structuralism, formalism, gender theory and postcolonialism, I was far too busy shuffling through my iPod to see what the patriarchal world order of capitalist oppression had to do with "Ethan Frome." But when we began to study postmodernism, something struck a chord with me and made me sit up and look anew at the seemingly blasé college-age literati of which I was so self-consciously one.

2 According to my textbook, the problem with defining postmodernism is that it's impossible to. The difficulty is that it is so...post. It defines itself so negatively against what came before it—naturalism, romanticism and the wild revolution of modernism—that it's sometimes hard to see what it actually is. It denies that anything can be explained neatly or even at all. It is parodic, detached, strange and sometimes menacing to traditionalists who do not understand it. Although it arose in the postwar West, the generation that has witnessed its rise has yet to come up with an explanation of what postmodern attitudes mean for the future of culture or society. The subject intrigued me because, in a class otherwise consumed by dead-letter theories, postmodernism remained an open book, tempting to the young and curious. But it also intrigued me because the question of what postmodernism—what a movement so posteverything, so reticent to define itself—is spoke to a larger question about the political and popular culture of today, of the other jaded sophomores sitting around me who grew up in a postmodern world.

3 In many ways, my generation is also extremely post: post-cold war, postindustrial, post-baby boom, post-9/11. At one point in his famous text "Postmodernism, or the Cultural Logic of Late Capitalism," the literary critic Fredric Jameson even calls us postliterate. We are a generation that is riding on the tail end of a century of war and revolution that toppled civilizations, overturned repressive social orders and left us with more privilege and opportunity than any other society in history. Ours could be an era to accomplish anything.

4 And yet do we take to the streets and the airwaves and say, "Here we are, and this is what we demand"? Do we plant our flag of youthful rebellion on the Mall in Washington and say: "We are not leaving until we see change! Our eyes have been opened by our education, and our conception of what is possible has been expanded by our privilege and we demand a better world

because it is our right"? It would seem that we do the opposite. We go to war without so much as questioning the rationale; we sign away our civil liberties; we say nothing when the Supreme Court cites Brown v. Board of Education in restricting efforts to combat segregation; and we sit back to watch the carnage on the evening news.

[5] On campus, we sign petitions, join organizations, put our names on mailing lists, make small-money contributions, volunteer a spare hour to tutor and sport an entire wardrobe's worth of LiveStrong-like bracelets advertising our moderately priced opposition to everything from breast cancer to global warming. But what do we really stand for? A true postmodern generation, we refuse to weave together an overarching narrative to our own political consciousness, to present a cast of inspirational or revolutionary characters on our public stage or to define a specific philosophy. We are a story seemingly without direction or theme, structure or meaning—a generation defined negatively against what came before us. When Al Gore once said, "It's the combination of narcissism and nihilism that really defines postmodernism," he might as well have been echoing his entire generation's critique of our own. We are a generation for whom even revolution seems trite, and therefore as fair a target for bland imitation as anything else. We are the generation of the Che Guevara T-shirt.

[6] Jameson calls it "pastiche": "the wearing of a linguistic mask, speech in a dead language." In literature, this means an author speaking in a style that is not his own—borrowing a voice and continuing to use it until the words lose all meaning and the chaos that is real life sets in. It is an imitation of an imitation, something that has been re-envisioned so many times that the original model is no longer relevant or recognizable. It is mass-produced individualism, anticipated revolution. It is

why postmodernism lacks cohesion, why it seems to lack purpose or direction. For us, the posteverything generation, pastiche is the use and reuse of the old clichés of social change and moral outrage—a perfunctory rebelliousness that has culminated in the age of rapidly multiplying nonprofits and relief funds. We live our lives in masks and speak our minds in a dead language—the language of a society that expects us to agitate because that's what young people do.

[7] But how do we rebel against a generation that is expecting, anticipating, nostalgic for revolution? How do we rebel against parents who sometimes seem to want revolution more than we do? We don't. We rebel by not rebelling. We wear the defunct masks of protest and moral outrage, but the real energy in campus activism is on the Internet, with Web sites like MoveOn.org. It is in the rapidly developing ability to communicate ideas and frustration in chat rooms instead of on the streets, and to channel them into nationwide projects striving earnestly for moderate and peaceful change. We are the generation of Students Taking Action Now Darfur. We are the Rock the Vote generation, the generation of letter-writing campaigns and public-interest lobbies, the alternative-energy generation.

[8] College as America once knew it—as an incubator of radical social change—is coming to an end. To our generation the word "radicalism" evokes images of Al Qaeda, not the Weathermen. "Campus takeover" sounds more like Virginia Tech in 2007 than Columbia University in 1968. Such phrases are from a dead language to us. They are words from another era that do not reflect the realities of today. The technological revolution, however—the MoveOn.org revolution, the revolution of the Organization Kid—is just as real and just as profound as the revolution of the 1960s; it is just not as visible. It is a work in progress, but it is there. Perhaps when our parents finally

stop pointing out the things that we are not, the stories that we do not write, they will see the threads of our narrative begin to come together. They will see that behind our pastiche, the postgeneration speaks in a language that does make sense. We are writing a revolution. We are just putting it in our own words.

SUMMARIZE AND RESPOND

What is the central argument Handler is trying to make about his generation? Do you think his essay is effective? Why or why not?

ANALYZE

Which of the rhetorical appeals (to ethos, pathos, or logos) does Handler use most effectively in his essay? Make sure you point to specific examples of the appeal at work in the text to support your analysis.

DISCUSS

What do you think Swann means when he writes, "How do we rebel against parents who sometimes seem to want revolution more than we do? We don't. We rebel by not rebelling." How does he use this passage to develop his central argument?

Alan Finder writes about higher education for the New York Times, *where this article was published on May 2, 2007. In his piece, notice how Finder uses several different sources to explore the causes behind what he reports is a growth in religious life on campuses. Notice, too, the critical difference between the acknowledgment of sources in journalistic and academic writing: Journalists almost never use in-text citations or works cited pages, which are requirements in the writing you'll do in most of your classes.*

MATTERS OF FAITH FIND A NEW PROMINENCE ON CAMPUS

Alan Finder

[1] Peter J. Gomes has been at Harvard University for 37 years, and says he remembers when religious people on campus felt under siege. To be seen as religious often meant being dismissed as not very bright, he said.

[2] No longer. At Harvard these days, said Professor Gomes, the university preacher, "There is probably more active religious life now than there has been in 100 years."

[3] Across the country, on secular campuses as varied as Colgate University, the University of Wisconsin and the University of California, Berkeley, chaplains, professors and administrators say students are drawn

to religion and spirituality with more fervor than at any time they can remember.

4 More students are enrolling in religion courses, even majoring in religion; more are living in dormitories or houses where matters of faith and spirituality are a part of daily conversation; and discussion groups are being created for students to grapple with questions like what happens after death, dozens of university officials said in interviews.

5 A survey on the spiritual lives of college students, the first of its kind, showed in 2004 that more than two-thirds of 112,000 freshmen surveyed said they prayed, and that almost 80 percent believed in God. Nearly half of the freshmen said they were seeking opportunities to grow spiritually, according to the survey by the Higher Education Research Institute at the University of California, Los Angeles.

6 Compared with 10 or 15 years ago, "there is a greater interest in religion on campus, both intellectually and spiritually," said Charles L. Cohen, a professor of history and religious studies at the University of Wisconsin, Madison, who for a number of years ran an interdisciplinary major in religious studies. The program was created seven years ago and has 70 to 75 majors each year.

7 University officials explained the surge of interest in religion as partly a result of the rise of the religious right in politics, which they said has made questions of faith more talked about generally. In addition, they said, the attacks of Sept. 11 underscored for many the influence of religion on world affairs. And an influx of evangelical students at secular universities, along with an increasing number of international students, means students arrive with a broader array of religious experiences.

8 Professor Gomes (pronounced like "homes") said a more diverse student body at Harvard had meant that "the place is more representative of mainstream America."

9 "That provides a group of people who don't leave their religion at home," he said.

10 At Berkeley, a vast number of undergraduates are Asian-American, with many coming from observant Christian homes, said the Rev. Randy Bare, the Presbyterian campus pastor. "That's new, and it's a remarkable shift," Mr. Bare said.

11 There are 50 to 60 Christian groups on campus, and student attendance at Catholic and Presbyterian churches near campus has picked up significantly, he said. On many other campuses, though, the renewed interest in faith and spirituality has not necessarily translated into increased attendance at religious services.

12 The Rev. Lloyd Steffen, the chaplain at Lehigh University, is among those who think the war in Iraq has contributed to the interest in religion among students. "I suspect a lot of that has to do with uncertainty over the war," Mr. Steffen said.

13 "My theory is that the baby boomers decided they weren't going to impose their religious life on their children the way their parents imposed it on them," Mr. Steffen continued. "The idea was to let them come to it themselves. And then they get to campus and things happen; someone dies, a suicide occurs. Real issues arise for them, and they sometimes feel that they don't have resources to deal with them. And sometimes they turn to religion and courses in religion."

14 Increased participation in community service may also reflect spiritual yearning of students. "We don't use that kind of spiritual language anymore," said Rebecca S. Chopp, the Colgate president. "But if you look at the students, they do."

15 Some sociologists who study religion are skeptical that students' attitudes have changed significantly, citing a lack of data to compare current students with those of previous generations. But even some of those concerned about the data say something has shifted.

16 "All I hear from everybody is yes, there is growing interest in religion and spirituality and an openness on college campuses," said Christian Smith, a professor of sociology at the University of Notre Dame. "Everybody who is talking about it says something seems to be going on."

17 David D. Burhans, who retired after 33 years as chaplain at the University of Richmond, said many students "are really exploring, they are really interested in trying things out, in attending one another's services."

18 Lesleigh Cushing, an assistant professor of religion and Jewish studies at Colgate, said: "I can fill basically any class on the Bible. I wasn't expecting that."

19 When Benjamin Wright, chairman of the department of religion studies at Lehigh, arrived 17 years ago, two students chose to major in religion. This year there are 18 religion majors, and there were 30 two and three years ago.

20 At Harvard, more students are enrolling in religion courses and regularly attending religious services, Professor Gomes said. Presbyterian ministries at Berkeley and Wisconsin have built dormitories to offer spiritual services to students and encourage discussion among different faiths. The seven-story building on the Wisconsin campus, which will house 280 students, is to open in August.

21 At Colgate, five Buddhist and Hindu students received permission to live in a new apartment complex on the edge of campus this year. They call their apartment Asian Spirituality House and they use it for meetings and occasional religious events.

22 The number of student religious organizations at Colgate has grown to 11 from 5 in recent years. The university's Catholic, Protestant and Jewish chaplains oversee an array of programs and events. Many involve providing food to students, a phenomenon that the university chaplain, Mark Shiner, jokingly calls "gastro-evangelism."

23 Among the new clubs is one created last year to encourage students to hold wide-ranging dialogues about spirituality and faith. Meeting over lunch on Thursdays in the chapel's basement, the students talk about what happens when you die or the nature of Catholic spirituality.

24 Called the Heretics Club (the chaplains were looking to grab students' attention), the group listened to John Gattuso talk about his book, "Talking to God: Portrait of a World at Prayer" (Stone Creek Publications, 2006), a collection of essays and photos about prayer in world religions.

25 "Do you need to believe in God in order to pray?" Mr. Gattuso asked.

26 The discussion was off and running, with one student saying one needed only to believe in "something outside yourself" and another saying that "sometimes 'Thank you' can be a prayer."

27 Afterward, several students talked about what attracted them to the sessions, besides the sandwiches, chips and fruit. Gabe Conant, a junior, said he wanted to contemplate personal questions about his own faith. He described them this way: "What are these things I was raised in and do I want to keep them?"

SUMMARIZE AND RESPOND

Write a 50- to 100-word summary of Finder's article, followed by a 100-word response in which you address the following question: Do you find the author's portrayal of students' interests and needs to be accurate?

Richard Just was the online editor of The American Prospect *when he wrote this piece for the October 2005 edition of the publication, which describes itself as "an authoritative magazine of liberal ideas." In his article, Just explores political activism on college and university campuses nationwide. As you read, think about how the election of Barack Obama as president might affect some of Just's findings and arguments.*

SCHOOLS OF THOUGHT: THE LIBERAL-CONSERVATIVE DIVIDE ON COLLEGE CAMPUSES

Richard Just

[1] During her first two years at the University of Pennsylvania, Stephanie Steward became convinced that she was being treated unfairly because of her political views. In her class on diversity and the law, a professor seemed obsessed with the evils of slavery. Another professor's defense of the estate tax struck her as excessively one-sided. *The Daily Pennsylvanian*, where she worked, seemed to exhibit subtle political bias. Eventually Steward decided that she had taken enough abuse. So last year the junior launched a newspaper of her own, *The Pennsylvania Independent*, and this year she will take the publication biweekly. Starting a newspaper costs money (her budget for this school year will run about $15,000). Fortunately for Steward, a portion of that money will come from the Intercollegiate Studies Institute (ISI), a conservative organization that funds college publications.

[2] Steward's story will sound familiar to anyone who has talked to college conservatives. "It takes a little oppression to really get engaged and involved," says Evan Baehr, a junior at Princeton University, where he is editor in chief of the conservative *Princeton Tory* and president of the College Republicans. Like Steward, Baehr sees himself as an oppressed minority on his campus—and he, too, has turned to national conservative organizations for remedy. The *Tory* received tens of thousands of dollars last year from groups such as the Leadership Institute, the Young America Foundation and the ISI to fund its printing costs and

to host speakers such as Jonah Goldberg, George Will and Daniel Flynn, author of *Why the Left Hates America*. Baehr says such speakers are necessary to counterbalance the influence of an overwhelmingly liberal faculty, many of whom he believes exhibit left-wing tendencies in their course materials. Don't conservative college professors also indulge their biases in the classroom? "I'm sure there are equally absurd cases on the other side," Baehr says, mentioning the faculty at Bob Jones University.

[3] Although conservatives currently run the national government and are enjoying an upswing in media influence, conservative activists on campus still draw energy from feeling like a beleaguered minority—and they're not entirely wrong. In last year's American Freshman Survey, conducted annually by the University of California, Los Angeles, 27.8 percent of college freshmen nationwide identified themselves as liberal or far left while 21.3 percent identified themselves as conservative or far right. It was the first time since 1996 that the percentage of students identifying themselves as liberal or left in the survey decreased; the year before, 29.9 percent had identified themselves as liberal or far left, the most since 1975.

[4] Liberal dominance is more pronounced at elite schools. Dartmouth is widely considered to be the most conservative school in the Ivy League. And yet, according to a voluntary e-mail poll by *The Dartmouth*, the school's student newspaper, 62 percent of students voted for Al Gore in 2000 compared with 23 percent for George W. Bush. At Princeton, generally considered the second-most conservative Ivy, 55 percent voted for Gore compared with 26 percent for Bush, according to a 2000 poll by *The Daily Princetonian* (of which I was then editor in chief). At the University of Pennsylvania, probably the third-most conservative Ivy, 67 percent chose Gore while 20 percent chose Bush, according to *The Daily Pennsylvanian*.

[5] If these broad measurements—liberal vs. conservative, Gore voter versus Bush voter—were the only campus trends that mattered to the future health of progressive politics, liberals would be in reasonably strong shape. But unfortunately for progressives, college politics are more complex. I recently spoke to about 30 student leaders at universities throughout the country. Their perspectives on campus activism varied from school to school, but most agreed that though the right is still a minority on many campuses, it is undoubtedly an energized one. Like Steward and Baehr, conservatives are often fueled by two forces: their own sense of righteous indignation at professors, administrators and peers whom they believe have made college campuses inhospitable territory for conservative ideas; and the availability of funding from outside organizations, which allows them to channel this indignation into publications, speaker series—and, they hope, converts.

[6] The siege mentality of campus conservatives and the substantial financial support they receive from outside groups have not escaped media notice. In May, *The New York Times Magazine* published a story about the rise of "hip" conservatives at Bucknell University. *The Economist* followed with a shorter piece in July on the growth of College Republicans, which has tripled its national membership in the last three years. "The leftists who seized control of the universities in the 1960s have imposed their worldview on the young with awesome enthusiasm, bowdlerizing textbooks of anything that might be considered sexist or racist, imposing draconian speech codes and inventing pseudo-subjects such as women's studies," *The Economist* wrote, offering a concise illustration of the current conservative mind-set on many campuses. As a student from Pennsylvania State University told the *Pittsburgh Post-Gazette* while attending a Young America Foundation

conference in Washington this summer, "Our group is much smaller than the college Democrats, but at least we are making our voices known."

[7] Campus conservatives have made the most of their self-conception as an oppressed minority. Their insurgency is just a natural "reaction against the professors and the administration, which tend to be liberal," says Dan Gomez, chairman of Penn's College Republicans. Alicia Washington, president of Yale University's College Democrats, agrees. Yale conservatives, she says, "knock a lot louder because there are so few of them." And if conservatives find that knocking louder helps them generate publicity, well, that's part of the point.

[8] By contrast, campus progressives, though still more numerous, have two big problems: funding and fragmentation. Yoni Applebaum, who led the Columbia University organization that dispenses funding to student groups and worked with the nonpartisan Columbia Political Union (CPU), said the disparity was noticeable. "It was far easier for us at the Gee to locate external sources of funding to bring conservative speakers to campus than it was to locate sources of funding to bring Democratic speakers to campus," he says. The funding gap manifests itself in more subtle ways, too. "The liberal magazines don't look anywhere near as nice as the conservative magazines," says Emily Regan Wills, a senior at Yale and a leader of the school's Women's Center. Zac Frank, president of Columbia's College Democrats, marvels at the outside support available to conservative groups. "The national network they have is just astounding," he says. That national network serves as a pipeline for young conservatives, and it has churned out its share of success stories: Ralph Reed, Grover Norquist and, most famously, Karl Rove all held national positions in the College Republicans organization.

[9] The number of progressive campus groups often dwarfs the number of conservative organizations, but that is both a strength and a weakness. Harvard's Web site, for instance, displays numerous student groups running the gamut from liberal to radical: the Environmental Action Committee; AIDS Education and Outreach; the Bisexual, Gay, Lesbian and Transgendered Supporters Alliance; the Black Students Association; the Black Men's Forum; the Coalition Against Sexual Violence; the Coalition for Drug Policy Reform; the Harvard-Radcliffe Women's Leadership Project; Youth at Harvard Against Handgun Violence; Students for Choice; Amnesty International; the Initiative for Peace and Justice and so on. The conservative counterparts are much fewer in number. This phenomenon exists at many schools, and on some campuses, student leaders say, the proliferation of liberal groups can lead to divisions in the progressive community.

[10] It's not simply the number of organizations that matters—the ideological range of progressive groups tends to be much wider than those on the right. That fragmentation can be healthy, of course—what is college about, if not debating ideas?—but it can also create bitter and disabling divisions, particularly at schools with strong cultures of radicalism. Ethan Ris, president of Brown University's College Democrats, says that this past spring the Young Communist League took over efforts to organize protests against the war in Iraq. "We would show up to these meetings and be shouted down and called idiots....My members would show up and have such a terrible time, they'd never want to go again." Yale's Wills, who is herself no centrist—she voted for Gore only because she lived in the swing state of Pennsylvania and would have voted for Ralph Nader elsewhere—says the progressive community often ends up being dominated by its most extreme voices.

"I am shocked often by what I am called moderate for saying," she says. "And 'moderate' in the activist community is a dirty word." Describing some activists as "hard-line" and "off-putting," she adds, "People who get committed to Yale activism often end up being very far to the left."

[11] At Columbia, a school with a long tradition of radicalism, liberal students say that the vocal student chapter of the International Socialist Organization (ISO) has a chilling effect on more mainstream progressive activism. "I've met freshmen who've been wary of joining a political group because what they see on campus are these far-left groups who are not their cup of tea," says Samir Arora, who just graduated from Columbia and was president of the CPU. Frank, of the College Democrats, says, "People see any identification with progressive issues as being, 'Oh, that's the ISO again.'"

[12] Progressive students engaged in narrowly focused organizations may ignore liberal electoral politics. "Sometimes it's difficult to work with single-issue groups," says Gerard McGeary, president of Harvard's College Democrats. Alicia Washington of Yale agrees that the strength of identity groups "in some ways does kind of detract." But other campus liberal leaders see identity groups as valuable gateways to political awareness for students who might otherwise remain on the sidelines. "It's a big group of people to get our message out to," says Rich Eisenberg, president of Penn's College Democrats.

[13] Another problem for the liberal side is durability. Single issue liberal organizations often ride on the energy of a handful of students and may not outlive their graduations. Changes in world events may also make narrowly defined groups obsolete, scattering to the wind the political energy they briefly harnessed. Groups that sprang up to oppose the Iraq War this past spring are a prime example. "Things form as news forms, and then they die as news dies," Lucretia Fernandez, press secretary of Indiana University's College Republicans, says of some progressive groups on her campus.

[14] Still, campus conservatives say that the sheer number of liberal groups gives progressives more opportunities to lure students to campus activism. "Any sort of liberal issue has a group at Penn, as opposed to the conservatives, who, as of now, have us," says Gomez of Penn's College Republicans. With more groups, he says, "you can mobilize so many more people, even though they may not be united by a common leadership." As a result, conservatives at Penn and Princeton say they are trying to emulate the left by encouraging the formation of new right-of-center political groups more narrowly tailored around specific issues.

[15] A bigger nemesis for both groups is a familiar one: apathy. Getting the message out about political issues is a particular challenge when great swaths of the student body aren't listening. To have a conversation with current college students about political activism, it's practically a precondition to acknowledge that many students simply don't care about the great debates of our time, or don't think that political engagement is worth the trouble. There is, of course, some sample bias at work here: It makes sense that the average activist would view his or her peers as politically apathetic, just as the typical cellist would probably view other students as insufficiently interested in attending orchestra concerts. And yet it is impossible to avoid the fact that conversations about politics at colleges big and small, liberal and conservative, urban and rural, private and public invariably turn toward the fact that "the majority of students are apathetic," as Josh Fisher of the Bucknell Caucus for Economic Justice put it in speaking about his campus. Asked whether students at Bucknell are generally

left or right of center, he says he doesn't know. "I couldn't say definitively because most people avoid topics of conversation like that," he says. "It's sort of an anti-intellectual environment." Katerina Seligmann of Columbia's Amnesty International chapter acknowledges that most of her peers are politically left of center. But, she adds, "There's a difference between people being liberals and people being activists."

[16] Cutting through this apathy is the greatest challenge faced by campus activists, left and right—and possibly the one idea that unites the two sides. "When we're registering people by ourselves, we get 10 people per hour," says Eisenberg of Penn's College Democrats. "When we're registering with the College Republicans, we get 50 people an hour." Gomez, his Penn counterpart on the right, says that debates between the two groups—which take place once or twice a year—draw "the most participation of any one event that either of us do."

[17] Humor is another way to coax students out of apathy, and a little effort goes a long way. Conservatives have been out in front on this one, probably because it's easier to poke fun at the establishment when you perceive yourself as being outside it. *The New York Times Magazine* documented how Bucknell conservatives have made a rite of annually penning something called "Penis Monologues," a response to the feminist play *The Vagina Monologues*, popular on many campuses. The stunt generates outrage and publicity, which is exactly what conservative students want.

[18] Liberals may be watching and learning. Shortly after this year's State of the Union address, Peter Hackeman, opinions editor of *The Bucknellian*, the student newspaper, wrote a satirical draft of Bush's speech that wasn't bad. "Our intelligence sources tell us that Saddam has attempted to purchase high-strength aluminum tubes suitable for nuclear weapons production," he wrote, "but they were actually to be used for those low-tech phones with string connecting two aluminum cans. . . . Saddam Hussein has not credibly explained these activities. He clearly has much to hide. Just what are these string-and-can phones to be used for? If this is not evil, then evil has no meaning." Not as outrageous as the "Penis Monologues," to be sure, but give Bucknell's liberals points for effort.

[19] The Iraq War was fertile ground for campus activism on both sides of the political spectrum. But most students agree that national politics in the last two years has moved into territory where campus conservatives feel more comfortable than their liberal peers. "It became a lot easier to be a conservative at college after September 11," says Angel Rivera, president of Indiana University's College Republicans. Following the terrorist attacks, groups with names such as the Princeton Committee Against Terrorism and Columbia's Students United for America sprang up. Though many of these groups had bipartisan memberships, they clearly leaned right.

[20] Many see this trend not as evidence that undergraduates have converted to neoconservatism en masse but rather as a manifestation of how contemporary college students feel about institutions—such as the military—that were largely opposed by their parents. In the most recent nationwide UCLA survey, 45 percent of students agreed "strongly" or "somewhat" with the idea of increasing military spending. In 1993, that number was 21.4 percent. Supporters of the Iraq War understood this situation. At Columbia, for instance, the College Republicans chapter was careful to advertise its rally as a "pro-troops" event rather than a "pro-war" one, explained Dennis Schmelzer, the organization's executive director. "The war in Iraq has been a great issue for us," says the group's president, Ganesh Betanabhatla.

[21] A debate raged at the school over whether to bring the ROTC back to campus. And some liberals—revealing, perhaps, the inclinations of their generation—have found it difficult to dismiss the arguments of their more conservative peers. Dina Schorr, a founder of Toward Reconciliation, a Columbia group that advocates peaceful resolutions to international conflicts, struggled with the question of whether to sign a petition advocating the ROTC's return.

[22] "If all of these liberal campuses don't have ROTC," she explained, "then how can you expect the military to change?" In the end, she signed.

[23] On social issues, however, college students remain generally liberal. "Social issues [are] really our best shot among young, educated kids," says Owen Conroy, president of Princeton's College Democrats. Whatever else characterizes today's college students, this is surely the Tolerant Generation. The percentage of students supporting gay rights has consistently grown in UCLA's survey in recent years. Last year a record high of 59.3 percent supported gay marriage while a record low of 24.8 percent favored laws limiting homosexual rights. It is well documented that students are growing more ambivalent about ever having an abortion or personally approving of one, yet recently a majority still favored abortion rights. And 39.7 percent support legalizing marijuana, up from 16.7 percent in 1989. "It's definitely harder to sell them on socially conservative ideas," says Gomez of Republican efforts to enlist Penn students.

[24] Whatever frustrations Gomez has experienced haven't sapped his sense of mission. Last year, to spark interest in their group, Republicans put up signs around campus that asked, "What Would Reagan Do?" When many were torn down—as campus posters often are—Gomez took it as a sign of anti-conservative bias. "If there were posters saying, 'What Would Carter Do?'

they wouldn't have gotten torn down," he says. The deeply held belief that they are being persecuted on college campuses may make some conservatives seem a little paranoid. But it may also be strengthening their resolve.

[25] College liberals confront a paradox: Their parents won many aspects of the battle for campuses some decades ago—freer sexuality, affirmative action, greater curricular and cultural diversity. Liberals of that generation came to dominate faculties, notably in the liberal arts. Today it's conservatives who feel like the opposition, and it's a lot easier to be outraged, dogmatic and zealously energized if you're not in charge.

[26] But it's not clear that liberals are completely in charge. It's true that professors in departments like English, sociology and women's studies are disproportionately left of center, but in the parts of universities that lead directly to real power—business schools, law faculties, economics departments—the opposite is often true. Diversity of ideological views is, of course, healthy. When conservatives complain that their sociology professors teach from a liberal vantage point, liberals can retort that it's good for conservatives to challenge themselves by studying with liberal sociologists—just as it's good for liberals to challenge themselves by taking economics courses with market fundamentalists.

[27] To spur activism, liberals have no shortage of topics to tap. The anti-sweatshop movement, which crested on campuses about four years ago, placed progressive activists in direct confrontation with their school administrations and also garnered sympathy from large portions of normally apathetic student bodies. Campaigns for higher wages for the lowest-paid workers at colleges have achieved similar results.

[28] There are any number of other issues—from the death grip of commercialized athletic departments on university decision making

to the outrageous use of federal work-study money to fund menial campus jobs rather than meaningful service opportunities—that are ripe for exploration by thoughtful, progressive undergrads. When campus liberals have enjoyed success and garnered publicity in recent years, they have carved out creative positions on issues that have allowed them to challenge both the institutions where they study and the larger society. Their victories have suggested that beneath the apathy, idealism is still the natural condition of youth.

SUMMARIZE AND RESPOND

Summarize Just's article in 100 to 150 words, taking care to accurately and fairly convey his central idea.

DISCUSS

In his article, Just writes: "To have a conversation with current college students about political activism, it's practically a precondition to acknowledge that many students simply don't care about the great debates of our time, or don't think that political engagement is worth the trouble." Do you think this is an accurate statement, especially given the election in 2008 of President Barack Obama? Support your response with evidence from your own experiences.

ARGUE

Write a brief causal argument in which you answer the following question: Why are many college students apathetic when it comes to politics?

from reading to writing

1. Michiko Kakutani and Alex Williams paint very different pictures of Millennials' civic engagement. With a partner or in a small group, discuss how you think these authors would respond to each other. Taking into account each author's claims and counterclaims, write a hypothetical dialogue between Kakutani and Williams. What might their discussion sound like? Whose argument do you find more convincing? Why?

2. The following articles each incorporate research using the Narcissistic Personality Inventory. How does each writer evaluate and use this evidence?
   a. Larry Gordon and Louis Sahagun ("Gen Y's Ego Trip Takes a Bad Turn")
   b. Melissa Ludwig ("LOOK@ME: Generation Next Is Living Out Loud and Online")
   c. Jonah Goldberg ("Isn't That Special?")

3. Jonah Goldberg, in "Isn't That Special?" and Nicholas Handler, in "The Posteverything Generation," present responses to the commonly held view of

college-aged students as selfish and unmotivated. Compare their essays and how they challenge this stereotype. Which writer do you find more persuasive? Why?

4.   Several of the authors in this chapter identify technology as a defining characteristic of college students today. Using pertinent readings from this chapter as a reference point, discuss the role(s) that technology plays in your life. Do you think devices like the iPod and sites like MySpace define you? Explain.

5.   Writers in this chapter posit shifts in college populations in matters of faith (Alan Finder's "Matters of Faith Find a New Prominence on Campus") and political orientation (Richard Just's "Schools of Thought: The Liberal-Conservative Divide on College Campuses"). Identify the causal argument in each of these articles. What do the authors see as the reasons for these changes? Do you find their arguments valid?

the heat is on

"It may sound odd to ask of global warming, What's in it for me? But the question is neither crass nor tongue-in-cheek. The ways in which climate change could skew the world's distribution of wealth should help us appreciate just how profoundly an artificial greenhouse effect might shake our lives. Moreover, some of the lasting effects of climate change are likely to come not so much from the warming itself but from how we react to it . . ."

—Gregg Easterbrook, *Global Warming: Who Loses—and Who Wins?*

"Are humans like frogs in a simmering pot, unaware that temperatures have reached the boiling point?" asks writer Andrew C. Revkin. "Or has global warming been spun into an 'alarmist gale'..." The answer is difficult to gauge, given that so much about our relationship with, and effects on, the environment is up for debate. But one thing is certain, as these readings show: Global warming, ignored for so long by the public and government at all levels, demands our immediate attention. Public discussion about the issue, now that the warming of Earth's atmosphere has been documented, tends to focus on three questions: What's causing the phenomenon? What will its consequences be? And what can and should be done to address the problems associated with global warming? The pieces in this chapter deal with these and other issues related to the problem.

Writing about the state of the global warming debate in 2007, journalist Jerry Adler focuses on the ways that language shapes how we think and talk about issues. He wrote this piece for the April 16, 2007, issue of Newsweek *magazine.*

THE WAR OF THE WORDS

Whether it's climate 'chaos', 'change' or 'crisis,' language comes first in the environment fight.

Jerry Adler

[1] What is the most pressing environmental issue we face today? "Global warming"? The "greenhouse effect"? At the Oscar ceremonies, Al Gore referred to a "climate crisis," but in his State of the Union address President Bush chose the comparatively anodyne phrase "climate change." They all refer to the same thing, but the first rule of modern political discourse is that before addressing any empirical problem each side must "frame the debate" in the most favorable way. If you doubt it, just try to get a Republican to utter the phrase "estate tax" rather than "death tax." Behind the overt campaign to head off whatever it is—environmental heating? thermal catastrophe?—is a covert struggle over what we should even call it.

[2] In recent years this has played out largely as a contest between "global warming" and "climate change." Bush's use of the latter was consistent with Republican practice, which calls for de-emphasizing the urgency of the situation, as recommended in a 2002 memo by strategist Frank Luntz. Unlike the "catastrophic" connotations of global warming, Luntz wrote, "climate change sounds a more controllable and less emotional challenge." So should activists favor "global warming"? Well, not necessarily. Richard C. J. Somerville, a leading researcher on—um, worldwide calorification?—at Scripps Institution of Oceanography, thinks "global warming" is problematic because it puts the focus on worldwide average temperature, rather than the more serious regional dangers of storms, floods and drought. More pointedly, a leading Democratic strategist, Celinda Lake, actually endorsed "climate change" in 2004 on the grounds that "global warming" only works for half the year. "Every time we'd use the term in the winter, people would say, 'It doesn't feel that warm to me'," she said. (For the record, she now believes the issue has penetrated the public's awareness to the point where it doesn't matter

much what it's called.) Similarly, it's been suggested that Americans have been slower than Europeans to grasp the magnitude of the impending disaster because they think of temperature in Fahrenheit, while scientists—and most of the rest of the world—use the Celsius scale, on which the numbers are smaller. A predicted temperature rise of, say, 3 degrees Celsius sounds less alarming than the equivalent swing of 5.4 degrees in the units most Americans are familiar with.

[3] In any case, "global warming" seems to have won out over its rivals, if one can judge by *The New York Times*, where for each of the last three years "global warming" has outpaced references to "climate change" by almost exactly two to one—or an even bigger margin if you throw out articles that are actually about changes in the economic or cultural climate. Both of these phrases have triumphed over "greenhouse effect," which was the most common term in the early 1980s, when the phenomenon of—atmospheric pyrogenesis?—first came to public attention. Arguably, if your goal is to affect public attitudes and policies, "greenhouse effect," which refers to the buildup of heat-trapping gases in the atmosphere, puts the emphasis in the wrong place, on the mechanism rather than the outcome. George Lakoff, the Berkeley professor of linguistics and cognitive science, is a strong backer of the dark horse "climate crisis,"

which is also favored by Gore (along with the rather more cumbersome term he used in his congressional testimony last month, "planetary emergency"). "'Climate change' doesn't suggest immediate action," says Lakoff. "'Climate crisis' says immediate action needed. The framing is not just a matter of labels, it's modes of thought. In Europe they use 'climate chaos'."

[4] So that ought to settle it, except, of course, that this is a kind of crisis for which neither human experience nor language has quite prepared us: a slow-motion crisis, requiring heroic action now to head off disaster decades down the road. Somerville was on the losing side of a public debate last month in New York, sponsored by Intelligence Squared U.S., and he believes he lost in part because the proposition was framed as "Global Warming Is Not a Crisis." The other side, which included the novelist and, uh, meteorological-calamity skeptic Michael Crichton, was able to convince a narrow majority of the audience that "crisis" is the wrong term for whatever it is humanity is dealing with. "I don't like words that leave me vulnerable to charges of being alarmist," says Somerville. "Using crisis conveys the notion this is hopeless. But there's a lot that can be done about this. I'm still looking for the right words to describe what's happening, but it's not keeping me from trying to stop it."

SUMMARIZE AND RESPOND

Write a 50-word summary of Adler's piece, followed by a 100-word response to Adler's central argument. Do you agree with his position?

ANALYZE

Examine a few news media sites or blogs to see how people talk about global warming. How would you characterize the language that you find? Is it even-handed? Or does it try to evoke emotional responses (such as guilt or anger or fear) from the audience? Based on your findings, and on Adler's essay, briefly discuss what might drive authors to make the language choices they make (think in terms of the rhetorical appeals discussed in Chapters 2 and 3).

Johnny Johnson/Getty Images

GLOBAL
WARMING =
EXTINCTION
GREENPEACE

Nicholas Kamm/Getty Images

FIGURES 7-1 AND 7-2

"Polar bears are drowning," Andrew C. Revkin says in his essay "Yelling 'Fire' on a Hot Planet." His goal? To make us pay attention to his essay and care about the issue he's addressing by appealing to our concerns for the polar bear, one of the most recognizable members of the animal kingdom (think Coca-Cola commercials and *The Golden Compass*, for example). In the rhetorical terms you learned in Part 1, Revkin is making an appeal based on pathos—he wants us to respond emotionally to the plight of the polar bear so that we will be more open to the topic of his essay, global warming. His is a common strategy in the public discourse surrounding global warming: Advocates for the environment often, as journalists say, "put a face on the problem" to make it seem less abstract and more immediate. In Figure 7-2, members of the environmental group Greenpeace go even further, donning entire polar bear costumes to make a statement at an Interior Department news conference in the spring of 2008. Do you think this is an effective rhetorical strategy? Or are there better ways to make us care about the problems associated with global warming?

In the following article, from the April 23, 2006, edition of the New York Times, *Andrew C. Revkin examines the state of the debate over global warming. Although he doesn't present an explicit argument, he does reveal a position on the issue.*

YELLING 'FIRE' ON A HOT PLANET

Andrew C. Revkin

[1] Global warming has the feel of breaking news these days.

[2] Polar bears are drowning; an American city is underwater; ice sheets are crumbling. *Time* magazine proclaimed that readers should be worried. Very worried. There are new hot-selling books and a batch of documentaries, including one starring former Vice President Al Gore and his climate-evangelist slide show that is touted as "the most terrifying movie you will ever see."

[3] Are humans like frogs in a simmering pot, unaware that temperatures have reached the boiling point? Or has global warming been spun into an "alarmist gale," as Richard S. Lindzen, a climatologist at M.I.T. wrote in a recent *Wall Street Journal* op-ed article?

[4] There is enough static in the air to simultaneously confuse, alarm and paralyze the public. Is global warming now a reality? What do scientists know for sure and when are they just guessing?

[5] And what can truly be accomplished by changing behavior? After all, there are still the traditional calls to limit heat-trapped greenhouse-gas emissions, but a growing number of experts are also saying what was once unthinkable: humans may have to adapt to a warmer globe.

[6] Here, an attempt to shed a little light in all the heat.

What We Know

[7] Between the poles of real-time catastrophe and nonevent lies the prevailing scientific view: without big changes in emissions rates, global warming from the buildup of greenhouse gases is likely to lead to substantial, and largely irreversible, transformations of climate, ecosystems and coastlines later this century.

[8] The Earth's average surface temperature rose about 1 degree over the 20th century, to around 59 degrees, but the rate of warming from the 1970's until now has been three times the average rate of warming since 1900. Seas have risen about six to eight inches globally over the last century and the rate of rise has increased in the last decade.

[9] In 2001, a large team of scientists issued the latest assessment of climate change and concluded that more than half of the recent warming was likely to have been caused by people, primarily because we're adding tens of billions of tons of carbon dioxide and other long-lived greenhouse gases to the atmosphere, mainly by burning coal and oil.

[10] There is no serious debate any more about one thing: more of these gases will cause more warming. Dr. Lindzen, who contends any human climate influence is negligible and has long criticized those calling global warming a catastrophe, agreed on this basic fact in his article.

[11] At the same time, few scientists agree with the idea that the recent spate of potent hurricanes, European heat waves, African drought and other weather extremes are, in essence, our fault. There is more than enough natural variability in nature to mask a direct connection, they say.

[12] Even recent sightings of drowned polar bears cannot be firmly ascribed to human influence on climate given the big cyclical fluctuations of sea ice around the Arctic.

What Is Debated

[13] The unresolved questions concern the pace and extent of future warming and the impact on wildlife, agriculture, disease, local weather and the height of the world's oceans—in other words, all of the things that matter to people.

[14] The latest estimates, including a study published last week in the journal *Nature*, foresee a probable warming of somewhere around 5 degrees should the concentration of carbon dioxide reach twice the 280-parts-per-million figure that had been the norm on earth for at least 400,000 years. This is far lower than some of the apocalyptic projections in recent years, but also far higher than mild warming rates focused on by skeptics and industry lobbyists.

[15] As a result, by 2100 or so, sea levels could be several feet higher than they are now, and the new normal on the planet for centuries thereafter could be retreating shorelines as Antarctic and Greenland ice sheets relentlessly erode.

[16] Rivers fed by mountain glaciers, including those nourishing much of south Asia, could shrivel. Grand plans to restore New Orleans and the Everglades would be rendered meaningless as seawater advances. Manhattan would become New Orleans—a semi-submerged city surrounded by levees. In summers, polar bears would be stuck on the few remaining ice-clotted shores around the largely blue Arctic Ocean.

[17] Projections of how patterns of drought, deluges, heat and cold might change are among the most difficult, and will remain laden with huge uncertainties for a long time to come, said M. Granger Morgan, a physicist and policy expert at Carnegie Mellon University in Pittsburgh.

[18] For example, while computer simulations of the climate consistently show that the centers of big continents are likely to grow drier, and winters and nights generally warmer, they cannot reliably predict conditions in Chicago or Shanghai.

What's the Rush?

[19] By the clock of geology, this climate shift is unfolding at a dizzying, perhaps unprecedented pace, but by time scales relevant to people, it's happening in slow motion. If the bad stuff doesn't happen for 100 years or so, it's hard to persuade governments or voters to take action.

[20] And there is the rub. Many scientists say that to avoid a doubling of carbon dioxide concentrations, energy efficiency must be increased drastically, and soon. And by midcentury, they add, there must be a complete transformation of energy technology. That may be why some environmentalists try to link today's weather to tomorrow's problem. While scientists say they lack firm evidence to connect recent weather to the human influence on climate, environmental campaigners still push the notion.

[21] "The issue clearly has an urgency problem," said Billy Parish, a founder of Energy Action, a coalition of student groups. "Maybe I'm just a paranoid that sees global warming everywhere, but the here-and-now effects do seem to be mounting, and I think we need to connect the dots for people."

[22] A Gallup survey last month shows that people are still not worried about climate change. When participants were asked to rank 10 environmental problems, global

warming was near the bottom, far below water pollution and toxic waste (both now largely controlled).

23 Without a connection to current disasters, global warming is the kind of problem people, and democratic institutions, have proved singularly terrible at solving: a long-term threat that can only be limited by acting promptly, before the harm is clear.

24 Problems that get attention are "soon, salient and certain," said Helen Ingram, a professor of planning, policy and design at the University of California, Irvine.

25 Stressing the problem's urgency could well be counterproductive, according to *Americans and Climate Change*, a new book by the Yale School of Forestry and Environmental Studies.

26 The book notes that urgency does not appear to be something that can be imposed on people. Moreover, it says, "Urgency is especially prone to being discounted as unreasoned alarmism or even passion."

27 Among its recommendations, the Yale book suggests something radical: drop the reluctance to accept adaptation as a strategy. Adaptation to climate extremes has long been derided by many environmentalists as defeatism. But, the book says, adaptation may help people focus on the reality of what is coming—and that may motivate them to cut emissions to limit chances of bigger changes to come.

28 Actions could range from developing drought-resistant crops to eliminating federal insurance and other subsidies that have long encouraged coastal development.

29 Could stressing adaptation work? The Yale group calls global warming "the perfect problem"—meaning that a confluence of characteristics make it hard, if not impossible, to solve. Its impact remains clouded with scientific uncertainty, its effects will be felt over generations, and it is being amplified by everything from microwaving a frozen dinner to bringing electricity to an Indian village.

30 "I wish I were more optimistic of our ability to get a broad slice of the public to understand this and be motivated to act," said David G. Hawkins, who directs the climate program at the Natural Resources Defense Council, a private group.

31 In an e-mail message, he wrote: "We are sensory organisms; we understand diesel soot because we can smell it and see it. Getting global warming is too much of an intellectual process. Perhaps pictures of drowning polar bears (which we are trying to find) will move people but even there, people will need to believe that those drownings are due to our failure to build cleaner power plants and cars."

SUMMARIZE AND RESPOND

Write a 100-word summary of Revkin's article. Because it is itself a kind of summary (of the debate over global warming), doing this might prove challenging. But as you compose your summary, try to cover all of the main points Revkin presents in his article.

DISCUSS

Revkin quotes *Americans and Climate Change* as saying that urgency as a rhetorical appeal is "prone to being discounted as unreasoned alarmism or even passion."

Do you agree? Is passion necessarily unsuccessful in scientific arguments? Are there other instances where science and passion are equally present in public debate?

ARGUE

Revkin says that the "prevailing scientific view" is that, "without big changes in emissions rates, global warming from the buildup of greenhouse gases is likely to lead to substantial, and largely irreversible, transformations of climate, ecosystems and coastlines later this century." Still, there are people and organizations who dispute this. Write a brief argument in which you make the case for calling Revkin's claim into question.

Jeffrey Kluger's article, like Andrew C. Revkin's, presents an overview of the global warming debate. Kluger's is different, however, in that it starts from the position that we all have roles to play in dealing with the problem and then examines how businesses, governments, and individuals are responding. This article was first published in the April 9, 2007, edition of Time *magazine, with reporting by Aryn Baker, Pune; David Bjerklie; Adam Graham-Silverman, New York; Carolyn Sayre, New York; Dan Cray, Los Angeles; and Bryan Walsh, Tokyo.*

WHAT NOW?

Our feverish planet badly needs a cure. Climate change is caused by a lot of things, and it will take a lot of people to fix it. There's a role for big thinkers, power players, those with deep pockets—and the rest of us.

Jeffrey Kluger

[1] It was probably always too much to believe that human beings would be responsible stewards of the planet. We may be the smartest of all the animals, endowed with exponentially greater powers of insight and abstraction, but we're animals all the same. That means that we can also be shortsighted and brutish, hungry for food, resources, land—and heedless of the mess we leave behind trying to get them.

[2] And make a mess we have. If droughts and wildfires, floods and crop failures, collapsing climate-sensitive species and the images of drowning polar bears didn't quiet most

of the remaining global-warming doubters, the hurricane-driven destruction of New Orleans did. Dismissing a scientist's temperature chart is one thing. Dismissing the death of a major American city is something else entirely. What's more, the heat is only continuing to rise. This past year was the hottest on record in the U.S. The deceptively normal average temperature this winter masked record-breaking highs in December and record-breaking lows in February. That's the sign not of a planet keeping an even strain but of one thrashing through the alternating chills and night sweats of a serious illness.

3 The U.N.'s Intergovernmental Panel on Climate Change issued a report on the state of planetary warming in February that was surprising only in its utter lack of hedging. "Warming of the climate system is unequivocal," the report stated. What's more, there is "very high confidence" that human activities since 1750 have played a significant role by overloading the atmosphere with carbon dioxide hence retaining solar heat that would otherwise radiate away. The report concludes that while the long-term solution is to reduce the levels of CO_2 in the atmosphere, for now we're going to have to dig in and prepare, building better levees, moving to higher ground, abandoning vulnerable floodplains altogether. When former Vice President Al Gore made his triumphant return to Capitol Hill on March 21 to testify before Congress on climate change, he issued an uncompromising warning: "We do not have time to play around with this."

4 Some lingering critics still found wiggle room in the U.N. panel's findings. "I think there is a healthy debate ongoing, even though the scientists who are in favor of doing something on greenhouse gases are in the majority," says Republican Congressman James Sensenbrenner of Wisconsin. But when your last good position is to debate the difference between certain and extra certain, you're playing a losing hand. "The science," says Christine Todd Whitman, former administrator of the Environmental Protection Agency (EPA), "now is getting to the point where it's pretty hard to deny." Indeed it is. Atmospheric levels of CO_2 were 379 parts per million (p.p.m.) in 2005, higher than at any time in the past 650,000 years. Of the 12 warmest years on record, 11 occurred between 1995 and 2006.

5 So if the diagnosis is in, what's the cure? A crisis of this magnitude clearly calls for action that is both bottom-up and top-down. Though there is some debate about how much difference individuals can make, there is little question that the most powerful players—government and industry—have to take the lead.

6 Still, individuals too can move the carbon needle, but how much and how fast? Different green strategies, after all, yield different results. You can choose a hybrid vehicle, but simply tuning up your car and properly inflating the tires will help too. Buying carbon offsets can reduce the impact of your cross-continental travel, provided you can ensure where your money's really going. Planting trees is great, but in some parts of the world, the light-absorbing color of the leaves causes them to retain heat and paradoxically increases warming.

7 Even the most effective individual action, however, is not enough. Cleaning up the wreckage left by our 250-year industrial bacchanal will require fundamental changes in a society hooked on its fossil fuels. Beneath the grass-roots action, larger tectonic plates are shifting. Science is attacking the problem more aggressively than ever. So is industry. So are architects and lawmakers and urban planners. The world is awakened to the problem in a way it never has been before. Says Carol Browner, onetime administrator of the EPA: "It's a sea change

from where we were on this issue." Here are the ways that sea is shifting the most:

The Scientists' Solutions

[8] If the Earth is choking on greenhouse gases, it's not hard to see why. Global carbon dioxide output last year approached a staggering 32 billion tons, with about 25% of that coming from the U.S. Turning off the carbon spigot is the first step, and many of the solutions are familiar: windmills, solar panels, nuclear plants. All three technologies are part of the energy mix, although each has its issues, including noise from windmills and radioactive waste from nukes.

[9] Biofuels, however, are the real growth science, particularly after President George W. Bush, in his State of the Union address, called for the U.S. to quintuple its production of biofuels, primarily ethanol. That was good news to American corn farmers, who produce the crop from which the overwhelming share of domestic ethanol is made. But the manufacture of corn ethanol is still inefficient: the process burns up almost as much energy as it produces.

[10] A better answer is sugarcane ethanol, which yields eight times the energy it takes to make and provides 40% of all the fuel sold in Brazil. But such ethanol causes environmental problems of its own, as forests are cleared for cane fields. Better still would be to process ethanol from agricultural waste like wood chips or the humble summer grass called switchgrass. The cellulosic ethanol they produce packs more energy than corn ethanol, but it also takes more energy to manufacture. "If you make ethanol by burning coal, you defeat the purpose," says Sarah Hessenflow Harper, an analyst for the advocacy group Environmental Defense.

[11] Until we can dial down the carbon, a more immediate strategy might be to find somewhere to put it all—to sequester it underground. In the same way we store radioactive waste from nuclear reactors, so too could we collect the gaseous CO_2 from power plants.

[12] The earth is full of safe, stable places to store gases we don't want, and scientists know precisely where they are. The natural gas that heats homes, fires stoves and runs factories is found in deep, saline-rich limestone and sandstone cavities, where spongelike pores store gas and help keep it from leaking away. When the energy industry pumps a deposit clean, the chambers stand empty. Not only are the shape and capacity of the cavities mapped, but also in many cases equipment is still on hand that could easily be repurposed from extraction to injection.

[13] The U.S. Department of Energy is funding seven research partnerships to test sequestration technologies. This summer, one of those projects will inject a modest 2,000 metric tons of CO_2 into the sandstone subsurface beneath a spread of tomato fields near Thornton, Calif., where it would stay, in effect, forever.

[14] Would that be safe? Carbon dioxide can be lethal, a fact grimly illustrated in 1986 when a giant surge of the stuff bubbled up from Lake Nyos in Cameroon, asphyxiating 1,700 people as they slept. Nonetheless, investigators involved in the Thornton project insist there is little cause for worry. "The fields held oil and gas for millennia," says Larry Myer, an earth scientist with Lawrence Berkeley National Laboratory in Berkeley, Calif., and the project's director, "so geologically we know they're going to hold CO_2."

[15] Even if researchers master the mechanics of sequestration, they must still develop a way to separate CO_2 from power-plant exhaust so that there will be something to stash in the cavities in the first place. There are two promising methods. One is to gasify coal before it's burned, reducing it to a high-pressure synthetic gas that can be stripped of its carbon, leaving mostly hydrogen behind. The alternative is to pulverize coal as power-plant operators do now but then rely on new hardware to separate the CO_2 after burning. Both methods are at

least 20 years away from being fully developed, predicts Ernest Moniz, co-director of the M.I.T. Laboratory for Energy and the Environment and a former Under Secretary of the Department of Energy. "We're very early in the process," he says.

Building a Better Skyscraper

[16] If you want to see what the future of architecture looks like, take a look at the new federal building in San Francisco, but don't look too long. If you're like a lot of folks, you won't much care for it. The glinting, 18-story steel tower jangles badly against the gentle skyline of San Francisco, but it's beautiful on the inside. There's the absence of conventional heating and air conditioning in 70% of the floor space. There's the natural light that fills the workspace during much of the day. There are the windows that actually open and close, and the awninglike fins that filter out heat and glare.

[17] It's easy to overlook how important a building like this one could be. While the power and auto industries get the bulk of the blame for the planet's carbon crisis, the business of operating office buildings and homes is responsible for 38% of U.S. CO_2 emissions. In the case of offices, mid-20th century technology worked against us, as the development of low-temperature fluorescent lights and high-powered air conditioning made it possible to design sealed structures that you could drop into any climate. "It gave architects the power to design anything, then hand it over to engineers and say, 'Here, you heat and cool it,'" says Gail Brager of the Center for the Built Environment at the University of California, Berkeley.

[18] The new federal building, by contrast, sits lightly on its site and does so using technology that is available. Computer-operated floor vents open and close automatically in response to temperature sensors; interior walls and cubicle partitions are kept to a minimum to increase circulation; automated panels that filter out glare also

help air move around the building, creating what the designers call a circulation engine. "Buildings can use passive as well as active energy," says architect Thom Mayne of the firm Morphosis, which designed the building.

[19] Certainly, if you're going to design a green building, it's smart to do it in San Francisco, where the generally mild weather makes it easier to let your surroundings set your temperature. But what about a place like New York City, with its 100°F summers and 10° winters? Bank of America is currently tackling that challenge, with a 945-foot tower in the heart of Manhattan that will use both wind energy and recirculated heat to generate some of its own power. Higher ceilings and insulating glass will reduce temperature changes and maximize available sunlight. The basement will even be equipped with a thermal-control system that will manufacture ice in the evenings, when energy demands are lowest, and use it to cool the building during the day, when power plants are running at peak capacity.

[20] The Pearl River Tower, under construction in Guangzhou, China, is aiming for a net energy footprint of zero by relying on such features as on-site wind turbines and recovery and recycling of condensed water. In Paris, a new tower will rely on wind turbines to provide its heating and cooling for the equivalent of five months of the year. And if you're a corporation planning a skyscraper, don't assume you can't afford to go green. The new buildings typically cost about 5% more to construct than conventional ones but quickly exceed that outlay in energy savings. "I think what we're doing now will be commonplace in five years," Mayne says.

The Green Company

[21] When a business with more than 7,000 stores, 1.8 million employees and $345 billion in sales changes its ways, it's hard not to notice. Wal-Mart has made itself the darling of greens with its pledge to install solar panels on many of its stores, switch to

hybrid vehicles, conserve water and even buy wild-caught salmon. More important, its mandates are having an incalculable ripple effect through its 60,000 suppliers, which are being asked to join Wal-Mart's effort to reduce packaging, waste and energy use. And when Wal-Mart asks, there's little question what the answer will be.

[22] But Wal-Mart is not alone. In January the U.S. Climate Action Partnership, a group that includes some of the biggest corporate players and energy users in the world—Alcoa, BP America, Duke Energy, General Electric, Lehman Brothers, Caterpillar and PG&E—asked the Federal Government to act aggressively on climate change, not least by imposing legal limits on the amount of industrial carbon dioxide emissions. The corporations know there's a virtue in going green, but they're also looking for some regulatory certainty before they make massive investments. What's more, there's money to be made in the enviro game.

[23] Take General Electric. Its Ecomagination initiative centers on a line of 45 green products, including wind turbines and next-generation jet engines that go easy on the earth but land nicely on the balance sheet. Chairman and CEO Jeffrey Immelt set a goal of generating more than $20 billion in revenue from Ecomagination by 2010, and by 2006 the company had hit the $12 billion mark.

[24] DuPont, which suffered twin hits to both revenue and reputation in the late 1980s and early 1990s, when it had to phase out its production of ozone-destroying chlorofluorocarbons, has made a similar environmental pledge. It sold its Dacron, Lycra and Nylon division—all fossil-fuel-based fabrics—and is concentrating on bio-based materials like Sorona polymer made from starch found in the kernels of corn. DuPont hopes to more than double its revenue from nondepletable resources, to $8 billion by 2015. The company has also cut its greenhouse-gas emissions 72% since 1990 and is aiming for more. That puts DuPont in position to respond nimbly if Washington eventually acts to cap carbon. "We learned that we have to be ahead of legislation," says Linda Fisher, DuPont's chief sustainability officer, a title of growing significance in corporate America. "That is truer today than it was 20 years ago."

[25] Not surprisingly, some companies talk a green game but don't really play one. Ford Motor Co. made a big show of performing a $2 billion environmental overhaul of its River Rouge factory in Dearborn, Mich., but still turns out SUVs like the elephantine Expedition, which gets a puny 14 m.p.g. in city driving. Toyota, famous for its hybrid Prius, has nonetheless joined the U.S. Big Three in lobbying Washington against stricter fuel standards.

[26] This kind of environmental posing—greenwashing is the term of art—will not be a viable business strategy in a world transformed by climate change. The smart money is betting on the need for real innovation—clean technology that lowers costs or improves output. Venture capital is increasingly flowing to green start-ups: $474 million in the first three quarters of 2006 in Silicon Valley alone. That's sparking the interest of everyday investors, who see green technology as—dare they wish it?—the next Internet. Says Ray Lane, a partner at the KPCB venture-capital firm: "If you consider the sheer scale of the problem, I think this is an order of magnitude bigger."

Change on the Hill

[27] Jubilant Democrats crowed about big changes to come when they won majorities in the House and Senate last November, and the arena in which they can make the greatest change—at least domestically—is the environment. Part of the reason is the people who will wield the new power.

[28] The Jurassic James Inhofe, the Oklahoma Republican who has referred to global

warming as the "greatest hoax ever perpetrated on the American people," has been replaced as chair of the Senate Committee on Environment and Public Works. In his four years in the post, Inhofe held a total of five hearings on climate change, and the star witness was a science-fiction fabulist: Michael Crichton, a critic of warming theory. Now holding the gavel is California's Barbara Boxer, who has had five hearings on climate change in less than three months. While more hearings are a certainty, she must also help field a flock of green bills being offered by newly empowered Democratic members.

[29] Michigan Democrat John Dingell will be a key player in the debate about lowering carbon dioxide emissions—not just on cars, but economy-wide. The new chairman of the House Committee on Energy and Commerce, Dingell comes from a state congenitally opposed to any measure that could pinch the auto industry. Democrats hope to spin that in their favor, arguing that any climate-change legislation that gets through his committee will have the legitimacy of having cleared a high bar.

[30] The true measure of success for the party will be whether Congress finally passes a law to limit greenhouse emissions. That effort began in earnest in 2003, when Senators John McCain and Joe Lieberman sponsored a bill that would set limits on industrial greenhouse gases and let companies that do better than required sell pollution credits to those that fail to meet targets. One credit worth of extra pollution from a dirty company is offset by one credit worth of extra cleanliness from a more environmentally conscious company, and the clean company is paid for its effort too. This is just the kind of strategy that was implemented in 1990 to curb sulfur dioxide—the leading cause of acid rain—and has resulted in a 35% reduction of the pollutant since.

[31] McCain and Lieberman's bill was soundly defeated that year and in 2005 suffered an even worse Senate smackdown, 60 to 38. With a new Congress in place, McCain and Lieberman will try again. This time they will face competition from Senators Jeff Bingaman and Arlen Specter, whose version would set higher caps and more gradual reductions. "The McCain-Lieberman proposal was very credible," Bingaman says. "[But] this draft has more prospect of actually being adopted." Yet another cap-and-trade bill will probably come out of Boxer's committee, and more bills still will be considered in the House of Representatives.

[32] What all the measures have in common is that they will ultimately have to find their way to hostile territory—Bush's desk. Still, Bush 2007 is not Bush 2004, and the embattled President may decide that vetoing a piece of broadly popular legislation is not a fight worth picking now, especially since corporations see value in it. Kristin Hellmer, a spokeswoman for the White House Council on Environmental Quality, will not rule out the President's signing onto cap-and-trade or any other green bill. "It's a bit premature to have that conversation," she says.

[33] States and cities aren't waiting for Congress to act. California Governor Arnold Schwarzenegger committed the state to a 25% reduction in greenhouse gases by 2020; he was promptly sued by carmakers that would have to increase fuel efficiency to sell there. If California prevails, the size of its market could turn its regulations into a de facto national standard. While no other states have passed limits as strict as California's, about one-third of the U.S. population lives in areas where there are automotive-carbon limits in place or under consideration, with curbs in place in 11 states so far.

[34] States are also joining hands to curb emissions from power plants—the coal burned in Pennsylvania, after all, doesn't pause at the New Jersey state line. In 2003 then Governor George Pataki of New York launched the Regional Greenhouse Gas Initiative,

a confederation of northeastern and mid-Atlantic states that has created its own cap-and-trade program, with the goal of reducing emissions 10% below the current level by 2019. Nine states are part of the group, with Maryland set to join in June. In February five Western states embraced a similarly ambitious goal.

[35] At the local level, Mayor Greg Nickels of Seattle, who was incensed after the Senate walked away from the international Kyoto global-warming accords, began what has become a nationwide movement to bring U.S. cities into compliance. As of last month, 431 mayors representing more than 61 million Americans had signed on, imposing higher parking taxes, buying hybrid vehicles for the municipal fleet, helping local businesses audit their energy use and even converting traffic lights from incandescents to LEDs, which are 90% more efficient. Says Nickels: "I think this sends a message that there is intelligent life in America."

The Twin Elephants

[36] No matter how aggressively the U.S. tackles its carbon problem, the global outlook hinges on the coal-fired economies of the world's two looming giants: China and India. Between 1990 and 2004, energy consumption rose 37% in India and 53% in China. Beijing is building new coal-fired power plants at the startling rate of one every week. While the most technologically sophisticated coal plants operate at almost 45% efficiency, China's top out at just 33%.

[37] But China and India are hardly energy hogs—not if you consider the amount of emissions that any single person living there generates. Americans' per capita emission of carbon dioxide is about 21.75 tons. In China it's just 4.03; in India it's an even smaller 1.12. Yet that is going to change. Up to 50% of the Indian population lives almost entirely off the grid, and the government is determined to bring them aboard. The Chinese economy has been growing at the rate of 10% a year,

and Beijing is not inclined to slow down. China is expected to pass the U.S. in total greenhouse emissions before 2010.

[38] Not all is bleak. The U.S.-based Natural Resources Defense Council is trying to help the Chinese clean up, working with their businesses to audit energy consumption and developing a fund to bankroll the installation of more efficient equipment in factories. Barbara Finamore of the China Clean Energy Program estimates that this could eliminate the need for 3,000 new power plants over the next few decades. China also imposes higher taxes on large cars than on small ones; subsidizes wind, solar and other renewables; and has passed a law that aims to make 15% of the country's power come from renewables by 2020.

[39] India is further behind China in developing renewable-energy sources, but the need for power is spurring innovation. India has an aggressive solar and wind industry, with one company, Suzlon, generating $1.5 billion in wind-turbine revenue in 2006. But India, with its less-developed economy, cannot as easily afford the cost of going green—or at least greener. "The Indian government has not taken the problem seriously," says Steve Sawyer, a policy adviser for Greenpeace International.

[40] It sometimes seems that the same can be said for the entire world. It's not surprising that faced with a problem of this magnitude, people will yield to the impulse to lay blame. Voters blame politicians. Politicians blame industry. Industry blames an overweening government. Prius owners blame Hummer drivers. But never mind who caused the problem, its very enormity means that all of the finger pointers will have a role in cleaning it up. It took generations to foul the planet as badly as we have, and it will surely take generations to reverse things. The difference is, we had the leisure of beginning our long industrial climb whenever we wanted to. We don't have the leisure of waiting to clean up after it.

SUMMARIZE AND RESPOND

Write a 100-word summary of this piece, followed by a 100-word response. In your response, focus on Kluger's effectiveness in making his central point: that we all have roles to play in responding to global warming.

ANALYZE

Choose one of the rhetorical appeals (to ethos, pathos, or logos) and briefly analyze how Kluger uses it in his article. Ask yourself, for example, how the appeal affects the audience and why the author might have chosen to do this. Make sure you point to specific examples of the appeal at work in the text to support your analysis.

In this article, which he wrote for the April 2007 issue of The Atlantic Monthly, *Gregg Easterbrook looks beyond the debate over whether global warming is happening and how it might be stopped to examine how life might look—and who the winners and losers might be—in a climatically altered future.*

GLOBAL WARMING: WHO LOSES—AND WHO WINS?

Climate change in the next century (and beyond) could be enormously disruptive, spreading disease and sparking wars. It could also be a windfall for some people, businesses, and nations. A guide to how we all might get along in a warming world.

Gregg Easterbrook

[1] Coastal cities inundated, farming regions parched, ocean currents disrupted, tropical diseases spreading, glaciers melting—an artificial greenhouse effect could generate countless tribulations.

[2] If Earth's climate changes meaningfully—and the National Academy of Sciences, previously skeptical, said in 2005 that signs of climate change have become significant—there could be broad-based disruption of

the global economy unparalleled by any event other than World War II.

[3] Economic change means winners as well as losers. Huge sums will be made and lost if the global climate changes. Everyone wonders what warming might do to the environment—but what might it do to the global distribution of money and power?

[4] Whether mainly natural or mainly artificial, climate change could bring different regions of the world tremendous benefits as well as drastic problems. The world had been mostly warming for thousands of years before the industrial era began, and that warming has been indisputably favorable to the spread of civilization. The trouble is that the world's economic geography is today organized according to a climate that has largely prevailed since the Middle Ages—runaway climate change would force big changes in the physical ordering of society. In the past, small climate changes have had substantial impact on agriculture, trade routes, and the types of products and commodities that sell. Larger climate shifts have catalyzed the rise and fall of whole societies. The Mayan Empire, for instance, did not disappear "mysteriously"; it likely fell into decline owing to decades of drought that ruined its agricultural base and deprived its cities of drinking water. On the other side of the coin, Europe's Medieval Warm Period, which lasted from around 1000 to 1400, was essential to the rise of Spain, France, and England: Those clement centuries allowed the expansion of farm production, population, cities, and universities, which in turn set the stage for the Industrial Revolution. Unless greenhouse-effect theory is completely wrong—and science increasingly supports the idea that it is right—21st-century climate change means that sweeping social and economic changes are in the works.

[5] To date the greenhouse-effect debate has been largely carried out in abstractions—arguments about the distant past (what *do* those 100,000-year-old ice cores in Greenland really tell us about ancient temperatures, anyway?) coupled to computer-model conjecture regarding the 22nd century, with the occasional Hollywood disaster movie thrown in. Soon, both abstraction and postapocalyptic fantasy could be pushed aside by the economic and political realities of a warming world. If the global climate continues changing, many people and nations will find themselves in possession of land and resources of rising value, while others will suffer dire losses—and these winners and losers could start appearing faster than you might imagine. Add artificially triggered climate change to the volatility already initiated by globalization, and the next few decades may see previously unthinkable levels of economic upheaval, in which fortunes are won and lost based as much on the physical climate as on the business climate.

[6] It may sound odd to ask of global warming, What's in it for me? But the question is neither crass nor tongue-in-cheek. The ways in which climate change could skew the world's distribution of wealth should help us appreciate just how profoundly an artificial greenhouse effect might shake our lives. Moreover, some of the lasting effects of climate change are likely to come not so much from the warming itself but from how we react to it: If the world warms appreciably, men and women will not sit by idly, eating bonbons and reading weather reports; there will be instead what economists call "adaptive response," most likely a great deal of it. Some aspects of this response may inflame tensions between those who are winning and those who are losing. How people, the global economy, and the international power structure adapt to climate change may influence how we live for generations. If the world warms, who will win? Who will lose? And what's in it for you?

Land

[7] Real estate might be expected to appreciate steadily in value during the 21st century, given that both the global population and global prosperity are rising. The supply of land is fixed, and if there's a fixed supply of something but a growing demand, appreciation should be automatic. That's unless climate change increases the supply of land by warming currently frosty areas while throwing the amount of *desirable* land into tremendous flux. My hometown of Buffalo, New York, for example, is today so déclassé that some of its stately Beaux-Arts homes, built during the Gilded Age and overlooking a park designed by Frederick Law Olmsted, sell for about the price of one-bedroom condos in Boston or San Francisco. If a warming world makes the area less cold and snowy, Buffalo might become one of the country's desirable addresses.

[8] At the same time, Arizona and Nevada, blazing growth markets today, might become unbearably hot and see their real-estate markets crash. If the oceans rise, Florida's rapid growth could be, well, swamped by an increase in its perilously high groundwater table. Houston could decline, made insufferable by worsened summertime humidity, while the splendid, rustic Laurentide Mountains region north of Montreal, if warmed up a bit, might transmogrify into the new Poconos.

[9] These are just a few of many possible examples. Climate change could upset the applecarts of real-estate values all over the world, with low-latitude properties tanking while high latitudes become the Sun Belt of the mid-21st century.

[10] Local changes in housing demand are only small beer. To consider the big picture, examine a Mercator projection of our planet, and observe how the Earth's landmasses spread from the equator to the poles. Assume global warming is reasonably uniform. (Some computer models suggest that

warming will vary widely by region; for the purposes of this article, suffice it to say that all predictions regarding an artificial greenhouse effect are extremely uncertain.) The equatorial and low-latitude areas of the world presumably will become hotter and less desirable as places of habitation, plus less valuable in economic terms; with a few exceptions, these areas are home to developing nations where living standards are already low.

[11] So where is the high-latitude landmass that might grow more valuable in a warming world? By accident of geography, except for Antarctica nearly all such land is in the Northern Hemisphere, whose continents are broad west-to-east. Only a relatively small portion of South America, which narrows as one travels south, is high latitude, and none of Africa or Australia is. (Cape Town is roughly the same distance from the equator as Cape Hatteras; Melbourne is about the same distance from the equator as Manhattan.) More specifically, nearly all the added land-value benefits of a warming world might accrue to Alaska, Canada, Greenland, Russia, and Scandinavia.

[12] This raises the possibility that an artificial greenhouse effect could harm nations that are already hard pressed and benefit nations that are already affluent. If Alaska turned temperate, it would drive conservationists to distraction, but it would also open for development an area more than twice the size of Texas. Rising world temperatures might throw Indonesia, Mexico, Nigeria, and other low-latitude nations into generations of misery, while causing Canada, Greenland, and Scandinavia to experience a rip-roarin' economic boom. Many Greenlanders are already cheering the retreat of glaciers, since this melting stands to make their vast island far more valuable. Last July, *The Wall Street Journal* reported that the growing season in the portion of Greenland open to cultivation is already two weeks longer than it was in the 1970s.

[13] And Russia! For generations poets have bemoaned this realm as cursed by enormous, foreboding, harsh Siberia. What if the region in question were instead enormous, temperate, inviting Siberia? Climate change could place Russia in possession of the largest new region of pristine, exploitable land since the sailing ships of Europe first spied the shores of what would be called North America. The snows of Siberia cover soils that have never been depleted by controlled agriculture. What's more, beneath Siberia's snow may lie geologic formations that hold vast deposits of fossil fuels, as well as mineral resources. When considering ratification of the Kyoto Protocol to regulate greenhouse gases, the Moscow government dragged its feet, though the treaty was worded to offer the Russians extensive favors. Why might this have happened? Perhaps because Russia might be much better off in a warming world: Warming's benefits to Russia could exceed those to all other nations combined.

[14] Of course, it could be argued that politicians seldom give much thought—one way or the other—to actions whose value will become clear only after they leave office, so perhaps Moscow does not have a grand strategy to warm the world for its own good. But a warmer world may be much to Russia's liking, whether it comes by strategy or accident. And how long until high-latitude nations realize global warming might be in their interests? In recent years, Canada has increased its greenhouse-gas output more rapidly than most other rich countries. Maybe this is a result of prosperity and oil-field development—or maybe those wily Canadians have a master plan for their huge expanse of currently uninhabitable land.

[15] Global warming might do more for the North, however, than just opening up new land. Temperatures are rising on average, but *when* are they rising? Daytime? Nighttime? Winter? Summer? One fear about artificially triggered climate change has been that global warming would lead to scorching summer-afternoon highs, which would kill crops and brown out the electric power grid. Instead, so far a good share of the warming—especially in North America—has come in the form of nighttime and winter lows that are less low. Higher lows reduce the harshness of winter in northern climes and moderate the demand for energy. And fewer freezes allow extended growing seasons, boosting farm production. In North America, spring comes ever earlier—in recent years, trees have flowered in Washington, D.C., almost a week earlier on average than a generation ago. People may find this creepy, but earlier springs and milder winters can have economic value to agriculture—and lest we forget, all modern societies, including the United States, are grounded in agriculture.

[16] If a primary impact of an artificially warmed world is to make land in Canada, Greenland, Russia, Scandinavia, and the United States more valuable, this could have three powerful effects on the 21st-century global situation.

[17] First, historically privileged northern societies might not decline geopolitically, as many commentators have predicted. Indeed, the great age of northern power may lie ahead, if Earth's very climate is on the verge of conferring boons to that part of the world. Should it turn out that headlong fossil-fuel combustion by northern nations has set in motion climate change that strengthens the relative world position of those same nations, future essayists will have a field day. But the prospect is serious. By the middle of the 21st century, a new global balance of power may emerge in which Russia and America are once again the world's paired superpowers—only this time during a Warming War instead of a Cold War.

[18] Second, if northern societies find that climate change makes them more wealthy, the quest for world equity could be dealt a

huge setback. Despite the popular misconception, globalized economics have been a positive force for increased equity. As the Indian economist Surjit Bhalla has shown, the developing world produced 29 percent of the globe's income in 1950; by 2000 that share had risen to 42 percent, while the developing world's share of population rose at a slower rate. All other things being equal, we might expect continued economic globalization to distribute wealth more widely. But if climate change increases the value of northern land and resources, while leaving nations near the equator hotter and wracked by storms or droughts, all other things would not be equal.

[19] That brings us to the third great concern: If climate change causes developing nations to falter, and social conditions within them deteriorate, many millions of jobless or hungry refugees may come to the borders of the favored North, demanding to be let in. If the very Earth itself turns against poor nations, punishing them with heat and storms, how could the United States morally deny the refugees succor?

[20] Shifts in the relative values of places and resources have often led to war, and it is all too imaginable that climate change will cause nations to envy each other's territory. This envy is likely to run both north-south and up-down. North-south? Suppose climate change made Brazil less habitable, while bringing an agreeable mild clime to the vast and fertile Argentinean pampas to Brazil's south. São Paulo is already one of the world's largest cities. Would a desperate, overheated Brazil of the year 2037—its population exploding—hesitate to attack Argentina for cool, inviting land? Now consider the up-down prospect: the desire to leave low-lying areas for altitude. Here's an example: Since its independence, in 1947, Pakistan has kept a hand in the internal affairs of Afghanistan. Today Americans view this issue through the lens of the Taliban

and al-Qaeda, but from Islamabad's perspective, the goal has always been to keep Afghanistan available as a place for retreat, should Pakistan lose a war with India. What if the climate warms, rendering much of Pakistan unbearable to its citizens? (Temperatures of 100-plus degrees are already common in the Punjab.) Afghanistan's high plateaus, dry and rocky as they are, might start looking pleasingly temperate as Pakistan warms, and the Afghans might see yet another army headed their way.

[21] A warming climate could cause other landgrabs on a national scale. Today Greenland is a largely self-governing territory of Denmark that the world leaves in peace because no nation covets its shivering expanse. Should the Earth warm, Copenhagen might assert greater jurisdiction over Greenland, or stronger governments might scheme to seize this dwarf continent, which is roughly three times the size of Texas. Today Antarctica is under international administration, and this arrangement is generally accepted because the continent has no value beyond scientific research. If the world warmed for a long time—and it would likely take centuries for the Antarctic ice sheet to melt completely—international jockeying to seize or conquer Antarctica might become intense. Some geologists believe large oil deposits are under the Antarctic crust: In earlier epochs, the austral pole was densely vegetated and had conditions suitable for the formation of fossil fuels.

[22] And though I've said to this point that Canada would stand to become more valuable in a warming world, actually, Canada and Nunavut would. For centuries, Europeans drove the indigenous peoples of what is now Canada farther and farther north. In 1993, Canada agreed to grant a degree of independence to the primarily Inuit population of Nunavut, and this large, cold region in the country's northeast has been mainly self-governing since 1999. The Inuit

believe they are ensconced in the one place in this hemisphere that the descendants of Europe will never, ever want. This could turn out to be wrong.

23 For investors, finding attractive land to buy and hold for a warming world is fraught with difficulties, particularly when looking abroad. If considering plots on the pampas, for example, should one negotiate with the current Argentinian owners or the future Brazilian ones? Perhaps a safer route would be the contrarian one, focused on the likelihood of falling land values in places people may leave. If strict car bon-dioxide regulations are enacted, corporations will shop for "offsets," including projects that absorb carbon dioxide from the sky. Growing trees is a potential greenhouse-gas offset, and can be done comparatively cheaply in parts of the developing world, even on land that people may stop wanting. If you jump into the greenhouse-offset business, what you might plant is leucaena, a rapidly growing tree species suited to the tropics that metabolizes carbon dioxide faster than most trees. But you'll want to own the land in order to control the sale of the credits. Consider a possible sequence of events: First, climate change makes parts of the developing world even less habitable than they are today; then, refugees flee these areas; finally, land can be snapped up at Filene's Basement prices—and used to grow leucaena trees.

Water

24 If Al Gore's movie, *An Inconvenient Truth*, is to be believed, you should start selling coastal real estate now. Gore's film maintains that an artificial greenhouse effect could raise sea levels 20 feet in the near future, flooding Manhattan, San Francisco, and dozens of other cities; Micronesia would simply disappear below the waves. Gore's is the doomsday number, but the scientific consensus is worrisome enough: In 2005, the National Academy of Sciences warned that oceans may rise between four

inches and three feet by the year 2100. Four inches may not sound like a lot, but it would imperil parts of coastal Florida and the Carolinas, among other places. A three-foot sea-level rise would flood significant portions of Bangladesh, threaten the national survival of the Netherlands, and damage many coastal cities, while submerging pretty much all of the world's trendy beach destinations to boot. And the Asian Tigers? Shanghai and Hong Kong sit right on the water. Raise the deep a few feet, and these Tiger cities would be abandoned.

25 The global temperature increase of the last century—about one degree Fahrenheit—was modest and did not cause any dangerous sea-level rise. Sea-level worries turn on the possibility that there is some nonlinear aspect of the climate system, a "tipping point" that could cause the rate of global warming to accelerate markedly. One reason global warming has not happened as fast as expected appears to be that the oceans have absorbed much of the carbon dioxide emitted by human activity. Studies suggest, however, that the ability of the oceans to absorb carbon dioxide may be slowing; as the absorption rate declines, atmospheric buildup will happen faster, and climate change could speed up. At the first sign of an increase in the rate of global warming: Sell, sell, sell your coastal properties. Unload those London and Seattle waterfront holdings. Buy land and real property in Omaha or Ontario.

26 An artificial greenhouse effect may also alter ocean currents in unpredictable ways. Already there is some evidence that the arctic currents are changing, while the major North Atlantic current that moves warm water north from the equator may be losing energy. If the North Atlantic current falters, temperatures could fall in Europe even as the world overall warms. Most of Europe lies to the north of Maine yet is temperate because the North Atlantic current

carries huge volumes of warm water to the seas off Scotland; that warm water is Europe's weathermaker. Geological studies show that the North Atlantic current has stopped in the past. If this current stops again because of artificial climate change, Europe might take on the climate of present-day Newfoundland. As a result, it might depopulate, while the economic value of everything within its icy expanse declines. The European Union makes approximately the same contribution to the global economy as the United States makes: Significantly falling temperatures in Europe could trigger a worldwide recession.

[27] While staying ready to sell your holdings in Europe, look for purchase opportunities near the waters of the Arctic Circle. In 2005, a Russian research ship became the first surface vessel ever to reach the North Pole without the aid of an icebreaker. If arctic sea ice melts, shipping traffic will begin transiting the North Pole. Andrew Revkin's 2006 book, *The North Pole Was Here*, profiles Pat Broe, who in 1997 bought the isolated far-north port of Churchill, Manitoba, from the Canadian government for $7. Assuming arctic ice continues to melt, the world's cargo vessels may begin sailing due north to shave thousands of miles off their trips, and the port of Churchill may be bustling. If arctic polar ice disappears and container vessels course the North Pole seas, shipping costs may decline—to the benefit of consumers. Asian manufacturers, especially, should see their costs of shipping to the United States and the European Union fall. At the same time, heavily trafficked southern shipping routes linking East Asia to Europe and to America's East Coast could see less traffic, and port cities along that route—such as Singapore—might decline. Concurrently, good relations with Nunavut could become of interest to the world's corporations.

[28] Oh, and there may be oil under the arctic waters. Who would own that oil? The United States, Russia, Canada, Norway, and Denmark already assert legally complex claims to parts of the North Pole seas—including portions that other nations consider open waters not subject to sovereign control. Today it seems absurd to imagine the governments of the world fighting over the North Pole seas, but in the past many causes of battle have seemed absurd before the artillery fire began. Canada is already conducting naval exercises in the arctic waters, and making no secret of this.

[29] Then again, perhaps ownership of these waters will go in an entirely different direction. The 21st century is likely to see a movement to create private-property rights in the ocean (ocean property rights are the most promising solution to overfishing of the open seas). Private-property rights in the North Pole seas, should they come into existence, might generate a rush to rival the Sooners' settlement of Oklahoma in the late 1800s.

[30] Whatever happens to our oceans, climate change might also cause economic turmoil by affecting freshwater supplies. Today nearly all primary commodities, including petroleum, appear in ample supply. Freshwater is an exception: China is depleting aquifers at an alarming rate in order to produce enough rice to feed itself, while freshwater is scarce in much of the Middle East and parts of Africa. Freshwater depletion is especially worrisome in Egypt, Libya, and several Persian Gulf states. Greenhouse-effect science is so uncertain that researchers have little idea whether a warming world would experience more or less precipitation. If it turns out that rain and snow decline as the world warms, dwindling supplies of drinking water and freshwater for agriculture may be the next resource emergency. For investors this would suggest a cautious view of the booms in China and Dubai, as both places may soon face freshwater-supply problems. (Cost-effective desalinization continues to elude engineers.) On the

other hand, where water rights are available in these areas, grab them.

[31] Much of the effect that global warming will have on our water is speculative, so water-related climate change will be a high-risk/high-reward matter for investors and societies alike. The biggest fear is that artificially triggered climate change will shift rainfall away from today's productive breadbasket areas and toward what are now deserts or, worse, toward the oceans. (From the human perspective, all ocean rain represents wasted freshwater.) The reason Malthusian catastrophes have not occurred as humanity has grown is that for most of the last half century, farm yields have increased faster than population. But the global agricultural system is perilously poised on the assumption that growing conditions will continue to be good in the breadbasket areas of the United States, India, China, and South America. If rainfall shifts away from those areas, there could be significant human suffering for many, many years, even if, say, Siberian agriculture eventually replaces lost production elsewhere. By reducing farm yield, rainfall changes could also cause skyrocketing prices for commodity crops, something the global economy has rarely observed in the last 30 years.

[32] Recent studies show that in the last few decades, precipitation in North America is increasingly the result of a few downpours rather than lots of showers. Downpours cause flooding and property damage, while being of less use to agriculture than frequent soft rains. Because the relationship between artificially triggered climate change and rainfall is conjectural, investors presently have no way to avoid buying land in places that someday might be hit with frequent downpours. But this concern surely raises a red flag about investments in India, Bangladesh, and Indonesia, where monsoon rains are already a leading social problem.

[33] Water-related investments might be attractive in another way: for hydropower. Zero-emission hydropower might become a premium energy form if greenhouse gases are strictly regulated. Quebec is the Saudi Arabia of roaring water. Already the hydropower complex around James Bay is one of the world's leading sources of water-generated electricity. For 30 years, environmentalists and some Cree activists opposed plans to construct a grand hydropower complex that essentially would dam all large rivers flowing into the James and Hudson bays. But it's not hard to imagine Canada completing the reengineering of northern Quebec for hydropower, if demand from New England and the Midwest becomes strong enough. Similarly, there is hydropower potential in the Chilean portions of Patagonia. This is a wild and beautiful region little touched by human activity—and an intriguing place to snap up land for hydropower reservoirs.

Adaptation

[34] Last October, the treasury office of the United Kingdom estimated that unless we adapt, global warming could eventually subtract as much as 20 percent of the gross domestic product from the world economy. Needless to say, if that happens, not even the cleverest portfolio will help you. This estimate is worst-case, however, and has many economists skeptical. Optimists think dangerous global warming might be averted at surprisingly low cost (see "Some Convenient Truths," September 2006). Once regulations create a profit incentive for the invention of greenhouse-gas-reducing technology, an outpouring of innovation is likely. Some of those who formulate greenhouse-gas-control ideas will become rich; everyone will benefit from the environmental safeguards the ideas confer.

[35] Enactment of some form of binding greenhouse-gas rules is now essential both to slow the rate of greenhouse-gas accumulation and to create an incentive for

inventors, engineers, and businesspeople to devise the ideas that will push society beyond the fossil-fuel age. *The New York Times* recently groused that George W. Bush's fiscal 2007 budget includes only $4.2 billion for federal research that might cut greenhouse-gas emissions. This is the wrong concern: Progress would be faster if the federal government spent nothing at all on greenhouse-gas-reduction research— but enacted regulations that gave the private sector a significant profit motive to find solutions that work in actual use, as opposed to on paper in government studies. The market has caused the greenhouse-gas problem, and the market is the best hope of solving it. Offering market incentives for the development of greenhouse-gas controls—indeed, encouraging profit making in greenhouse-gas controls—is the most promising path to avoiding the harm that could befall the dispossessed of developing nations as the global climate changes.

36 Yet if global-warming theory is right, higher global temperatures are already inevitable. Even the most optimistic scenario for reform envisions decades of additional greenhouse-gas accumulation in the atmosphere, and that in turn means a warming world. The warming may be manageable, but it is probably unstoppable in the short term. This suggests that a major investment sector of the near future will be climate-change adaptation. Crops that grow in high temperatures, homes and buildings designed to stay cool during heat waves, vehicles that run on far less fuel, waterfront structures that can resist stronger storms—the list of needed adaptations will be long, and all involve producing, buying, and selling. Environmentalists don't like talk of adaptation, as it implies making

our peace with a warmer world. That peace, though, must be made—and the sooner businesses, investors, and entrepreneurs get to work, the better.

37 Why, ultimately, should nations act to control greenhouse gases, rather than just letting climate turmoil happen and seeing who profits? One reason is that the cost of controls is likely to be much lower than the cost of rebuilding the world. Coastal cities could be abandoned and rebuilt inland, for instance, but improving energy efficiency and reducing greenhouse-gas emissions in order to stave off rising sea levels should be far more cost-effective. Reforms that prevent major economic and social disruption from climate change are likely to be less expensive, across the board, than reacting to the change. The history of antipollution programs shows that it is always cheaper to prevent emissions than to reverse any damage they cause.

38 For the United States, there's another argument that is particularly keen. The present ordering of the world favors the United States in nearly every respect— political, economic, even natural, considering America's excellent balance of land and resources. Maybe a warming world would favor the United States more; this is certainly possible. But when the global order already places America at No. 1, why would we want to run the risk of climate change that alters that order? Keeping the world economic system and the global balance of power the way they are seems very strongly in the U.S. national interest—and keeping things the way they are requires prevention of significant climate change. That, in the end, is what's in it for us.

SUMMARIZE AND RESPOND

Summarize the winners and losers that Easterbrook explores in his article. Do you find his argument plausible?

In this column, which she wrote for the January 3, 2007, edition of the New York Times, *Kim Severson examines the marketing of environmentalism.*

BE IT EVER SO HOMESPUN, THERE'S NOTHING LIKE SPIN

Kim Severson

1 Something made me uneasy when I dropped a box of gluten-free EnviroKidz organic Koala Crisp cereal in my shopping cart. But it's hard to suspect a cartoon koala, so I moved on.

2 The unsettling sensation came back when I bought a bag of my favorite organic frozen French fries. Why did the verdant fields in the Cascadian Farm logo make me feel so smug?

3 Then I got really suspicious. A bag of natural Cheetos seemed so much more appealing than the classic cheese puff. Why? Was it the image of a subdued Chester Cheetah rising gently from a farm field bathed in golden sunlight?

4 Like clues to a murder that suddenly point to a single culprit, the mystery in my shopping cart revealed itself. Wheat sheaf by wheat sheaf, sunrise by sunrise, the grocery store shelves had been greenwashed.

5 And I was falling for it.

6 The kind of greenwashing I'm talking about is not just a fake environmental ethos. Greenwashing, it seems to me, can also describe a pervasive genre of food packaging designed to make sure that manufacturers grab their slice of the $25 billion that American shoppers spend each year on natural or organic food.

7 As a design shorthand, it makes subtle use of specific colors, images, typefaces and the promise of what marketers call "an authentic narrative" to sell food. Especially in recent years, greenwashing has spilled out well past the organic section of the

grocery store. Even the snack aisle at the gas station isn't immune.

8 "Somebody becomes successful with a specific point of view, and the consumer begins to identify with it and it spreads like a virus," said Paula Scher, a partner in Pentagram, an international design firm. From there it's only a matter of time before Cap'n Crunch shows up in a hemp jacket, raising money to save the manatees.

9 Buy a greenwashed product and you're buying a specific set of healthy environmental and socially correct values.

10 If the package does its work, then the food inside doesn't actually have to be organic, only organic-ish. The right cues on a package free mass-market consumers from doing any homework, said Elizabeth Talerman, a branding analyst. They can assume that a group she calls the green elite—those early adopters who pushed for organic food laws and who helped make Whole Foods markets a success—have done the work for them.

11 "The mass market wants an instant identifier," said Ms. Talerman, a longtime New York advertising consultant.

12 So what are the identifiers? After shopping for dozens of products in places as varied as food co-ops and convenience stores, I've uncovered the essential elements of a greenwashed product. Start with a gentle image of a field or a farm to suggest an ample harvest gathered by an honest, hardworking family. To that end, strangely oversize vegetables or fruits are good. If they are dew-kissed and nestled in a basket, all the better. A little red tractor is O.K. Pesticide tanks and rows of immigrant farm laborers bent over in the hot sun are not.

13 Earth's Best, a baby and toddler food company, offers a delicious example. Its whole grain rice cereal features two babies working the rice fields. One is white and one is black. (A greenwashed package would never show the black child working in the fields alone.)

A sign that looks hand-hewn declares "No GMO's." There is a barn, a butterfly and a typeface that could have come from the back room of a general store.

14 A good greenwashed product should show an animal displaying special skills or great emotional range. Some Organic Valley packages feature a sax-playing, environmentally friendly earthworm. Jaunty cows on Stonyfield Farm yogurt wear sunglasses and headbands. The cows on Horizon's milk cartons dance a bovine jig, despite challenges by organic purists that some Horizon cows see precious little pasture.

15 A little family history helps, too. My Family Farm of Fort Thomas, Ky., sells packaged cookies and crackers and promises to give some of the money to charity. On the back of the box is a story that begins, "With careers as licensed social workers, my sister and I are committed to improving the lives of children." A carton of Country Hen omega-3 eggs, which cost $3.69 for six, had a fuzzy black-and-white photograph inside showing the company's owner, George Bass, and the entire Country Hen family, along with their favorite eggnog recipe.

16 A cause is important. Nature's Path, the maker of Koala Crisp, promises that 1 percent of sales will be spent saving endangered species. Barbara's Bakery, maker of Puffins cereal, pays for the National Audubon Society's live "puffin cams" in the Gulf of Maine. Buy a box of Peace Cereal's raspberry ginger crisp, and a percentage of the profit helps pay for International Peace Prayer Day in New Mexico.

17 The actual health benefits of a product don't always matter. A package of organic Naturepops from College Farm shows a field of lollipops and a barn, suggesting a well-educated farmer tending her candy. The sugar might come from cane juice and tapioca syrup, but it's sugar just the same.

18 And although "organic" is losing its power as a code word for certain cultural values,

it doesn't hurt to flaunt it if you've got it. The word appears 21 times on a box of Cascadian Farm Vanilla Almond Crunch.

19 Having established a design paradigm that succeeds in selling food that is often more expensive than conventional groceries, the design world should perhaps rejoice. This is not the case. Some top brand and package designers find the cartoonish animals and bad hippie typefaces as grating as a self-righteous vegan at a barbecue.

20 But then, they didn't like American food package design that much to begin with.

21 "It's the bottom of the barrel," said Ms. Scher, who works in the New York office of Pentagram design.

22 Riskier designs, like the clean lettering and curvy bottle of Pom Wonderful pomegranate juice, are rare. Food manufacturers usually agonize over changing the size of a box or shifting the background color from teal to aquamarine.

23 But when a trend starts to show success, it's a design pileup. That's what happened with the natural and organic category, which makes up about 10 percent of the food at the grocery store and has been growing by more than 20 percent a year since 2000. In the grocery business, a 4 percent jump is considered a victory.

24 "It's aisle after aisle of design desperation," said Brian Collins, chairman and chief creative officer of the design group at Ogilvy, the international advertising and public relations company. He called the look "phony naïveté" and predicted that its demise was close because consumers are wising up. There is value in telling a story, but it must be true, he said.

25 Merely dressing up the package is not enough, he said. Nonetheless, manufacturers are eager to project a wholesome image.

26 "It's the halo effect," said Caren Wilcox, executive director of the Organic Trade Association. "That's why we encourage consumers to look for the U.S.D.A. organic seal."

27 But even the organic seal doesn't necessarily offer assurances that the item is produced in a way that jibes with consumer expectations for something that comes in a greenwashed package.

28 "All the ingredients being used in items with the organic seal are produced using the organic system," Ms. Wilcox said. "It doesn't mean they don't sometimes end up in products some people think other people shouldn't eat."

29 Design and packaging experts fix the start of sincerity and authenticity in food package design in the 1970s. Mo Siegel began selling Celestial Seasonings tea in boxes with sleepy bears. Tom and Kate Chappell gave up the corporate life to create Tom's of Maine toothpaste. Ben Cohen and Jerry Greenfield sold ice cream in Vermont, using goofy hand-rendered graphics to tell their story.

30 The trend grew in the 1980s, when corporate America entered a noncorporate phase. "Companies began to try to not look like big companies," Ms. Scher said.

31 By the late 1990s, anything with a hint of natural organic goodness sold in big numbers. Today, many companies that started with a humble story line have been purchased by larger interests. Unilever owns Ben and Jerry's, the Hain Celestial Group is traded on Nasdaq and Tom's of Maine is controlled by Colgate-Palmolive.

32 The kind of imagery that once marked a brand as an alternative to corporate food conglomerates has now been incorporated into Lay's potato chips. Consumers can buy classic Lay's in the shiny yellow bag, or Natural Lay's, with a thicker cut, expeller-pressed oil and sea salt. The package has a brown harvest graphic design, old-timey typefaces and a matte bag. The natural chips cost about 10 cents an ounce more than the classics. A handful of either still offers 150 calories and 10 grams of fat.

³³ "When it gets to Lay's," Ms. Scher said, "its time to change."

³⁴ Ms. Talerman, the New York advertising consultant, predicted that the fascination with what she called the green identifiers will last about five years longer. Then, she said, green-elite food consumers will push companies for even more information about environmental impact, labor practices and community involvement, and mass market consumers will start reading labels instead of just searching out easy identifiers.

³⁵ Food manufacturers might begin to copy the new nutrition-style labels that Timberland is putting on its shoe boxes. Each one lists the amount of energy it took to make the shoes, how much of that was renewable, whether child labor was used and how many hours per pair Timberland dedicated to community service.

³⁶ "As soon as the mass market starts to understand these issues more," Ms. Talerman predicted, "we'll get away from the fields and the giant vegetables and get back to better design."

SUMMARIZE AND RESPOND

Write a 50-word summary of Severson's column, followed by a 100-word response in which you take a position on her central argument.

ANALYZE

Which rhetorical appeal (to ethos, pathos, or logos) do you find to be most apparent in Severson's essay? How does this appeal work on the audience? Make sure you point to specific examples of the appeal at work in the text to support your analysis.

As Kim Severson does in the preceding column, Jamie Lincoln Kitman, the New York bureau chief for Automobile Magazine *and a columnist for* Top Gear, *questions the motives behind and value of certain strains of environmental consumerism. Kitman's column was first published in the April 16, 2006, edition of the* New York Times.

LIFE IN THE GREEN LANE

Jamie Lincoln Kitman

¹ If you make your way over to the Javits Convention Center for the New York International Automobile Show—or if you've gone to any auto show in the last year or so—you'll know that hybrid cars are the hippest automotive fashion statement to come along in years. They've become synonymous with the worthy goal of reducing gasoline consumption and dependence on foreign oil and all that this means for a better environment and more stable geopolitics.

2 And yet like fat-free desserts, which sound healthy but can still make you fat, the hybrid car can make people feel as if they're doing something good, even when they're doing nothing special at all. As consumers and governments at every level climb onto the hybrid bandwagon, there is the very real danger of elevating the technology at the expense of the intended outcome—saving gas.

3 Few things these days say "environmentally aware consumer" so loudly as the fuel-sipping Toyota Prius. With its two power sources—one a gasoline-powered internal combustion engine, the other a battery-driven electric motor—the best-selling Prius (and other hybrids sold by Honda and Ford and due soon from several other car makers) can go further on a gallon and emit fewer pollutants in around-town use than most conventional automobiles because under certain circumstances they run on battery power and consume less fuel. For this reason, federal, state and local governments have been bending over backward to encourage the sale of hybrids, with a bewildering array of tax breaks, traffic lanes and parking spaces dedicated to hybrid owners.

4 But just because a car has so-called hybrid technology doesn't mean it's doing more to help the environment or to reduce the country's dependence on imported oil any more than a nonhybrid car. The truth is, it depends on the hybrid and the nonhybrid cars you are comparing, as well as on how you use the vehicles. There are good hybrids and bad ones. Fuel-efficient conventional cars are often better than hybrid S.U.V.'s—just look at how many miles per gallon the vehicle gets.

5 Being a professional car-tester, which is to say a person who gets asked for unpaid car-buying advice practically every day, I know these distinctions have already been lost on many car buyers. And I fear they're well on their way to being lost on our governments, too.

6 Lately, right-minded people have been calling me and telling me they're thinking about buying the Lexus 400H, a new hybrid S.U.V. When I tell them that they'd get better mileage in some conventional S.U.V.'s, and even better mileage with a passenger car, they protest, "But it's a hybrid!" I remind them that the 21 miles per gallon I saw while driving the Lexus is not particularly brilliant, efficiency-wise—hybrid or not. Because the Lexus 400H is a relatively heavy car and because its electric motor is deployed to provide speed more than efficiency, it will never be a mileage champ.

7 The car that started the hybrid craze, the Toyota Prius, is lauded for squeezing 40 or more miles out of a gallon of gas, and it really can. But only when it's being driven around town, where its electric motor does its best and most active work. On a cross-country excursion in a Prius, the staff of Automobile Magazine discovered mileage plummeted on the Interstate. In fact, the car's computer, which controls the engine and the motor, allowing them to run together or separately, was programmed to direct the Prius to spend most of its highway time running on gasoline because at higher speeds the batteries quickly get exhausted. Indeed, the gasoline engine worked so hard that we calculated we might have used less fuel on our journey if we had been driving Toyota's conventionally powered, similarly sized Corolla—which costs thousands less. For the owner who does the majority of her driving on the highway, the Prius's potential for fuel economy will never be realized and its price premium never recovered.

8 For years, most of the world's big car makers have shied away from building hybrids because while they are technologically intriguing, they are also an inelegant engineering solution—the use of two energy sources assures extra weight, extra complexity and extra expense (as much as $6,000 more per car.) The hybrid car's electric battery packs rob space from passengers and cargo and although they can be recycled, not every owner can be counted on to do the right thing at the end of their vehicle's service

life. And an unrecycled hybrid battery pack, which weighs more than 100 pounds, poses a major environmental hazard.

9 So the ideal hybrid car is one that is used in town and carefully disposed of at the end of its days. Hybrid taxis and buses make enormous sense. But the market knows no such distinctions. People think they want hybrids and they'll buy them, even if a conventional car would make more sense for their pocketbook and for the environment. The danger is that the automakers will co-opt the hybrids' green mantle and, with the help of a government looking to bail out its troubled friends in Detroit, misguidedly encourage the sale of hybrids without reference to their actual effect on oil consumption.

10 Several bills floating around Congress, for instance, have proposed tax incentives to buyers of hybrid cars, irrespective of their gas mileage. Thus, under one failed but sure to resurface formulation, the suburbanite who buys a hypothetical hybrid Dodge Durango that gets 14 miles per gallon instead of 12 thanks to its second, electric power source would be entitled to a huge tax incentive, while the buyer of a conventional, gasoline-powered Honda Civic that delivers 40 miles per gallon on the open road gets none.

11 And under some imaginable patchwork of state and local ordinances, the Durango buyer might get a special parking space at the train station and the right to use a high occupancy vehicle lane, despite appalling fuel economy and a car full of empty seats, while the Honda driver will have to walk to the train from a distant parking lot after braving the worst of morning rush hour traffic on the highway just like everybody else.

12 Pro-hybrid laws and incentives sound nice, but they might just end up subsidizing companies that have failed to develop truly fuel-efficient vehicles at the expense of those that have had the foresight to design their cars right in the first place. And they may actually punish citizens who save fuel the old-fashioned way—by using less of it, with smaller, lighter and more efficient cars. All the while, they'll make a mockery of a potentially useful technology.

SUMMARIZE AND RESPOND

Write a 50-word summary of Kitman's column, followed by a 150-word response in which you comment on the effectiveness of his argument.

ANALYZE

How does Kitman use appeals to logos, or the audience's intellect, to bolster his argument? Point to specific examples from the text in your analysis.

ARGUE

Kitman points out what he sees as flaws in the incentive-based approach to selling the public on environmentally friendly vehicles. Write a brief essay in which you propose a course of action to address some of these problems.

Patrick Moore, a co-founder of the environmental group Greenpeace and chairman and chief scientist of Greenspirit Strategies Ltd, wrote this column for the April 16, 2006, edition of the Washington Post. *As you read, notice the rhetorical effect of his position as an environmentalist who now favors nuclear power.*

GOING NUCLEAR: A GREEN MAKES THE CASE

Patrick Moore

[1] In the early 1970s when I helped found Greenpeace, I believed that nuclear energy was synonymous with nuclear holocaust, as did most of my compatriots. That's the conviction that inspired Greenpeace's first voyage up the spectacular rocky northwest coast to protest the testing of U.S. hydrogen bombs in Alaska's Aleutian Islands. Thirty years on, my views have changed, and the rest of the environmental movement needs to update its views, too, because nuclear energy may just be the energy source that can save our planet from another possible disaster: catastrophic climate change.

[2] Look at it this way: More than 600 coal-fired electric plants in the United States produce 36 percent of U.S. emissions—or nearly 10 percent of global emissions—of CO_2, the primary greenhouse gas responsible for climate change. Nuclear energy is the only large-scale, cost-effective energy source that can reduce these emissions while continuing to satisfy a growing demand for power. And these days it can do so safely.

[3] I say that guardedly, of course, just days after Iranian President Mahmoud Ahmadinejad announced that his country had enriched uranium. "The nuclear technology is only for the purpose of peace and nothing else," he said. But there is widespread speculation that, even though the process is ostensibly dedicated to producing electricity, it is in fact a cover for building nuclear weapons.

[4] And although I don't want to underestimate the very real dangers of nuclear technology in the hands of rogue states, we cannot simply ban every technology that is dangerous. That was the all-or-nothing mentality at the height of the Cold War, when anything nuclear seemed to spell doom for humanity and the environment. In 1979, Jane Fonda and Jack Lemmon produced a frisson of fear with their starring roles in *The China Syndrome*, a fictional evocation of nuclear disaster in which a reactor meltdown threatens a city's survival. Less than two weeks after the blockbuster film opened, a reactor core meltdown at Pennsylvania's Three Mile Island nuclear power plant sent shivers of very real anguish throughout the country.

[5] What nobody noticed at the time, though, was that Three Mile Island was in fact a success story: The concrete containment structure did just what it was designed to do—prevent radiation from escaping into the environment. And although the reactor itself was crippled, there was no injury or death among nuclear workers or nearby residents. Three Mile Island was the only serious accident in the history of nuclear energy generation in the United States,

but it was enough to scare us away from further developing the technology: There hasn't been a nuclear plant ordered up since then.

[6] Today, there are 103 nuclear reactors quietly delivering just 20 percent of America's electricity. Eighty percent of the people living within 10 miles of these plants approve of them (that's not including the nuclear workers). Although I don't live near a nuclear plant, I am now squarely in their camp.

[7] And I am not alone among seasoned environmental activists in changing my mind on this subject. British atmospheric scientist James Lovelock, father of the Gaia theory, believes that nuclear energy is the only way to avoid catastrophic climate change. Stewart Brand, founder of the "Whole Earth Catalog," says the environmental movement must embrace nuclear energy to wean ourselves from fossil fuels. On occasion, such opinions have been met with excommunication from the anti-nuclear priesthood: The late British Bishop Hugh Montefiore, founder and director of Friends of the Earth, was forced to resign from the group's board after he wrote a pro-nuclear article in a church newsletter.

[8] There are signs of a new willingness to listen, though, even among the staunchest anti-nuclear campaigners. When I attended the Kyoto climate meeting in Montreal last December, I spoke to a packed house on the question of a sustainable energy future. I argued that the only way to reduce fossil fuel emissions from electrical production is through an aggressive program of renewable energy sources (hydroelectric, geothermal heat pumps, wind, etc.) plus nuclear. The Greenpeace spokesperson was first at the mike for the question period, and I expected a tongue-lashing. Instead, he began by saying he agreed with much of what I said—not the nuclear bit, of course, but there was a clear feeling that all options must be explored.

[9] Here's why: Wind and solar power have their place, but because they are intermittent and unpredictable they simply can't replace big baseload plants such as coal, nuclear and hydroelectric. Natural gas, a fossil fuel, is too expensive already, and its price is too volatile to risk building big baseload plants. Given that hydroelectric resources are built pretty much to capacity, nuclear is, by elimination, the only viable substitute for coal. It's that simple.

[10] That's not to say that there aren't real problems—as well as various myths—associated with nuclear energy. Each concern deserves careful consideration:

- Nuclear energy is expensive. It is in fact one of the least expensive energy sources. In 2004, the average cost of producing nuclear energy in the United States was less than two cents per kilowatt-hour, comparable with coal and hydroelectric. Advances in technology will bring the cost down further in the future.

- Nuclear plants are not safe. Although Three Mile Island was a success story, the accident at Chernobyl, 20 years ago this month, was not. But Chernobyl was an accident waiting to happen. This early model Soviet reactor had no containment vessel, was an inherently bad design and its operators literally blew it up. The multi-agency U.N. Chernobyl Forum reported last year that 56 deaths could be directly attributed to the accident, most of those from radiation or burns suffered while fighting the fire. Tragic as those deaths were, they pale in comparison to the more than 5,000 coal-mining deaths that occur worldwide every year. No one has died of a radiation-related accident in the history of the U.S. civilian nuclear reactor program. (And although hundreds of uranium mine workers did die from radiation exposure underground in the early years of that industry, that problem was long ago corrected.)

- Nuclear waste will be dangerous for thousands of years. Within 40 years, used fuel has less than one-thousandth of the radioactivity it had when it was removed from the reactor. And it is incorrect to call it waste, because 95 percent of the potential energy is still contained in the used fuel after the first cycle. Now that the United States has removed the ban on recycling used fuel, it will be possible to use that energy and to greatly reduce the amount of waste that needs treatment and disposal. Last month, Japan joined France, Britain and Russia in the nuclear-fuel-recycling business. The United States will not be far behind.

- Nuclear reactors are vulnerable to terrorist attack. The six-feet-thick reinforced concrete containment vessel protects the contents from the outside as well as the inside. And even if a jumbo jet did crash into a reactor and breach the containment, the reactor would not explode. There are many types of facilities that are far more vulnerable, including liquid natural gas plants, chemical plants and numerous political targets.

- Nuclear fuel can be diverted to make nuclear weapons. This is the most serious issue associated with nuclear energy and the most difficult to address, as the example of Iran shows. But just because nuclear technology can be put to evil purposes is not an argument to ban its use.

[11] Over the past 20 years, one of the simplest tools—the machete—has been used to kill more than a million people in Africa, far more than were killed in the Hiroshima and Nagasaki nuclear bombings combined. What are car bombs made of? Diesel oil, fertilizer and cars. If we banned everything that can be used to kill people, we would never have harnessed fire.

[12] The only practical approach to the issue of nuclear weapons proliferation is to put it higher on the international agenda and to use diplomacy and, where necessary, force to prevent countries or terrorists from using nuclear materials for destructive ends. And new technologies such as the reprocessing system recently introduced in Japan (in which the plutonium is never separated from the uranium) can make it much more difficult for terrorists or rogue states to use civilian materials to manufacture weapons.

[13] The 600-plus coal-fired plants emit nearly 2 billion tons of CO_2 annually—the equivalent of the exhaust from about 300 million automobiles. In addition, the Clean Air Council reports that coal plants are responsible for 64 percent of sulfur dioxide emissions, 26 percent of nitrous oxides and 33 percent of mercury emissions. These pollutants are eroding the health of our environment, producing acid rain, smog, respiratory illness and mercury contamination.

[14] Meanwhile, the 103 nuclear plants operating in the United States effectively avoid the release of 700 million tons of CO_2 emissions annually—the equivalent of the exhaust from more than 100 million automobiles. Imagine if the ratio of coal to nuclear were reversed so that only 20 percent of our electricity was generated from coal and 60 percent from nuclear. This would go a long way toward cleaning the air and reducing greenhouse gas emissions. Every responsible environmentalist should support a move in that direction.

Write a 100-word summary of Moore's argument.

Moore stakes much of his argument on his own credibility, part of his ethical appeal. Pointing to specific examples in the text to support your response, analyze how he wants to be perceived by the audience. Why is this appeal so important to the success of his argument?

from reading to writing

1. Characterize the ethos presented by three of the following writers, supporting your responses with evidence from their texts. Which do you find most persuasive? Why?
   a. Jeffrey Kluger in "What Now?"
   b. Greg Easterbrook in "Global Warming: Who Loses—and Who Wins?"
   c. Kim Severson in "Be It Ever So Homespun, There's Nothing Like Spin."
   d. Patrick Moore in "Going Nuclear: A Green Makes the Case."
2. How do Jeffrey Kluger and Kim Severson define "greenwashing"? Based on their reporting and on your own experience as a consumer, what do you think are the implications of the practice?
3. As people who support protecting the environment, Patrick Moore and Jamie Lincoln Kitman make surprising arguments in their essays concerning the effectiveness of hybrid vehicles and nuclear energy, respectively. Working individually or with a partner, outline their arguments and responses to counterarguments. How do you think an author's biography influences his or her persuasiveness?
4. Working with a partner or in a small group, make a list of modern conveniences you would be willing to sacrifice in order to stem global warming.
5. Using the pieces you've read as a starting point, write a brief essay in which you explain what you think is the best way for individuals to help solve the global warming crisis.

body images

"Males...appear to be vulnerable to social pressures to achieve the perfect body similar to those that have long plagued women. But unlike the female ideal, which tends to focus on a 'goal weight,'...men's focus is nearly always on achieving 'six-pack' abs."

—**Sandra G. Boodman,** *"Eating Disorders: Not Just for Women"*

America clearly has a problem—or lots of different problems—with eating, weight, and body image. The authors in this chapter present several different perspectives on these complicated and interrelated issues. Some argue that those who are obese need to take responsibility for their weight and do something about it. Others contend that deceptive marketing and irresponsible advertising by the food and fashion industries are to blame. And still others suggest that society as a whole should alter its perception of ideal body weight. As you read this chapter, consider whether our country has a prejudice against overweight citizens, whether there is really any such thing as an ideal body image, and whether you agree with the causal links presented in these essays and articles.

Reporter Shari Roan wrote the following article for the January 14, 2008, edition of the Los Angeles Times. *In it, she explores a recent trend in research that sees environmental causes—such as the availability of poor food options—at the root of America's obesity epidemic. One of the primary sources Roan cites is Deborah Cohen, whose article "A Desired Epidemic: Obesity and the Food Industry" starts on page 47.*

HEAVY HABITS

Don't blame yourself for that extra weight, a new theory says. Blame your environment. Cues to eat are all around—and we're only human.

Shari Roan

[1] Here's an interesting thought: What if you're not to blame for your weight problem?

[2] What if the fault could be laid squarely at the feet of food manufacturers and marketers, grocery store managers, restaurant operators, food vendors—the people who make food so visible, available and mouthwatering?

[3] Several recent studies, papers and a popular weight-loss book argue that eating is an automatic behavior triggered by environmental cues that most people are unaware of—or simply can't ignore. Think of the buttery smell of movie theater popcorn, the sight of glazed doughnuts glistening in the office conference room or the simple habit of picking up a whipped-cream-laden latte on the way to work.

[4] Accepting this "don't blame me" notion may not only ease the guilt and self-loathing that often accompanies obesity, say the researchers behind the theory, but also help people achieve a healthier weight.

[5] To make Americans eat less and eat more healthily, they contend, the environment itself needs to be changed—with laws regulating portion size, labeling or the places where food can be sold or eaten. That would be much easier, the researchers add, than overcoming human nature. The theory that our society—not us—is to blame for our overall expanding waist size is garnering support from health and nutrition experts. To recap the dismal statistics: In the last 25 years, the number of obese Americans has increased from 14.5% to 32.2%. Two out of

three adults are overweight, as are 19% of children, according to the Centers for Disease Control and Prevention.

6 "Almost everybody is gaining weight in almost all socioeconomic groups. It's not limited to certain people. It's everywhere," says Dr. Deborah A. Cohen, a senior natural scientist at Rand Corp. and the author of a recent paper on the environmental theory of obesity. "Look at doctors, nurses and dietitians who are overweight or obese. If it has anything to do with how much we know about nutrition or how much we're motivated, we would never see people with such expertise be overweight or obese."

7 But defining obesity as an environmental issue is a little like comparing it to global warming: The problem is all around us—part of us—but we, as individuals, can do little about it. Big actions by governments and societies will be needed for much to change, according to some researchers who study obesity.

8 Other health experts say that view is too extreme. Individuals can exert control over their own environment and lose or maintain weight despite the temptation of venti lattes, super-sized French fries and all-you-can-eat pasta bowls, they say.

9 "The environment, I think, to a large extent explains the obesity epidemic," says Dr. Robert H. Eckel, a professor of medicine at the University of Colorado and past president of the American Heart Association. "But should we change the environment to alter the obesity epidemic? And how much do we need to change it? Those are difficult questions. To blame it all on the environment is a mistake. There is individual responsibility."

Eating on autopilot

10 To explain how so many people have become overweight, researchers start with the urge to eat.

11 Eating is an automatic behavior that has little to do with choice, willpower or even hunger, Cohen says. Her paper, with co-author Thomas Farley of Tulane University's Prevention Research Center, was published online last month in *Preventing Chronic Disease*, the peer-reviewed health journal of the Centers for Disease Control and Prevention.

12 Cohen and Farley argue that automatic behaviors can be controlled, but only for a short time (the reason most diets ultimately fail). A more effective approach, they say, would be to decrease the accessibility, visibility and quantities of food people are exposed to, and the environmental cues that promote eating.

13 The fact that most people cannot maintain a weight loss is proof that nutrition knowledge and willpower don't work, they and other researchers contend.

14 "We've thought for a long time that if we just suggested to people that there are negative effects from obesity and if we provided reminders, they would be able to gain control over their behavior and act healthy," says Wendy Wood, a Duke University psychologist who studies habits. "There isn't much evidence that works."

15 Instead, ample research demonstrates that much of human behavior is automatic. Studies of people keeping activity diaries show that about 45% of daily human behavior is repetitive and unthinking. In a study published recently in the *Journal of Consumer Psychology*, Wood showed that people fall back on their habits—such as buying fast food—even when they intend to do otherwise.

16 Several recent studies depict the folly of human food consumption. A 2006 study in the *International Journal of Obesity* found that when candy was placed in a clear dish, people ate 71% more than when it was in

an opaque dish. The same study found that the closer the food, the more likely it would be eaten.

[17] The same research group, headed by Brian Wansink, director of Cornell University's Food and Brand Lab, also found that people don't necessarily stop eating when full. People eating from soup bowls that were secretly refilled ate 73% more soup. That study was published in 2005 in *Obesity Research*.

[18] "Eating behaviors are like a lot of other lifestyle behaviors; you tend to repeat them, often in the same context, same location, with the same people, at the same time of day," Wood says. "When people repeat behaviors in that way, they become automatic. They are cued by the context and no longer involve decision-making."

[19] That doesn't mean people are weak or stupid, however. Human brains have to operate on autopilot sometimes in order to accomplish more difficult mental tasks that involve analytical, creative or abstract thought, Cohen says. "There is a benefit to being automatic," she says. "It frees us up to do what is more important. Trying to change automatic behavior is going to be an exercise in frustration."

[20] The fact that food is everywhere in today's society is a problem, Cohen says, because people appear to be biologically configured to eat, eat, eat. "People are designed to overeat," she says. "We have a mechanism to store extra calories when we are given too much to eat. When you increase portion sizes, whether someone is fat or thin, neurotic or not neurotic, we eat too much."

[21] The fact that many people are not overweight is due to individual differences in environments and sensitivity to environmental cues. Genes vary too. Knowledge and self-control have little to do with it, she says. "Do you think people are less responsible than they were 20 years ago?" Cohen says. "What has happened in our environment between now and 20 years ago? I don't think responsibility has anything to do with this. That is the wrong emphasis."

A long-term struggle

[22] Good intentions are often a poor foil to such overwhelming environmental and biological cues.

[23] "I think a lot of people know what they should be eating," says Ruth Frechman, a spokeswoman for the American Dietetic Association who has a private practice in Burbank, California. "But because of their habits, they aren't doing it."

[24] Changing routine behavior is painstaking and slow, Frechman says. She asks clients to start by focusing on one small habit. For example, instead of going to the vending machine for candy at 3 o'clock each afternoon, she advises them to go to the office cafeteria and buy fruit. "It's hard," she says. "I sometimes work with people for years to get them to change one little thing."

[25] Louise Paziak, 54, of Burbank says she had some success losing weight only after she began keeping a food diary. "I would think, 'Well, I'm not eating that much.' But what I found out was that I was nibbling a lot," she says. She has lost 20 pounds over the last two years through nutritional counseling, strict shopping rules that prohibit snacks and eating only half of what she is served in a restaurant. "I'm so aware of it now, I notice what other people are eating too," she says with a laugh.

[26] Whether individuals can buck their environment is hotly debated. Some experts think it's just too hard for most people.

[27] "It's not that people can't think about what they're doing. Of course they can," Wood says. "That's one of the things that makes this so complex. If you ask people to limit their diet and eat healthful, everyone can do that for a short amount of time. It's when you have to inhibit a response over a long period of time, that is where we have

difficulty. It involves not just a decision to do something new, it also involves inhibiting the old one. If people rely on willpower alone, they are expecting too much of themselves."

28 It's easier to change the environment than it is to change people, Cohen says. In her paper, she says people need protection from the "toxic environment" and calls on governments, communities and organizations to solve the obesity problem. She advocates downsizing portions, limiting access to ready-to-eat foods and curbing food advertising. "We've created an environment that has resulted in our being overweight and obese and now we have to create an environment that helps us be healthy," she says.

29 The antismoking campaign is a good model, Cohen says. Smoking rates have been reduced by restricting where cigarettes can be sold and used, by taxing them and by media campaigns depicting smoking as harmful.

30 Eckel, the past president of the American Heart Association, agrees that an out-of-control environment, along with the biological propensity to retain weight, has caused Americans to gain weight. But he doubts change through legislation is necessary. "There are success stories in dieting, and we have sufficient data from studies to show it begins with a high level of motivation," Eckel says.

Rules don't fit all

31 It's clear, however, that applying strict rules to eating behavior doesn't work for most people, says Wansink, who was appointed in November as head of the Department of Agriculture's Center for Nutrition Policy & Research. The office is responsible for overseeing the "Dietary Guidelines for Americans" publication and other nutrition programs. But people can have success by making small changes. Demanding sweeping environmental changes is impractical and strict dieting is too overtaxing, he says.

32 "I think the answer lies somewhere in the middle," says Wansink, author of the 2006 book "Mindless Eating: Why We Eat More Than We Think." "We need to make small changes in our environment. That can be as small as moving fruits and vegetables to the middle shelf in the refrigerator. You won't lose 30 pounds in a month, but these small changes can make a big difference over time."

33 Changes can also be profound if people focus on their immediate environment. As he points out: Families usually have a "nutrition gatekeeper" who, through shopping, cooking and serving food, controls about 73% of what everyone in the family eats.

34 Eating is strongly influenced by the environment, but each person can still exert some conscious control over it, says Dr. Harvey J. Widroe, a Walnut Creek psychiatrist and author of the 2007 book "The Smart Dieter's Cheating Guide." He tells his clients to start with a few simple principles, such as to eat only two-thirds of their usual portions or to replace a favorite food, such as ice cream, with a similar but healthier alternative, such as sorbet.

35 "People can do this," he says. But environmental changes, such as taking vending machines out of schools and office buildings, won't work. "People cheat. They'll find a way to eat."

ANALYZE

The author spends much of this essay presenting, linking, and contextualizing the arguments of other writers, medical professionals, and nutrition experts. Is her piece simply informative, or does she manage to present an argument of her own? How would you characterize her position, and what clues cause you to come to this conclusion?

DISCUSS

In her essay, Roan cites Dr. Deborah A. Cohen, a scientist who argues for an environmental theory of obesity (an article by Cohen starts on page 47). Do you think environmental factors lead people to overeat? If so, is there a manageable way to control these environmental factors?

ARGUE

Using Roan's essay as a starting point, write a cause-and-effect argument about what would happen to obesity rates if vending machines featuring unhealthy snacks were removed from our public schools.

In this piece from the January 22, 2006, edition of the Washington Post, *Michael S. Rosenwald examines some less publicized consequences of America's battle with weight. As you read, notice how his use of the first person works on the audience.*

WHY AMERICA HAS TO BE FAT

Michael S. Rosenwald

[1] I am fat. Sixty pounds too hefty, in my doctor's opinion. Probably 80 pounds, in my fiancée's view.

[2] Being fat makes me a lot of things—a top contender for type II diabetes, for instance, or a heart attack, or stroke, maybe even a replacement knee or hip. My girth also puts me in familiar company, with about two-thirds of the U.S. population now considered overweight.

[3] But in many ways, my being fat also makes me pretty good for the economy.

[4] You've read the headlines: America's problem with bulging waistlines has reached pandemic proportions, according to federal health officials, who warn that obesity is becoming society's No. 1 killer. But as doctors wrestle with the problem, economists have been pondering which corporations and industries benefit, and the role that changes in the overall economy have played in making us fat to begin with.

[5] It turns out, economists say, that changes in food technology (producing tasty, easy-to-cook food, such as French fries)

and changes in labor (we used to be paid to exercise at work, now we pay to exercise after work) combined with women's importance in the workforce, not the kitchen, have combined to produce industries able to cheaply and efficiently meet the demands of our busy lives. The cookie industry. The fast-food industry. Potato chips. Soda. The chain-restaurant industry, with its heaping portions of low-priced, high-calorie foods.

6 In some ways, we are better off in this Fat Economy. Many people work in easier, better-paying jobs, which help pay for their big homes in the suburbs. Women don't have to spend two hours preparing dinner every night; many have risen to unprecedented levels of corporate and political power. Flat-panel plasma TVs hang over fireplaces, which can be lit using the same remote control for flipping channels. But the unintended consequence of these economic changes is that many of us have become fat. An efficient economy produces sluggish, inefficient bodies.

7 "The obesity problem is really a side effect of things that are good for the economy," said Tomas J. Philipson, an economics professor who studies obesity at the University of Chicago, a city recently named the fattest in America. "But we would rather take improvements in technology and agriculture than go back to the way we lived in the 1950s when everyone was thin. Nobody wants to sweat at work for 10 hours a day and be poor. Yes, you're obese, but you have a life that is much more comfortable."

8 For many corporations, and even for physicians, Americans' obesity has also fattened the bottom line. William L. Weis, a management professor at Seattle University, says revenue from the "obesity industries" will likely top $315 billion this year, and perhaps far more. That includes $133.7 billion for fast-food restaurants, $124.7 billion for medical treatments related to obesity, and $1.8 billion just for diet books—all told, nearly 3 percent of the overall U.S. economy.

9 Did you know, according to consumer-research firm Mintel Group, that we guzzled $37 billion in carbonated beverages in 2004? The same year, we spent $3.9 billion on cookies—$244 million of which were Oreo cookies sold by Kraft Foods for about $3.69 a package. In 2003, we splurged $57.2 billion on meals at restaurants such as Denny's, Chili's and Outback Steakhouse (a personal favorite). Potato chip sales hit $6.2 billion in 2004.

10 "Put simply, there is a lot of money being made, and to be made, in feeding both oversized stomachs and feeding those enterprises selling fixes for oversized stomachs," Weis wrote in 2005 in the Academy of Health Care Management Journal. "And both industries—those selling junk food and those selling fat cures—depend for their future on a prevalence of obesity."

11 And the prevalence of obesity won't fade anytime soon. According to David M. Cutler, an economist at Harvard University, Americans' waistlines are caught in a simple accounting quagmire. In a 2003 paper titled "Why Have Americans Become More Obese?" Cutler wrote: "As an accounting statement, people gain weight if there is an increase in calories taken in or a decrease in calories expended."

12 On the calories-expended side of the Fat Economy, economists have noted that changes in the workplace have caused us to burn fewer calories. Prior to the 1950s, jobs often meant hard labor. We lifted heavy things. We worked outside. Our desks—if we had them—did not come equipped with computers. We lived in urban environments, walking most places.

13 Now many Americans work in offices in buildings with elevators. If we walk anywhere, it's to lunch—to TGI Friday's or the corner burrito shop. We live in the suburbs,

we drive to and from work and—in my case—to and from the mailbox. We pay $60 a month for the privilege of lifting something heavy in a gym we have to drive to. (I belong to two gyms, in the hope that guilt will cause me to visit at least one.) And we also must pay to exercise by giving up our free time. Do we work out, or do we drive the kids to their soccer game, where we can sit and watch? Do we work out, or do we download new songs from iTunes?

[14] "People are just not willing to give up their leisure time," Philipson said. "People don't want to pay to exercise with their leisure time."

[15] Which brings us to the calories-consumed side of the ledger. If we don't expend calories, they add up and turn into pounds. Thirty-five hundred calories generally equals one pound. So behold, for argument's sake, the French fry. An order of large fries at McDonald's puts 520 calories into one's body. It is well known, at least by this consumer, that an order of large fries can generally be placed, filled and consumed in a matter of minutes.

[16] But this was not always so, Cutler said.

[17] Before World War II, if you wanted a French fry, you went to the store, bought potatoes, took them home, washed them, peeled them, sliced them and fried them. "Without expensive machinery, these activities take a lot of time," Cutler said. "In the postwar period, a number of innovations allowed the centralization of French fry production." Now fries are prepped in factories using sophisticated technologies, then frozen at sub-40-degree temperatures and shipped to a restaurant, where they are deep-fried, or to someone's home, where they are microwaved. Either way, they are served up in a matter of minutes.

[18] French fries helped drive up U.S. potato consumption by 30 percent between 1977 and 1995, but they mean more than that—they symbolize the convergence of the economic and technological changes that have made us fat. Cutler and Philipson have noted that when women joined the workplace, they left behind some of the labor that traditionally went into cooking meals. This happened as technology increasingly allowed for mass production and preparation of food. Much of this type of food—be it French fries, potato chips, frozen dinners or quick meals at restaurants—contains more calories.

[19] We expend fewer calories and take more in. The pounds add up. Hence, the Fat Economy.

[20] "The structure of the economy has made us more obese," Cutler said. "That is clearly true. What businesses do is they cater to what we want, whether what we want is really in our long-term interests or not. So people are obese and they want to diet, but they also want things to be immediately there. Manufacturers and store-owners make that possible. The upside is nobody spends two hours a day cooking anymore."

[21] So do Americans have to be fat for the economy to thrive? The economy would not exactly crash if people stopped spending money on French fries and meals at TGI Friday's. Economists think the money would just be spent differently or in different places. Specific industries would adapt—as many have already, offering more healthful choices—to meet changing demands. No business can survive by selling things people don't want.

[22] In fact the overall long-term economic costs of obesity are many. The $10,000 of extra medical care that the overweight require over their lifetimes certainly makes a doctor's wallet fatter, but it could bankrupt the health insurance industry. Also, research shows that while more women have entered the workforce, their wages, particularly for white women, sink if they are overweight.

[23] Much of the long-term financial burden for obesity will fall on the shoulders of U.S. corporations, which already fork out billions of dollars a year in sick time and insurance costs related to obesity illnesses, and on American taxpayers, through their contributions for programs such as Medicare and Medicaid. What's more, shorter life spans will more quickly take millions of educated people out of the workforce.

[24] For that last problem, the Fat Economy has already found ways to innovate and profit. In Lynn, Ind., there is a company called Goliath Casket that makes caskets up to 52 inches wide. The company's Web site, which can be found at www.oversizecasket.com/, notes that Goliath's founder quit his job as a welder in 1985, saying. "Boys, I'm gonna go home and build oversize caskets that you would be proud to put your mother in."

SUMMARIZE AND RESPOND

Write a 100-word summary of Rosenwald's article, focusing on the causal links he establishes to show how obesity fuels the U.S. economy.

ANALYZE

Analyze Rosenwald's use of the first person ("I" and "we") in his article. How does this kind of ethical appeal affect the audience? Make sure you point to specific examples of the appeal at work in the text to support your analysis.

DISCUSS

What is the Fat Economy? Do you agree with Rosenwald's characterization of it? Explain your answer.

In the next article, Sandra G. Boodman, writing in the March 13, 2007, edition of the Washington Post, *examines a less recognized problem in our image-conscious society—boys and men who suffer from eating disorders.*

EATING DISORDERS: NOT JUST FOR WOMEN

Sandra G. Boodman

[1] They exercise for hours, devise rigid rituals surrounding food, obsessively monitor their weight and yearn to resemble the taut-bodied celebrities whose images grace magazine covers. But the models and actors this group typically emulates are not

the skeletal Kate Moss or wispy Nicole Kidman but the chiseled muscularity of soccer superstar David Beckham and actor Daniel Craig, the latest screen incarnation of James Bond.

[2] The reason: These eating disorder sufferers are male.

[3] Long regarded as a women's problem, the trio of serious eating disorders—the self-starvation of anorexia, the gorging and purging that characterize bulimia and the uncontrolled consumption of large amounts of food that is binge eating—are increasingly affecting males.

[4] Last month, Harvard researchers reported the results of the first national study of eating disorders in a population of nearly 3,000 adults and found that 25 percent of those with anorexia or bulimia and 40 percent of binge eaters were men.

[5] The authors called the rate "surprisingly high" because earlier studies had estimated that males accounted for about 10 percent of the cases of bulimia and anorexia, which can be fatal. Binge eating is not officially recognized as a psychiatric disorder and is not considered life-threatening, but its prevalence among men surprised some eating disorders specialists.

[6] Although disordered eating is well-known among teenage girls and young women, experts say the problem among boys and young men is frequently overlooked by parents and coaches and under-treated by doctors. Males, they now believe, appear to be vulnerable to social pressures to achieve the perfect body similar to those that have long plagued women. But unlike the female ideal, which tends to focus on a "goal weight" or overall skinniness, men's focus is nearly always on achieving "six-pack" abs.

[7] "Men are more reluctant to admit losing control" about food, said James I. Hudson, lead author of the study, which estimated that about 9 million Americans suffer from an eating disorder at some point in their lives. The research was published last month in the journal *Biological Psychiatry*.

[8] Stigma, Hudson added, remains a major barrier: Many men are loath to admit having a problem that is so strongly associated with women, fearing they will seem unmanly. Even if they do, they may have trouble finding treatment: Some eating disorder programs admit only women. And in sharp contrast to the parade of female celebrities who have publicly discussed their eating disorders, few well-known men have come forward.

[9] The most notable exception is actor Dennis Quaid, who has talked about his battle with what he termed "manorexia," for which he sought treatment. Quaid said his problem started when he lost 40 pounds to play Doc Holliday in the 1994 movie "Wyatt Earp." Actor Billy Bob Thornton has said he, too, has battled anorexia, at one point losing 59 pounds, and singer Elton John has said he suffered from bulimia. Former male model Ron Saxen has written a new book describing his ordeal with binge eating.

[10] Some men have suffered from all three. Among them is Matt Gaebel, 22, who was hospitalized for anorexia during his sophomore year at North Carolina State University after his weight plummeted from 155 to 106 pounds. Gabel, who is 6 feet 3 inches tall, said he subsequently developed bulimia to cope with the weight he gained during treatment for anorexia, then turned to binge eating out of concern that self-induced vomiting would ruin his teeth. Binge eating, said Gaebel, who lives with his parents in Cary, N.C., "calms me down." It has also left him feeling fat as well as "very isolated and depressed"; he now weighs 225 pounds.

[11] Isolation is not a new feeling. Gaebel said he was the only male eating disorder patient most of the months he was hospitalized at the University of North Carolina. The only male he met there, he said, was a very young boy struggling with his homosexuality.

Gaebel said he worried that people might erroneously think he was gay, because male homosexuality is associated with the development of eating disorders. (Experts say the increased risk is not intrinsic, but stems from the emphasis on weight and appearance among gay men.)

[12] "I really didn't have anyone to talk to," Gaebel recalled. Although not overweight when he developed anorexia, he had been teased in middle school for his "baby fat" and "love handles." Such experiences are common among men with eating disorders, said psychologist Cynthia Bulik, director of UNC's eating disorders program.

[13] Psychiatrist Arnold Andersen, director of the eating disorders program at the University of Iowa and a widely recognized expert on male eating problems, said he has treated teenagers who developed bulimia or anorexia after failing to make a sports team where weight is paramount, such as wrestling. Other patients include men who began dieting to meet job requirements—and couldn't stop. "We've had a number of military people like colonels," said Andersen, who was formerly on the staffs of Johns Hopkins Hospital and the National Institutes of Health. "The military is very strict, and they're afraid they're going to get chucked out" or fail to win a promotion if they don't lose weight to meet certain requirements.

[14] Adelaide Robb, associate professor of psychiatry at George Washington University School of Medicine, said that many of the risk factors for males are the same as for females, although boys are more likely to be overweight and are typically older than girls when they develop an eating disorder.

[15] In both sexes there is often a family history of eating disorders—Gaebel said that is true in his family—as well as perfectionist and obsessive behaviors and a history of dieting.

[16] Treatment for males and females involves cognitive therapy to overcome a distorted body image, which is at the core of eating disorders. Depression and substance abuse may also be present.

[17] Parents of boys, Robb said, are much less likely to recognize the problem and more apt to deny it. Pediatricians, she said, often don't suspect it, either. "Boys say, 'I'm getting into shape,'" Robb said, "not, 'I'm fat and gross and need to go on a diet,'" as do girls. Initially, she added, many parents are thrilled that their teenage son who could polish off huge quantities of food in short order has sworn off junk food, carbohydrates or pizza in favor of turkey sandwiches, broiled salmon and fruit. "They often think he's adopted healthy eating habits."

[18] "A teenage boy shouldn't be eating what his 110-pound, dieting mother would eat," Robb cautioned. "It's normal for a half-gallon of milk and a loaf of bread to disappear every 48 hours if there's a teenage boy in the house." A notable change in eating habits, she noted, should prompt a call to a physician or nutritionist. Parents, Robb said, should model healthy behavior and avoid lamenting how chubby they are or trying to run a "fat-free" household. "When parents are hung up on their own weight issues, their kids are at higher risk," she said. "Boys can be as susceptible as girls."

[19] Eating disorders, Robb and other experts say, appear to be caused by a combination of genetic and environmental factors. "Genes load the gun, and environment pulls the trigger," said North Carolina's Bulik. "But one of the problems I see for male eating disorder patients is just being taken seriously."

ANALYZE

Identify at least three elements of pathos from Boodman's article. What is the rhetorical effect of these instances? How does it make you feel about the problem of eating disorders among men? Why do you think the author included them?

China Photos/Getty Images

FIGURE 8-1

The fashion industry—from designers to modeling agencies to retailers and advertisers—has long been a target of those trying to deal with eating disorders and poor body image. Many in the industry say they want to help solve these problems, as *Vogue* editor Rebecca Johnson points out in her article "Walking a Thin Line." But the standard for the beautiful body remains tall, thin, and well-toned—and not just on the catwalk and in glossy fashion magazines. Consider, for example, this collection of mannequins awaiting shipment at a wholesaler in China. What do these facsimiles of the human body say about the look we as a culture seem to value? How might you read this image as a statement about the issues covered in this chapter?

Just as fast-food restaurants are popular targets in the fight against obesity, the fashion industry frequently is accused of contributing to eating disorders and problems with body image. In this April 2007 article from the fashion magazine Vogue, *contributing editor Rebecca Johnson examines the way the industry responds to these charges.*

WALKING A THIN LINE

As the average runway sample dropped from a size 6 to a size 2 over the past decade, models were expected to shrink to fit.

Rebecca Johnson

[1] As job interviews go, the model casting call has to be the world's quickest.

[2] "Can I see you walk?" James Scully, a 20-year industry veteran, asked the tall, thin brunette standing in the foyer of designer Derek Lam's showroom. It was the week before the New York fall shows, and Scully needed to cast 26 models.

[3] The girl took a deep breath, dropped her shoulders, jutted her hips forward, and took off. After ten feet, she stopped, pivoted, and returned, eyes focused vacantly on the middle distance.

[4] "If you could stand against the wall." Scully pointed to a pink slash of tape six feet from the floor. He didn't say so, but if her head hit too far below that mark, she probably wouldn't get the job. This one cleared it by a good two inches. There was no scale, but you hardly needed it. Like the 20 or 30 girls who had come before her, she hadn't an inch of visible fat on her body.

[5] As the flash of the Polaroid went off, she looked into the camera's eye, struggling for an expression that would convey something. Anything.

[6] "How old are you?" Scully asked.

[7] "Sixteen," she answered in a thick Eastern European accent.

[8] After she left, Scully waved a developing Polaroid and shook his head (time elapsed: one minute, 57 seconds). "It's their ages," he said in response to the question of the day: Have runway models gotten too thin? "We're seeing girls as young as thirteen on the runway. When you're that age and that tall, you can be that thin naturally, but in two years, that girl's body is going to start changing. She's going to get hips, and then she's going to start hearing she's too big."

[9] It would be impossible for one person to change the vast and complex machine that is fashion but, in his own small way, Scully is trying. "This is the first year I am asking their ages," he said. "Both aesthetically and philosophically, I'd rather cast older girls. There have been times in the last year when I have felt like a high school math teacher. I don't even think girls begin to blossom until they're at least nineteen. You ask one of these girls to 'look sexy' and they don't know what that means. A lot of them have never had a boyfriend."

[10] More troubling for him is the thought of what will happen to that girl when the industry is done with her. "The turnover has gotten so quick. Girls are gone in one or two seasons. How do you tell a sixteen-year-old girl her career is over?" he asked. "They've spent the last two years living the lifestyle of a 35-year-old. It's hard for them to go back to where they came from."

[11] In the foyer outside, three new girls, all of whom looked more or less identical, had arrived. While Scully zoomed through the casting, I went outside to ask the girls what they thought about the weight issue, especially the health regulations issued by Spanish authorities requiring minimum BMIs (body-mass index) for models, and the Italian requirement for a medical certificate. The sameness of their replies was striking.

[12] "It's crazy," they all answered. "I eat!" On the table next to them were plates heaped with food—raspberries, chunks of pineapple, kiwis, croissants, bagels, brioche. Nothing had been touched.

[13] Later that day I sent an email to Cynthia Bulik, Ph.D., past president of the Academy for Eating Disorders and currently director of the University of North Carolina eating-disorders program. When the Council of Fashion Designers of America (CFDA) issued its own guidelines last January to protect the health of the models, Bulik had applauded some measures—such as limiting the use of girls under sixteen—but in general she had been critical of the initiative, calling it "an anemic response" to a serious occupational concern.

[14] *Dear Dr. Bulik,*

[15] *Today I attended a casting for a designer in which about 50 models came in and got quickly photographed. The agent doing the casting told me he believes he can tell in a second if a girl is sick. It's in "the skin, the eyes, the hands," he said. The girls who came in seemed very young, very tall, and very skinny, but they didn't seem sick.*

[16] *When I interviewed them, they all insisted they eat. They seemed so earnest, I can't believe they were lying. Was I missing something?*

[17] I got a response within hours.

[18] *You can't always tell just by looking! I am sure that agent had no data to actually check his/her observations with. . . .*

[19] *And there's not ONE question you can ask— especially if someone is afraid they might lose their job! Plus, they might indeed eat, but then vomit or use laxatives or other methods to try to get rid of the food.*

[20] I took her point. An eating disorder is a complex, multifaceted disease mediated by both genetic and psychosocial factors. But the irony couldn't help escaping me: If you can't tell whether a person has an eating disorder by looking at her, why are lawmakers from Spain to Milan and, more recently, New York trying to mandate models' health based on the way they look?

[21] Some history. It's a fact: Clothes look better on a thin person. Models are therefore, by definition, thinner than the average person. Always have been. Always will be. Even the so-called Amazon supermodels of the eighties, curvy women recognizable by only one name, were a lot thinner than the average woman. Then, suddenly, around the early nineties, the models got thinner still. Nian Fish, the creative director of KCD, the company that produces fashion shows for designers such as Marc Jacobs, Ralph Lauren, and Zac Posen, and one of the people most concerned about the trend, thinks she can pinpoint the precise moment it happened. "It was at a Calvin Klein go-see where I was working as a stylist," she remembers. "The big girls were there—Cindy, Nadja. And then Kate Moss walked in. She must have been fifteen or sixteen at the time. She put on this beige chiffon slip dress, and it just fell on her body. We put her in flat shoes, and when she walked, the fabric was like liquid flowing around her body. I got goose

bumps. We all knew we were witnessing one of those fashion moments." (A former dancer who herself once struggled with an eating disorder, Fish was one of the guiding forces behind the CFDA's push to address the issue.)

22 In the years that followed, as clothes became less structured and less formfitting, the "glamazons" suddenly found themselves out of work. Or, more precisely, out of high fashion. Because they had recognizable personae—"Those girls used to skip down the runway," says Fish—they were able to parlay their careers into even more lucrative perfume or makeup campaigns, options that don't exist nearly as much for the blank-faced girls walking today's runway. If you can name a runway model today, you probably work in the industry. "After Kate," says Tonne Goodman, fashion director of *Vogue*, "there have been schools of girls who have swum through like fish, but none of them have really stuck. Good models have to have sex appeal, but to feel sexy, you have to feel good about your body. At the magazine, we're looking for that. A few of the models are so thin I worry about them. I'm a mother; you feel for them."

23 So does photographer Arthur Elgort. "When I see those skinny girls, I just hope they don't put a bathing suit on them," he says.

24 Then, about two or three years ago, the average size of the models seemed to slip again, from a size 2 to a size 0. Until the local government in Madrid kicked up a fuss, nobody seemed to notice. But among the agents who represent the models and the models themselves, the shift has been devastating. "I went to a fitting the other day," says a top model who asked that her name not be used for fear of retribution, "and the stylist kept talking about how the show was supposed to be so 'sexy.' Then she handed me a pair of size 0 jeans, which did not fit. I said to her, 'What's sexy about a size 0?' The designers say models are naturally thin, but these are extreme sizes. I think half the girls walking the runway today have some kind of eating disorder." When the models themselves were famous, designers would gladly alter a dress to fit the girl. But when the models are generically interchangeable, it's easier to find a girl who fits the dress.

25 Speaking out on the issue is what you might call a no-win situation for people in such a highly competitive business. In the days preceding New York Fashion Week, one very powerful agent sounded pretty sanguine on the topic once I finally got him on the phone. "These girls are naturally thin," he said dismissively. "They were the Olive Oyls in high school, the ones who got teased for being a beanpole. If there's a problem, we'll talk to the girl. Everyone wants her to be healthy. We work with trainers and nutritionists. Maybe it's just a matter of cutting down on carbohydrates."

26 But a few days into Fashion Week, his tone changed. "I just got a call from a designer about a top girl they cut because the clothes don't fit," he said angrily one evening from his cell phone. "I asked them, 'Is she too large?' and all they said was 'The clothes don't fit.' I'm not talking about 25 pounds here, I'm talking about two or three pounds! This is the new era? I really thought things were going to change."

27 Still, he did not want his name used. "This is a very competitive business," he explained. "I want my clients to have long and prosperous careers. Managed correctly, these women can continue to make good money into their 30s. If she has a problem, the last thing we would ever do is talk about it publicly."

28 "It's the paradox of the model," said Natalia Vodianova, one of the few models who have been outspoken on the issue. "You're supposed to be projecting this image of fun and health. If you talk about

having a problem, you know it's going to affect your career, so you don't say anything. The girls talk about dieting all the time, but they never talk about problems."

29 If people don't talk, it's hard to know the true extent of the issue or where it begins and ends. "Why are the agents even sending these girls?" Donna Karan asked at the CFDA forum on the topic this past February. Answer: because those are the girls who are getting booked. "I know one of my girls has a problem," one anguished agent asked, "but every designer in town wants that girl in their show, so what am I supposed to tell her? If I tell her she can't work, she'll just go to someone else."

30 It's not as if the fashion industry wants to create eating disorders in young women. "Contrary to what people believe, this industry does have a heart," said Robin Givhan, fashion editor of *The Washington Post*. "Look at all the work it has done on AIDS. I think what happened was our eyes changed slowly over time. It's like the frog in the water: If you slowly turn up the heat, it doesn't know it's being boiled to death. After a while, a size 0 starts to seem normal, not cadaverous." But eventually, said Givhan, the zombie-like quality of some superskinny models began to detract from the aesthetic appreciation of the clothes themselves. "Fashion is about fantasy and aspiration," she said. "Women look to it for inspiration. But somewhere along the way the industry went from long and lean to something you wouldn't want to aspire to. It became unattractive."

31 The controversy might never have become the international story it did had it not been for the deaths of two South American models due to complications from anorexia nervosa. Neither Luisel Ramos nor Ana Carolina Reston got anywhere close to the runways in New York or Paris. At five feet eight inches—and friends says that was stretching it—Reston's head would have hit far below Scully's pink slash on the wall, but fashion is a global business, and for several years she was able to support her middle-class family by modeling for catalogs and fashion shows in Brazil. Her dream, however, was to travel abroad, living the glamorous life of an international model. When she went to China, she was told she was too fat. To get work, she thought she only needed to get thinner. By 2006, when she entered the Brazilian hospital where she died at 88 pounds, she was allegedly living on a diet of apples and tomatoes.

32 Reston's agents stopped booking her when she got seriously sick. In the weeks before her death, she was supporting herself by handing out fliers for nightclubs, but her death seemed to touch off a simmering anger against the fashion industry, as evidenced by this post on Live Journal, one of the most popular fashion blogs.

33 *I CANNOT *BELIEVE!!!* THE 'FASHION INDUSTRY' *STILL* DOESN'T THINK THERE IS A "PROBLEM."*

34 *What the #$#??! I feel bad for the girl, but hopefully, this will help show (or even FORCE) this industry to see how badly they need to DO SOMETHING!!!*

35 *(And this is coming from a model herself. If I had a penny for every time I heard my agent telling me or other models at the agency to "lose some inches in the hips," I could quit modeling and just be a millionaire....)*

36 Fellow Brazilian Gisele Bundchen made international headlines after Reston's death when she said parents are responsible for anorexia, not the fashion industry, but others were more empathetic. "I didn't know her personally," said Vodianova, "but when I read about her story, I could understand. At home, girls are the little princesses, but then you get this opportunity and you think, OK, this is my job now. This is what I am supposed to do. Nobody is nurturing them, and suddenly, everything

becomes about the weight. If you do allow yourself to eat something, you become nervous because you think the clothes won't fit. It's not that people even say things to your face; it's more like a tension in the air during a fitting. Or you overhear something. In your off-time, you start to overeat because you are so hungry, so now your normal relationship with food is gone."

[37] It's no coincidence that many of the youngest, thinnest girls on the runway come from countries where economic opportunities for them are limited. Reston's family was initially middle class, but after her family's savings were stolen, she felt an added pressure to be a breadwinner. "My parents saw an opportunity for me to have a better life," Vodianova said, explaining why her parents let her leave home alone at seventeen. To make money in Russia, she used to sell fruit on the street next to engineers and professors, people with advanced degrees who needed cash to feed their families. The money she made from her first fashion show—$50—was equal to a month's salary for a teacher. "If I had stayed, finished school, and become a doctor, so what?" She shrugged. "I still would have been selling fruit on the street."

[38] After Reston's death, the CFDA decided to address the issue. But if models are hired for their tall and skinny genetic phenotype, fashion designers succeed through an equally rigorous process of Darwinian selection. Creative people with robust egos don't like being told what to do. Some were sympathetic to the idea of regulation, especially women with children. "We have a big responsibility with this disease," said Carolina Herrera. Another prominent designer called the idea "revolting." Some were simply flummoxed by the practicalities—how do you regulate a worldwide industry composed of freelance workers who steadfastly maintain, "It's crazy! I eat!"

[39] In Spain, they tried instituting minimum weights calculated by BMI. The measurement, which takes into consideration height and weight, was invented by a nineteenth-century Belgian scientist who believed that the human condition could be better understood through the use of statistics—he was among the first to quantify a correlation between age and gender in crime—but while BMI may be a useful tool for tracking the growing obesity epidemic in the developed world, it's not so useful for screening models. The Spanish chose a BMI of eighteen as the cutoff for a working model, which, according to the Centers for Disease Control (CDC) growth charts, would mean that 17 percent of all sixteen-year-olds would be considered too thin to model. Not surprisingly, the regulation had little effect. England, Australia, and France all rejected mandatory minimums as discriminatory or inappropriate—as UK culture secretary Tessa Jowell said, "Government legislation is a very blunt instrument to address an issue this complex."

[40] Realistically, today's working models have BMIs closer to sixteen. When she was nineteen and weighed 117 pounds, five-foot-ten-inch Vodianova had a BMI of 16.8. (That was when several fashion houses complained about her weight.) When she weighed 106 pounds and her hair was beginning to fall out, she had a BMI of 15.2, which would put her off the CDC charts (they stop at the bottom 5 percent). Still, you can't definitively say someone with a low BMI has anorexia. "I would assume these models have a subclinical eating disorder," said Johannes Hebebrand, M.D., of the University of Essen, Germany, one of the world's leading experts on BMI, "but I wouldn't bet on it. There are a lot of very skinny people who can't gain weight. Nobody really knows why—maybe they have a higher body temperature, a faster metabolism; maybe they fidget more, or maybe they just don't eat."

[41] Some critics pushed for a mandatory annual doctor's examination, but anorexia

is both a psychological and physical disease. The fact that Uruguayan model Luisel Ramos had a sister who died less than a year after her—allegedly from complications of anorexia—confirms what twins studies have shown: Anorexia has a strong genetic component. Hebebrand could one day imagine a blood test—he has found that anorexics have lowered levels of leptin, a hormone produced by fat that is instrumental in regulating the hypothalamus and pituitary glands—but that's a long way off. Eating-disorder experts like Bulik say the best way to screen is an exam, including a face-to-face interview with a clinician trained at cutting through the denial of "It's crazy! I eat!" "I usually start with a weight history," said Bulik. "Then I might ask, 'How would you feel if you gained five pounds?' At that point, you look in their face, and you can usually tell from the expression of horror."

42 In the end, the best you can do is plant a seed and hope it grows. The eye may adjust, but the eye also grows restless and ready for change. "I've been thinking about it," Derek Lam said after his casting was over. "I travel the country for trunk shows and meet these successful women who have the means to really take care of themselves. They're working out, they look great. As designers, I think, we sometimes wait for technology to tell us what to do, but maybe the technology is there, in their bodies. Already I am giving my clothes more structure this year and making it less about something limp hanging on a rail."

SUMMARIZE

Write a 100-word summary of Johnson's article.

ANALYZE

Given that *Vogue* is one of the world's leading fashion magazines, who would you say is Johnson's target audience? How does this audience affect the ethos Johnson presents in her article?

DISCUSS

Johnson writes at one point: "It's a fact: Clothes look better on a thin person." Do you agree with this "fact"? How might Johnson's presentation of this "fact" affect readers who don't agree with her?

ARGUE

Write a brief essay in which you propose a course of action to deal with the problems Johnson presents in her article.

In this essay and the next, the authors talk about weight and body image on a much more personal level than most of the other readings in this chapter. In the first, Carla Broyles, a metro deputy news editor for the Washington Post, *invites readers into her world—"a culture where there [is] no shortage of love and acceptance for the girls with the curves." This piece was first published in the Post on November 12, 2006.*

A WELL-ROUNDED WOMAN

Carla Broyles

1 *Thank God for tiny kitchens.* Somewhere between the stove and the refrigerator, I get my daily confirmation from my husband, Stephen, that he is well pleased with what God gave me.

2 "What's that, baby? I didn't hear you," is my standard comeback, because I always want to hear him say it again—and he does.

3 "Lord, have mercy. Look at what I got. All mine, mine, mine."

4 And so our dance begins. And dinner is put on hold.

5 You love these? I whisper as I point to the dozens of freckles on my face.

6 "Yes," he says.

7 "And these? You love these?" I ask, bringing my lips to a full pout.

8 "Yes, I love those," he says with his trademark brow raise.

9 "But what about this and this and this and that and...?"

10 "All of you," Stephen interjects, pulling both my hands in to his chest. Still I continue like a stock boy taking inventory. Kinky hair balls on the back of my neck...check...stretch marks on the back of my upper arms...check... hips...check...thighs...check. And how about the scar on my knee I got when I was 13, running full speed to the corner store when I was supposed to stay on the porch?

11 "That, too," he says, nodding.

12 "All of this, huh?" I ask, tracing my silhouette—all 5-foot-5-inch, 188-pound, D-cup wearing me, with my 30-inch waist and 43-inch hips.

13 "All of that," my husband says, grinning.

14 Then I claim my place in his arms, and we resume kitchen duty all up in each other's way.

15 *It's no surprise that I married a man who loves—* no, adores—me in all of my glory. That's because, like many African American women, I grew up in a culture where there was no shortage of love and acceptance for the girls with the curves.

16 Growing up on the West Side of Chicago in my own insular world provided a model for how I saw me. You see, Tina Turner got her legs from my Grandma. And by the time I reached high school, where the demographics were different, it was too late. I was already grounded and stubborn and on the verge of being, as some folk refer to it, "full-figured."

17 Here, in America, where the standard of beauty is single-digit dress sizes, and grown women are praised for their boyish good looks, my childhood narrative featured the daily declarations of a mother with whom skinny didn't sit well, and the compilation of way too many sidewalk serenades.

18 My mother also grew up on the West Side, and as a wispy, 98-pound teenager in 1970 surrounded by black women with hourglass figures and generous backsides, she decided she wasn't curvy enough. "Twiggy wasn't in; hips were," she tells me. My Aunt Bonnie was the brick house, Mom says. "She had lots of boyfriends. I wanted to be a brick house, too."

19 So Mom set out to get herself some hips. A friend introduced her to Wate-On, a drug-store supplement that promised to fill her out. She picked up a bottle and kept her fingers crossed. A Wate-On ad from that time featured a black woman with ample thighs and bust in a black leotard, and boasted that one tablet provided more calories than a broiled steak, a baked potato, wax beans or carrots, a slice of bread, ice cream as dessert, and a cup of coffee with milk and sugar. But it didn't work for Mom.

20 It wasn't until her early 30s that she managed to get past 120 pounds. As I was growing up, she'd always compliment me on having "big, pretty legs, like your grand-mother's," and she was just as vocal about my potential.

21 "I wanted to make sure you understood that nobody could tell you what you couldn't do," she tells me now. For me, that translated into more than what I could accomplish. It also meant that one's opinion about my looks was just that, an opinion. It was what I thought that mattered, and I was comfort-able with the standard set on my side of town, on my block, in my house.

22 Of course, everybody there was black, and now as an adult I wonder how, exactly, race played into it.

23 I turn to Kathleen LeBesco, a scholar in the emerging academic field of fat studies, for insight. LeBesco's students are a diverse lot, so she has a front row seat on how people from different racial and ethnic groups view weight.

24 "White students may say that a person is too fat. Black students will say, no, she's not; she carries it well," says LeBesco, who is white and has struggled with her weight her entire life. LeBesco points out that, even today, many African tribes engage in the process of fattening a woman before she marries. Plumpness, LeBesco says, equals affluence and fertility in African culture, and that equals beauty.

25 LeBesco has found that, for her African American students, being attractive is "partly an attitude thing and partly where the fat is distributed." She also reminds me that while blacks are generally more accepting of girth than whites, that acceptance is not unlimit-ed. Translation: "It's fine to have a big butt, but not a big stomach."

26 As my Cousin Mimi's maid of honor in 1993, it was my duty to look as stunning as possible on a college student's budget. I carefully chose my sage green suit—my way of sup-porting Mimi, who had to be talked out of wearing a green wedding dress that Christ-mas season. The music began, and I strutted down the aisle, taking my place out front. There were no other bridesmaids. The best man, who also stood alone, was a chiseled Morehouse man I deemed worthy to stand as my equal.

27 Then I got the pictures back from Walgreens.

28 My face! Round and plump and ugh. Clearly, I hadn't intended for my weight to show up here. And just like that, I convinced myself that mommas say nice stuff just because they're mommas, and that men really don't know what they like. I decided to drop some pounds, and did.

29 Over the years, my weight fluctuated by 10 or 20 pounds, depending on my social calendar. I still wasn't model-thin, but I decided I was okay with that. You see, the positive feedback from friends, relatives and even strangers never stopped. Plus,

American culture is fickle, and I'm not one to keep jumping through hoops. Look at poor Nicole Richie, who, after being called out for having a little meat on her bones, is now tabloid fodder for being too thin.

30 With my self-esteem back in working order, I was doing my thing—working, hanging out with my girls, dating. Then came my annual checkup three years ago with Dr. B.

31 The ritual was always the same: The physician's assistant would ask me to step on the scale. She'd push the bar to the weight I appeared to be. A little sarcastically, I'd say, "Keep going." She'd try hard not to look astonished as she kept sliding. I'd rescue her, saying "Just put it at 200, then go forward a bit." She'd write down the number and tell me to take my place on the table. Dr. B would come in, pronounce me "heavy" and gently encourage me to lose weight.

32 But this time was different. Dr. B had gotten my blood work back and called me in for a consultation. She motioned me to get on a fancy new digital scale. She left and came back in carrying a readout from the scale with my body mass index and the results of my lab work.

33 "Carla, you've got to lose weight," 51.21 pounds, according to the scale, she told me.

34 I was stunned.

35 "Do you know how skinny I'd be if I lost that much weight?" I asked.

36 My body mass index, or estimated percentage of body fat based on height and weight, was 34.6, outside the healthy range of 18.5 to 24.9 percent. My total cholesterol was 245, Dr. B. said, and more than 200 is considered unhealthy. Convinced it was the Red Lobster shrimp feast I had inhaled the night before, I blew it off. Obviously, I was too young to have what I called "old man issues." Dr. B ordered another test, and the number came back a few points lower, but remained well over 200.

37 She told me I was going to have to stick to a low-fat, low-cholesterol diet. She also repeated that I'd need to lose 50 pounds. I read up on the ill effects of high cholesterol—possible heart attack or stroke—and that did it. I vowed to change my eating habits and fashion a fitness routine for a woman determined to live a long, healthy life.

38 But with her curves.

39 Every morning, I ate a breakfast of assorted fruit, whole grains and soy, and headed off to Bally's for my workout. One morning on the way back home, I stopped in at Honda to get my car checked. Ernest, my service consultant, seemed disturbed. So much so that he felt the need to warn me.

40 "Okay, now, whatever you're doing, don't lose too much."

41 "Shut up, Ernest," I said and took my place in the customer lounge.

42 We've gone back and forth like this for the past three years. During that time, I've lost some of the weight—including a nice bit right before my wedding last year—and my cholesterol is now below 200. But I'm trying to focus more on building and maintaining healthy habits than on the number on the scale. Maybe healthy for me doesn't mean losing 50 pounds. Maybe I'm in denial. We'll see.

43 During a recent visit, Ernest explained why he gives me such a hard time. "Women today are too concerned with being thinner," he laments, recalling Pam Grier and Jayne Kennedy, the voluptuous black celebrities of his youth. Without going into too much detail, I tell him I'm trying to lose for health reasons.

44 "I bet your husband's got something to say about that," he says.

45 *Stephen's position is very clear, and he lets me know mostly with his hands. It is good to be here, in a place where my body is fully appreciated.*

[46] So, at this very moment, how do I appear to myself?

[47] It's the morning after my rendezvous in the kitchen with Stephen. In the door mirror of our home office, I stand straight, feet together and shoulders back. I see an attractive woman in a white linen blouse and an apple green cardigan that fits her full bust to a T. The blazer drapes gracefully over her waist. The skirt will soon sway like the perfect pendulum over her ample hips. The sweet chocolate open-toed wedgies on her feet keep her balanced. The look she gets from her husband makes her late for work.

SUMMARIZE AND RESPOND

What do you think is Broyles' main point in this essay? Do you think she makes her point effectively? Explain your answer.

ANALYZE

What differences does Broyles point out in the ways that women's weight is viewed in white communities and African American communities? How does she make this comparison? Do you think the support she provides for her claims is sufficient?

DISCUSS

Early in her essay, Broyles writes: "Here, in America, where the standard of beauty is single-digit dress sizes, and grown women are praised for their boyish good looks, my childhood narrative featured the daily declarations of a mother with whom skinny didn't sit well." How does this sentence help explain the often competing pressures that African American women face when it comes to weight, beauty, health, and self-image?

ARGUE

Write a brief essay in which you argue for a new way of defining beauty that takes into account different cultural standards as well cross-cultural health concerns.

In the following excerpt, from the introduction to her 2004 book The Fat Girl's Guide to Life, *comedian and writer Wendy Shanker speaks directly to her audience, explaining her decision to take control of the word* fat. *Like the essay by Carla Broyles that precedes it, Shanker's is a personal account that seeks to address an issue affecting many people besides the writer.*

FROM 'fat' TO FAT

Wendy Shanker

"Wendy is a fat girl's name."
—*Monica (Courteney Cox Arquette) on* Friends

1 I start by telling the friend or coworker or acquaintance that I'm writing a book called *The Fat Girl's Guide to Life.* He or she usually looks me over from head to toe before choosing words carefully. "But Wendy, I don't think of you as—." This generally takes a second, because it's hard to say the word—"fat."

2 I know, sweetie, because you think fat is something really awful. You think fat means "loserish" and "lame" and "disgusting" and "hopeless." None of those words describe me. But I'm here to tell you that "fat" is a word. It's an adjective. Like "tall" or "brunette" or "female" or "Jewish" or "smart," which are other adjectives that describe me. By any standard you can find—societal norms, a doctor's chart, a clothing rack, my own personal ideals—I am most definitely fat. So go ahead and start thinking of me that way.

The F-Word

3 "Fat."

4 If you ever want to make people visibly uncomfortable, just say the f-word out loud.

5 You can refer to yourself as fat ("Hi, I'm fat!") or acknowledge that someone else is fat ("She's pretty, but she sure is fat!"), but either way, you're pretty much guaranteed to freak someone out.

6 "Fat" is the word I use to describe my physical stature. I use it without apology. The more I use it, the more comfortable I feel with it, and the less power it has to hurt me when someone else uses it as an insult. When I describe myself to someone else, I like to say I'm fat, but it usually scares the hell out of 'em. I don't know what they picture—maybe one of those people Richard Simmons has to suck out of a house with a forklift. By now I've said the word so many times that it really doesn't bother me anymore. I don't mind the word; it's the associations I can do without. What's the worst thing someone can say to me? "You're fat!"? No duh. I just told you that.

7 "Fat" literally means "containing or full of fat; oily; greasy…said of meat." It also means "prosperous; profitable; lucrative; valuable." Screw the dictionary definitions; in our society, "fat" means bad. Unless you're on one of those high-fat, no-carb diets, that is. In that case, set yourself up with a slab of bacon and some eggs Benedict on the side—without the English muffin, of course.

8 "But Wendy," says my poor innocent friend/relative/victim, "since 'fat' is such a

loaded word, isn't there a different one you can use?"

[9] Sure. I could use "overweight," or "plus size," or "curvaceous," or any of a million others, and I do. But why not call it like I see it? The word that I like the most, and the one that I think aptly describes my body, is "fat." The opposite of thin. I like it. It's short, it's sweet, it's surprisingly compact.

[10] But why do I call myself a fat girl instead of a fat woman? Personally, using the word "girl" conjures up the energy of "girl power," aka the fun side of feminism. "Fat girl" is also one of those phrases in our collective unconscious—like "the fat kid"—that's desperately in need of a mental makeover. One night—and this is recently—I was on a packed subway train minding my own business. As the train pulled into my stop I said "Excuse me," so I could start weaving my way through a knot of people. Right behind me, this teenage girl who had been making out with her boyfriend the whole ride said in a really loud voice, "FAT GIRL COMING THROUGH!" I can't begin to tell you how surprised I was, how humiliated I felt. I didn't get my composure back until I was off the train and it was too late to say something in response. I mean, I'm ME. Fantastic ME. I'm the thirty-one-year-old you-go-girl, writing the book you are reading this very minute, but that little phrase cut me to the quick. I don't know why she said it. I'm pretty sure that it was about her and not me—maybe she wanted to impress her boyfriend, maybe she needed to let him know that she would never get fat (like me), maybe I reminded her of her mother or sister or friend or ex-friend or some girl at school she hates. Maybe she was pissed that my big fat ass was taking up valuable subway seat space and I had been too lost in my own thoughts to notice.

[11] And what was I supposed to say to her? I know what I would have asked her if I had the moment back again. I'd calmly ask her why. "Why say that? What are you trying to accomplish? I'm not going to be mean to you, like you were to me, I just want to know why." It's not my job to defend myself against this girl. It's her job not to attack me.

[12] Still, it's hard to be called "fat" and just roll with it. I think of poor Fergie. You know, Sarah Ferguson, flame-haired duchess and current spokesmodel for Weight Watchers. British tabloids regularly referred to her as "the Duchess of Pork." Journalists printed a story that said 82 percent of men would rather sleep with a goat than Fergie. But a recent news story from Reuters revealed that Fergie "recently came face to face with the author of the 'Duchess of Pork' headline that most haunted her, only to find that her enemy was a jovial, balding, middle-aged man who had no idea of the years of distress he had caused. Before long she was joking with him, realizing suddenly that the writer bore her no malice and never had. 'He was paid to be clever, end of story. It occurred to me that we survive our critics by knowing that their agendas, at heart, may have little to do with us,' she said." Kind of like my little lady on the subway. Props to Fergie for calling her tormentor out, but what a shame that she had to hurt for so many years. Can you relate?

[13] Words are just a bunch of letters in a row. A word isn't negative, it's our connotation that is. The words can stay the same; it's our attitudes about them that have to change. You've seen this evolution happen in the gay community with the word "queer." Once reviled, the word "queer" now demands respect and pride. Only a few years ago, would you have thought that a show called *Queer Eye for the Straight Guy* would be a hit on network television? Could *The Fat Pick on the Skinny Chick* be far behind?

[14] Like gay men have, we need to reappropriate "fat" and take back the power

of the word. But just because I'm opening the floodgates on "fat" doesn't mean that someone outside the fold is allowed to take it too far. Yes, I am a Fat Girl. And I am coming through. But to the rest of you riding the train with me, I hope this is what will come through loud and clear: Keep your insults to yourself.

SUMMARIZE AND RESPOND

Write a 100-word summary of this piece, followed by a 100-word response. In your response, focus on Shanker's tone. Is her direct way of speaking to the audience effective?

ANALYZE

How does Shanker use humor in this excerpt? Use examples from the text to support your response.

DISCUSS

Do you agree with Shanker's contention that reappropriating the word *fat* can help people who are obese feel better about themselves? Explain your response.

This essay, published on December 4, 2005, in the Chicago Sun Times, *is an excerpt from* Fat Politics: The Real Story Behind America's Obesity Epidemic *by J. Eric Oliver, an associate professor of political science at the University of Chicago. In it, Oliver presents an unconventional causal argument that explores why so many people react negatively to people with weight problems.*

WHY WE HATE FAT PEOPLE

J. Eric Oliver

[1] "Obesity! Ugh. Those people are so gross. It's sick. How could they let themselves get that way?"

[2] It is remarkable how often I've heard comments like this one when I tell people about the book I am writing, *Fat Politics*. Most thin people I've met seem to have a pretty harsh view toward the obese. Over the past three years, I've heard scores of unsolicited invectives of disgust and contempt for fat people, particularly from educated, middle-class folks who otherwise pride themselves on being rational and fair-minded. Even more interesting is how they assume that I, as an affluent thin person, naturally share in their horror. Like a group of white folks surreptitiously

Public Domain

FIGURE 8-2

While our cultural ideas about beauty may have changed over the past century, the pressure to conform—especially for women—clearly has not. This newspaper ad from 1890 touts the benefits of Professor Williams' "Fat-Ten-U" Foods to women who are too thin to measure up to the body standard of the time. The smaller text on the ad includes the following sales pitch, accompanied by before-and-after drawings on either side:

"Why suffer tortures with inferior mechanical devices that artificially fatten? Don't look like the poor unfortunate on the left who, shorn of her artificial inflationary devices & pads, must, in the confines of the bedroom, through shame, try to cover her poor thin figure from the gaze of her beloved spouse."

The marketing sounds familiar, doesn't it? How many modern products can you think of that prey on women's fears of being seen as undesirable? Of course, the critical difference lies in the desired results: in 1890, Professor Williams' product promised to make "the thin plump and rosy with honest fleshiness of form." Today, diet and beauty products promise the opposite. What kinds of rhetorical appeals do you see at work in this ad? Do modern diet ads use similar appeals? Explain your response with a few examples.

sharing a racist joke, many thin middle-class people will easily convey their disdain for the obese if no fat people are around.

3 Although there is a logic to why thinness is valued, it does not sufficiently explain the vehemence against fat people. Clearly, the loathing of fatness comes from another source, and that source is fear. As with any type of prejudice, the animosity toward fat people originates in some much deeper anxieties over self and social status. For not only is thinness a convenient way for middle-class people to assert their moral superiority and boost their self-image, it also serves to rationalize the social inequalities that exist between various social groups.

4 Find this hard to believe? Listen closely to how Americans criticize fat people and you'll find rationalizations that are remarkably similar to those historically used to justify negative attitudes toward all marginalized groups in America. Fat people are thought to be gluttonous, lustful, greedy, lazy, weak-willed, and lacking any kind of self-control. If fat people are targets of our contempt, it is only because they have brought this on themselves with their unwillingness to take responsibility for their own actions.

5 The ideology that underscores this prejudice is an ethos of individualism and self-reliance. As with blacks and the poor, fat people are thought to violate some of the most fundamental tenets in American political culture: that all people are fundamentally responsible for their own welfare; that self-control and restraint are the hallmarks of virtue; and that all Americans are obliged to work at improving themselves. These views derive partly from our liberal political tradition that emphasizes the importance of individual freedom and rights and the restraint of government power. And, as we've seen, they also come from America's Anglo-Protestant heritage that emphasized individuals' unique responsibility for demonstrating their worth before God. This individualism has also been accentuated by two hallmarks of American economic development—laissez-faire capitalism and entrepreneurship—which both celebrate the good that individual initiative promotes in the free market. Whether it is the rugged frontiersman, the lonesome cowboy, or the Horatio Alger stories of the self-made man, American heroes are notable for their individual pluck, initiative, and isolation.

6 The importance of this individualistic ethos continues to be evident in contemporary American attitudes toward the poor. Most Americans dislike welfare programs, not because they are opposed to helping others, but because they think that relying on government aid betrays a lack of self-reliance and individual responsibility. In situations in which poverty is seen to be beyond the person's control (such as with children or the elderly), Americans are quite willing to embrace government spending. Programs including Head Start and Social Security enjoy wide support because they are seen to assist the "deserving" poor. Conversely, able-bodied adults are held responsible for their own condition and are thought not to be deserving of aid or government redistribution of wealth. This individualistic ethos thus serves as an important rationale for justifying the tremendous gulf between rich and poor in the United States: barring a few exceptions, if people are poor, they only have themselves to blame.

7 Nor does this individualistic ethos stop with the poor—it is also at the heart of many white Americans' racial attitudes. Most whites know that it is no longer publicly acceptable to express racist stereotypes and, unlike a generation ago, most whites no longer publicly voice negative stereotypes of blacks, support segregation or oppose interracial marriage. When surveyed, most white Americans strongly

endorse the principle of racial equality. But this does not mean racial bias has disappeared. Instead, according to many race scholars, whites now couch their racial resentment in rhetoric of individual responsibility. Blacks are not denigrated because they are fundamentally less intelligent, lazy, or some other stereotype; rather, blacks are denigrated because they fail to embrace principles of individual self-reliance and self-control. Like the poor, blacks are held accountable for racial disparities in income, employment, and wealth because of their own moral failure. Policies that promote racial equality, such as affirmative action, are discredited because blacks are believed to be unable to live up to the individualistic norms of self-reliance.

We blamed the fat person

[8] The same individualistic ethos that underscores Americans' attitudes toward race and class is also at the heart of their antipathy toward fat people. As with their views of poor people and blacks, most white Americans see fat people as violating the tenets of discipline and self-control. In two national surveys I conducted for this book, more than 64 percent of Americans believe overweight people are "fat because they lack self-control," and more than 70 percent ranked individual laziness as the most important cause of obesity. The University of Kansas psychologist Christian Crandall has shown that most Americans also believe that fat people are morally deviant, self-indulgent, and unwilling to correct their own behavior. Not surprisingly, people who express a prejudice against fat people also endorse a worldview that emphasizes traditional values, individual responsibility, and the notion that "people get what they deserve."

[9] Conversely, if someone is believed to be fat for reasons beyond their control, then the contempt quickly changes to sympathy and compassion. Experiments have shown that anti-fat attitudes diminish when people think that obesity is glandular in origin. Americans dislike fatness because they think it indicates a person's unwillingness to be responsible and self-monitoring: as with the poor, if someone is fat, they only have themselves to blame. In fact, people who have strong anti-fat attitudes also tend to be more hostile toward minorities and the poor. In the national survey I conducted, more than 80 percent of people who believed that blacks are "welfare dependent" or that the poor are "irresponsible" also believed that overweight people are fat because they lack self-control, much higher rates than the general population.

[10] Given the confluence of racial and class prejudice with anti-fat sentiments, it is not surprising that apprehension of body fat is strongest among middle-class whites. Whites are five times more likely to report feeling ashamed of their weight than blacks or Latinos, even though the latter two groups have much higher body weights on average. Nor are anti-fat attitudes about others nearly as strong or prevalent among minorities as they are among whites. The similarity between modern racism and anti-fat attitudes may also explain these racial differences. As blacks or Latinos experience racial stigmatization in the same terms as the moral condemnation that is applied to the obese, it is logical that body size as well skin color have become intertwined as a part of their cultural identity.

[11] But perhaps the greatest reason why fat prejudice is so intertwined with class and racial prejudice is because America's poor and minorities are much fatter, on average, than its middle-class whites. Nearly one in three African Americans and one in four Latinos are obese, compared with only one in five non-Latino whites. Body sizes also vary consistently by education

and income—27 percent of high school dropouts are obese compared to only 16 percent of college graduates; people below the poverty line are nearly 15 percent more likely to be obese than those not in poverty. Indeed, the very highest levels of obesity are among people in both categories—nearly 50 percent of poor black and Latino women are technically obese (that is, have a Body Mass Index of 30 or above).

[12] With obesity so prevalent among minorities and the poor, condemning fatness is an effective way of highlighting their "moral failure" and justifying their continued marginalization. After all, if poor black people are unable to control their weight, the reasoning goes, then it is surely another indication of their inability to exercise self-control in general. Thereby, they deserve whatever low social conditions they live in and should be subject to greater restriction in terms of their moral behaviors. In truth, the higher body weights of minorities and the poor have little to do with their own "moral weakness." The logic of America's food industry almost predetermines that the poor will have higher body weights than the affluent. Meanwhile, genetic evidence suggests that people of non-European ancestry are more biologically predisposed toward weight retention. Yet, despite these facts, minorities and the poor are still blamed for weighing "too much" while thin, middle-class people can view their slenderness as a signal of their own superiority.

The real problem of obesity

[13] America is a society gripped by fear. We are afraid of crime, terrorism, drugs, environmental collapse, economic decline, moral erosion, and numerous other threats. Much of this fear, however, is directed at the wrong things. For example, the economist Steven Levitt has shown that, despite all the hoopla over gun control, guns are much less dangerous, statistically speaking, for children than something far more benign: swimming pools. The average American child is one hundred times more likely to die by drowning in a pool than from a gun. Nevertheless, most parents would be much more concerned about their children playing at a house where they think a gun might be than they would be about them playing at a house with a swimming pool.

[14] A similar type of misperception is happening with obesity. There is perhaps no greater fiction in the United States than the idea that we are worried about being fat because of its implications for our health. While the media and public health establishment may be sounding ever more hysterical alarms over the growing weight of the population, it is not because our obesity actually represents a verifiable health threat. Rather, it is because we are afraid of fat.

[15] Compare how obesity is being handled as a public health issue versus another major killer, automobiles. Last year more than 43,000 Americans died in automobile wrecks, far more than the numbers estimated to have died from "weighing too much." Moreover, unlike the estimated figures with obesity, these are verifiable numbers. Yet, outside of a handful of environmentalists, few people are talking about an epidemic of driving in this country. We have no pejorative terms like "overdriven" in our language. Although we have numerous mechanisms for ensuring driver safety, we still allow increasingly dangerous vehicles including Hummers and SUVs to roam largely unrestricted despite the threats they pose to our collective health.

[16] Given the general lack of concern about driving relative to its real impact on deaths, it seems highly implausible that we are worried about obesity because of its health consequences or its medical costs. In fact,

in terms of our collective health or economic well-being, we shouldn't worry. Yet, it is obesity, not other, more demonstrable risks to health and mortality, such as driving, that are capturing the headlines.

[17] This obsession with weight and obesity goes beyond the financial interests of the health-industrial complex and taps into something much more powerful: the racial and economic anxieties of America's middle class. One reason Americans so readily accept that obesity must be a major problem is because obesity is associated with those at the bottom end of America's social ladder. Thus, if obesity is growing, it surely must be a sign of American decline.

[18] Indeed, it is precisely because it is such a powerful symbol that obesity has been adopted by so many different groups. Among conservatives, it is evidence of the growing moral degeneration of America: the fact that we are getting fatter only shows that we are getting lazier, and more lustful, and moving farther away from the Anglo-Protestant tradition that defined American greatness. Among liberals, obesity represents the increasing power of international corporations and food companies in making us heavy against our will.

Among whites, it taps into latent racial fears that come with America's growing ethnic diversity—the growth of obesity parallels the increasing numbers of Latinos and African Americans relative to a shrinking white majority. And among the economic elite (the group in America most preoccupied with weight), obesity taps into a sense of social insecurity.

[19] Ultimately, however, the reason that so many people think the rise of obesity is a cause for alarm is because of our own chronic feelings of helplessness. In an era of corporate downsizing, globalization, and mass marketing, Americans often report that more and more of their lives seem beyond their control. Our bodies remain one of the last areas where we feel that we should be able to exercise some autonomy—a view that is only stoked by the diet, fitness, and cosmetic industries. Yet the fact that we continue to gain weight despite all our dieting, nutrition advice, and working out belies just how little control we may actually have. It is our anxiety with our own powerlessness and status much more than any health issue that is driving the perception that our growing weight is an epidemic disease.

SUMMARIZE AND RESPOND

Write a 100-word summary of Oliver's piece, making sure you accurately and fairly convey the author's central argument, and then write a 100-word response.

ANALYZE

How does Oliver use the rhetorical appeals to connect with his audience and to make his argument? Which of the appeals (to ethos, pathos, or logos) do you think is most effective? Why?

In his piece, Oliver writes, "[N]ot only is thinness a convenient way for middle-class people to assert their moral superiority and boost their self-image, it also served to rationalize the social inequalities that exist between various social groups." What do you think he means by this? Do you agree or disagree with this claim? Why?

from reading to writing

1. What is your definition of "overweight"?
2. Identify the ways in which the readings in this chapter present causal arguments. Then, use details from the readings to develop your own position on the cause of America's obesity problem.
3. What steps do you think the government could take to help Americans eat a better diet? What role should the food industry play? How about individuals?
4. Compare the ethos presented by Wendy Shanker and Carla Broyles. Who do you think are their target audiences? How do they appeal to these audiences? Which author do you think is more successful? Why?
5. Find a current advertisement—in a newspaper, magazine, or online—for a weight-loss or exercise product. Then, compare the rhetorical situation and appeals in the modern ad with those used in the 1890 ad for Professor William's "Fat-Ten-U" Foods on page 248. Which appeals are strongest in the two ads? Do you find one ad more or less effective than the other? Why? Do you find either ad offensive or dangerous? Explain your response.

modern love . . . and other social studies

CHAPTER 9

"Communication has been streamlined by the Internet, and something essential to the process of falling in love has been lost. We can type up carefully crafted statements rather than go face-to-face and improvise from the heart, thereby risking embarrassment, vulnerability or Oscar-worthy dialogue. We can Google our way into the museums of each other's identities—and fall in love there. . . . Flirting has been transformed into a digital process. We don't even have to touch each other to 'hook up.' We can just hook up to the Internet."

—Alice Mathias, *"Love in the Digital Age"*

What does it mean to have a friend or to be a friend? How would you define being in love? Whether we dwell on them or not—whether we take them for granted or fret about them obsessively—relationships help define who we are. Our encounters and engagement (or lack thereof) with others affect how they see us and how we see ourselves. But, according to the writers in this chapter, the nature of relationships—and especially of love—is changing. Henry Fountain reports in "The Lonely American Just Got a Bit Lonelier" that adults have fewer close relationships than ever. In "Do Smart Girls Finish Last in Love?" Laura Vanderkam tries to debunk the idea that smart, successful women can't find love. And in "Love in the Digital Age," Alice Mathias worries about the effects that technology is having on the ways we interrelate. What's happening here? Are we doomed to shallow relationships and artificial love? You read and decide for yourself.

Reporter Henry Fountain explores the fate of close adult friendships in this article from the July 2, 2006 edition of the New York Times. *In it, he presents possible causes and consequences of the decline in the number and quality of such friendships. You may wish to compare this article with the one that follows, in which reporter Joel Garreau examines the ways that online social networking sites are redefining what it means to be "friends."*

THE LONELY AMERICAN JUST GOT A BIT LONELIER

Henry Fountain

[1] For as long as humans have gathered in groups, it seems, some people have been left on the outside looking in. In postwar America in particular, the idea that loneliness pervades a portion of society has been a near-constant. Only the descriptions have changed: the "lonely crowd" alienation of the 1950's; the grim career-driven angst of the 70's and 80's; the "Bowling Alone" collapse of social connections of the 90's.

[2] There is a new installment in the annals of loneliness. Americans are not only lacking in bowling partners, now they're lacking in people to tell their deepest, darkest secrets. They've hunkered down even more, their inner circle often contracting until it includes only family, only a spouse or, at worst, no one.

[3] And that is something the Internet may help ease, but is unlikely to cure.

[4] A recent study by sociologists at Duke and the University of Arizona found that, on average, most adults only have two people they can talk to about the most important subjects in their lives—serious health problems, for example, or issues like who will care for their children should they die. And about one-quarter have no close confidants at all.

[5] "The kinds of connections we studied are the kinds of people you call on for social support, for real concrete help when you need it," said Lynn Smith-Lovin, a sociologist at Duke and an author of the study, which analyzed responses in interviews that

mirrored a survey from 1985. "These are the tightest inner circle."

[6] The study "should provide a wake-up call to our society," said Bill Maier, a vice president and psychologist in residence with Focus on the Family, the evangelical Christian group. "We're missing out on deep, meaningful interpersonal relationships."

[7] Yet within the analysis there was at least a suggestion of hope.

[8] "The one type of relationship that actually went up was talking over personally important things with your spouse," Dr. Smith-Lovin said.

[9] Like "Bowling Alone," the essay and, later, book by Robert D. Putnam, a public policy professor a Harvard, the Duke study suggested that a weakening of community connections is in part responsible for increasing social isolation. More people are working and commuting longer hours and have little time for the kinds of external social activities that could lead to deeper relationships.

[10] So the closest ties increasingly are limited to family members, in particular to spouses.

[11] "That's probably a result of the fact that men's and women's lives are more structurally similar now than in 1985," Dr. Smith-Lovin said. It's more likely that both spouses are working at jobs that are important to them, and men are more involved around the house. "Spouses literally have more to talk about," she said.

[12] Dr. Maier, for one, sees that as cause for at least some optimism in a society whose fast pace generally bodes badly for family life. "To hear that people are investing more in their nuclear family is a positive thing," he said.

[13] The Internet is also cause for some optimism, because it has made it easier to maintain ties among family members who

have become scattered. Those ties inevitably developed over long-term, face-to-face contact, but e-mail can help keep them strong.

[14] "E-mail really does help maintain your social networks," said John Horrigan, associate director of the Pew Internet and American Life Project. Recent Pew surveys, he said, found that "when you contact family by e-mail, you share important and serious things."

[15] Still, Dr. Smith-Lovin said, any optimism must be tempered. For one thing, having only one confidant, even if that confidant is a spouse, leaves a person extremely vulnerable if the spouse dies or the marriage disintegrates.

[16] And in the end, she and others pointed out, e-mail or instant messaging is no substitute for face-to-face contact. "E-mailing somebody far way is not the same as them going to pick up your child at daycare or bringing you chicken soup," she said.

[17] Dr. Putnam said the new study reinforced much of what he had reported in "Bowling Alone," which had been criticized by some academics as a faulty analysis that ignored other social and economic trends. And even if the new study points to a rise in spouses as confidants, that is not especially cause to rejoice, he said. "It's like with global warming, if we learn that temperatures are going to rise slightly less than we thought," he said. "It's still a problem."

[18] "Sure, you might say, we've still got our wives or husbands or mothers," he said. "That's true. But gosh, the number of friends you have is a strong predictor of how long you live."

[19] The impact goes beyond the individual, as well. "There are effects on my neighbors of my not knowing them," he said. For one thing, "If I don't know them well and they don't know me, that has a demonstrable effect on the crime rate."

[20] Dr. Horrigan said there was anecdotal evidence that some members of a community use e-mail and the Internet "to keep up with people very close by." The Internet can help expand social networks, although the ties it creates are not as strong as those the Duke researchers are concerned with. Yet they can be useful.

[21] His group's research has shown that the Internet is increasingly being used during life's "major moments"—to gather information or advice when making a big financial investment, deciding where to live, or choosing a college for a child. The research has shown that "people were more likely to get help through their social network" for those kinds of decisions.

[22] Still, Dr. Putnam said, "The real interesting future is how can we use the Net to strengthen and deepen relationships that we have offline."

SUMMARIZE AND RESPOND

Write a 50-word summary of this piece, followed by a 150-word response in which you compare your experience with friendships to the points that Fountain makes in his article.

DISCUSS

Fountain ends his article with this quote from Professor Robert D. Putnam: "The real interesting future is how can we use the Net to strengthen and deepen relationships that we have offline." Do you see e-mail, text messages, and instant messaging as a good way to develop and strengthen off-line relationships? Explain your answer.

In this article, which appeared in the April 20, 2008 edition of the Washington Post, *reporter Joel Garreau explores the effects that online social networking sites are having on relationships.*

FRIENDS INDEED?

As We Click With More Pals Online, The Idea of Friendship Multiplies

Joel Garreau

[1] Shadee Malaklou has lots of friends. A whole lot—1,295, according to her latest Facebook count. But whom exactly can she count on?

[2] Malaklou, 22, acknowledges that if she ran into some of her "friends" on the street, she might not remember their names. When she went to Duke, where "I was quote unquote

FIGURE 9-1

As several of the readings in this chapter point out, the Internet has changed the way we pursue and maintain all kinds of relationships, from the casual to the romantic. Social networking sites such as Facebook and MySpace make it easy to line up hundreds of "friends," but for many people, the true nature of these relationships isn't clear. And, as Alice Mathias says in "Love in the Digital Age," it's easier than ever to make contact with potential romantic partners online. But, she writes, we might be in danger of becoming "trapped in the Age of the Emoticon." What do you think Mathias means by this? Do you see any drawbacks to developing and maintaining online relationships?

popular," social life was so competitive that sometimes invitations were based only on online determinations of how hot a person was, and whether her "friends" were cool.

3 Now that she is working at a Washington nonprofit, Malaklou is planning on pruning her "friends" as a rite of spring cleaning, defriending people who have come to mean little to her.

4 She does stay Facebook friends, however, with professors who might be good for letters of recommendation to graduate school. "The biggest value-added is that it helps maintain relationships—somewhat superficial but not worth getting rid of," she says.

5 The word "friend" has long covered a broad range of relationships—roommates, army buddies, pals from the last law firm, old neighbors, teammates, people you used to smoke dope with in back of your high school, people you see once a year at the Gold Cup, scuba instructors and carpool members, along with fellow gun collectors, Britney fans and cancer victims. The Oxford English Dictionary traces "freondum" back to "Beowulf" in 1018, and "to be frended" to 1387.

6 But MySpace and all the hundreds of other social networking Web sites, from Flickr to Twitter to Bebo, have caused us to think afresh about the boundaries and intensities of these relationships. Never before in history has it been so easy to keep up with so many people with whom you otherwise would have lost contact. These new electronic meshes are more than mere improvements over alumni magazines, holiday cards with pictures of families and those horrible letters about their lives, Rolodexes, yearbooks, organizational newsletters, and birth and death notices in the newspaper.

7 Summer friendships, for example, have been transformed. The ritual of meeting again at the beach after a long winter was once marked by hours of catching up. Not today. Networked people who haven't seen each other in forever already know about the new boyfriend, and what happened to the old one—in very great detail. They also know about the old school and the new job. They have known, every day, no matter where in the world they roamed, the instant that emotional change occurred. Now, after the initial squeals and swaying hugs, conversations pick up in mid-sentence. It's a mind-meld uncanny to watch.

8 This is a world of "participatory surveillance," says Anders Albrechtslund of Denmark's Aalborg University in the online journal *First Monday*.

9 Real online friends watch over each other—mutually, voluntarily and enthusiastically, in ways that can be endearing.

10 Others have referred to it as "empowering exhibitionism," Albrechtslund says.

11 Call it Friends Next.

You Can Pick Your Friends, but . . .

12 Life was once so simple. "I'll be there for you, when the rain starts to pour," went the "Friends" theme. "I'll be there for you, 'cause you're there for me too."

13 Today, when you join a social network, the first thing you start questioning is if you really want to embrace every "friend" request. Such promiscuity's downside quickly becomes obvious. Do you really want every petitioner—no matter how unclear his identity or intent—to see your revealing personal information? Much less those pictures of Ashley, Courtney and Jason from last Saturday night?

14 There's this girl at school "who won't even say 'hi' in the hallway," says a 16-year-old junior at a Washington high school who desires anonymity for fear of social ostracism. The aloof girl keeps asking to be a virtual "friend" on Facebook, arguably the most sophisticated popular site, no matter how often the answer is no.

15 This junior struggles with the relationship dilemma. "Why would I want to be 'friends' with this person? I occasionally smile at her. I guess it's kind of really impersonal to me, if she's not even going to say 'hi.'" The high schooler says she's "selective in acceptance of friends"—she has "only" 131 on Facebook. But if she had a relationship blow up, on the shoulders of how many could she cry?

16 "Probably like 20," she says.

17 For two decades, online social networks have been touted as one of the finest flowerings of our new era. But what is the strength of ties so weak as to barely exist? Who will lend you lunch money? Who will bail you out of jail? Who's got your back?

18 A remote Wyoming cattle ranch was home to Internet pioneer John Perry Barlow when he was a boy in the '50s. In the '80s, when he encountered the first settlers of online communities such as the Well, he felt like he was back in the small towns he once knew. He reveled in the throngs "gossiping, complaining . . . comforting and harassing each other, bartering, engaging in religion . . . beginning and ending love affairs, praying for one another's sick kids,"

he once wrote. "There was, it seemed, about everything one might find going on in a small town, save dragging Main or making out on the back roads."

[19] He has since developed a more jaundiced view of the Internet's utopian promise to dissolve barriers between people—"the reason I got involved in that stuff" in the first place, he says. Barlow hoped for "a distinctly 19th-century understanding of what community was. Where it was not just bail you out of jail, but stand behind you with a loaded gun—the Wyoming version." Instead, he sees people collecting and displaying enormous numbers of "friends" on MySpace, "for the same reason that elk grow antlers, I expect."

[20] As part of his firm's "online strategy," James C. Courtovich, 42, managing partner of a Washington lobbying and public relations outfit, recently joined Facebook and had a small team take the 3,000 names in his address book and cross-reference them with everyone there. The overlap was "shocking," he reports. "I expected my niece, but not the chairman of *The Washington Post*. At my age I expected a tenth of a percent." Instead, he found 7 percent of his world there: "Capitol Hill types, journalists, friends I'd not seen in years."

[21] Do you consider these people your friends? "Some friends are more equal than others," Courtovich says. To him, this network is no more than Washington business-as-usual—"an online cocktail party without having to stay up late or drink alcohol."

[22] Some encounters can be novel and strange. Jessica Smith, 23, remembers the time someone she'd never heard of from Vassar tried to friend her. It happened when Smith was an undergraduate at George Washington University and had just started dating her boyfriend, Peter. Turned out the stranger was Peter's ex.

[23] "There was nothing friendly about this," she says. "She only wanted to know about me." When Smith didn't fall for this probe—like it was the ex's business how cute she might be, or clever—"a friend of hers friended me. Like that would trick me—'Ooo, a new friend from Vassar!' It was weird. Really creepy." Before social networks, "she wouldn't have called me, or written me a letter."

Worlds Colliding

[24] You know all those separate lives you lead? When you're not being the FTC lawyer, or the hair-metal band freak, you're the wife of a glassblower and mother of two who likes to spend every vacation she can on the black-sand beaches of Dominica?

[25] Forget about keeping those lives neatly partitioned in Friends Next.

[26] "It's the postmodern nightmare—to have all of your selves collide," says Rebecca G. Adams, a sociologist at the University of North Carolina at Greensboro who edits *Personal Relationships*, the journal of the International Association for Relationship Research.

[27] In villages of the agrarian age, you wouldn't even have developed those various personalities. In Friends Next you can't escape them. "If you really welcome all of your friends from all of the different aspects of your life and they interact with each other and communicate in ways that everyone can read," Adams says, "you get held accountable for the person you are in all of these groups, instead of just one of them."

[28] This became dramatically clear in September 2003, on an early site called Friendster. Two 16-year-old students approached a young San Francisco teacher with two questions: Why do you do drugs, and why are you friends with pedophiles? So reports danah boyd, a PhD candidate at the University of California at Berkeley's School of Information who has become renowned for her research into online social networks, and who insists on rendering her name without capital letters.

[29] The teacher's profile was nothing extraordinary or controversial. Her picture showed her hiking. But she had a lot of friends who were devotees of Burning Man—the annual weeklong festival in the Nevada desert that attracts tens of thousands of people experimenting with community, artwork, self-expression, self-reliance, absurdity and clothing-optional revelry.

[30] "The drug reference came not from her profile but from those of her Friends, some of whom had signaled drug use (and attendance at Burning Man, which for the students amounted to the same thing)," boyd writes. "Friends also brought her the pedophilia connection—in this case via the profile of a male Friend who, for his part, had included an in-joke involving a self-portrait in a Catholic schoolgirl outfit and testimonials about his love of young girls. The students were not in on this joke."

[31] In Friends Next, all your lives and circles of relationships are collapsed. Extreme cases of friend mash-ups resemble the barroom scene in "Star Wars."

[32] "You can be friends with someone you know well and don't like," reports Susannah Clark, a sophomore at the University of Mary Washington. "You read their profiles and blogs and are well aware of their life. It's a love-to-hate type arrangement."

[33] "I even agreed to be one person's friend because he's so psychotic I was scared of what would happen if I said no," writes blogger Dan Kaufman.

Stitched Together

[34] We're inventing Friends Next every day.

[35] "For most people, when they thought of their close friends, it was people with whom they would share personal things," says Sherry Turkle, a sociologist and psychologist at MIT who has studied online social networks from their beginnings. "What's changing now is that people who are not in the other person's physical life meet in this very new kind of space. It is leaving room for new hybrid forms."

[36] The weirdness of Friends Next is that it comes at you like a melodrama: "Is he married yet?" "Is he still straight?" "She's changed her religious views to 'rain dancing'? I thought she had a cross tattooed on her hip."

[37] "Facebook is more about entertainment than work," says Nicholas A. Christakis, a physician and sociologist who studies social networks at Harvard. "Instead of watching soap operas, they're watching soap operas of people they sort of know."

[38] "It sucks you in," says Mary Washington's Clark. "The public conversations—it's digital eavesdropping."

[39] Losing friends in this new world is as fraught as making them. "Real-world friendships are not usually intentionally ended," Adams says. "Folks just let things naturally cool off. On Facebook, decisive action has to be taken." Defriending cements that a friendship is over.

[40] The best soap operas occur when a couple breaks up. Change your profile from "In a Relationship" to "Single"—or even more ominously, "It's Complicated"—and little press releases blast out to all your gossip-hound "friends." Massive e-mailing and tongue-wagging ensues.

[41] It's futile to try to erase latent traces of Friends Next. "The digital trails of an online friendship—true or not—really do last forever," Albrechtslund says. Its evidence is stored on servers indefinitely, beyond the control of the persons involved.

[42] While many are still trying to figure out how to make Friends Next work for us, Todd Huffman is trying to harness this new social form to save us.

[43] The Phoenix software developer is creating a company called sStitch. In times of

crisis, like the recent San Diego wildfires, Huffman notes, there are vast quantities of useful information buzzing among Friends Next. They turn to their social tech—text-messaging, blogs, e-mail, Web networks—to announce: "I'm okay." "I'm evacuating to this city." "This freeway is shut down." "That road is flooded." They send pictures on the fly. Their cell phones' global positioning locates them precisely.

[44] This is all instant bottom-up information from hundreds of thousands of eyes not now available to the people trying to manage the disaster. How great would it be, Huffman thinks, if you could aggregate all that into a comprehensive and sensible God's-eye picture of what's going on that would allow instantaneous and effective response?

[45] Huffman, 28, sees the potential in this because Friends Next is at the heart of his personal life. "I'm one of the first in that generation of people very defined by friends obtained and maintained through social technologies," he says. "Almost all my close friends, I originally met over the Internet. They're very geographically spread out."

[46] The one thing he's learned is Friends Next is not enough to sustain relationships. "A lot of friendship is sharing experiences, not necessarily planned. It's people going through the world, negotiating a pathway together."

[47] But Huffman has discovered Friends Next can be a gateway to genuine intimacy.

[48] Recently he organized a ski trip to British Columbia with his core group of buddies, and for the hell of it announced on Facebook that anybody who could read his profile was invited to come along. To his surprise, an acquaintance from Texas took him up on it. Houston-boy started off not knowing anybody else, but intense bonds ensued. "Now he's going with us to Burning Man—he's become a de facto member of the core group," Huffman says.

[49] The novel ties of Friends Next have caused Huffman to think hard about what the word "friend" means.

[50] "You can maintain a friendship over a distance. Once the person is a friend, it takes very little data to communicate very complex things. You can send a five-word e-mail" that, for someone else, "would take a two-hour conversation."

[51] "A friend," however, he has decided, "is someone who you like a lot who understands you at a pretty deep level."

The Real Thing

[52] So in Friends Next, what matters? Is being good company enough? Is trust a key ingredient? Or loyalty? Or self-sacrifice?

[53] "Go through your phone book, call people and ask them to drive you to the airport," Jay Leno once said. "The ones who will drive you are your true friends. The rest aren't bad people; they're just acquaintances."

[54] "It's the friends you can call up at 4 a.m. that matter," said Marlene Dietrich.

[55] While Facebook will allow you as many as 5,000 "friends," enduring realities impose far more significant limits.

[56] No matter how thick your soup of constant communication, sooner or later you may have to decide who will be your bridesmaid.

[57] No matter how easily you can get Facebook on your iPhone, sooner or later you may have to decide who will be the godfather of your child.

[58] And no matter how extensive your profile, it is certain that someday, someone is going to have to decide who will be your pallbearers.

Write a 100-word summary of Garreau's explanation of what he calls "Friends Next." Then, write a brief response in which you critique this phenomenon.

Who do you think is Garreau's target audience? What does he do in his article to appeal to this audience? Do you think he is successful? Explain your response.

How does Garreau compare the ending of "real-world" friendships with "defriending" online? Do you agree with his comparison?

In his essay, Garreau quotes a source who describes social networking sites in two ways: as a world of "participatory surveillance" and as a place of "empowering exhibitionism." What do you think is the difference between these two descriptions? Which more accurately describes your experience with such sites?

Alice Mathias was a columnist for The Dartmouth *at Dartmouth College, in Hanover, N.H., when she wrote this piece for a* New York Times *online series called "The Graduates: Eight College Seniors Face the Future" on April 17, 2007. As you read her piece, pay attention to how she creates her distinctive voice.*

LOVE IN THE DIGITAL AGE

Alice Mathias

[1] This winter I was in a class called Romantic Comedy. Shakespeare, you might ask? Umm... no. We're talking "You've Got Mail." I figured this had to be the Rocks for Jocks of the film department, but as it turned out, Rom-Com was no sunset stroll down the beach. We dragged our feet through Freudian readings of "Bringing Up Baby" and analyzed the shift from modernism to postmodernism by contrasting "The Apartment" with "Annie Hall." All I wanted to do was kick back with some popcorn and take a vacation from my not-so-"Moonstruck" freezing-cold Dartmouth winter, but unfortunately there would be an exam.

[2] For this exam, we had to bust out our crystal balls and write an essay predicting

the future of the romantic comedy genre. Our professor raised several issues to consider. Among them was the fact that zero Renaissance Dartmouth men had signed up for this pretty-big class. Our professor was a guy. He liked sappy movies. Was this a generational thing?

[3] One of my classmates suggested a revealing answer. Perhaps a heterosexual Romeo might be paranoid about listing Romantic Comedy as one of his courses in his Facebook profile. He might imagine that Juliet was out there somewhere, stalking through cyberspace looking for the One. What if she were to check out his course load, see that he was in Chick Flicks 101, and assume he was therefore "interested in: men"? This stereotype-fueled miscommunication could be the dagger that might murder their chances of ever meeting face-to-face! Talk about tragedy.

[4] My classmate's hypothesis demonstrates how young people today think about relationships and identity—that is, in terms of Facebook.com. Men (and women!) of my generation are undergoing an unprecedented emotional crisis that has little to do with gender roles. We are trapped in the Age of the Emoticon :(

[5] Young people today are more inclined than ever to drool over love stories in the flickering privacy of the movie theater, because in our own realities, the classic process of romance is as endangered as—well, the movie theater. We have entered a post-butterflies era. Romantic comedy's nerve-wracking meet cutes, blind dates, love letters and eye contact have been kicked out of our love lives by MySpace, Match.com, AOL Instant Messenger and e-mail. The mystery man has been expelled from our virtual paradise. His identity has been unveiled by Google, and guess what? He's no Cary Grant.

[6] My first (and arguably most notable) fauxmance started in seventh grade when a boy in my class asked me to be his girlfriend on AOL.

That relationship came to an abrupt end days later when we accidentally bumped into each other in the cafeteria and failed to overcome the challenge of improvising un-spell-checked conversation. (I had just had my braces tightened, so I got away with pretending my teeth were too sore for me to talk.)

[7] Communication has been streamlined by the Internet, and something essential to the process of falling in love has been lost. We can type up carefully crafted statements rather than go face-to-face and improvise from the heart, thereby risking embarrassment, vulnerability or Oscar-worthy dialogue. We can Google our way into the museums of each other's identities—and fall in love there.

[8] If we get up the nerve to e-mail or IM our love interests, we can correspond at a comfortable pace (i.e., however long it takes us to come up with witty, well-crafted messages). They will assume we're taking our time to respond because we're busy fighting off that parade of knights in shining armor who are begging to be listed with us in a Facebook relationship. They don't know we're staring longingly at that one picture that pops up when we Google them, and we don't have to worry about whether or not they're staring longingly back! (Bonus: No one has to deal with that awkward "who's paying?" question.)

[9] Flirting has been transformed into a digital process. We don't even have to touch each other to "hook up." We can just hook up to the Internet.

[10] The difficulty of negotiating what happens in each arena of reality probably explains why the word "awkward" has shot to the top of my generation's lexicon. My classmates and I charade our way through first dates, trying to keep track of what's been said versus what's been read on the Internet ahead of time. We have to fake it through "Where are you from?" conversation, and if we let something slip that reveals we've done our research, it's awkward.

[11] It gets even more complicated than that.

[12] That real-life Archibald Leach was probably no Cary Grant (the pseudonym under which Archie was advertised to adoring audiences). But today, we are all walking, breathing Cary/Archie complexes—part public, part (we hope) private.

[13] We are all so submerged in one another's gazes that it's almost natural to act as though we're always in a movie. (Thanks to all those security cameras out there, we pretty much are!) Like movie stars, we are sensitive to the fact that everything we do and say (every mistake we make and every triumph at which we "boo-yah") could be witnessed and speculated about in public forums by just about anyone in the world.

[14] Granted, many of us have not yet established much of a reputation on the Internet; as we get older we will undoubtedly accumulate more and more hits on our Google resumes. But we cannot separate ourselves from our Internet alter egos. Both are relevant players in our job searches, friendships and love lives.

[15] Our children may even Google us someday. We're never going to be able to ground them for doing anything without being exposed as hypocrites. Whoops.

[16] The truth is, my greatest concern is not with how the Internet will influence romance. Romance is a privilege. One can get through life without it. I'm concerned about emotion in general.

[17] I'm worried that we are becoming desensitized to the fact that there are actual human beings whose lives and feelings are being shaped by things that are so easy to mindlessly type into e-mails, chat rooms, Facebook wall posts and blogs.

[18] Maybe I'm just skeptical about emotional relationships because I haven't met the right person, i.e. "Entourage" star Adrian Grenier. (Cut to: me swooning.) Who knows, Adrian might be hypnotized by fate to read this online declaration of my love for him and consider e-mailing me, thereby unleashing a flood of digital interactions that might culminate in a (mind-bogglingly awkward) real-life encounter. Of course, this is never going to happen because just before he e-mails me, he'll Google my name (just to make sure I'm not a freak), and find out that I am, indeed, apparently quite appalling, according to recent comments on blogs in response to my April 1st post on this site. Everyone's ability to "get to know Alice Mathias" online may very well be the beginning and end of my social life and my chances at scoring that M.R.S. I'm purportedly looking for. (From Mr. Grenier or any other Internet-savvy, earth-dwelling guy for that matter.)

[19] All joking aside, I am willingly putting myself out there for criticism in a public forum. That said, it is important to understand that similar attempts at identity destruction are happening to innocent people in every corner of cyberspace—to people who aren't asking for it.

[20] For example, Dartmouth students have recently had to deal with the construction of the Web site boredatbaker.com (which has cousins at the other Ivies, the Massachusetts Institute of Technology, New York University and Stanford). Intended as a community tool, this Web site has mutated into a forum for the anonymous publication of very personal attacks on students who must try their best not to be emotionally affected when people publicly question their sexuality, comment on their physical appearance and speculate about their value as humans.

[21] In anonymous Internet attacks, people can say things they would never mention aloud while looking their target in the eye. No one need take any personal responsibility. The victims of these unfortunate manifestations

of free speech must suspend their emotions and try to trust that people around them (including love interests) aren't the ones who are writing or consuming this stuff. The safest thing to do in our boredatbaker-shadowed community is to be emotionally isolated from everyone until graduation brings escape.

22 So I guess the question remains: what does all this mean for the future of romantic comedy?

SUMMARIZE AND RESPOND

Write a one-paragraph response to this quotation from Mathias' essay: "I'm worried that we are becoming desensitized to the fact that there are actual human beings whose lives and feelings are being shaped by things that are so easy to mindlessly type into e-mails, chat rooms, Facebook wall posts and blogs." In your response, discuss why you think social networking sites are, or, if you disagree with her claim, are *not* desensitizing us to real human emotion.

ANALYZE

Go back through Mathias' piece, and identify what types of evidence she uses to help make her point (Does she rely primarily on statistical data? On observations of the student body on which she writes? On personal experience?). Once you have identified the types of evidence she uses here (she uses more than one type), consider why she has chosen these approaches. Which elements of her support are most effective and why?

DISCUSS

Based on evidence from her essay, discuss what audience (or audiences) Mathias had in mind when she composed this piece. Do you think her argument would be as effective on a person who does not regularly browse the Web?

ARGUE

Write a brief argument in opposition to Mathias' piece. In your essay, try to make the case that social networking sites actually draw us closer together with our fellow online denizens.

A former associate editor of National Review, *Travis Kavulla wrote this essay for the August 8, 2007 edition of the magazine's online edition. Like Joel Garreau and Alice Mathias in the two pieces that precede his, Kavulla examines the effects social networking sites have on personal relationships. Kavulla's focus, however, is on how these sites enable a new kind of mourning after the deaths of friends and acquaintances.*

DEATH ON FACEBOOK: A DIFFERENT KIND OF FUNERAL

Travis Kavulla

[1] I didn't know him that well. So when I received an e-mail telling me my classmate Harry was dead—aged 24, a suicide—I did what I could. I turned to Facebook, the social-networking website where we were (indeed still are) "friends."

[2] The farewell messages on his Wall, the space on a Facebook profile where one's friends can add notes, had just begun to filter in. At first, they had been ambiguous and spare: "I miss you!" said one. "Love you," another. Then, posted at 10:33 a.m.: "Goodbye [Harry], we love you and miss you. I hope you are laughing and talking forever and making music in heaven."

[3] Facebook had made it a matter of record—it was all over for our friend Harry.

[4] I had not thought much about him lately. Ours was one of those acquaintanceships forged in college that would endure as only a small, if crystalline, memory. A trove of amusing anecdotes had informed my enduring mental image of Harry: the sometime womanizer and accomplished boozer–turned–homosexual devotee of worthy causes. There was the time, for instance, when Harry disappeared with my friend into a darkroom known popularly as "the Orgasmatron 3000" at the office of Harvard's student newspaper, *The Crimson*. Harry emerged some time later with an emptied bottle of Brut in hand; I believe my friend walked away with a bite mark.

[5] These miscellaneous happenings were hardly glue for a lasting friendship. Once past the Ivy gates, Harry and I spent little effort keeping each other abreast of our lives. Ours was a situation, in short, ripe for an enduring Facebook "friendship."

[6] Had Harry and I been classmates in 1907 and not today, I suppose weeks would have passed before I met a common friend able to inform me of the tragedy. I can almost imagine the quiet, meandering recollection that would follow: the inescapable speculation on the matters of mental health and happiness, then the retelling of our undisturbed and (since two friends in the same sphere perceive much the same thing) consonant college memories of Harry.

[7] Facebook provides an antidote to the ambiguities this earlier generation endured. Whether in matters of a classmate's employment, or marriage, or death, Facebook makes so much information readily available.

⁸ It has taken only a few days for Harry's online profile to be transformed into a continuously updated obituary. Many seem to want it that way—one friend pleaded on his Wall, "Facebook Please Do Not Erase This Profile."

⁹ And Facebook is happy to oblige. When the company learns of a death, it immediately purges the record of the deceased's erstwhile contact information, membership in online groups, and "personal info" (favorite books, movies, quotations, and so on). But, for a month, the user's Wall, photographs, and basic information (hometown, birthdate, religion) are retained.

¹⁰ As I read the outpouring of remembrance on Harry's Wall, I marveled at the detail my mental image of him had missed. A huge number of e-mourners thanked him for his "bear hugs"—I'd never received one. And at the end of his life, he apparently had a girlfriend, who seems charming from all the photos—I'd had no idea he swung that way still. Because I'm in the same Facebook "network" as she, I could even see her profile and read the consolations others had written on her Wall.

¹¹ But there I stopped. All alone in the early-morning hours, I couldn't help but feel almost prurient—or in any case, not mournful—as I perused Harry's and his close friends' profiles. Facebook is a place where users offer up details of themselves for the private consumption of others; I've always found that creepy, a feeling exacerbated by the circumstances. One could be unclothed, or eating a bowl of cereal, or listening to Cher and still electronically mourning the passing of Harry.

¹² I thought I should post something, to leave a mark that I had been to Harry's profile, and had come with the intention to mourn, not just to observe. But what could I say?

¹³ Many of the comments others left seemed glib. Someone wrote: "We're going to miss you and your fun-spirited ways. I'll collect my $10 loan plus interest from you in Heaven!" Another wrote of Harry's apparent girlfriend, who is black: "I will drink [her] hot chocolate for you. That sounds dirty but you know what I'm talking about." Exclamation marks and frowning emoticons, the telltale marks of Internet prose, were abundant.

¹⁴ Accompanying these comments were photographs of their authors. Nearly all the e-mourners, like most Facebook users, have profile pictures that capture them in a moment of revelry: smiling wide or winking for the camera, an intoxicating substance of choice in hand. My own profile picture shows me "undercover"—wearing an ostentatious peace-sign necklace, black-rim glasses, and corduroy aplenty—at a Howard Dean campaign rally in 2003. Collectively, our faces look fit for a frat party or a masquerade ball, but not a funeral.

¹⁵ Once before, I had dealt with a suicide amongst friends, when I was in middle school and my next-door neighbor, barely a teenager, shot himself. I was at home when it happened, watching *The Simpsons*. My mother came downstairs, and it was immediately clear that an extraordinary tragedy had occurred. She couldn't speak at first, and I feared the worst—that my father, perhaps, had died. At last, she blurted out my friend's name, gave a pause that said everything, and finally sobbed, "He's dead."

¹⁶ I was called back to that cataclysmic moment every day for years afterward. But Harry's was different: I heard of the suicide through an e-mail within 48 hours of the event, confirmed through Facebook that Harry had died, and thereafter stood witness at my laptop as electronic condolences were filed by his college friends, now scattered by graduation or summer break. Absent were those feelings that attend one's close proximity to a friend's suicide. There was no guilt, except at my capacity for voyeurism. There was a certain shock, but it was dulled by the physical distance of others who had known Harry.

[17] In the era of online social networking, one often hears about how MySpace, Facebook, and similar websites desensitize young people to their everyday interactions. Online, the fights are more frequent and venomous, the flirtations more direct and lascivious. But until Harry, I had not yet been called upon to imagine what footprint Facebook would leave on the solemn act of remembering the dead.

[18] Here lay our friend Harry: inside an electronic network that brings disparate mourners together, even while making them feel emotionally distant and, when they powered down the laptop, utterly alone.

[19] It was very late at night when I concluded not to post anything at all on Harry's Wall, much less to trumpet the hope, as many of the e-mourners had, to see him again in the afterlife. News of Harry's death had left me inert, silent—only the fingers moved, only the keystrokes could be heard. I needed to give this mournfulness I felt a physical dimension, and remedy what Facebook had wrought. When I pray, I typically assume no special posture, but now I got down on my knees and began, "Our Father, I pray for the repose of . . ." It was the least I could do.

SUMMARIZE

How does Kavulla characterize his reaction to reading about his former classmate's death on Facebook and to the outpouring of grief that followed almost immediately? How, in the end, did he decide to respond to the death?

DISCUSS

Kavulla writes that "Facebook is a place where users offer up details of themselves for the private consumption of others; I've always found that creepy . . ." What bothers him about this situation? Do you agree with his point? Explain your response.

ARGUE

Some critics of social networking spaces contend that sites such as MySpace and Facebook enable self-absorbed behavior by creating a false sense of community and caring. Using Kavulla's essay as a starting place, write a brief essay in which you either agree or disagree with this claim.

In the following piece, Laura Vanderkam, an author and member of the board of contributors for USA Today, *argues that the "success penalty" for well-educated and successful women has "nearly disappeared." The piece was first published in* USA Today *on October 17, 2006.*

DO SMART GIRLS FINISH LAST IN LOVE?

Laura Vanderkam

1 Back in my single days, my friends and I used to joke about a dating dilemma we called "dropping the P-bomb."

2 "Where did you go to school?" a gentleman would inquire at a party.

3 "Oh, in New Jersey." We'd smile and try to change the subject. No luck.

4 "Where in New Jersey?"

5 "Um, Princeton?"

6 We'd grip our drinks and wait. Would he scurry away? That's what we expected—especially as we began collecting graduate degrees and serious paychecks.

7 Growing up as a smart, ambitious girl in America, you can't miss the assumption that neither of those attributes wins you points in the love game.

8 In 2002, Sylvia Ann Hewlett's book, *Creating a Life: Professional Women and the Quest for Children*, claimed that only 60% of high-achieving women in their 40s and early 50s were married vs. 76% of men and 83% of extremely high-earning men. Pulitzer Prize–winning columnist Maureen Dowd subsequently rued that despite succeeding beyond the dreams of her Irish maid ancestors, her odds of landing a husband might have jumped if she, too, never aspired to anything beyond keeping house.

9 Dumb it down, we learned. Men don't make passes at girls who wear glasses.

10 There's just one problem. It's not true—not anymore. A growing body of research finds that the success penalty—the lower marriage rates among high-achieving women vs. their lower-achieving sisters—has nearly disappeared.

'Volley with an equal'

11 "While there are certainly some men who want a woman to play fetch for them, the majority of men, and certainly the ones we would want to date, are definitely looking to volley with an equal," says Christine Whelan, author of the new book *Why Smart Men Marry Smart Women*. As children of egalitarian baby boomer moms and dads hit their 20s and 30s, high-achieving women now marry at the same rate as others, they just do so a few years later. The first part of that sentence is reason to celebrate. The latter is more worrisome. Later marriages tend to mean later and fewer births, and this country needs the bright kids bright moms raise. Though given how quickly society has changed on the first count, there's every reason to hope that soon young women will succeed in changing the second part, too.

[12] Whelan, herself a Princeton grad who's getting married next summer, combed through years of Census data, studies and a Harris poll that she commissioned. The finding? Hewlett and Dowd missed a big shift that's just showing up on the radar among high achievers, whom Whelan defines as women with graduate degrees and/or incomes in the top 10% for their age.

[13] In the bad old days—alas, as recently as the 1980s—a woman with a graduate degree was 16% less likely to be married by age 44 than a woman with a high school diploma. Now, while 55% of women with graduate degrees marry by age 29 vs. 61% of other women, after 30, the odds reverse. A single, 30-year-old woman with a graduate degree has about a 75% chance of getting married. A single 30-year-old woman with less education has about a 66% chance.

[14] The Center for Economic and Policy Research reports that women ages 28 to 35 who earn more than $55,000 a year (roughly the top 10%) are just as likely to be married as other women who work full-time. Indeed, Whelan's survey found that 90% of high-achieving men want a spouse who is as smart as they are, and 71% say a woman's success makes her more desirable as a wife. Maybe it's because these men do want to marry Mommy—72% of moms of high-achieving men worked outside the home as they raised their sons.

[15] So why does the myth persist? Blame the higher age of first marriage for women with graduate degrees or high paychecks—fueled by a belief that starting a family during grad school, or during the early years of a "big" job, is impossible. These women marry, on average, around age 30; women overall first marry at about 25. From ages 25 to 30, Whelan notes, "you'll go to many weddings on your own," believing bad news after bad bouquet tosses.

Reason to worry

[16] But though it's reassuring to know the odds of marrying are good, the older age of first marriage for high-achieving women is not so reassuring. Despite headlines about professional women becoming single moms by choice, most won't have children out of wedlock, so later marriages mean later births. Indeed, America's brightest people—men and women—tend to delay childbearing.

[17] This may be a choice, though it's too bad for society that successful people aren't so successful in the Darwinian sense.

[18] But even this, I believe, will change. New York's sidewalks these days are clogged with $700 double strollers pushed by the nannies of high-achieving parents who can afford such wheels. Trendsetting Manhattan's pre-school age population soared 26% from 2000–04; from Britney Spears to Angelina Jolie, young moms are becoming hip.

[19] When women decide that they want to get married, they tend to make it happen. They approach dates with open minds. They ask to be set up. They seal the deal.

[20] Until now, young women haven't adopted that mind-set in graduate school or in the early years of their big careers because they believe the myth that it's impossible to have it all.

[21] If the marriage penalty can disappear in a generation, though, there's no reason that young women can't demand that suitors, schools and employers work on a different timetable when it comes to families, too.

[22] That will take guts, but so does being honest during party chitchat. In time, we can learn to do both.

Summarize the problem to which Vanderkam seems to be responding. With what issues is she concerned? What claims does she make about marriage and the professional woman?

Identify the evaluative criteria (these can be explicit or implied) that guide Vanderkam's argument. How do these criteria enable her to make claim that it's beneficial for women to marry while they are young?

Does Vanderkam do an adequate job of persuading you that there is a problem to be addressed? What assumptions does she make about marriage? In what ways do these help or hurt her argument?

Using humor and wit, Frank Paiva, a 2005 high school graduate, describes one of the crucial roles he played as "the gay best friend" of young women who needed last-minute prom dates. As you read his essay, first published in the May 29, 2005 edition of the New York Times, *try to look beyond his lighthearted approach to see the underlying issues he is addressing.*

A PRINCE CHARMING FOR THE PROM (NOT EVER AFTER, THOUGH)

Frank Paiva

1 Lately I've become wary of the question "Frank, what are you doing next Saturday night?" In the month of May it can only mean one thing: I'm going to yet another prom. And no, I'm not doing a favor for a cousin. Cousins are out. I'm this century's new answer to the last-minute prom date: the gay best friend.

2 By the end of June I'll have worn the tuxedo I swiped from the school drama department three or four times. While most 18-year-old guys are preparing for their one big night, I'm whipping up more magical evenings than Lance Burton or David Copperfield.

³ I am also swimming in corsages. I went to the florist today for the second time this week, and she gave me a suspicious look. Does she know what I'm up to? After all, I can't be the only one who understands that gay is the new cousin.

⁴ Until recently this wasn't really possible, because most gay men postponed coming out until college or later, if they came out at all. But now more and more young men are coming out in high school. I knew I was gay in sixth grade and came out in eighth. Originally I didn't plan to tell anyone until ninth grade, when I would enroll in a new school, but I decided I needed to let people know who I really was.

⁵ My decision had a traumatic aftermath. How is a school supposed to handle the coming out of an eighth grader? My middle school also contained an elementary school, and alarmed parents feared for their little children, worried, I suppose, that I might convert them or something.

⁶ I endured a set of excruciating meetings with school administrators during which parameters for my behavior were discussed. That and the cruelty of my classmates left me feeling isolated and scared, and I found myself turning mostly to girls for support and friendship.

⁷ Although things improved in high school, I still found myself relying primarily on friendships with girls, some of whom I met at summer drama camps and who attended different schools.

⁸ As I see it, these girls saved me, and now it's my turn to save them. Dancing a few steps in a beautified gymnasium is the least I could do to thank the girls who helped me become who I am.

⁹ I don't even have to go broke doing this. Any girl who's progressive enough to go to her prom with a gay guy understands that it's no longer the 1950's and that I shouldn't have to pay for everything.

¹⁰ They also understand I won't turn into a drunken, groping creep in the middle of the evening, so I figure it's an even trade.

¹¹ And unlike the goofy cousin who might arrive in a ruffled, powder-blue tux and tell embarrassing stories about computer camp, I'm a safe, chic choice. Neither of us will blush with sexual tension when it comes time to attach corsage to bosom. I won't make a fool of my date or myself with awkward straight-boy dancing. And I'll help her figure out the details of her dress and hairstyle. After all, we wouldn't want anyone committing social suicide on the biggest night of our tender young lives.

¹² As the gay date, I also make one of the evening's most unpleasant moments a breeze. I have no problem meeting the girl's parents, a typical sticking point for most guys, because I know that wise and open-minded parents are smart enough to realize that a gay guy is their daughter's best and safest prom bet.

¹³ If I were a worried mother of a dateless daughter, I would scour the hip coffee shops of my town waving a rainbow flag in search of recruits. It might cause my daughter to die of embarrassment, but at least she would have a fabulous night out and wouldn't make me a grandmother anytime soon.

¹⁴ At the proms themselves, though, I'm supposed to be straight, so I do my best. Am I ever worried about being found out? Not really. My friend Katie goes to a Catholic high school, and at her prom I even passed rigid nun interrogation.

¹⁵ On our way through the lineup of nun inspectors, they shook my hand and eyed me up and down before pronouncing me a fit suitor. So what do I have to worry about? Then again, maybe nuns aren't known for their finely tuned gay-dar.

¹⁶ One thing I've discovered in my brief barrage of proms is that they're all pretty much the same. There's that sense of finality, of going out with a bang.

Peter Dazeley/Getty Images

FIGURE 9-2

As several writers in this chapter explain, there is no template for finding—and maintaining—a romantic relationship. In his essay "A Prince Charming for the Prom," Frank Paiva, who calls himself "this century's new answer to the last-minute prom date: the gay best friend," wonders why many of his "female friends, who are charming, attractive and fun to be with," can't find dates. He also admits to having unfulfilled prom dreams of his own—namely, being able to go with a date of his own choosing. But, he writes, "I just don't feel ready to take a boy to prom. I once tried to take a boy to a school dance, and it was just too weird. It felt like every eye was focused on us for all the wrong reasons." What details in Figure 9-2 mirror the institutional and cultural difficulties that many people in same-sex relations face? What argument do you think the image makes?

17 Gay or not, there's still that stomach-churning feeling of anticipation as you and your date see each other in your formal dress for the first time. There's the poor couple wearing the absolute wrong ensemble. There's that burned-out feeling in the early morning from so much fun packed into so little time. Rest assured that the onset of horror from wondering what the pictures will look like decades from now is there every time as well.

18 But sometimes our expectations get the better of us, and the prom's real purpose is lost. It's one of the last times to be together and have fun as a class before everyone scatters and comes back to the reunion 10 years later balding, divorced, wildly successful or exactly, pathetically the same.

19 Whether you loved your own prom, hated it, missed it, only made it to the parking lot or were too drunk to remember, there's no denying it's a milestone that happens only once. Or, in my case, several times.

20 The one thing I can't understand is why many of my female friends, who are charming, attractive and fun to be with, don't have straight male suitors to accompany them. Surely the school halls aren't filled with date-snatching floozies offering the one thing no teenage guy, except the gay best friend, can say no to. So I've got to believe I see things in these girls that straight guys can't because with me the element of sexual attraction was never there to begin with.

21 Many young gay men make friends with the cool girls who fly under the radar because they don't possess conventional good looks and they don't put out. We get to know these girls for the things about them that matter.

22 Sometimes I want to hold up a sign that says: "Here! Date this girl, you idiot!" Of course if they aren't smart enough to figure out a girl is worth dating, they probably aren't worthy of the girl in the first place.

23 Perhaps this is why certain girls and certain gay guys become such good friends in high school. They're waiting for an environment that isn't based on popularity or games, an atmosphere where they can thrive.

24 While I've had an excellent time in high school these past four years, I have to believe there is something better out there for me in years to come. I know many of my friends feel the same way.

25 We've all heard famous women talk about how they were ostracized in high school or unpopular with the boys, only later to become gorgeous and desired. Even though they ended up successful, they never had that high school experience of the prom, that one magical time that can never be taken away. I'm here to provide this to many future famous women, even if I don't get it for myself.

26 As much as I'd like to, I will not be attending my own school's prom with a guy. My florist must know this because each time I walk in, she always flips past the boutonniere section of her prom accessories book.

27 I wish this weren't the case. I wish I could take someone with me, because I've got prom dreams of my own. They involve buying expensive ingredients at the gourmet food store and spending the entire day making dinner with my date. We would enjoy the food even more knowing we put all the effort into making it ourselves.

28 When we walked into the dance, the two of us would initially stun people, not because we were two guys but just because we looked great. I wouldn't care if I had to learn to make clothes myself if it meant avoiding that awkward "I rented this, and it doesn't quite fit" look. I would be able

to hold his hand all night without feeling weird or attracting attention. By the time it was over, we would be so tired we wouldn't even care.

29 Right now, however, my prom dream is just that. My school is a great place, but out of about 500 students, there are only a few other openly gay kids. (There are also a handful of openly bisexual girls, but that's considered trendy, so they don't count.)

30 I'm pretty brave, but sorry, I just don't feel ready to take a boy to prom. I once tried to take a boy to a school dance, and it was just too weird. It felt like every eye was focused on us for all the wrong reasons.

31 Maybe things will be better for younger guys. I hope so.

32 At my school, attending the prom in groups of friends is normal and acceptable, so that's what I'm doing. Time to drag out that tuxedo again. But I'm looking forward to it. I will thank my friends for the great times and try not to focus on the thing I cannot yet have. I'll walk in feeling sad and knowing that, for better or worse, I'll be leaving these people in the fall. We'll all go off to our own lives. Who knows what'll happen in mine?

33 All proms have their cheesy themes, and ours is no exception. "Let the Dreams Begin!" cries out from invitations and prom updates throughout our school.

34 My dream began a long time ago. I'm just waiting for it to come true.

RESPOND

Based on your experience in high school, respond to the following quote from Paiva: "Perhaps this is why certain girls and certain gay guys become such good friends in high school. They're waiting for an environment that isn't based on popularity or games, an atmosphere where they can thrive."

ANALYZE

Identify the elements of pathos in Paiva's piece. What emotions does he evoke and how does he evoke them? How does this appeal strengthen his overall argument?

DISCUSS

Why do you think that Paiva waits until the last part of his essay to discuss his own desires for taking a real date to the prom? How does this strategy position you as an audience member?

Justin Britt-Gibson, a freelance journalist and screenwriter working in Los Angeles, wrote this piece for the March 18, 2007 edition of the Washington Post. *In it, he explores what he sees as a more tolerant attitude toward race among his generation.*

WHAT'S WRONG WITH THIS PICTURE?

Race isn't a factor when my generation chooses friends.

Justin Britt-Gibson

[1] "It's no big deal," I tell myself. I'm sitting on the subway in Manhattan with Caroline, a woman I'm seeing. Her head rests on my shoulder, her auburn hair tangled in my scarf. Though it should be the last thing on my mind, I can't help but wonder what inspires the elderly African American woman across from us to shake her head disapprovingly: the Detroit Tigers cap I'm wearing or the company I'm keeping. After all, my beloved Tigers had recently defeated the New York Yankees in the American League playoffs. Then again, I'm also a young black man sharing an affectionate arm with a white woman.

[2] As a 25-year-old member of the post–Gen X generation dubbed the "Millennials," I'm used to displays of warmth between interracial couples being ignored or barely noticed. They're hardly on our minds at all.

[3] A similar carefree attitude toward racial mixing reigned at Springbrook High School in Silver Spring, Maryland, where I shared cafeteria tables and Nintendo controls with friends whose parents hailed from Pakistan, Haiti, Ethiopia, Colombia—and Pittsburgh. To my parents' generation, our devil-may-care attitude toward diversity is striking, a symbol of racial progress. Ninety-five percent of 18- to 29-year-olds have friends from different racial backgrounds, according to a Washington Post-Kaiser-Harvard poll. Many Millennials take it further: To us, differences in skin color are largely irrelevant. That's not to say that young minorities never experience racial inequality. Prejudices still exist, and serious economic gaps still yawn between racial and cultural groups. But I feel fortunate to live in an era when, in choosing friends or dates, race can be among the least of my concerns. Essentially, it's no big deal.

[4] But it felt like a big deal on that subway—much as it did two years ago in Rome when Federico, a new Italian acquaintance, casually inquired, "Do you listen to black music?" I was a Temple University senior studying art and film in Italy's eternal city. It was my first night out with fellow students. We ended up at a small, smoke-filled dive where we met five 20-something men who spoke in stilted English and didn't hide their attraction to the women in our pack. Eager to ingratiate ourselves with the locals, we accepted their invitation to join them.

⁵ I had been told by a black student previously with the program that many Italians don't take kindly to people of color, so Federico's question set off an alarm. Lowering my beer, I calmly asked what "black music" was. When Federico admiringly cited artists such as Tupac, Notorious B.I.G. and Snoop Dogg, I realized this was his way of describing hip-hop, that his intention was no different from my own clumsy attempts to describe my adoration of Italian cinema. Federico just hoped to make a new hip-hop-appreciating friend—and he did.

⁶ In Rome, I learned that whatever I was told to expect, it was best to assume nothing. My five months there also taught me that the indifference to skin color stretches way beyond American soil. Federico and his crew treated me like a brother—they even referred to me as "brother." Not once during my stay did anyone ever treat me as unequal; my skin color was never a subject of discussion—at least not to my face.

⁷ Weeks after that first meeting, Federico's posse took us to an underground club in the city's college district. Throngs of dreadlocked Italians were smoking joints, drinking beer, grooving to the rhythms of Bob Marley, Steel Pulse and other reggae icons. Most striking was how comfortable these Italians seemed in their appropriated shoes, adopting a foreign culture and somehow making it theirs. The scene reinforced my sense of how far we've come since the days when people dressed, talked and celebrated only that which sprang from their own background. For the first time in my life, I was fully aware of the spiritual concept that we're all simply one.

⁸ That sense hasn't left me. Everywhere I look, I see young people—such as my two younger brothers, a Japanese-anime-obsessed 11-year-old and a pastel-Polo-sporting 21-year-old—adopting styles, hobbies and attitudes from outside the culture in which they were raised. Last month in a Los Angeles barbershop, I was waiting to get my trademark Afro cut when I noticed a brother in his late teens sitting, eyes closed, as the barber clipped his hair into a " 'frohawk," the punk-inspired African American adaptation of the mohawk. Asked why he chose the look, the guy, without looking up, shrugged, "Something different." Immediately, I understood. Minutes later, his "different" cut became my new look.

⁹ Sporting a 'frohawk doesn't mean I'll be pulling kickflips in a pair of Vans at the local skate park anytime soon—I favor Gap jeans, European-cut shirts, British Wallabees and street-smart hoodies. Increasingly, fashion is a mix of everything. My generation's embrace of various subcultures makes once-autonomous racial groups difficult to categorize. Friends who live in different parts of the country all report seeing blacks, whites, Latinos and Asians adopting facets of one another's cultures without taking flak from members of their own group.

¹⁰ Just a decade ago, Matthew Hencke, a biracial independent filmmaker who grew up in Washington, was called "Uncle Tom" by black students at schools he attended, he said, "because of the music I listened to or the clothes I wore." Hencke, who now lives in Manhattan, was scorned for wearing Rolling Stones and Lynyrd Skynyrd T-shirts—even though he adored the Fugees and Scarface. "My problem was, why couldn't I like everything?" said Hencke, who believes that hip-hop artists such as Kanye West, Pharrell and Lupe Fiasco have made diverse choices acceptable by saying, "Yeah I'm black, but I love rock music, skateboarding and wearing preppy clothes—and that's okay."

¹¹ Millennials' cross-cultural tastes don't just affect how we dress or wear our hair; they influence our romantic choices. In my

case, it isn't about seeking the most exotic woman. It's about liking whom I like—black, brown, white or yellow. Dating outside the bounds of our own ethnicity is fairly common among people my age, as indicated by a 2005 Gallup poll finding that about 60 percent of 18- to 29-year-olds say they have dated outside their race. The general consensus among my diverse body of friends is: Who cares?

[12] For the record, I've dated black women and expect to date more of them. My high school sweetheart happened to be Korean; I don't recall ever being criticized for our relationship, perhaps because so many other kids had similar ones. Reactions were equally blasé to cross-cultural relationships I had in college and beyond. In fact, the only disapproval I've noted when I'm with a woman who isn't black has been from black women.

[13] Last fall, I was in a shoe store with Caroline when I noticed a beautiful sister staring at us. As we passed her, she muttered "Too bad" to her girlfriend. "It's sad," said Hencke, whose wife of six years is white. "I come from a family where my mother's black and my father's white . . . my own upbringing was colorblind. Race was never an issue in my family." I can relate. Having been raised by progressive, racially tolerant parents, I never feared incurring their wrath for bringing home a girl who didn't have a matching tan. Lately at movies, bars and restaurants in New York, Los Angeles and the Washington area, friends and I have seen an increase in black women dating men of other races. Still, considering black men's high rates of unemployment and incarceration, I understand black women's concerns about "losing" eligible brothers to women of other ethnicities.

[14] So does my friend Majeedah Johnson, a 25-year-old African American writer living in the District of Columbia. "If you meet someone you're compatible with who's outside your ethnic background, that's great," she said. "But if [the attraction] is based on self-hatred or prejudice, I have a problem with it." No kidding. A former college roommate of mine dated white women exclusively. His rationale: Because of the stereotype that black women are too strong, difficult and self-righteous, he perceived white women as an easier option. His skewed perception is very un-Millennial. Brothers who reject black women—or any group of women—are as foolish and repugnant as the white racists whom they despise. As Majeedah put it, "They're the ones missing out."

[15] Of course, having been raised in a diverse middle-class neighborhood in Silver Spring and having attended a large, urban university probably has everything to do with my viewpoint. Barry Canty, 33, is a black Los Angeles filmmaker whose upcoming indie-comedy "L.A. Proper" features a racially diverse cast of 20- and 30-somethings. Canty said that although many in our generation live or were raised in comparatively colorblind settings, those in more segregated communities probably see things differently. "What separates many minorities from embracing diversity is their socioeconomic background," he said.

[16] In Mecklenburg County, N.C., where Canty grew up in a diverse middle-class neighborhood, the lower you were on the economic totem pole, the more segregated your neighborhood was. "In high school, many of the poorer blacks were shocked at how easy it was for me to interact with people of other races," he said. "I think their point of view was affected by their economic status."

[17] Perhaps it seems that Millennials like me are deaf, dumb and blind to the continuing injustices that people of color face. Racism isn't extinct; its effects are ongoing. Earlier this month in East Texas, Chris Wright, a 26-year-old African American, was hospitalized in critical condition after being

dragged by a truck driven by a 24-year-old white man who turned himself in and faces assault charges. Wright's girlfriend is white, and according to his family, the incident marked the brutal conclusion of racial taunts the couple has endured for months. The NAACP is pushing to have the assault classified as a hate crime.

[18] As horrific as that incident was, it's important to acknowledge progress and to keep fighting for an even more tolerant society. Although popular, multiethnic TV shows such as "Grey's Anatomy," "Heroes" and "Lost" reflect our nation's and world's ever-increasing diversity, the most powerful force for bringing diversity into American homes is the Internet. Web sites such as MySpace, Friendster and Facebook have created multicultural and ethnic social networks that have made it possible to connect with and befriend people from a universe of cultures just a click away.

[19] The recent uproar over journalist Kenneth Eng's infamous article "Why I Hate Blacks" in *AsianWeek* showed that some Millennials—Eng is 23—aren't there yet. Eng's abusive grocery list of reasons why people should continue to "discriminate against blacks" was outrageous—and instructive. My initial reaction wasn't anger but pity for the author, who probably constructed his hateful assumptions based on his negative encounters with African Americans. His article, however wrongheaded, was like this one—observations drawn from scenes of his own unique experiences.

[20] As strongly as I disagree with his statements, I have no problem with him freely speaking his mind. Everyone in this country has a right to be heard. It's his opinion. Considering how many real advances Americans have made when it comes to tolerance, I have to say:

[21] No big deal.

SUMMARIZE

Write a 100-word summary of Britt-Gibson's essay.

ANALYZE

Which rhetorical appeal (to ethos, pathos, or logos) does Britt-Gibson use most effectively in his essay? Make sure you point to specific examples of the appeal at work in the text to support your analysis.

DISCUSS

What do you think of Britt-Gibson's contention that, no matter how hateful our opinions might be, all Americans have the right to express their opinions openly and freely? Do you see any possible negative consequences of allowing people to openly express prejudice?

from reading to writing

1. Write a brief essay in which you define "friend." To support your claim, make sure you include examples of relationships that fit your criteria and of some that don't fit.

2. Do you have a page on a social networking site like Facebook or MySpace? If so, go visit your profile and take some time to analyze it as if you have never seen it before. What ethos or persona emerges from your page? What kind of argument do you make about who you are? To answer this question, consider what your posted photos; self-selected club memberships; specially downloaded interactive games and quizzes; and featured tastes in film, music, and books say about you. If you wanted to drastically change the ethos that's constructed there (or perhaps target a prospective employer instead of a group of friends), what would you change and why? If you don't have a site, you can choose the site of a classmate, a teacher, or even a total stranger and try this exercise there.

3. As many of the authors in this chapter suggest, our expectations for love and romance are changing. Drawing on at least two pieces from this chapter in your discussion, explain why you think this might be (and, more specifically, what might be transforming these expectations). Do you think these changes are a good thing? Why or why not?

4. Define a successful romantic relationship. Be sure to provide specific criteria. Do you know a couple who fit this definition?

5. Laura Vanderkam and Frank Paiva suggest that evolving gender roles have altered our ideas on modern love. According to these authors, how have gender roles changed? How do the authors evaluate these changes?

6. How have the media and technology influenced our various kinds of relationships? Use evidence from your own experience and from at least two of the readings in this chapter to support your response.

7. Compare the intended audiences of Joel Garreau's "Friends Indeed?" and Justin Britt-Gibson's "What's Wrong with This Picture?" Who are the target audiences? Why do you think this? What do the authors do to appeal to their audiences? Do you think they are successful? You may need to do a little research about the writers and the original places of publication to get started.

air waves

"Let's just say it outright: AC/DC is God's most beautiful and significant gift to humankind. . . . I personally spent upward of 3.6 billion hours (give or take) as a happy, rebellious, well-fed, surly, middle-class teen pounding my delicate eardrums and grinding my nerves to this glorious Aussie rock band's dizzy, brain-churning music, shaking my pale fist to its monster-arena blues and soaking my burgeoning id in the profound lyrics of songs like 'Dirty Deeds Done Dirt Cheap' and 'What Do You Do for Money Honey.'"

—Mark Morford, *"Which Came First: the Lyrics or Libidos?"*

Although this chapter is not organized around a single issue, the essays that follow do have a few things in common: All address elements of that fuzzy category called "pop culture" and all are provocative, whether in content, style, or both. In short, the writers here investigate some of the things we watch and listen to, why and how we watch and listen to them, and the effect all of this has on us. Although these writers may reach different conclusions, they share a common understanding of the influence that pop culture has in our lives. As you read these pieces, think about the consumer and entertainment choices you make and how the products you embrace affect you and your world.

Steven Johnson adapted this piece from his 2005 book Everything Bad Is Good for You: How Today's Popular Culture Is Actually Making Us Smarter. *In his book, he argues that "the most debased forms of mass diversion—video games and violent television dramas and juvenile sitcoms—turn out to be nutritional after all." Here, in an essay published in the April 24, 2005 edition of the* New York Times Magazine, *he presents an abbreviated version of his argument about the intellectual value of television shows that many people dismiss as lightweight.*

WATCHING TV MAKES YOU SMARTER

Steven Johnson

SCIENTIST A: Has he asked for anything special?

SCIENTIST B: Yes, this morning for breakfast . . . he requested something called "wheat germ, organic honey and tiger's milk."

SCIENTIST A: Oh, yes. Those were the charmed substances that some years ago were felt to contain life-preserving properties.

SCIENTIST B: You mean there was no deep fat? No steak or cream pies or . . . hot fudge?

SCIENTIST A: Those were thought to be unhealthy.

—*From Woody Allen's* Sleeper

¹ On Jan. 24, the Fox network showed an episode of its hit drama *24*, the real-time thriller known for its cliffhanger tension and often-gruesome violence. Over the preceding weeks, a number of public controversies had erupted around *24*, mostly focused on its portrait of Muslim terrorists and its penchant for torture scenes. The episode that was shown on the 24th only fanned the flames higher: in one scene, a terrorist enlists a hit man to kill his child for not fully supporting the jihadist cause; in another scene, the secretary of defense authorizes the torture of his son to uncover evidence of a terrorist plot.

² But the explicit violence and the post-9/11 terrorist anxiety are not the only elements of *24* that would have been unthinkable on prime-time network television 20 years ago. Alongside the notable change in content lies an equally notable change in form. During its 44 minutes—a real-time hour, minus 16 minutes for commercials—the episode

connects the lives of 21 distinct characters, each with a clearly defined "story arc," as the Hollywood jargon has it: a defined personality with motivations and obstacles and specific relationships with other characters. Nine primary narrative threads wind their way through those 44 minutes, each drawing extensively upon events and information revealed in earlier episodes. Draw a map of all those intersecting plots and personalities, and you get structure that—where formal complexity is concerned—more closely resembles *Middlemarch* than a hit TV drama of years past like *Bonanza*.

3 For decades, we've worked under the assumption that mass culture follows a path declining steadily toward lowest-common-denominator standards, presumably because the "masses" want dumb, simple pleasures and big media companies try to give the masses what they want. But as that *24* episode suggests, the exact opposite is happening: the culture is getting more cognitively demanding, not less. To make sense of an episode of *24*, you have to integrate far more information than you would have a few decades ago watching a comparable show. Beneath the violence and the ethnic stereotypes, another trend appears: to keep up with entertainment like *24*, you have to pay attention, make inferences, track shifting social relationships. This is what I call the Sleeper Curve: the most debased forms of mass diversion—video games and violent television dramas and juvenile sitcoms—turn out to be nutritional after all.

4 I believe that the Sleeper Curve is the single most important new force altering the mental development of young people today, and I believe it is largely a force for good: enhancing our cognitive faculties, not dumbing them down. And yet you almost never hear this story in popular accounts of today's media. Instead, you hear dire tales of addiction, violence, mindless escapism. It's assumed that shows that promote smoking or gratuitous violence are bad for us, while those that thunder against teen pregnancy or intolerance have a positive role in society. Judged by that morality-play standard, the story of popular culture over the past 50 years—if not 500—is a story of decline: the morals of the stories have grown darker and more ambiguous, and the antiheroes have multiplied.

5 The usual counterargument here is that what media have lost in moral clarity, they have gained in realism. The real world doesn't come in nicely packaged public-service announcements, and we're better off with entertainment like *The Sopranos* that reflects our fallen state with all its ethical ambiguity. I happen to be sympathetic to that argument, but it's not the one I want to make here. I think there is another way to assess the social virtue of pop culture, one that looks at media as a kind of cognitive workout, not as a series of life lessons. There may indeed be more "negative messages" in the mediasphere today. But that's not the only way to evaluate whether our television shows or video games are having a positive impact. Just as important—if not more important—is the kind of thinking you have to do to make sense of a cultural experience. That is where the Sleeper Curve becomes visible.

Televised Intelligence

6 Consider the cognitive demands that televised narratives place on their viewers. With many shows that we associate with "quality" entertainment—*The Mary Tyler Moore Show, Murphy Brown, Frasier*—the intelligence arrives fully formed in the words and actions of the characters on-screen. They say witty things to one another and avoid lapsing into tired sitcom clichés, and we smile along in our living rooms, enjoying the company of these smart people. But assuming we're bright enough to understand the sentences they're saying, there's no intellectual labor involved in enjoying the show as a viewer. You no more challenge your mind by watching these intelligent shows than you challenge

your body watching *Monday Night Football*. The intellectual work is happening on-screen, not off.

[7] But another kind of televised intelligence is on the rise. Think of the cognitive benefits conventionally ascribed to reading: attention, patience, retention, the parsing of narrative threads. Over the last half-century, programming on TV has increased the demands it places on precisely these mental faculties. This growing complexity involves three primary elements: multiple threading, flashing arrows and social networks.

[8] According to television lore, the age of multiple threads began with the arrival in 1981 of *Hill Street Blues*, the Steven Bochco police drama invariably praised for its "gritty realism." Watch an episode of *Hill Street Blues* side by side with any major drama from the preceding decades—*Starsky and Hutch*, for instance, or *Dragnet*—and the structural transformation will jump out at you. The earlier shows follow one or two lead characters, adhere to a single dominant plot and reach a decisive conclusion at the end of the episode. Draw an outline of the narrative threads in almost every *Dragnet* episode, and it will be a single line: from the initial crime scene, through the investigation, to the eventual cracking of the case. A typical *Starsky and Hutch* episode offers only the slightest variation on this linear formula: the introduction of a comic subplot that usually appears only at the tail end of the episode.

[9] A *Hill Street Blues* episode complicates the picture in a number of profound ways. The narrative weaves together a collection of distinct strands—sometimes as many as 10, though at least half of the threads involve only a few quick scenes scattered through the episode. The number of primary characters—and not just bit parts—swells significantly. And the episode has fuzzy borders: picking up one or two threads from previous episodes at the outset and leaving one or two threads open at the end.

[10] Critics generally cite *Hill Street Blues* as the beginning of "serious drama" native in the television medium—differentiating the series from the single-episode dramatic programs from the 50's, which were Broadway plays performed in front of a camera. But the *Hill Street* innovations weren't all that original; they'd long played a defining role in popular television, just not during the evening hours. The structure of a *Hill Street* episode—and indeed of all the critically acclaimed dramas that followed, from *thirtysomething* to *Six Feet Under*—is the structure of a soap opera. *Hill Street Blues* might have sparked a new golden age of television drama during its seven-year run, but it did so by using a few crucial tricks that *Guiding Light* and *General Hospital* mastered long before.

[11] Bochco's genius with *Hill Street* was to marry complex narrative structure with complex subject matter. *Dallas* had already shown that the extended, interwoven threads of the soap-opera genre could survive the weeklong interruptions of a prime-time show, but the actual content of *Dallas* was fluff. (The most probing issue it addressed was the question, now folkloric, of who shot J.R.) *All in the Family* and *Rhoda* showed that you could tackle complex social issues, but they did their tackling in the comfort of the sitcom living room. *Hill Street* had richly drawn characters confronting difficult social issues and a narrative structure to match.

[12] Since *Hill Street* appeared, the multithreaded drama has become the most widespread fictional genre on prime time: *St. Elsewhere*, *L.A. Law*, *thirtysomething*, *Twin Peaks*, *N.Y.P.D. Blue*, *E.R.*, *The West Wing*, *Alias*, *Lost*. (The only prominent holdouts in drama are shows like *Law and Order* that have essentially updated the venerable *Dragnet* format and thus remained anchored to a single narrative line.) Since the early 80's, however, there has been a noticeable increase in narrative complexity in these dramas. The most ambitious

show on TV to date, *The Sopranos*, routinely follows up to a dozen distinct threads over the course of an episode, with more than 20 recurring characters.

13 The total number of active threads equals the multiple plots of *Hill Street*, but on *The Sopranos* each thread is more substantial. The show doesn't offer a clear distinction between dominant and minor plots; each story line carries its weight in the mix. Episodes also display a chordal mode of storytelling entirely absent from *Hill Street*: a single scene in *The Sopranos* will often connect to three different threads at the same time, layering one plot atop another. And every single thread in many *Sopranos* episodes builds on events from previous episodes and continues on through the rest of the season and beyond.

14 Taken together, these programs show the Sleeper Curve rising over the past 30 years of popular television. In a sense, this is as much a map of cognitive changes in the popular mind as it is a map of on-screen developments, as if the media titans decided to condition our brains to follow ever-larger numbers of simultaneous threads. Before *Hill Street*, the conventional wisdom among television execs was that audiences wouldn't be comfortable following more than three plots in a single episode, and indeed, the *Hill Street* pilot, which was shown in January 1981, brought complaints from viewers that the show was too complicated. Fast-forward two decades, and shows like *The Sopranos* engage their audiences with narratives that make *Hill Street* look like *Three's Company*. Audiences happily embrace that complexity because they've been trained by two decades of multi-threaded dramas.

15 Multi-threading is the most celebrated structural feature of the modern television drama, and it certainly deserves some of the honor that has been doled out to it. And yet multi-threading is only part of the story.

The Case for Confusion

16 Shortly after the arrival of the first-generation slasher movies—*Halloween*, *Friday the 13th*—Paramount released a mock-slasher flick called *Student Bodies*, parodying the genre just as the *Scream* series would do 15 years later. In one scene, the obligatory nubile teenage babysitter hears a noise outside a suburban house; she opens the door to investigate, finds nothing and then goes back inside. As the door shuts behind her, the camera swoops in on the doorknob, and we see that she has left the door unlocked. The camera pulls back and then swoops down again for emphasis. And then a flashing arrow appears on the screen, with text that helpfully explains: *Unlocked!*

17 That flashing arrow is parody, of course, but it's merely an exaggerated version of a device popular stories use all the time. When a sci-fi script inserts into some advanced lab a nonscientist who keeps asking the science geeks to explain what they're doing with that particle accelerator, that's a flashing arrow that gives the audience precisely the information it needs in order to make sense of the ensuing plot. ("Whatever you do, don't spill water on it, or you'll set off a massive explosion!") These hints serve as a kind of narrative hand-holding. Implicitly, they say to the audience, "We realize you have no idea what a particle accelerator is, but here's the deal: all you need to know is that it's a big fancy thing that explodes when wet." They focus the mind on relevant details: "Don't worry about whether the babysitter is going to break up with her boyfriend. Worry about that guy lurking in the bushes." They reduce the amount of analytic work you need to do to make sense of a story. All you have to do is follow the arrows.

18 By this standard, popular television has never been harder to follow. If narrative threads have experienced a population explosion over the past 20 years, flashing arrows have grown correspondingly

scarce. Watching our pinnacle of early 80's TV drama, *Hill Street Blues*, we find there's an informational wholeness to each scene that differs markedly from what you see on shows like *The West Wing* or *The Sopranos* or *Alias* or *E.R.*

[19] *Hill Street* has ambiguities about future events: will a convicted killer be executed? Will Furillo marry Joyce Davenport? Will Renko find it in himself to bust a favorite singer for cocaine possession? But the present-tense of each scene explains itself to the viewer with little ambiguity. There's an open question or a mystery driving each of these stories—how will it all turn out?—but there's no mystery about the immediate activity on the screen. A contemporary drama like *The West Wing*, on the other hand, constantly embeds mysteries into the present-tense events: you see characters performing actions or discussing events about which crucial information has been deliberately withheld. Anyone who has watched more than a handful of *The West Wing* episodes closely will know the feeling: scene after scene refers to some clearly crucial but unexplained piece of information, and after the sixth reference, you'll find yourself wishing you could rewind the tape to figure out what they're talking about, assuming you've missed something. And then you realize that you're supposed to be confused. The open question posed by these sequences is not "How will this turn out in the end?" The question is "What's happening right now?"

[20] The deliberate lack of hand-holding extends down to the microlevel of dialogue as well. Popular entertainment that addresses technical issues—whether they are the intricacies of passing legislation, or of performing a heart bypass, or of operating a particle accelerator—conventionally switches between two modes of information in dialogue: texture and substance. Texture is all the arcane verbiage provided to convince the viewer that they're watching Actual Doctors at Work; substance is the material planted amid the background texture that the viewer needs to make sense of the plot.

[21] Conventionally, narratives demarcate the line between texture and substance by inserting cues that flag or translate the important data. There's an unintentionally comical moment in the 2004 blockbuster *The Day After Tomorrow* in which the beleaguered climatologist (played by Dennis Quaid) announces his theory about the imminent arrival of a new ice age to a gathering of government officials. In his speech, he warns that "we have hit a critical desalinization point!" At this moment, the writer-director Roland Emmerich—a master of brazen arrow-flashing—has an official follow with the obliging remark: "It would explain what's driving this extreme weather." They might as well have had a flashing "Unlocked!" arrow on the screen.

[22] The dialogue on shows like *The West Wing* and *E.R.*, on the other hand, doesn't talk down to its audiences. It rushes by, the words accelerating in sync with the high-speed tracking shots that glide through the corridors and operating rooms. The characters talk faster in these shows, but the truly remarkable thing about the dialogue is not purely a matter of speed; it's the willingness to immerse the audience in information that most viewers won't understand. Here's a typical scene from *E.R.*:

[WEAVER AND WRIGHT *push a gurney containing a 16-year-old girl. Her parents, JANNA AND FRANK MIKAMI, follow close behind. CARTER AND LUCY fall in.*]

WEAVER: 16-year-old, unconscious, history of biliary atresia.

CARTER: Hepatic coma?

WEAVER: Looks like it.

MR. MIKAMI: She was doing fine until six months ago.

CARTER: What medication is she on?

MRS. MIKAMI: Ampicillin, tobramycin, vitamins a, d and k.

LUCY: Skin's jaundiced.

WEAVER: Same with the sclera. Breath smells sweet.

CARTER: Fetor hepaticus?

WEAVER: Yep.

LUCY: What's that?

WEAVER: Her liver's shut down. Let's dip a urine. [To CARTER] Guys, it's getting a little crowded in here, why don't you deal with the parents? Start lactulose, 30 cc's per NG.

CARTER: We're giving medicine to clean her blood.

WEAVER: Blood in the urine, two-plus.

CARTER: The liver failure is causing her blood not to clot.

MRS. MIKAMI: Oh, God. . . .

CARTER: Is she on the transplant list?

MR. MIKAMI: She's been Status 2a for six months, but they haven't been able to find her a match.

CARTER: Why? What's her blood type?

MR. MIKAMI: AB.

[This hits CARTER like a lightning bolt. Lucy gets it, too. They share a look.]

23 There are flashing arrows here, of course—"The liver failure is causing her blood not to clot"—but the ratio of medical jargon to layperson translation is remarkably high. From a purely narrative point of view, the decisive line arrives at the very end: "AB." The 16-year-old's blood type connects her to an earlier plot line, involving a cerebral-hemorrhage victim who—after being dramatically revived in one of the opening scenes—ends up brain-dead. Far earlier, before the liver-failure scene above, Carter briefly discusses harvesting the hemorrhage victim's organs for transplants, and another doctor makes a passing reference to his blood type being the rare AB (thus

making him an unlikely donor). The twist here revolves around a statistically unlikely event happening at the E.R.—an otherwise perfect liver donor showing up just in time to donate his liver to a recipient with the same rare blood type. But the show reveals this twist with remarkable subtlety. To make sense of that last "AB" line—and the look of disbelief on Carter's and Lucy's faces—you have to recall a passing remark uttered earlier regarding a character who belongs to a completely different thread. Shows like E.R. may have more blood and guts than popular TV had a generation ago, but when it comes to storytelling, they possess a quality that can only be described as subtlety and discretion.

Even Bad TV Is Better

24 Skeptics might argue that I have stacked the deck here by focusing on relatively high-brow titles like The Sopranos or The West Wing, when in fact the most significant change in the last five years of narrative entertainment involves reality TV. Does the contemporary pop cultural landscape look quite as promising if the representative show is Joe Millionaire instead of The West Wing?

25 I think it does, but to answer that question properly, you have to avoid the tendency to sentimentalize the past. When people talk about the golden age of television in the early 70's—invoking shows like The Mary Tyler Moore Show and All in the Family—they forget to mention how awful most television programming was during much of that decade. If you're going to look at pop-culture trends, you have to compare apples to apples, or in this case, lemons to lemons. The relevant comparison is not between Joe Millionaire and MASH; it's between Joe Millionaire and The Newlywed Game, or between Survivor and The Love Boat.

26 What you see when you make these head-to-head comparisons is that a rising tide of complexity has been lifting programming at the bottom of the quality spectrum and

at the top. *The Sopranos* is several times more demanding of its audiences than *Hill Street* was, and *Joe Millionaire* has made comparable advances over *Battle of the Network Stars*. This is the ultimate test of the Sleeper Curve theory: even the junk has improved.

27 If early television took its cues from the stage, today's reality programming is reliably structured like a video game: a series of competitive tests, growing more challenging over time. Many reality shows borrow a subtler device from gaming culture as well: the rules aren't fully established at the outset. You learn as you play.

28 On a show like *Survivor* or *The Apprentice*, the participants—and the audience—know the general objective of the series, but each episode involves new challenges that haven't been ordained in advance. The final round of the first season of *The Apprentice*, for instance, threw a monkey wrench into the strategy that governed the play up to that point, when Trump announced that the two remaining apprentices would have to assemble and manage a team of subordinates who had already been fired in earlier episodes of the show. All of a sudden the overarching objective of the game—do anything to avoid being fired—presented a potential conflict to the remaining two contenders: the structure of the final round favored the survivor who had maintained the best relationships with his comrades. Suddenly, it wasn't enough just to have clawed your way to the top; you had to have made friends while clawing. The original *Joe Millionaire* went so far as to undermine the most fundamental convention of all—that the show's creators don't openly lie to the contestants about the prizes—by inducing a construction worker to pose as man of means while 20 women competed for his attention.

29 Reality programming borrowed another key ingredient from games: the intellectual labor of probing the system's rules for weak spots and opportunities. As each show discloses its conventions, and each participant reveals his or her personality traits and background, the intrigue in watching comes from figuring out how the participants should best navigate the environment that has been created for them. The pleasure in these shows comes not from watching other people being humiliated on national television; it comes from depositing other people in a complex, high-pressure environment where no established strategies exist and watching them find their bearings. That's why the water-cooler conversation about these shows invariably tracks in on the strategy displayed on the previous night's episode: why did Kwame pick Omarosa in that final round? What devious strategy is Richard Hatch concocting now?

30 When we watch these shows, the part of our brain that monitors the emotional lives of the people around us—the part that tracks subtle shifts in intonation and gesture and facial expression—scrutinizes the action on the screen, looking for clues. We trust certain characters implicitly and vote others off the island in a heartbeat. Traditional narrative shows also trigger emotional connections to the characters, but those connections don't have the same participatory effect, because traditional narratives aren't explicitly about strategy. The phrase "Monday-morning quarterbacking" describes the engaged feeling that spectators have in relation to games as opposed to stories. We absorb stories, but we second-guess games. Reality programming has brought that second-guessing to prime time, only the game in question revolves around social dexterity rather than the physical kind.

The Rewards of Smart Culture

31 The quickest way to appreciate the Sleeper Curve's cognitive training is to sit down and watch a few hours of hit programming

from the late 70's on Nick at Nite or the SOAPnet channel or on DVD. The modern viewer who watches a show like *Dallas* today will be bored by the content—not just because the show is less salacious than today's soap operas (which it is by a small margin) but also because the show contains far less information in each scene, despite the fact that its soap-opera structure made it one of the most complicated narratives on television in its prime. With *Dallas*, the modern viewer doesn't have to think to make sense of what's going on, and not having to think is boring. Many recent hit shows—*24, Survivor, The Sopranos, Alias, Lost, The Simpsons, E.R.*—take the opposite approach, layering each scene with a thick network of affiliations. You have to focus to follow the plot, and in focusing you're exercising the parts of your brain that map social networks, that fill in missing information, that connect multiple narrative threads.

[32] Of course, the entertainment industry isn't increasing the cognitive complexity of its products for charitable reasons. The Sleeper Curve exists because there's money to be made by making culture smarter. The economics of television syndication and DVD sales mean that there's a tremendous financial pressure to make programs that can be watched multiple times, revealing new nuances and shadings on the third viewing. Meanwhile, the Web has created a forum for annotation and commentary that allows more complicated shows to prosper, thanks to the fan sites where each episode of shows like *Lost* or *Alias* is dissected with an intensity usually reserved for Talmud scholars. Finally, interactive games have trained a new generation of media consumers to probe complex environments and to think on their feet, and that gamer audience has now come to expect the same challenges from their television shows. In the end, the Sleeper Curve

tells us something about the human mind. It may be drawn toward the sensational where content is concerned—sex does sell, after all. But the mind also likes to be challenged; there's real pleasure to be found in solving puzzles, detecting patterns or unpacking a complex narrative system.

[33] In pointing out some of the ways that popular culture has improved our minds, I am not arguing that parents should stop paying attention to the way their children amuse themselves. What I am arguing for is a change in the criteria we use to determine what really is cognitive junk food and what is genuinely nourishing. Instead of a show's violent or tawdry content, instead of wardrobe malfunctions or the F-word, the true test should be whether a given show engages or sedates the mind. Is it a single thread strung together with predictable punch lines every 30 seconds? Or does it map a complex social network? Is your on-screen character running around shooting everything in sight, or is she trying to solve problems and manage resources? If your kids want to watch reality TV, encourage them to watch *Survivor* over *Fear Factor*. If they want to watch a mystery show, encourage *24* over *Law and Order*. If they want to play a violent game, encourage Grand Theft Auto over Quake. Indeed, it might be just as helpful to have a rating system that used mental labor and not obscenity and violence as its classification scheme for the world of mass culture.

[34] Kids and grown-ups each can learn from their increasingly shared obsessions. Too often we imagine the blurring of kid and grown-up cultures as a series of violations: the 9-year-olds who have to have nipple broaches explained to them thanks to Janet Jackson; the middle-aged guy who can't wait to get home to his Xbox. But this demographic blur has a commendable side that we don't acknowledge enough. The kids are forced to think

like grown-ups: analyzing complex social networks, managing resources, tracking subtle narrative intertwinings, recognizing long-term patterns. The grown-ups, in turn, get to learn from the kids: decoding each new technological wave, parsing the interfaces and discovering the intellectual rewards of play. Parents should see this as an opportunity, not a crisis. Smart culture is no longer something you force your kids to ingest, like green vegetables. It's something you share.

SUMMARIZE AND RESPOND

Summarize Johnson's argument in 100 to 150 words, and then respond to his contention that "the culture is getting more cognitively demanding, not less."

ANALYZE

Although logos is an important appeal in Johnson's argument, it isn't the only one. How, for example, does Johnson establish his persona as the author? How does he want to be perceived by the audience? What does he do to achieve this? Pathos plays a role in the text, too. How does he appeal to the audience's emotions and imagination? What effect do these appeals have?

DISCUSS

In his essay, Johnson writes: "Of course, the entertainment industry isn't increasing the cognitive complexity of its products for charitable reasons. The Sleeper Curve exists because there's money to be made by making culture smarter." Write a brief essay in which you define the "Sleeper Curve" and explain how, according to Johnson, "there's money to be made by making culture smarter."

ARGUE

In her essay "The Dumbing of America" (on page 135), Susan Jacoby criticizes Johnson's claims about the intellectual value of pop culture. While Johnson argues that pop culture is getting more "cognitively demanding," Jacoby claims that we're a nation of dunces, in part because of our turn away from books and toward video. Write a brief essay in which you argue against Johnson's position, Jacoby's, or both, in favor of a third alternative.

FIGURE 10-1

Television—reality TV in particular—is getting a bad rap, according to essayists Steven Johnson and Michael Hirschorn. As critics call for more culture and less sex, violence, and public humiliation, Johnson and Hirschorn argue, in different ways, that TV is better than a lot of people think. Johnson writes, for example, that the cognitive demands made by much of today's television programming are far greater than ever before. "[E]ven the junk has improved," he says. And Hirschorn argues that knee-jerk criticism of reality TV misses the point: "Creative endeavors . . . should be measured not by how literally they replicate actual life but by how effectively they render emotional truths." Have you ever heeded the common call to stop watching TV? Do you think you could? Or do you, like Johnson and Hirschorn, see value in popular television programming?

Michael Hirschorn, VH1's executive vice president for original programming and production, uses this essay from the May 2007 issue of The Atlantic Monthly *to defend reality TV from critics he claims don't understand or appreciate the genre's contributions to the industry.*

THE CASE FOR REALITY TV: WHAT THE SNOBS DON'T UNDERSTAND

Michael Hirschorn

[1] This past January, I had the pleasure of serving as official spear-catcher for a *CBS Evening News* report on the increasing levels of humiliation on *American Idol* and other reality-TV shows, including some on my channel, VH1. The segment featured snippets of our shows *I Love New York* (a dating competition with an urban vibe) and *Celebrity Fit Club* (which tracks the efforts of overweight singers and actors to get back in shape, and, by extension, reignite their careers). "VH1, among other things, showcases faded celebrities who are fat," said the CBS correspondent Richard Schlesinger.

[2] In between shots of me fake working at my computer and fake chatting with the amiable Schlesinger while fake strolling down our corporate-looking hallway, I took my best shot at defending the alleged horrors of *AI* and *Celebrity Fit Club*. But it was clear that CBS News was set on bemoaning what it saw as yet another outrage against the culture. The central complaint, per Katie Couric's intro to the report, was that more people had watched *American Idol* the previous week than watched the State of the Union address on all the broadcast networks combined. When the segment ended, Couric signed off with an extravagant eye roll. "We're doing our part here at CBS News," she seemed to be saying, "but the barbarians are massing at the gates, people." A line had been drawn in the sand, as if the news were now akin to an evening at the Met.

[3] Is there an easier position to take in polite society than to patronize reality TV? Even television programmers see the genre as a kind of visual Hamburger Helper: cheap filler that saves them money they can use elsewhere for more-worthy programming. Reality shows cost anywhere from a quarter to half as much to produce as scripted shows. The money saved on *Extreme Makeover: Home Edition*, the logic goes, allows ABC to pay for additional gruesome medical emergencies and exploding ferries on *Grey's Anatomy*. NBC's crappy *Fear Factor* pays for the classy *Heroes*.

[4] As befits a form driven largely by speed and cost considerations, reality TV is not often formally daring. Fifteen years after MTV's *The Real World* set the template for contemporary reality TV by placing seven strangers in a downtown Manhattan loft, reality television has developed its own visual shorthand: short doses of documentary footage interspersed with testimonials (often called OTFs, for "on-the-fly" interviews) in which the participants describe, ex post facto, what they were thinking during the action you are watching.

[5] The current boom may be a product of the changing economics of the television business, but reality TV is also the liveliest genre on the set right now. It has engaged hot-button cultural issues—class, sex, race— that respectable television, including the august *CBS Evening News*, rarely touches.

And it has addressed a visceral need for a different kind of television at a time when the Web has made more traditionally produced video seem as stagy as Molière.

[6] Reality TV may be an awkward admixture of documentary (with its connotations of thousands of hours of footage patiently gathered, redacted by monk-like figures into the purest expression of truth possible in 90 to 120 minutes) and scripted (with its auteurs and Emmys and noble overtones of craft). But this kludge also happens to have allowed reality shows to skim the best elements of scripted TV and documentaries while eschewing the problems of each. Reality shows steal the story structure and pacing of scripted television, but leave behind the canned plots and characters. They have the visceral impact of documentary reportage without the self-importance and general lugubriousness. Where documentaries must construct their narratives from found matter, reality TV can place real people in artificial surroundings designed for maximum emotional impact.

[7] Scripted television is supposedly showing new ambition these days, particularly in the hour-long drama form. *Studio 60 on the Sunset Strip* was going to bring the chatty intelligence of *The West Wing* back to prime time. *Lost* was going to challenge network audiences like never before, with complex plots, dozens of recurring characters, and movie-level production values. Shows are bigger now: On *24* this season, a nuclear bomb exploded. But network prime-time television remains dominated by variants on the police procedural (*Law & Order*, *CSI*, *Criminal Minds*), in which a stock group of characters (ethnically, sexually, and generationally diverse) grapples with endless versions of the same dilemma. The episodes have all the ritual predictability of Japanese Noh theater: Crimes are solved, lessons are learned, order is restored.

[8] Reality shows have leaped into this imaginative void. Discovery's *Deadliest Catch*, which began its third season in April, is an oddly transfixing series about . . . crab fishermen in the Bering Sea. As a straightforward documentary, *Catch* would have been worthy fodder, but the producers have made it riveting by formatting the whole season as a sporting event, with crab tallies for each of the half dozen or so boats and a race-against-the-clock urgency that, for all its contrivance, gives structure and meaning to the fishermen's efforts.

[9] Narrative vibrancy is not the only thing that electrifies these shows. Reality TV presents some of the most vital political debate in America, particularly about class and race. Fox's *Nanny 911* and ABC's *Supernanny* each offer object lessons on the hazards of parenting in an age of instant gratification and endless digital diversion. ABC's *Extreme Makeover: Home Edition* features intensely emotional tales of people who have fallen through the cracks of Bush-era America—often blue-collar families ravaged by disease, health-care costs, insurance loopholes, layoffs, and so forth. My channel's *The (White) Rapper Show* turned into a running debate among the aspiring white MCs over cultural authenticity—whether it is more properly bestowed by class or race.

[10] Class realities are plumbed to remarkable effect on *The Real Housewives of Orange County*, a "docu soap" that completed its second season on Bravo this spring. The show is inspired by a trio of suburban dramas: *The O.C.*, *Desperate Housewives*, and the 1999 movie *American Beauty*. Lacking the visual panache, or the budgets, of its scripted forebears, *Real Housewives* nonetheless goes deeper, charting the spiritual decay of life in gated communities, where financial anxieties, fraying families, and fear of aging leave inhabitants grasping for meaning and happiness as they steer their Escalades across Southern California's perfectly buffed, featureless landscape. *Crash*, the 2006 Oscar winner, trafficked in similar white California dread, but with all the nuance of a two-by-four to the face.

11 In *Real Housewives*, businessman Lou Knickerbocker stages a photo shoot to promote his new "highly oxygenated" water, variously called "Aqua Air" and "O.C. Energy Drink" ("We have patented technology that produces water from air"). The models are attractive-ish teen and 20-something girls: Lou's daughter Lindsey, by ex-wife Tammy; a few other daughters of O.C. housewives; and a newcomer whom Lou apparently found waitressing at a local restaurant.

12 Lou and Tammy made piles of money—it's not clear how—but their finances seem to have fractured along with their marriage. The photo shoot, therefore, is throwing off more than the normal amount of flop sweat. Lou apparently has personally selected the girls, which means he has declined to showcase his other daughter, Megan, because of her tattoos and lack of physical fitness. Lou believes the "Aqua Air Angels" should embody the Aqua Air ideal, which is why they can't drink or smoke and must have grade-point averages higher than 3.5. "This is a photo shoot," he barks after a fight breaks out between one of the girls and the waitress, "not a gang bang, for chrissakes."

13 The detail is what puts the scene over: Lou's lip-smacking focus on the girls, the girls' bland acquiescence. "That's it, baby, smile," Lou urges his daughter. "Show those teeth," says Tammy. A similar scenario on *Desperate Housewives* could never have been quite this preposterous, quite this blandly amoral. The characters would have been scripted with softening, redeeming qualities, or been rendered comically evil. Lou would've gotten his comeuppance, like Wallace Shawn's money-siphoning literary agent in that series. Here, the apparent willingness of the young women and at least some of the parents to indulge Lou's bottom-of-the-barrel scheming outlines, in a few short brushstrokes, a community's shared value system.

14 Value systems are smashed into each other, like atoms in an accelerator, on ABC's *Wife Swap*, where the producers find the most extreme pairings possible: lesbian mommies with bigots, godless cosmopolites with Bible thumpers. On one February show, a Pentacostal family, the Hoovers, was paired with the family of a former pastor, Tony Meeks, who has turned from God to follow his rock-and-roll dreams (mom Tish rocks out as well). "I feel by being there," Kristin Hoover said, "I was able to remind Tony that God still loves him and is not finished with him." The episode took seriously the Hoovers' commitment to homeschooling and their rejection of contemporary culture (a rejection not taken to the extreme of declining an invitation to appear on reality TV). Compare this with the tokenism of "born-again Christian" Harriet Hayes on NBC's dramedy *Studio 60 on the Sunset Strip*. Harriet's but a cipher, a rhetorical backboard against which ex-boyfriend Matt Albie can thwack his heathen wisecracks.

15 The competitions and elimination shows are latter-day Milgram experiments that place real people in artificial situations to see what happens. *The Apprentice* is Darwinism set loose inside an entrepreneurial Habitrail. Post-9/11, *Survivor* became less a fantasy and more a metaphor for an imagined postapocalyptic future. What happens on these shows might be a Technicolor version of how we behave in real life, but so is most fiction. Creative endeavors—written, scripted, or produced—should be measured not by how literally they replicate actual life but by how effectively they render emotional truths. The best moments found on reality TV are unscriptable, or beyond the grasp of most scriptwriters. It's no coincidence that 2006's best scripted dramas—*The Wire*, HBO's multi-season epic of inner-city Baltimore; and *Children of Men*, Alfonso Cuarón's futuristic thriller—were studies in meticulously crafted "realness," deploying naturalistic dialogue, decentered and chaotic action, stutter-step pacing, and a reporter's eye for the telling detail. *The Wire*'s season and Cuarón's movie both ended on semi-resolved novelistic notes, scorning the tendency in current television and cinema toward easy narrative closure. Watching them only threw into higher relief the inability of so much other scripted product

to get beyond stock characterizations and pat narrative.

[16] For all the snobbism in the doc community, reality TV has actually contributed to the recent boom in documentary filmmaking. The most successful docs of recent vintage have broken through in part by drawing heavily from reality television's bag of tricks, dropping the form's canonical insistence on pure observation. In *Fahrenheit 9/11*, Michael Moore brings an Army recruiter with him to confront legislators and urge them to enlist their children in the Iraq War effort. In *Bowling for Columbine*, Moore takes children who were shot at Columbine to a Kmart, where they ask for a refund on the bullets that are still lodged in their bodies. Of course, Moore's never been a doc purist. *TV Nation*, his short-lived 1994 television series, prefigured a long line of gonzo reality, from *Joe Millionaire* to *Punk'd*. Having the Serbian ambassador sing along to the Barney theme song ("I love you, you love me") while statistics about the number of Bosnians killed during the breakup of Yugoslavia appeared on the screen was not only ur-reality; it was ur-Borat. And speaking of talking animals, *March of the Penguins* turned stunning footage of mating and migrating penguins into an utterly contrived Antarctic version of *Love Story*.

[17] The resistance to reality TV ultimately comes down to snobbery, usually of the generational variety. People under 30, in my experience, tend to embrace this programming; they're happy to be entertained, never mind the purity of conception. As an unapologetic producer of reality shows, I'm obviously biased, but I also know that any genre that provokes such howls of protest is doing something interesting. Try the crab.

SUMMARIZE AND RESPOND

In 50 words or less, summarize Hirschorn's central argument. Do you think he presents an effective case?

ANALYZE

Who do you think is Hirschorn's target audience (TV watchers? Reality TV fans? People who don't watch reality TV, or any TV at all?)? Why do you think this? What does he do to appeal to this audience—in other words, to make them more likely to read and consider his argument? Offer specific examples from the text in your response.

DISCUSS

Working with a partner or in a group, make a list of the reality TV programs you watch. Then, briefly explain what you find interesting or compelling about these shows. Finally, explain whether and how each show fits Hirschorn's claim that reality TV engages "hot-button cultural issues—class, sex, race—that respectable television . . . rarely touches."

ARGUE

Using Hirschorn's essay as a starting point, write a brief essay in which you argue against his central claim about reality TV.

In this next essay, television writer and producer Charlie Hauck identifies a problem in his industry and offers a specific solution to that problem. He wrote this essay for the September 16, 2006 edition of the New York Times.

MY PLAN TO SAVE NETWORK TELEVISION

Charlie Hauck

1 Let's say you've created a network television series for the 2006–2007 season. It's beautifully calibrated to appeal to the only viewers of any value to advertisers: young people. It's about a family of migrant lifeguards. They travel to beaches all over the world in revealing swimwear, saving lives and drinking popular beverages. They have a soon-to-be-famous catch phrase, which they use in the face of any adversity: "You can't stop progress."

2 The attractive brothers and sisters are in their late teens and early 20's. Mom is played by a movie hottie still in her 30's whose film career has stalled. Dad's reserve unit was called to Iraq. He can come home during sweeps week.

3 But after your premiere the Nielsen ratings bring distressing news: old people are watching your show. Maybe they like the family's pet cockatiel. Maybe one of the lifeguards reminds them of the young Alan Ladd. But they are wreaking havoc on your demographics, the lifeblood of a series. Your show is "skewing old."

4 Many assume that mature viewers, with their $2 trillion a year in spending power, would be welcomed by the networks. Well, they aren't. Advertisers want to lock in viewers' buying habits early in life, not struggle with them to change brands in their last few decades. The key demographic in the weekly Nielsen ratings report is 18–49. Anyone outside that range is undesirable. People over 49 do not buy interesting products. They detract from the hip environment advertisers seek. The shows they watch tend not to become "water cooler" shows. They are not, as one media buyer puts it, "an opportunity audience."

5 The majestic glacier that is network television is very gradually melting. Many young viewers, particularly males in their 20's, have been stolen away by such lures as the Internet, iPods, the Xbox and opera. This makes the young people who do watch all the more valuable to advertisers. They have far greater disposable income than older people, and they actually dispose of it. Advertisers gladly pay steep premiums for those young eyes. But it is more difficult to single them out when older viewers clutter the demographics.

6 The fact is, mature viewers are threatening the well-being of network television. I have a bold but common-sense suggestion: old people should not be allowed to watch TV.

7 I anticipate the predictable charges of "discriminatory," "unfair," "idiotic." Well, millions of elderly people live in age-restricted retirement communities, and you don't hear young people whining about that. Right-thinking older Americans will see this as a chance to do something for their country.

Nurturing a nation's consumer base is as vital as protecting its streams and forests. It's time for people over 49 to "take one for the team." Besides, it's really not such a terrible sacrifice; they have Sudoku now.

[8] Once the necessary "49 and Out" federal legislation is enacted, we'll need a system in place to block older viewers' network access. Fingerprinting, iris scans, re-purposed V-chips, psychoacoustic masking? Perhaps it would be possible to borrow some of the amazing technology being developed in the Transportation Security Administration's laboratories; they aren't using it at the airports.

[9] Boomers will feel they should be exempt from this law. They're "younger" than previous old people. They're in tune with contemporary culture. If you're a boomer and thinking along those lines, take this simple test:

[10] "They combed out Ann Miller's hair and found the Lindbergh baby."

[11] If you laughed at that, if you understood the references, you have no business in front of a television set.

[12] This ban applies only to the Big Four broadcast networks. Older viewers would still be free to tune into the many cable channels. At programs like "The O'Reilly Factor," an onslaught of people still in their 50's will be greeted with flowers.

[13] A warning to certain lobbyists for the elderly, who may resort to selfish interpretations of the Constitution to thwart this needed legislation: beware the backlash. Nielsen Media Research, the keeper of the ratings, is owned by VNU, an increasingly powerful media conglomerate headquartered in the Netherlands. The Netherlands, where laws governing euthanasia are extremely lenient. "You can't stop progress." I'm just saying.

SUMMARIZE AND RESPOND

Write a 50-word summary of Hauck's essay, followed by a 100-word response in which you identify and comment on Hauck's central argument.

ANALYZE

Choose one of the rhetorical appeals (to ethos, pathos, or logos) and briefly analyze how Hauck uses this appeal in the essay. Ask yourself, for example, how the appeal affects the audience and why the author might have chosen to do this. Make sure you point to specific examples of the appeal at work in the text to support your analysis.

DISCUSS

Midway through his essay, Hauck writes: "I have a bold but common-sense suggestion: old people should not be allowed to watch TV." Is he really proposing such a restriction? What point do you think he is trying to make? Using a reliable source, look up the definition of *satire*. What are the defining characteristics of the genre? What is satire's chief purpose? Do you think Hauck's essay fits this definition? Do you think satire is an effective way to address social issues?

In this essay from the October 14, 2006 edition of Salon, Mary Elizabeth Williams investigates a causal question: Why is Food Network star and talk show host Rachael Ray so popular? As you read, notice how Williams weaves her own experiences with Ray's food shows into her larger exploration of the TV star's phenomenal success.

RACHAEL RAY, MY DINNER HOOKER

Mary Elizabeth Williams

[1] There is an entire industry built around the loathing of peppy media chef-phenomenon Rachael Ray. Google up "Rachael Ray" and "hate" and you'll uncover an enthusiastic community devoting considerable energy to "Raytard's" manic je ne sais quoi and dubious fashion sense. But does the "Joker faced" celebrity chef really merit that much scorn? This is a woman who, as far as we know, has never thrown a phone at an assistant, evaded her taxes, launched into any unfortunate, blood-alcohol-elevated tirades, or rapped at the Teen Choice Awards. If there ever comes a day that Rachael Ray is hospitalized for exhaustion, it'll be a safe bet that she really is exhausted. Why then is there such a thriving cult of antipathy toward the woman *Forbes* recently identified as the second most trusted person in America?

[2] Because there are two kinds of people in the world. There are those who leap out of bed smiling and eager to start the day, the kind who come up with team-building exercises for their departments, who stay out late into the evening line dancing because it's just so darn fun, and who wake up again the next morning still smiling and eager to start the day. These are the kind of people who sell T-shirts on their Web sites that say "Yum-O." Then there are the rest of us, the ones who see people like that and want to barf-o.

[3] Rachael Ray, the turbocharged personality who has built an entire career on the notion that anyone can pull dinner out of their ass in under a half-hour, has, in the past year, gone from high-profile basic cable star to full-blown media juggernaut. She is the face of her own magazine, the author of a string of bestselling cookbooks, and the host of approximately a bazillion Food Network series. In September, her eponymously named daytime talk show launched with the highest ratings for a syndicated debut since Dr. Phil hit the airwaves four years ago. Earlier this year, *Time* named Ray one of the 100 most influential people in the world. She has become, to crib from her bottomless supply of stock phrases, a big ta-da.

[4] Hers is a quintessentially self-made American success story. Small-town girl and specialty food buyer hits upon the idea to teach "30 Minute Meal" classes as a way of moving the merchandise. The classes lead to TV appearances, which lead to cookbooks and a Food Network gig, which lead to guesting on "Oprah" and subsequent total media domination. Ray has no formal culinary training, and a brash willingness to embrace pre-washed produce and canned broth. She has boasted that she's completely unqualified for every job she's ever had. Unsurprisingly, she pisses a lot of people off.

[5] Unlike some of her other Food Network compatriots, Ray brings no seductive charge,

no "food porn" element to her work. Jamie Oliver, Tyler Florence, Giada De Laurentiis and their ilk infuse their personas with the erotic decadence that comes from good cooking. Their newest colleague, Nigella Lawson, owes much of her fame to languorous finger licking. Ray, in contrast, is all brisk and bouncy. Even when she posed for FHM a few years ago in a series of skimpy outfits, her wholesome smile, her cheerful lack of subtext when nibbling a strawberry, remained firmly intact.

6 Ray does not exist to wine you and dine you. She is here to wham-bam thank-you-ma'am you, an abundantly useful strategy. I may find her personality considerably off-putting. I may feel guilty for turning to her again and again at that certain hour of the evening when I need gratification. Rachael Ray is my dinner hooker—fast, reliable, a sure bet. Her critics can bemoan the meteoric rise of the warp-speed dinner; they can turn up their noses at her "sammies" and burgers. But not every meal can be a truffle-infused work of art. Most nights, you're just grateful for a little culinary reach-around.

7 Therein lies the secret of her success. Perhaps she's a star because that breakneck energy and interjection-riddled vocabulary are genuinely appealing, although if that's the case I may have to move to another, far more dour corner of the globe. I prefer to believe she's made it despite the relentless ebullience, that she connects because she understands that for a whole lot of people, getting dinner on the table is a major accomplishment. You work late, you take care of your kids, you have no time to shop. You contemplate choking down a solitary Luna Bar or picking up a supersize bucket of trans fats at the drive-through. Rachael Ray says there's another option, and with her chipper, can-do attitude, she demystifies cooking. If she weren't sugarcoated to the gills, her message would be almost too tough to take. Suck it up, she's saying. If I can do it, you can do it. Take one lousy

half-hour and get a hot meal together, for yourself and for your family. A real meal, preferably the kind with some lean meat and fresh vegetables. No expensive equipment or specialty store ingredients; no fancy French terms or techniques. No excuses.

8 My own relationship with Ray began in her early days on Food Network, when I was a frazzled new mother and the sight of watching people cook was the most soothing thing I could imagine. Her "30 Minute Meals" offered a warm and accessible personality, a regular gal who, like me, was just trying to get dinner made without having a nervous breakdown. I enjoyed the repetitive lull of her drizzling "EVOO" (that's extra virgin olive oil to you and me) "twice around the pan" night after night after night, even as her patter about Grandpa Emmanuel and Daddy's Cajun cred wore thin. Our bond was truly fixed, however, when I was pregnant with my second child, and I was helpfully gifted with one of her cookbooks.

9 It was a fascinating read. On the one hand, what legitimate cookbook author uses more exclamation points than a month's worth of Craigslist postings? Who in her right mind actually writes out phrases like "h-e-double-hockey-sticks" or "WHOA! I can't find the time to do all that!"? I, a semi-competent, fairly snobby home chef with a subscription to Cooks Illustrated, was appalled. On the other hand, the annoying chick delivered. Mere speed and convenience alone do not a successful recipe make, as anyone who's ever watched the Cool Whip–wielding nightmare that is Sandra Lee will attest. In contrast, Ray's roast leg of lamb was a crusty, garlicky hit, and her rosemary grilled chicken was, according to my mate, "restaurant quality." The last thing I made before going into labor was Rachael Ray's green minestrone. In the weeks and months that followed, her other cookbooks appeared on the shelf, and became battered and grease-spattered

from constant abuse. She may grate on my nerves like a block of Parmesan on a blade, but dammit, she's my fix.

10 She wasn't always this irritating. Take a gander at the early episodes of "30 Minute Meals" that air regularly on Food Network, and you'll find a coherent personality putting together some pretty decent dinners. As her star has risen, so, apparently, has Ray's energy level and fondness for cutesy phrasing. The woman who could once do the "chop and drop" with a reasonable amount of serenity has been replaced by something resembling a hyperactive Red Bull addict going through a speed drill while delivering a stream of consciousness. Case in point: Her laid-back howdy-do of yore has been obliterated on her new show, which opens with a large metal gate parting to unleash Ray, bat-out-of-hell-style, upon the masses. As she patters a mile a minute and announces she's heading into her kitchen (emblazoned, à la Mary Richards, with the star's trademark monogram) to grab a cup of coffee, one can only pray that it's decaf. During the course of a recent episode, I heard the 38-year-old use the phrase "back in the day" twice in one minute, "awesome" in four staccato repetitions, and "girl" what felt like roughly 9,000 times. And when she settled down to nervously interrupt and giggle her way through the next interview, somewhere, I could hear the sound of a blogger's hands rubbing gleefully together.

11 But consider this: 66 percent of Americans are overweight or obese, while fast food and takeout consumption and portion sizes have ballooned. It's estimated that less than half of American families sit down to eat together every night. It doesn't take a genius to figure out how these things are related. So if the woman that Anthony Bourdain is not unjustified in referring to as a bobble-head can make dinner a little less intimidating, I can admit she may not be the antichrist. If she understands the vicissitudes of the dinner hour well enough to divide a recent tome into "Meals for the Exhausted," "Meals for the Not Too Tired" and "Bring It On! (But Be Gentle)," she can girlishly giggle herself all the way to the bank. And if, most important of all, a fair share of her recipes actually pass the taste test, she's welcome on my shelf any day.

12 Do the meals that have become my weeknight staples actually get made in under 30 minutes? Sometimes. My husband has been known to hopefully flip open a Ray recipe 30 minutes before he expects to eat, only to emerge considerably later, bathed in flop sweat and exasperation. But as Ray "eyeballs" her measurements, I do likewise with my time, and I can usually hit pretty close to her mark. The timing is realistically livable, and I'm not dialing for takeout or beating myself for not having a pot roast–compatible lifestyle. Our family sits down together. We eat our vegetables. We have time for the rest of the evening. The most frantic woman in America, ironically, brings a measure of peace and pleasure into my hummingbird-paced day. So I'll keep making Ray's seafood stew, her veal involtini, and, when the fear of a lingering, E. coli-related death leaves me, her spinach rolls. Just don't expect me to ever call them yum-o.

SUMMARIZE AND RESPOND

Write a 50- to 100-word summary of Williams' central argument. To what does she attribute Ray's popularity?

How would you characterize the ethos that Williams presents in her essay? How does she get her persona across to her readers? Do you think her ethical appeals are effective? Do they make you more likely to accept her argument?

In her essay, Williams writes, "Rachael Ray is my dinner hooker—fast, reliable, a sure bet." Given the backdrop of humor in the essay, discuss how Williams means this as a compliment—and how it might be misconstrued as an insult by some readers. Do you see any danger is using humor the way Williams does in this piece?

Kelefa Sanneh, a music writer and critic for the New York Times, *uses this essay to do two things: First, he defines the term* rockism, *and then he proceeds to investigate the effects rockism has on the musicians, fans, and the industry as a whole. Sanneh's piece was first published on October 31, 2004 in the* Times.

THE RAP AGAINST ROCKISM

Kelefa Sanneh

[1] Bad news travels fast, and an embarrassing video travels even faster. By last Sunday morning, one of the Internet's most popular downloads was the hours-old 60-second .wmv file of Ashlee Simpson on *Saturday Night Live*. As she and her band stood onstage, her own prerecorded vocals—from the wrong song—came blaring through the speakers, and it was too late to start mouthing the words. So she performed a now-infamous little jig, then skulked offstage, while the band (were a few members smirking?) played on. One of 2004's most popular new stars had been exposed as. . . .

[2] As what, exactly? The online verdict came fast and harsh, the way online verdicts usually do. A typical post on her Web site bore the headline, "Ashlee you are a no talent fraud!" After that night, everyone knew that Jessica Simpson's telegenic sister was no rock 'n' roll hero—she wasn't even a rock 'n' roll also-ran. She was merely a lip-synching pop star.

[3] Music critics have a word for this kind of verdict, this knee-jerk backlash against producer-powered idols who didn't spend years touring dive bars. Not a very elegant word, but a useful one. The word is rockism, and among the small but extraordinarily pesky group of people who obsess over this stuff, rockism is a word meant to start fights. The rockism debate began in earnest in the early 1980's, but over the past few years it has heated up, and today, in certain impassioned circles, there is simply nothing worse than a rockist.

[4] A rockist isn't just someone who loves rock 'n' roll, who goes on and on about Bruce Springsteen, who champions ragged-voiced

singer-songwriters no one has ever heard of. A rockist is someone who reduces rock 'n' roll to a caricature, then uses that caricature as a weapon. Rockism means idolizing the authentic old legend (or underground hero) while mocking the latest pop star; lionizing punk while barely tolerating disco; loving the live show and hating the music video; extolling the growling performer while hating the lip-syncher.

5 Over the past decades, these tendencies have congealed into an ugly sort of common sense. Rock bands record classic albums, while pop stars create "guilty pleasure" singles. It's supposed to be self-evident: U2's entire oeuvre deserves respectful consideration, while a spookily seductive song by an R&B singer named Tweet can only be, in the smug words of a recent VH1 special, "awesomely bad."

6 Like rock 'n' roll itself, rockism is full of contradictions: it could mean loving the Strokes (a scruffy guitar band!) or hating them (image-conscious poseurs!) or ignoring them entirely (since everyone knows that music isn't as good as it used to be). But it almost certainly means disdaining not just Ms. Simpson but also Christina Aguilera and Usher and most of the rest of them, grousing about a pop landscape dominated by big-budget spectacles and high-concept photo shoots, reminiscing about a time when the charts were packed with people who had something to say, and meant it, even if that time never actually existed. If this sounds like you, then take a long look in the mirror: you might be a rockist.

7 Countless critics assail pop stars for not being rock 'n' roll enough, without stopping to wonder why that should be everybody's goal. Or they reward them disproportionately for making rock 'n' roll gestures. Writing in *The Chicago Sun-Times* this summer, Jim DeRogatis grudgingly praised Ms. Lavigne as "a teen-pop phenom that discerning adult rock fans can actually admire without feeling (too) guilty," partly because Ms. Lavigne "plays a passable rhythm guitar" and "has a hand in writing" her songs.

8 Rockism isn't unrelated to older, more familiar prejudices—that's part of why it's so powerful, and so worth arguing about. The pop star, the disco diva, the lip-syncher, the "awesomely bad" hit maker: could it really be a coincidence that rockist complaints often pit straight white men against the rest of the world? Like the anti-disco backlash of 25 years ago, the current rockist consensus seems to reflect not just an idea of how music should be made but also an idea about who should be making it.

9 If you're interested in—O.K., mildly obsessed with—rockism, you can find traces of it just about everywhere. Notice how those tributes to "Women Who Rock" sneakily transform "rock" from a genre to a verb to a catch-all term of praise. Ever wonder why OutKast and the Roots and Mos Def and the Beastie Boys get taken so much more seriously than other rappers? Maybe because rockist critics love it when hip-hop acts impersonate rock 'n' roll bands. (A recent *Rolling Stone* review praised the Beastie Boys for scruffily resisting "the gold-plated phooey currently passing for gangsta.")

10 From punk-rock rags to handsomely illustrated journals, rockism permeates the way we think about music. This summer, the literary zine *The Believer* published a music issue devoted to almost nothing but indie-rock. Two weeks ago, in *The New York Times Book Review*, Sarah Vowell approvingly recalled Nirvana's rise: "a group with loud guitars and louder drums knocking the whimpering Mariah Carey off the top of the charts." Why did the changing of the guard sound so much like a sexual assault? And when did we all agree that Nirvana's neo-punk was more respectable than Ms. Carey's neo-disco?

11 Rockism is imperial: it claims the entire musical world as its own. Rock 'n' roll is the unmarked section in the record store,

a vague pop-music category that swallows all the others. If you write about music, you're presumed to be a rock critic. There's a place in the Rock and Roll Hall of Fame for doo-wop groups and folk singers and disco queens and even rappers—just so long as they, y'know, rock.

[12] Rockism just won't go away. The rockism debate began when British bands questioned whether the search for raw, guitar-driven authenticity wasn't part of rock 'n' roll's problem, instead of its solution; some new-wave bands emphasized synthesizers and drum machines and makeup and hairspray, instead. "Rockist" became for them a term of abuse, and the anti-rockists embraced the inclusive possibilities of a once-derided term: pop. Americans found other terms, but "rockist" seems the best way to describe the ugly anti-disco backlash of the late 1970's, which culminated in a full-blown anti-disco rally and the burning of thousands of disco records at Comiskey Park in Chicago in 1979: the Boston Tea Party of rockism.

[13] That was a quarter of a century and many genres ago. By the 1990's, the American musical landscape was no longer a battleground between Nirvana and Mariah (if indeed it ever was); it was a fractured, hyper-vivid fantasy of teen-pop stars and R&B pillow-talkers and arena-filling country singers and, above all, rappers. Rock 'n' roll was just one more genre alongside the rest.

[14] Yet many critics failed to notice. Rock 'n' roll doesn't rule the world anymore, but lots of writers still act as if it does. The rules, even today, are: concentrate on making albums, not singles; portray yourself as a rebellious individualist, not an industry pro; give listeners the uncomfortable truth, instead of pandering to their tastes. Overnight celebrities, one-hit-wonders and lip-synchers, step aside.

[15] And just as the anti-disco partisans of a quarter-century ago railed against a bewildering new pop order (partly because disco was so closely associated with black culture and gay culture), current critics rail against a world hopelessly corrupted by hip-hop excess. Since before Sean Combs became Puff Daddy, we've been hearing that mainstream hip-hop was too flashy, too crass, too violent, too ridiculous, unlike those hardworking rock 'n' roll stars we used to have. (This, of course, is one of the most pernicious things about rockism: it finds a way to make rock 'n' roll seem boring.)

[16] Much of the most energetic resistance to rockism can be found online, in blogs and on critic-infested sites like I Love Music <ilx. wh3rd.net>, where debates about rockism have become so common that the term itself is something of a running joke. When the editors of a blog called Rockcritics Daily noted that rockism was "all the rage again," they posted dozens of contradictory citations, proving that no one really agrees on what the term means. (By the time you read this article, a slew of indignant refutations and addenda will probably be available online.)

[17] But as more than one online ranter has discovered, it's easier to complain about rockism than it is to get rid of it. You literally can't fight rockism, because the language of righteous struggle is the language of rockism itself. You can argue that the shape-shifting feminist hip-pop of Ms. Aguilera is every bit as radical as the punk rock of the 1970's (and it is), but then you haven't challenged any of the old rockist questions (starting with: Who's more radical?), you've just scribbled in some new answers.

[18] The challenge isn't merely to replace the old list of Great Rock Albums with a new list of Great Pop Songs—although that would, at the very least, be a nice change of pace. It's to find a way to think about a fluid musical world where it's impossible to separate classics from guilty pleasures. The challenge is to acknowledge that music videos and reality shows and glamorous layouts can be as interesting—and as influential—as an old-fashioned album.

¹⁹ In the end, the problem with rockism isn't that it's wrong: all critics are wrong sometimes, and some critics (now doesn't seem like the right time to name names) are wrong almost all the time.

²⁰ The problem with rockism is that it seems increasingly far removed from the way most people actually listen to music.

²¹ Are you really pondering the phony distinction between "great art" and a "guilty pleasure" when you're humming along to the radio? In an era when listeners routinely—and fearlessly—pick music by putting a 40-gig iPod on shuffle, surely we have more interesting things to worry about than that someone might be lip-synching on *Saturday Night Live* or that some rappers gild their phooey. Good critics are good listeners, and the problem with rockism is that it gets in the way of listening. If you're waiting for some song that conjures up soul or honesty or grit or rebellion, you might miss out on Ciara's ecstatic electro-pop, or Alan Jackson's sly country ballads, or Lloyd Banks's felonious purr.

²² Rockism makes it hard to hear the glorious, incoherent, corporate-financed, audience-tested mess that passes for popular music these days. To glorify only performers who write their own songs and play their own guitars is to ignore the marketplace that helps create the music we hear in the first place, with its checkbook-chasing superproducers, its audience-obsessed executives and its cred-hungry performers. To obsess over old-fashioned stand-alone geniuses is to forget that lots of the most memorable music is created despite multimillion-dollar deals and spur-of-the-moment collaborations and murky commercial forces. In fact, a lot of great music is created because of those things. And let's stop pretending that serious rock songs will last forever, as if anything could, and that shiny pop songs are inherently disposable, as if that were necessarily a bad thing. Van Morrison's "Into the Music" was released the same year as the Sugarhill Gang's "Rapper's Delight"; which do you hear more often?

²³ That doesn't mean we should stop arguing about Ms. Simpson, or even that we should stop sharing the 60-second clip that may just be this year's best music video. But it does mean we should stop taking it for granted that music isn't as good as it used to be, and it means we should stop being shocked that the rock rules of the 1970's are no longer the law of the land. No doubt our current obsessions and comparisons will come to seem hopelessly blinkered as popular music mutates some more—listeners and critics alike can't do much more than struggle to keep up. But let's stop trying to hammer young stars into old categories. We have lots of new music to choose from—we deserve some new prejudices, too.

SUMMARIZE AND RESPOND

Write a 100-word summary of Sanneh's two central arguments: his definition of "rockism" and his claim about its negative consequences.

ANALYZE

Which of the rhetorical appeals do you think is strongest in this essay? How does Sanneh use this appeal to connect with his readers and to advance his argument? Make sure you point to specific examples of the appeal at work in the text to support your analysis.

Are you a "rockist"? Explain your response, using Sanneh's definition as a starting point.

Near the end of his essay, Sanneh writes, "The problem with rockism is that it seems increasingly far removed from the way most people actually listen to music." Explain what this means, in the context of his essay, and whether you agree with this claim.

Mark Morford, a reporter for the San Francisco Chronicle, *uses the following piece—infused with a healthy dose of humor—to challenge conventional wisdom about the relationship between raunchy music and teenage sexuality. You may want to compare Morford's essay—published August 11, 2006 in the* Chronicle—*with the one that follows by Tara Parker-Pope.*

WHICH CAME FIRST: THE LYRICS OR LIBIDOS?

Mark Morford

[1] Let's just say it outright: AC/DC is God's most beautiful and significant gift to humankind.

[2] Hey, it's a fact. I personally spent upward of 3.6 billion hours (give or take) as a happy, rebellious, well-fed, surly, middle-class teen pounding my delicate eardrums and grinding my nerves to this glorious Aussie rock band's dizzy, brain-churning music, shaking my pale fist to its monster-arena blues and soaking my burgeoning id in the profound lyrics of songs like "Dirty Deeds Done Dirt Cheap" and "What Do You Do for Money Honey." To their giant slab of divine truth, I hereby testify.

[3] Around the time of my initial AC/DC affection, I also had sex. And like many of the male teen persuasion, I enjoyed it quite a lot. So much so that—also like many of the male teen persuasion—I became passionately enamored of and reverential about the female gender, not to mention convinced that the overwhelming, mind-altering, time-space-bending force of my newfound enjoyment of this wondrous activity might somehow cause me to levitate and spontaneously combust and go absolutely insane. Simultaneously.

[4] This did not happen. At least, not yet. But the feeling, I have to say, remains to this day.

[5] But now I have a new understanding. Now I can attribute at least part of this mad hot desire, this otherworldly adoration, to my beloved AC/DC. In fact, I might even go so far as to claim that the Aussie rock gods added serious fuel to my lubricious fire, transformed my bones and shaped the arc of my life. Without them, I might never have evolved into the calm and Hitachi-advocating lightworker I am today. I am considering sending them a gift basket.

6 See, there is this new study, yet another one that says teens who listen to lots of sexually explicit music full of "degrading" lyrics are much more likely to have sex sooner than those who listen to, say, church hymns and banjo music and Carrie Underwood preening her way through "Jesus Take the Wheel." I know, it's shocking.

7 The study, from the nonprofit Rand think tank in Philly, surveyed about 1,200 kids who listen to hours upon hours of hip-hop, R&B and rock on their iPods. Apparently, among "heavy listeners" of raunchy and "degrading" songs, 51 percent started having sex within a couple years, versus only 29 percent who listened to, say, Coldplay. Or Beyoncé. George Benson. Whatever.

8 But the study might as well be referring to AC/DC. Or Elvis. Or the Starland Vocal Band belting out "Afternoon Delight." Hey, it's all devil music, right? It all objectifies women as sex objects and reduces men to dumb superstuds, and it all makes you want to have sex and do drugs and light stuff on fire and eat your own flesh and laugh maniacally. You know, same as it ever was.

9 Now, you may jump up and down and call this study silly, revealing nothing and only reminding you of the old days when networks refused to show Elvis from the waist down lest an entire nation quiver and explode and start grinding their pelvises against the TV. You may say it tries—and fails—to make a tenuous causal connection, isolating one influence on teens amid an ocean of frenzied influences, from music to TV to peer pressure to sexually terrified parents to MySpace to Internet porn to Red Bull to thong underwear. And you would be quite correct.

10 Let's flip it around: What would you have thought if it had concluded that listening to thousands of hours of raunchy lyrics had zero effect on teen attitudes and behaviors? "Those sure are some inept teens," you might've said, recalling how good it was to get it on in the backseat of that Trans Am to the dulcet sounds of, say, Van Halen's "Ice Cream Man." "Bring me my 'Sticky Fingers' LP and a hookah and a bottle of Goldschlager, stat!" you might've cried, revealing a bit too much information.

11 But aren't you also thinking, Wait, don't they have it exactly backward? Doesn't the fact that you're a sexually desperate, hormone-blasted teen make you that much more likely to crave music that reflects your surging desires?

12 Are you not, after all, just another misinformed and misled American teenager, weaned on a sickly diet of insidious abstinence programs, lousy sex ed and horribly mixed messages about sex and love and your body? But it does not matter, because all of that is easily crushed by a pile of hormones so raging you think you will jump out of your skin at any moment.

13 Hence, are you not merely seeking music to match this feeling? Is it not a case of which came first, the eager chicken or the throbbing, groovy egg? Of course it is.

14 From what I can recall, the music I loved (and still love) was as much a balm and mirror and therapist for my pimpled and tormented young soul as it was any sort of motivation or shaper of sexual attitude. And truly, the music was a minor accomplice when compared with, say, those early *Penthouse Forum* letters. Or the existence of tight jeans. Or Denet Whitaker's skin. Note to researchers: Isolate one aspect at your peril. If you divorce one random influence from the context of a teen's manic life, the significance of your point simply collapses.

15 But there is another tragedy hidden in this rather silly study, slipping away unnoticed. The report implies that the lyrics to many hip-hop and rock songs have become grossly raunchy, straight pornography, stripped entirely of even the playful

and juvenile double-entendres of AC/DC, Zeppelin and Run-DMC. And it's true.

16 There is no more "Squeeze my lemon till the juice runs down my leg." There is no more "She was holding a pair, but I had to try/Her deuce was wild, but my ace was high." There is no "The men don't know, but the little girls understand." There is only, well, the unprintable straight-porn versions thereof.

17 It is a case of kids being regularly assaulted by, well, really lousy lyrics. It is a heartbreaking case of songwriters with zero imagination, with a lack of appreciation for the craft of penning a cunning, puerile lyric that will attach itself like a sloppy kiss to the budding libidos of an entire generation.

18 Forget the problem of myopic adults who generate silly, brow-furrowed studies on teen behavior. Where is the next generation of lyrical pun masters? Whither double entendres and sticky innuendo with more than one layer? Who, pray who, will teach our children about, say, "giving the dog a bone"? It's an unsung tragedy is what it is.

RESPOND

In his essay, Morford asks the following question, which sums up part of his argument: "Doesn't the fact that you're a sexually desperate, hormone-blasted teen make you that much more likely to crave music that reflects your surging desires?" What do you think of his reasoning? Do you think he makes a valid point? Explain your answer.

ANALYZE

Based on the text itself, who do you think is Morford's target audience? Do you think he successfully connects with that audience? Point to specific elements in the essay to support your answer.

DISCUSS

Morford uses humor, much of it directed at himself, throughout his essay. Do you think this approach helps him present a persuasive argument? Be sure to refer to specific parts of the essay to support your response.

ARGUE

Near the end of his essay, Morford presents another argument, writing: "The report implies that the lyrics to many hip-hop and rock songs have become grossly raunchy, straight pornography, stripped entirely of even the playful and juvenile double-entendres of AC/DC, Zeppelin and Run-DMC. And it's true." Do you agree with his claim about the sorry state of rock and hip-hop lyrics today? Write a brief essay in which you explain and defend your position.

Tara Parker-Pope's piece, like Mark Morford's before it, examines what effects—if any—music has on sexual behavior. Parker-Pope wrote her article for the November 6, 2007 edition of the New York Times.

FOR CLUES ON TEENAGE SEX, EXPERTS LOOK TO HIP-HOP

Tara Parker-Pope

1 Hip-hop, with its suggestive lyrics, videos and dance moves, has long been criticized by public health experts and parents, who fear that it leads to risky sexual behavior among teenagers.

2 But it has never been clear whether there is something uniquely insidious about hip-hop or whether the problem is simply that most people over 40 just don't understand it. After all, nearly every generation seems troubled by the musical preferences of the next; remember, Elvis's gyrating hips were once viewed as a corrupting influence on the nation's youth. To solve that riddle, public health researchers are deconstructing hip-hop culture, venturing onto club dance floors and dissecting rap lyrics. The hope is that by understanding hip-hop, experts can design more effective health messages—and maybe even give parents insight into the often confounding music embraced by their children.

3 "There's definitely a popular opinion that hip-hop is music that is bad for you and makes people do crazy things," said Miguel A. Muñoz-Laboy, an assistant professor in the department of sociomedical sciences at Columbia University. "We need to try to see how youth understand their own culture without imposing our own adult judgments."

4 Dr. Muñoz-Laboy spent three years studying the hip-hop club scene, talking to dozens of teenagers and watching them dance. While hip-hop music has been widely assailed as misogynistic, the researchers found that young women were the "gatekeepers" of boundaries on the dance floor, according to research published this month in the journal *Culture, Health and Sexuality*. Even during the highly sexualized form of dance known as grinding, in which bodies rub against each other, the girls in the study "were consistently vigilant about maintaining control over their bodies and space," the study noted.

5 Most of the teenagers in the study were sexually experienced. But the researchers found that the overt sexuality of the music and dancing was not the main influence on sexual behavior. Rather it was the old standbys of alcohol, drugs and peer pressure that typically led them into sexual encounters.

6 The lesson for public health workers is that hip-hop is not just music but a support system and social structure that dominates youth culture, Dr. Muñoz-Laboy said. The language of hip-hop also may in fact be a more effective way to communicate with teenagers. One H.I.V. prevention ad that resonated with women, for instance, mirrored the sexualized lyrics of hip-hop, telling girls, "Don't take it laying down."

7 Questions remain about whether hip-hop's explicit lyrics encourage early sex. Last year, the journal *Pediatrics* published research from the RAND Corporation concluding that degrading lyrics, not sexual lyrics, were the problem.

8 The researchers interviewed more than 1,400 teenagers over two years, asking them about the music they listened to along with factors like peer pressure and parental supervision. They found that adolescents who were exposed to the highest levels of sexually degrading lyrics were twice as likely to have had sex by the end of the study.

9 The researchers defined degrading lyrics as those that portrayed women as sexual objects, men as insatiable and sex as inconsequential. One example they cited was from the rapper Ja Rule, whose song "Livin' It Up" includes the lyrics "Half the ho's hate me, half them love me." Notably, lyrics that celebrated sex, like those crooned by the band 98 Degrees—"I'm dreamin' day and night of making love"—had no effect on sexual behavior, the study found.

10 It may be that teenagers who are most interested in initiating sexual activity simply gravitate toward songs with edgier lyrics. But the research suggests that parents should focus less on whether their children listen to hip-hop and pay more attention to the content. "We need to teach teens that these portrayals of women and sex don't represent reality," said Steven C. Martino, a behavioral scientist at RAND.

11 This year, another paper in *Culture, Health and Sexuality* titled "Representin' in Cyberspace" studied the way black American girls used hip-hop terms like "freaks" and "pimpettes" to describe themselves on personal home pages. The research led the author, Carla E. Stokes, to form HotGirls (Helping Our Teen Girls in Real Life Situations), an Atlanta-based nonprofit group that holds workshops where girls talk about music, rewrite objectionable lyrics and even record their own music. "We're trying to build on the empowering aspects of the hip-hop culture," Dr. Stokes said.

12 In fact, many experts believe the keys to communicating with an entire generation of young people can be found in hip-hop. "That's far more powerful than any negative influence the music may be having," said Bakari Kitwana, an artist in residence at the University of Chicago whose book "The Hip-Hop Generation" is viewed as the leading scholarly work on the culture.

13 "Hip-hop is a generational phenomenon that has united young people," Mr. Kitwana added. "If that's not understood, you're going to miss a lot."

SUMMARIZE

Summarize the sources that Parker-Pope uses in her article. Whom does she quote? What expertise do these sources bring to the article?

ANALYZE

Compare the rhetorical situations of Parker-Pope's article and the Mark Morford essay that precedes it. How do each author's purpose and audience influence the rhetorical choices she or he makes? Think specifically about each author's ethos and use of evidence.

DISCUSS

What is the distinction Parker-Pope makes between sexually explicit lyrics and sexually degrading lyrics? Which do you think might be more harmful to young listeners? Why?

The next essay and the two that follow it respond to the uproar surrounding racially inflammatory comments made by radio personality Don Imus in 2007 with different arguments about who should be held accountable for violent, degrading, and offensive lyrics in hip-hop and rap. Journalist and commentator Jonetta Rose Barras wrote this first piece for the April 15, 2007 edition of the Washington Post.

WE'RE OUR OWN WORST IMUSES

Jonetta Rose Barras

1 They wanted to slay Don Imus and they did. Jesse Jackson and Al Sharpton, the NAACP, the National Association of Black Journalists and their posse knocked the shock jock off his throne at CBS Radio and MSNBC. But behind the scenes in the black community where I live and work, the outcry all along has been for something else.

2 Rather than blast the talk-show host for his derogatory description of the Rutgers University women's basketball team, many African Americans I spoke to in my work as a radio commentator said all along that black folks, including and perhaps chiefly those who led the charge against Imus, should take a long look in the mirror.

3 I think they're right.

4 The sensational indignation that got Imus fired last week struck many of us as hypocritical. It cast African Americans principally as the victims of discrimination—and ignored the fact that they are the chief purveyors of the demeaning language being decried. It ignored the realities of how culture gets transmitted in contemporary society and the prominent role that African Americans play in that transfer. It failed to recognize the market forces at play. And it held blacks unaccountable for any of the damage, saddling whites with all the blame.

5 I have no tears for Imus. His style of commentary is as outdated as black-and-white TV, and he deserved to be sent packing.

But here's the point: If African Americans wanted to hold Imus accountable and punish him, shouldn't they take similar actions against some in their own group?

6 Urban American pop culture is fast becoming a black—and sometimes Hispanic—thing, and a bunch of people are getting filthy rich from it. The dirty little secret here is that the fight over Imus may not have been so much about his terminal foot-in-mouth disease as about who has dominion over that culture and who collects the cash.

7 "Imus didn't say anything that hasn't been included in thousands of records," said Misty Brown, a local arts consultant. "We have been called far worse, and by our own people."

8 It was black rap artists who created the image of African American women as "bitches and hos." That image has been marketed and distributed by large corporations—Warner Brothers, Viacom, Black Entertainment Television—and purchased all over the world by regular folks, white and black, including, no doubt, some of the same people who called for Imus's head.

9 As a result, there isn't anything sacred in black culture anymore, said local hip-hop artist Bomani Armah, "because it isn't sacred among us."

10 Some black radio stations "allow songs to be played that clearly disrespect black

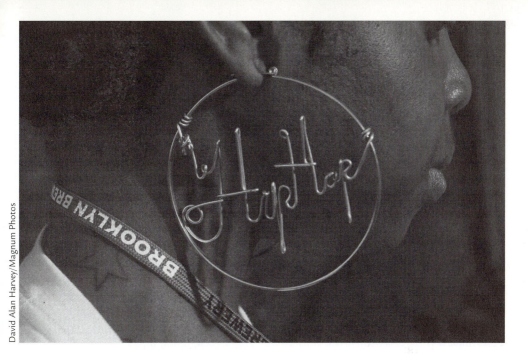

David Alan Harvey/Magnum Photos

FIGURE 10-2

While many purists bemoan the commercialization of hip-hop and rap, other critics see something far more dangerous going on. "The denigration of women has been a huge seller in the last 20 years," radio host Kojo Nnamdi says in Jonetta Rose Barras' essay "We're Our Own Worst Imuses." Do you agree with this comment? Can you think of other genres of music that face similar criticism for the content of their songs? The Barras essay and the two that follow it acknowledge that there is a problem with hip-hop and rap but present different culprits for the blame. Who, ultimately, do you think is responsible for the content of popular music? Do you think musicians have artistic and social obligations that should supersede their commercial aspirations?

women," said Michael Francis, a criminal justice expert and social commentator in the District, who cautions that not all the blame for the denigration of black women can be placed at rap's door. The antecedents can be found in slavery, when black women were bred, whipped and put on the block to work for others.

11 But even though it was poorly executed Imus-speak, "nappy-headed ho" is, in fact, a progeny of black street/thug culture. It is a culture whose symbols, idioms and fashions have not only seeped into

the American mainstream over the past 20 years but have been enthusiastically embraced. We see and hear this culture every day in the 'hood, in high schools, in the movie ticket line, in the upper-crust college dorm.

12 Consider that last year's Academy Award for Best Original Song went to "It's Hard Out Here for a Pimp" from the movie "Hustle and Flow." That Howard University gave rapper P. Diddy the same postgraduate achievement award that it once bestowed upon famed African American

author Zora Neale Hurston. Or that in 2001 the NAACP gave its prestigious Image Award to R. Kelly, a black singer accused of having sex with underage girls.

[13] We know this "thug" culture by its awful and extensive body tattoos; its denigrating language that sculpts every woman—regardless of color—into a sex object or a joke. We know it by its so-called urban fashion, which includes the butt-revealing pants, the flashy and often fake gold—around the neck, on the arms, in the mouth. And yes, by the lyrics we hear and the videos we see. Nowadays, it has also spread into comedy, said Armah, who notes a rise in politically incorrect jokes and skits.

[14] African Americans "have created the atmosphere where people feel comfortable making derogatory statements," said D.C. small-business owner Edwin Chin-Shue, who managed several record stores for years. "If we want to boycott Imus, then we have to boycott Warner Brothers and Sony. We have to boycott Spike Lee and radio stations that play rap music."

[15] The Imus controversy was an extension of the battle over use of the N-word. African Americans can throw around the most demeaning terminology, seeking to cash in at major record companies, production studios or publishing houses (check out the chick-lit phenom, which in many cases is just blaxploitation movies put to print). But the moment certain whites walk into that world, blacks are insulted, deeply offended. Spike Lee can use the word "jiggaboo" in his movie "School Daze." Imus and his producer sidekick had better step back.

[16] Who is caretaker of the authentic thug culture, including when and how to use the phrases "nappy head" or "bitches and hos"? That is the question.

[17] The day after Imus was fired, rapper Snoop Dogg was quoted as saying that what Imus did and what rappers do "are two separate things." Rappers "have these songs coming from our minds and our souls that are relevant to what we feel," he said. "I will not let them [expletive] say we in the same league as him."

[18] But as American society becomes more colorized, more reflective of its multicultural roots and features, blacks may be unable to retain sole rights of proprietorship, even through bullying and demonstrations. Expressions seep into mainstream culture and become universal property.

[19] "People start thinking [a phrase] is cool," said Deborah Tannen, professor of linguistics at Georgetown University. "You use it because you have the feeling of being with it, being on the cutting edge. It's also about the youth culture" and "the allure associated with youth."

[20] So we heard the aging Imus attempting to replicate the language of youthful African American thug culture. And we saw Bush adviser Karl Rove onstage at a recent radio correspondents' dinner, clumsily trying out the menacing gangsta pose and confrontational hand gestures as he shouted out the lame lyrics to a faux rap song. It was American street culture come to the White House.

[21] And street culture's introduction into mainstream America, though incremental, is not accidental. It is orchestrated by image- and opinion-makers—black and white—and corporations champing at the bit for new markets and the cash they promise. The public aids and abets the process. It's less about being cool and more about the money. Ka-ching.

[22] Each year rap/hip-hop brings more than $4 billion to the music industry. The urban apparel market racks up more than $2 billion in sales annually, according to various trade publications.

²³ "In a capitalist environment, what is mainstream is what sells," said WAMU Radio talk show host Kojo Nnamdi. "The denigration of women has been a huge seller in the last 20 years. Black men do it and even black women do it."

²⁴ And that denigration gets picked up and tossed around freely. "You should hear some of the things the young ladies I work with call themselves," said Janice Ferebee, president of Got It Goin' On, which provides self-esteem and life-skills services for girls and young women in the United States, South Africa and Ghana.

²⁵ So it's fair to ask: Why now? Why all the heat and bother? Surely it's not the first time that African Americans have heard rap-speak in mainstream America. And why won't blacks chastise their own?

²⁶ The same machine that fed Imus has made an awful lot of black folks millionaires. So this matter of who is paraded in the public square for an old-fashioned butt-kicking must be a finely executed dance. Although Sharpton and others may claim that they have flogged rap artists, one thing is certain: They haven't flogged P. Diddy, Snoop Dogg or many of the others with the same vengeance that they did Imus. They haven't sought to strip them of their sponsors and their livelihood. One reason may be that money from these trash-talkers keeps the wheels of more than a few black organizations turning. The last person who had the guts to challenge those within the race was the late C. Delores Tucker, who led the National Congress of Black Women.

²⁷ "People have been allowed to continue living out this most amazing double standard," said Nnamdi. It's time that double standard were slain.

SUMMARIZE

Who does Barras argue should be included on the list of those responsible for the creation, dissemination, and consumption of offensive and degrading hip-hop and rap music? What do you think of her claim?

ANALYZE

Compare the argument presented by Barras with Glen Ford's in the essay that follows this one. What common ground do they share? Where do their claims differ? Who's argument do you find more persuasive? Why?

Pioneering broadcaster and journalist Glen Ford is a co-founder and executive editor of Black Agenda Report, *an online journal of African-American political thought and action. Ford wrote this piece—in which he forcefully lays the blame for rap music's obscene and violent lyrics at the feet of corporations that control the music—for the May 2, 2007 edition of the journal.*

HIP-HOP PROFANITY, MISOGYNY AND VIOLENCE: BLAME THE MANUFACTURER

Glen Ford

[1] On a Spring day at McDonald's fast food restaurants all across Black America, counter clerks welcome female customers with the greeting, "What you want, bitch?" Female employees flip burgers in see-through outfits and make lewd sexual remarks to pre-teen boys while bussing tables. McDonald's managers position themselves near the exits, arms folded, Glocks protruding from their waistbands, nodding to departing customers, "Have a good day, motherf**kers. Y'all my niggas."

[2] Naturally, the surrounding communities would be upset. A portion of their anger would be directed at the young men and women whose conduct was so destructive of the morals and image of African Americans. Preachers would rail against the willingness of Black youth to debase themselves in such a manner, and politicians would rush to introduce laws making it a crime for public accommodations employees to use profanity or engage in lewd or threatening behavior. However, there can be no doubt that the full wrath of the community and the state would descend like an angry god's vengeance on the real villain: the McDonald's Corporation, the purveyor of the fast food experience product.

[3] Hip-hop music is also a product, produced by giant corporations for mass distribution to a carefully targeted and cultivated demographic market. Corporate executives map out multiyear campaigns to increase their share of the targeted market, hiring and firing subordinates—the men and women of Artists and Recordings (A&R) departments—whose job is to find the raw material for the product (artists), and shape it into the package upper management has decreed is most marketable (the artist's public persona, image, style and behavior). It is a corporate process at every stage of artist "development," one that was in place long before the artist was "discovered" or signed to the corporate label. What the public sees, hears and consumes is the end result of a process that is integral to the business model crafted by top corporate executives. The artist, the song, the presentation—all of it is a corporate product.

[4] Yet, unlike the swift and certain public condemnation that would crash down upon our hypothetical McDonald's-from-Da Hood, the bulk of Black community anger at hip-hop products is directed at foul-behaving artists, rather than the corporate Dr. Frankensteins that created and profit from them. As the great French author

and revolutionary Franz Fanon would have understood perfectly, colonized and racially oppressed peoples internalize—take ownership—of the social pathologies fostered by the oppressor. Thus, the anti-social aspects of commercial hip-hop are perceived as a "Black" problem, to be overcome through internal devices (preaching and other forms of collective self-flagellation), rather than viewed as an assault by hostile, outside forces secondarily abetted by opportunists within the group.

[5] In order for our nightmare McDonald's analogy to more closely fit the music industry reality, all the fast food chains would have to provide the same type of profane, low-life, hyper-sexualized, life-devaluing service/product: "Bitch-Burgers" from Burger King, served with "Chronic-Flavored Fries," "Ho Wings" from KFC, dipped in too-hot "187 Murder Sauce." If you wanted fast food, you'd have to patronize one or the other of these thug-themed chains. So, too, with hip-hop music.

[6] A handful of entertainment corporations exercise total control of the market, in incestuous (and illegal) conspiratorial concert with corporate-dominated radio. Successful so-called "independent" labels are most often mere subcontractors to the majors, dependent on them for record distribution and business survival. They are no more independent than the owner of a McDonald's franchise, whose product must conform to the standards set by global headquarters in Oak Brook, Illinois.

[7] As "conscious" rapper Paris wrote, there is no viable alternative to the corporate nexus for hip-hop artists seeking to reach a mass audience. "*What* underground?" said Paris. "Do you know how much good material is marginalized because it doesn't fit white cooperate America's ideals of acceptability? Independents can't get radio or video play anymore, at least not through commercial outlets, and most listeners don't acknowledge material that they don't see or hear regularly on the radio or on TV."

[8] The major record labels actively suppress positive hip-hop by withholding promotional support of both the above- and below-the-table variety. Hip-hop journalist and activist Davey D reported that Erykah Badu and The Roots' Grammy-winning hit "You Got Me" was initially rejected by the corporate nexus due to its "overtly positive" message "so palms were greased with the promise that key stations countrywide would get hot 'summer jam' concert acts in exchange for airplay. According to Questlove [of The Roots], more than $1 million in cash and resources were eventually laid out for the success of that single song."

[9] Black America's hip-hop problem cannot be laid at the feet of a few hundred wayward performers—and should certainly not be assigned to some inherent pathology in Black culture. African Americans do not control the packaging and dissemination of their culture: corporations and their Black comprador allies and annexes do. The mass Gangsta Rap phenomenon is a boardroom invention. I know.

[10] From 1987 to early 1994, I co-owned and hosted "Rap It Up," the first nationally syndicated radio hip-hop music program. During the first half of this period, the Rap genre accomplished its national "breakout" from New York and LA, spreading to all points in between. By 1990, the major labels were preparing to swallow the independent labels that had birthed commercial hip-hop, which had evolved into a wondrous mix of party, political and street-aggressive subsets. One of the corporate labels (I can't remember which) conducted a study that shocked the industry: The most "active" consumers of hip-hop, they discovered, were "tweens," the demographic slice between the ages of 11 and 13.

[11] The numbers were unprecedented. Even in the early years of Black radio, R&B

music's most active consumers were at least two or three years older than tweens. It didn't take a roomful of Ph.D.s in human development science to grasp the ramifications of the data. Early and pre-adolescents of both genders are sexual-socially undeveloped—uncertain and afraid of the other gender. Tweens revel in honing their newfound skills in profanity; they love to curse. Males, especially, act out their anxieties about females through aggression and derision. This is the cohort for which the major labels would package their hip-hop products. Commercial Gangsta Rap was born—a sub-genre that would lock a whole generation in perpetual arrested social development.

[12] First, the artists would have to be brought into the corporate program. The term "street" became a euphemism for a monsoon of profanity, gratuitous violence, female and male hyper-promiscuity, the most vulgar materialism, and the total suppression of social consciousness. A slew of child acts was recruited to appeal more directly to the core demographic.

[13] Women rappers were coerced to conform to the new order. A young female artist broke down at my kitchen table one afternoon, after we had finished a promotional interview. "They're trying to make me into a whore," she said, sobbing. "They say I'm not 'street' enough." Her skills on the mic were fine. "They" were the A&R people from her corporate label.

[14] Stories like this abounded during the transition from independent to major label control of hip-hop. The thug- and ho-ification of the genre is now all but complete.

[15] Blame the manufacturer.

SUMMARIZE AND RESPOND

Explain the extended analogy that Ford presents in his column using McDonald's restaurants and the rap music industry. Do you think his analogy is effective? Explain your response.

DISCUSS

Ford claims that "major record labels actively suppress positive hip-hop" and cites the Grammy-winning hit "You Got Me" as an example. How many hip-hop or rap songs with positive messages can you think of? Compare this with the number of songs you've heard with violent, obscene, or misogynistic lyrics. Even if you're not familiar with hip-hop, why do you think music companies would want to keep positive songs off the air?

ARGUE

Do you think we should "[b]lame the manufacturer" for harmful hip-hop lyrics, as Ford suggests? Develop your response into a brief essay. You may also wish to refer to the Jonetta Rose Barras essay that starts on page 312.

Justin D. Ross, a Democrat who represents Prince George's County in the Maryland House of Delegates, wrote this essay for the September 9, 2007 edition of the Washington Post. *In it, he takes a different tack in the debate over blame for objectionable lyrics in hip-hop and rap music.*

OFFENDED? THE RAP'S ON ME

Justin D. Ross

[1] When it comes to sexism and racism in hip-hop, I'm part of the problem.

[2] Let me explain. I love hip-hop—have ever since it first came on the scene when I was in elementary school. Over the years, I've bought hundreds of tapes, CDs and downloads, gone to countless rap concerts, even worn my favorite artists' clothing lines. We used to think of hip-hop as just a black thing, but it's not. The largest share of rap music sales in America goes to white listeners. That would be me.

[3] So I'm not just sounding off when I say this: It's time for a boycott of all rap music that stereotypes African Americans or insults and degrades women. And in particular, the people who need to be doing the boycotting are white fans like myself.

[4] In the current debate over whether hip-hop has become degrading to women and harmful to race relations, I've heard quite a bit from black activists, some of whom have fought for years against the sort of lyrics I'm writing about, and I've gotten several earfuls from black rap artists. But I haven't heard a peep from the white fans who essentially underwrite the industry by purchasing more than 70 percent of the rap music in this country, according to Mediamark Research Inc. I don't presume to tell any artist, studio executive or record label what to record or not record. But I will presume to ask young white customers: Why are we buying this stuff?

[5] Across the country, white kids in comfortable suburban neighborhoods (mine was Greenbelt) sit in their cars or bedrooms or studio apartments, listening to the latest rap music that glorifies violence, peddles racist stereotypes and portrays women as little more than animals. We look through the keyhole into a violent, sexy world of "money, ho's and clothes." We're excited to be transported to a place where people brag about gunplay, use racial epithets continually and talk freely about dealing drugs. And then we turn off whatever we're listening to and return to our comfy world in time for dinner.

[6] But music is powerful. You can't just turn it on and off with a switch. Back in 1989, rap music had this white kid wearing a leather African pendant and reading Malcolm X because Chuck D did. Before I graduated from Kenmoor Middle School, I was ready to "Fight the Power" because Public Enemy told me to (even though I didn't really know what that meant).

[7] But it has been a long time since Public Enemy. Some hip-hop artists (the Roots, Talib Kweli, D.C.'s own Wale) still succeed without using stereotypes and misogyny, but too much of today's rap goes another way: It's full of drug dealing and killing, and

it portrays women as sex objects. A generation ago, at least some element of hip-hop remained loyal to the civil rights movement. Now songs talk so casually about selling crack and committing murder that listeners are desensitized to the words' effect.

8 Let's be clear about what we—rap's huge white audience—are becoming insensitive to: crime against black people, drugs being sold in black neighborhoods, black people being killed. I think this desensitization is partly responsible for the absence of discussion about the cruel fact that, according to a 2001 study by the Department of Health and Human Services, the leading killer of African Americans ages 15 to 34 is homicide. It may also help explain why you'll seldom hear politicians talking about another awful statistic: According to the same study, African Americans are five times more likely than whites to be victims of homicide.

9 So who are the rappers really aiming at? Many rap songs use the "N-word" a dozen times or more. But I can count on two hands the number of times I've heard the words "whitey" or "cracker" in rap music. I wonder: If the Grand Wizard himself owned a record label, how much different would the music sound?

10 I also wonder what would happen if rap artists started talking about selling dope in the suburbs, or shooting white people or beating down white men. Would rap's comfortable white fans continue to consume it? I suspect the record companies wouldn't even sell it. Like the majority of people who buy rap music, the majority of people who get rich off it are white. That sort of thing might hit a little too close to home for hip-hop's fans and profiteers.

11 The other day, my 3-year-old wanted to listen to some music on my iPod. Before I let her, I checked out what I had on there. Much of it was trash I wouldn't let her listen to. I've been waxing intellectual for years about the state of rap and how it needs to change, and there I was, looking at my iPod and seeing songs such as "Hustlin'," "Bury Me a G" and "Poppin' My Collar," all of which are guilty of the very offenses I just decried and all of which I purchased within the past year.

12 That's when it hit me: I'm the problem. It's time for me and others like me to own up to our role in peddling degrading hip-hop. Of course, I can't legislate a boycott of offensive rap, except for myself. And that's exactly what I plan to do.

ANALYZE

How would you characterize the ethos, or persona, that Ross presents in this essay? How does he achieve this ethical position? Do you think his persona helps his argument? Explain.

DISCUSS

What do you think Ross wants his audience to do after reading his essay? Why do you think this?

from reading to writing

1. Compare the television essays by Steven Johnson and Michael Hirschorn. Which writer presents a more effective argument? Why? How do you think Johnson would respond to Hirschorn's central argument about reality TV?
2. Using the readings in this chapter as a framework, work with a partner or a small group to develop a definition of "pop culture." You may support your definition with evidence from your own experience.
3. In one way or another, all of the essays in this chapter deal with issues of cause and effect. Mary Elizabeth Williams, for example, wants to know the causes of Rachael Ray's popularity, whereas Kelefa Sanneh explores the effects that rockism has on the pop music industry. Compose an essay in which you examine the causes or consequences of a pop culture phenomenon or trend, such as the explosive growth of social networking sites or the ever-increasing levels of realistic violence in popular video and computer games.
4. Compare the readings on hip-hop and rap by Jonetta Rose Barras, Glen Ford, and Justin D. Ross. Where do the authors agree? Where do they disagree? Which author do you think presents the most compelling argument? Why?

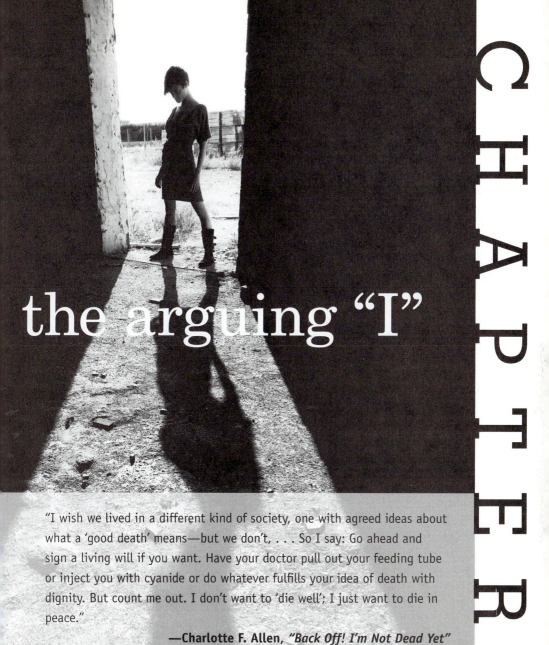

the arguing "I"

"I wish we lived in a different kind of society, one with agreed ideas about what a 'good death' means—but we don't, . . . So I say: Go ahead and sign a living will if you want. Have your doctor pull out your feeding tube or inject you with cyanide or do whatever fulfills your idea of death with dignity. But count me out. I don't want to 'die well'; I just want to die in peace."

—Charlotte F. Allen, *"Back Off! I'm Not Dead Yet"*

T his chapter is rooted in two simple ideas: First, even in our ever-more complicated and interconnected lives, one person, one voice, can still spur the world to action. Second—and this is probably the most important part—you don't have to stare down a line of tanks to make a difference. As the following essays show, writing in the first person—using your own voice and talking about your own experiences—can be a compelling way to present an argument on just about any subject. Though this perspective isn't always appropriate, these pieces are proof that there are times when it can help authors connect with readers and make them care as deeply as they do about their subjects.

Stuart Franklin/Magnum Photos

FIGURE 11-1

In one of the iconic images of the 20th century, a single protestor blocks the progress of a line of tanks during pro-democracy demonstrations in Beijing's Tiananmen Square in June 1989. In an essay honoring the man as one of *Time* magazine's "100 Most Important People of the Century," writer Pico Ayer described him as "[o]ne lone Everyman standing up to machinery, to force, to all the massed weight of the People's Republic [of China]—the largest nation in the world, comprising more than 1 billion people—while its all powerful leaders remain, as ever, in hiding somewhere within the bowels of the Great Hall of the People." Though China has never acknowledged any casualties, various media have reported that hundreds of people died during a crackdown on the demonstrators. What is your initial reaction to this image? Which of the rhetorical appeals—to ethos, pathos, or logos—do you think is most dominant in the image? How does the image argue for the power of individual action?

In the aftermath of the 2007 massacre at Virginia Tech, screenwriter Mike White wonders if he and others in the film business should "at least pause to consider what we are saying with our movies about the value of life and the pleasures of mayhem." White, whose credits include School of Rock *and* Year of the Dog, *wrote this piece for the May 2, 2007 edition of the* New York Times.

MAKING A KILLING

Mike White

[1] The first movie I ever made was called "Death Creek Camp." It told the age-old story of a group of teenage guys who set out on a fun-filled wilderness excursion only to be stalked and murdered by a psychopath disguised in a hockey mask and a blue kimono. It was no masterpiece of cinema.

[2] Most of the scenes played out the same way—one of the fresh-faced hikers would get separated from the group. He would hear a noise in the bushes. "Bob? Jerry, is that you? Charlie?" Suddenly, from behind a tree, the stalker would pounce and blood would fly.

[3] Why the killer wore a blue kimono was never explained nor why he wanted these nice campers dead. He was a deranged monster and that's what monsters do. As the filmmaker, I was more interested in how the ketchup would drip off the victim's cheek and where to plunge the retractable knife. I was 12.

[4] The inspirations for this home movie (and the centerpieces of many Saturday night sleepovers) were slasher films like "Friday the 13th," "Halloween" and "Terror Train." My friends and I would eat junk food, drink soda and watch these cinematic bloodbaths until we dozed off, visions of gore and mayhem dancing in our heads.

[5] Even though we all came from religious families—my father was a minister—it was rarely questioned whether our adolescent minds should be exposed to this kind of gruesome material. And clearly, we were the intended audience. My parents never sat and watched, nor did my sister, for that matter. The movies were titillating, shocking and dumb—and we teenage boys thought they were so cool. We devoured them and they, in turn, juiced us up.

[6] After the horrific events at Virginia Tech, the relationship between violence in our movies and violence in our realities is being examined once again. Was Seung-Hui Cho inspired by a movie (the South Korean revenge flick "Oldboy") when he murdered 32 of his classmates and teachers? Was Mr. Cho a deranged predator in a horror film, or was he a lost kid who could have been reached?

[7] Hollywood and defenders of violent films dismiss Virginia Tech as a "unique" event, arguing that Mr. Cho was profoundly alienated from our culture, not at all a product of it. They assert that there are law-abiding, sane American moviegoers who love the thrill of a visual bloodletting, and then there are mentally disturbed people like Mr. Cho, constitutionally wired to do damage—and never the twain shall meet.

[8] These commentators insist there's no point debating which came first, the violent chicken or her violent representational egg,

since no causal link has ever been proven between egg and chicken anyway. Besides, violent images can be found everywhere—on the news, in great art and literature, even Shakespeare!

9 For those who believe that violence in cinema consists of either harmless action spectacles or Martin Scorsese masterpieces, I might suggest heading down to the local multiplex and taking a look at some of the grotesque, morbid creations being projected on the walls. To defend mindless exercises in sadism like "The Hills Have Eyes II" by citing "Macbeth" is almost like using "Romeo and Juliet" to justify child pornography.

10 The notion that "movies don't kill people, lunatics kill people" is liberating to us screenwriters because it permits us to give life to our most demented fantasies and put them up on the big screen without any anxious hand-wringing. We all know there's a lot of money to be made trafficking in blood and guts. Young males—the golden demographic movie-makers ceaselessly pursue—eat that gore up. What a relief to be told that how we earn that money may be in poor taste, but it's not irresponsible. The average American teenage boy knows the difference between right and wrong and no twisted, sadistic movie is going to influence him.

11 My own experience as a teenager tells me otherwise. For my friends and me, movies were a big influence on our clothes and our slang, and on how we thought about and spoke to authority figures, our girlfriends and one another. Movies permeated our fantasy lives and our real lives in subtle and profound ways.

12 It's true nobody ever got shot in the face in my backyard, but there were acts of male bravado performed in emulation of our movie anti-heroes that ranged from stupid to cruel. And there were plenty of places where guys my age were shooting one another all the time. There still are. Can we really in good conscience conclude that the violence saturating our popular culture has no impact on our neighborhoods and schools?

13 The calamity at Virginia Tech is unfortunately not as unique an event as we'd like to think, but the sheer number of victims has grabbed our attention and inspired some collective soul-searching. As responsible Americans put their heads down on their desks and reflect, should the scribes of popular entertainment be excused to the playground? We screenwriters may be overgrown teenagers who still want to be cool, but we aren't 12 years old anymore. Maybe we're not responsible for Mr. Cho's awful actions, but does that abrogate our responsibility to the world around us?

14 Most of us who chose careers in this field were seduced by cinema's spell at an early age. We know better than anyone the power films have to capture our imaginations, shape our thinking and inform our choices, for better and for worse. At the risk of being labeled a scold—the ultimate in uncool—I have to ask: before cashing those big checks, shouldn't we at least pause to consider what we are saying with our movies about the value of life and the pleasures of mayhem?

SUMMARIZE AND RESPOND

Write a 50-word summary of White's essay. Then, respond to the following quote: "Can we really in good conscience conclude that the violence saturating our popular culture has no impact on our neighborhoods and schools?"

Although essayist David Sedaris is widely recognized for his wit and his ability to weave funny tales from the fabric of everyday life, he often uses humor to broach serious and sometimes difficult subjects. In "Chicken in the Henhouse," from his 2004 collection Dress Your Family in Corduroy and Denim, *he explores the stereotypes, expectations, intolerance, and misguided cultural judgment often heaped on gay men in the wake of well-publicized molestation cases involving Catholic clergy.*

CHICKEN IN THE HENHOUSE

David Sedaris

[1] It was one of those hotels without room service, the type you wouldn't mind if you were paying your own bill but would complain about if someone else was paying. I was not paying my own bill, and so the deficiencies stuck out and were taken as evidence of my host's indifference. There was no tub, just a plastic shower stall, and the soap was brittle and smelled like dishwashing detergent. The bedside lamp was missing a bulb, but that could have been remedied easily enough. I could have asked for one at the front desk, but I didn't want a lightbulb. I just wanted to feel put-upon.

[2] It started when the airline lost my luggage. Time was lost filling out forms, and I'd had to go directly from the airport to a college an hour north of Manchester, where I gave a talk to a group of students. Then there was a reception and a forty-five-minute drive to the hotel, which was out in the middle of nowhere. I arrived at 1 a.m. and found they had booked me into a basement room. Late at night it didn't much matter, but in the morning it did. To open the curtains was to invite scrutiny, and the people of New Hampshire stared in without a hint of shame. There wasn't much to look at, just me, sitting on the edge of the bed with a phone to my ear. The airline had sworn my suitcase would arrive overnight, and when it didn't, I called the 800 number printed on the inside of my ticket jacket. My choices were either to speak to a machine or to wait for an available human. I chose the human, and after eight minutes on hold I hung up and started looking for someone to blame.

[3] "I don't care if it's my son, my congressman, what have you. I just don't approve of that lifestyle." The speaker was a woman named Audrey who'd called the

local talk-radio station to offer her opinion. The Catholic Church scandal had been front-page news for over a week, and when the priest angle had been exhausted, the discussion filtered down to pedophilia in general and then, homosexual pedophilia, which was commonly agreed to be the worst kind. It was, for talk radio, one of those easy topics, like tax hikes or mass murder. "What do you think of full-grown men practicing sodomy on children?"

4 "Well, I'm *against* it!" This was always said as if it was somehow startling, a minority position no one had yet dared lay claim to.

5 I'd been traveling around the country for the past ten days, and everywhere I went I heard the same thing. The host would congratulate the caller on his or her moral fortitude, and wanting to feel that approval again, the person would rephrase the original statement, freshening it up with an adverb or qualifier. "Call me old-fashioned, but I just hugely think it's wrong." Then, little by little, they'd begin interchanging the words *homosexual* and *pedophile*, speaking as if they were one and the same. "Now they've even got them on TV," Audrey said. "And in the schools! Talk about the proverbial chicken in the henhouse."

6 "Fox," the host said.

7 "Oh, they're the worst," Audrey said. "*The Simpsons* and such—I never watch that station."

8 "I meant in the henhouse," the host said. "I believe the saying is 'the fox in the henhouse,' not 'the chicken in the henhouse.'"

9 Audrey regrouped. "Did I say chicken? Well, you get my point. These homosexuals can't reproduce themselves, and so they go into the schools and try to recruit our young people."

10 It was nothing I hadn't heard before, but I was crankier than usual and found myself in the middle of the room, one sock on and one sock off, shouting at the clock radio.

"Nobody recruited *me*, Audrey. And I *begged* for it."

11 It was *her* fault I was stuck in a basement room with no luggage, her and all the people just like her: the satisfied families trotting from the parking lot to the first-floor restaurant, the hotel guests with whirlpool baths and rooms overlooking the surrounding forest. *Why waste the view on a homosexual? He only looks at schoolboys' rectums. And a suitcase? Please! We all know what they do with those.* They might not have come out and said it, but they were sure thinking it. I could tell.

12 It stood to reason that if the world was conspiring against me, my Mr. Coffee machine was broken. It sat on the bathroom counter, dribbling cold water, and after a brief, completely unsatisfying cry, I finished getting dressed and left the room. There was a staircase at the end of the hall, and beside it a little cleared area where a dozen or so elderly women knelt upon the carpet, piecing together a patchwork quilt. They looked up as I passed, one of them turning to ask me a question. "Yoin' shurch?" Her mouth was full of pins and it took me a moment to realize what she was saying—You going to church? It was an odd question, but then I remembered that it was a Sunday, and I was wearing a tie. Someone at the college had loaned it to me the night before, and I'd put it on in hopes it might distract from my shirt, which was wrinkled and discolored beneath the arms. "No," I told her, "I am *not* going to church." Oh, I was in a horrible mood. Midway up the stairs I stopped and turned back around. "I *never* go to church," I said. "Never. And I'm not about to start *now*."

13 "Shute shelf," she said.

14 Past the restaurant and gift shop, in the center of the lobby, was a complimentary beverage stand. I thought I'd get a coffee and take it outdoors, but just as I approached, a boy swooped in and began mixing himself a cup of hot chocolate.

He looked like all of the kids I'd been seeing lately, in airports, in parking lots: the oversize sweatshirts stamped with team emblems, the baggy jeans and jazzy sneakers. His watch was fat and plastic, like a yo-yo strapped to his wrist, and his hair looked as if it had been cut with the lid of a can, the irregular hanks stiffened with gel and coaxed to stand at peculiar angles.

[15] It was a complicated business, mixing a cup of hot chocolate. You had to spread the powdered cocoa from one end of the table to the other and use as many stirrers as possible, making sure to thoroughly chew the wetted ends before tossing them upon the stack of unused napkins. This is what I like about children: complete attention to one detail and complete disregard of another. When finally finished, he scooted over to the coffee urn, filling two cups, black, and fitting them with lids. The drinks were stacked into a tower, then tentatively lifted off the table. "Whoa," he whispered. Hot chocolate seeped from beneath the lid of the bottom cup and ran down his hand.

[16] "Do you need some help with those?" I asked.

[17] The boy looked at me for a moment. "Yeah," he said. "Carry these upstairs." There was no *please* or *thank you*, just "I'll take the hot chocolate myself."

[18] He set the coffees back on the table, and as I reached for them it occurred to me that maybe this was not such a good idea. I was a stranger, an admitted homosexual traveling through a small town, and he was, like, ten. And alone. The voice of reason whispered in my ear. *Don't do it, buster. You're playing with fire.*

[19] I withdrew my hands, then stopped, thinking, *Wait a minute. That's not reason. It's Audrey, that crackpot from the radio.* The real voice of reasons sounds like Bea Arthur, and when it failed to pipe up, I lifted the coffees off the table and carried them toward the elevator, where the boy stood mashing the call button with his chocolate-coated fingers.

[20] A maid passed and rolled her eyes at the desk clerk. "Cute kid."

[21] Before the church scandal I might have said the same thing, only without the sarcasm. Now, though, any such observation seemed suspect. Though Audrey would never believe it, I am not physically attracted to children. They're like animals to me, fun to watch but beyond the bounds of my sexual imagination. That said, I am a person who feels guilty for crimes I have not committed, or have not committed in years. The police search the train station for a serial rapist and I cover my face with a newspaper, wondering if maybe I did it in my sleep. The last thing I stole was an eight-track tape, but to this day I'm unable to enter a store without feeling like a shoplifter. It's all the anxiety with none of the free stuff. To make things just that much worse, I seem to have developed a remarkable perspiration problem. My conscience is crosswired with my sweat glands, but there's a short in the system and I break out over things I didn't do, which only makes me look more suspect. Innocently helping to lighten a child's burden was a *good* thing—I knew this—yet moments after lifting the coffees off the table I was soaking wet. As usual, the sweat was fiercest on my forehead, under my arms, and, cruelly, on my ass, which is a great mystery to me. If the stress is prolonged, I'll feel the droplets inching down the back of my legs, trapped, finally, by my socks, which are cotton and bought expressly for their absorbent powers.

[22] If there was a security camera in the lobby, this is what it would have shown: A four-and-a-half-foot-tall boy stands mashing and then pounding the elevator call button. Beside him is a man, maybe a foot taller, dressed in a shirt and tie and holding a lidded cup in each hand. Is it raining outside?

If not, perhaps he just stepped from the shower and threw on his clothes without drying himself. His eyes shift this way and that, giving the impression that he is searching for somebody. Could it be this silver-haired gentlemen? He's just walked up, looking very dapper in his tweed jacket and matching cap. He talks to the boy and lays a hand on the back of his head, scolding him probably, which is good, as somebody needed to. The other man, the wet one, is just standing there, holding the cups and trying to wipe his forehead with his sleeve at the same time. A lid pops off and something—it looks like coffee—spills down the front of his shirt. He leaps about, prancing almost, and pulls the fabric away from his skin. The boy seems angry now and says something. The older gentleman offers a handkerchief, and the man sets down one of his cups and runs—literally runs, panting—off camera, returning thirty seconds later with another lidded cup, a replacement. By this time the elevator has arrived. The gentleman holds open the door, and he and the boy wait as the man picks the other cup off the floor and joins them. Then the door closes, and they are gone.

23 "So, who have we got here?" the gentleman asked. His voice was jovial and enthusiastic. "What do you call yourself, big fella?"

24 "Michael," the boy said.

25 "Well, that's a grown-up name, isn't it."

26 Michael guessed that it was, and the man caught my eye and winked, the way people do when they're establishing a partnership. *We'll just put on the small fry, what do you say?* "I bet a big guy like you must have a lot of girlfriends," he said. "Is that true?"

27 "No."

28 "You *don't?* Well, what's the problem?

29 "I don't know. I just don't have one. That's all," Michael said.

30 I had always hated it when men asked the girlfriend question. Not only was it corny, but it set you in their imaginations in a way that seemed private to me. Answer yes and they'd picture your wee courtship: the candlelit dinner of hot dogs and potato chips, the rumpled Snoopy sheets. Answer no and you were blue-balled, the frustrated bachelor of the second grade. It was an idea of children as miniature adults, which was about as funny to me as a dog in sunglasses.

31 "Well, there must be *someone* you have your eye on."

32 The boy did not answer, but the man persisted in trying to draw him out. "Is Mommy sleeping in this morning?"

33 Again, nothing.

34 The man gave up and turned to me. "Your wife," he said. "I take it she's still in bed?"

35 He thought I was Michael's father, and I did not correct him. "Yes," I said. "She's upstairs. . .passed out." I don't know why I said this, or then again, maybe I do. The man had constructed a little family portrait, and there was a pleasure in defacing it. Here was Michael, here was Michael's dad, and now, here was Mom, lying face-down on the bathroom floor.

36 The elevator stopped on three, and the man tipped his hat. "All right, then," he said. "You two enjoy the rest of the morning." Michael had pressed the button for the fifth floor no less than twenty times, and now he gave it an extra few jabs just for good measure. We were alone now, and something unpleasant entered my mind.

37 Sometimes when I'm in a tight situation, I'll feel a need to touch somebody's head. It happens a lot on airplanes. I'll look at the person seated in front of me, and within a moment the idea will have grown from a possibility to a compulsion. There is no option—I simply have to do it. The easiest method is to make like I'm getting up, to grab the forward seat for support and just sort of pat the person's hair with my fingers. "Oh, I'm sorry," I say.

³⁸ "No problem."

³⁹ Most often I'll continue getting out of my seat, then walk to the back of the plane or go to the bathroom and stand there for a few minutes, trying to fight off what I know is inevitable: I need to touch the person's head again. Experience has taught me that you can do this three times before the head's owner either yells at you or rings for the flight attendant. "Is something wrong?" she'll ask.

⁴⁰ "I don't think so, no."

⁴¹ "What do you mean 'no,'" the passenger will say. "This freak keeps touching my head."

⁴² "Is that true, sir?"

⁴³ It's not always a head. Sometimes I need to touch a particular purse or briefcase. When I was a child this sort of compulsive behavior was my life, but now I practice it only if I'm in a situation where I can't smoke: planes—as I mentioned—and elevators.

⁴⁴ *Just touch the boy's head*, I thought. *The old man did it, so why can't you?*

⁴⁵ To remind myself that this is inappropriate only makes the voice more insistent. The thing must be done *because* it is inappropriate. If it weren't, there'd be no point in bothering with it.

⁴⁶ *He won't even notice it. Touch him now, quick.*

⁴⁷ Were we traveling a long distance, I would have lost the battle, but fortunately we weren't going far. The elevator arrived on the fifth floor and I scrambled out the door, set the coffees on the carpet, and lit a cigarette. "You're going to have to give me a minute here," I said.

⁴⁸ "But my room's just down the hall. And this is non-smoking."

⁴⁹ "I know, I know."

⁵⁰ "It's not good for you," he said.

⁵¹ "That's true for a lot of people," I told him. "But it *really is* good for me. Take my word for it."

⁵² He leaned against a door and removed the **DO NOT DISTURB** sign, studying it for a moment before sticking it in his back pocket.

⁵³ I only needed to smoke for a minute, but realized when I was finished that there was no ashtray. Beside the elevator was a window, but of course it was sealed shut. Hotels. They do everything in their power to make you want to jump to your death, and then they make certain that you can't do it. "Are you finished with your cocoa?" I asked.

⁵⁴ "No."

⁵⁵ "Well, are you finished with the lid?"

⁵⁶ "I guess so."

⁵⁷ He handed it to me and I spit into the center—no easy task, as my mouth was completely dry. Fifty percent of my body water was seeping out my ass, and the other half was in transit.

⁵⁸ "That's gross," he said.

⁵⁹ "Yeah, well you're just going to have to forgive me." I stubbed the cigarette into the spit, set the lid on the carpet, and picked up the coffees. "Okay, where to?"

⁶⁰ He pointed down a long corridor and I followed him, gnawing on a question that's been troubling me for years. What if you had a baby and you just . . . you just needed to touch it where you knew you shouldn't. I don't mean that you'd want to. You wouldn't *desire* the baby any more than you desire a person whose head you've just touched. The act would be compulsive rather than sexual, and while to you there'd be a big difference, you couldn't expect a prosecutor, much less an infant, to recognize it. You'd be a bad parent, and once the child could talk and you told it not to tell anyone, you would become a manipulator—a monster, basically—and the reason behind your actions would no longer matter.

⁶¹ The closer we got to the end of the hall, the more anxious I became. I had not laid a finger on the boy's head. I have never

poked or prodded either a baby or a child, so why did I feel so dirty? Part of it was just my makeup, the deep-seated belief that I deserve a basement room, but a larger, uglier part had to do with the voices I hear on talk radio, and my tendency, in spite of myself, to pay them heed. The man in the elevator had not thought twice about asking Michael personal questions or about laying a hand on the back of his head. Because he was neither a priest nor a homosexual, he hadn't felt the need to watch himself, worrying that every word or gesture might be misinterpreted. He could unthinkingly wander the halls with a strange boy, while for me it amounted to a political act—an insistence that I was as good as the next guy. Yes, I am a homosexual; yes, I am soaking wet; yes, I sometimes feel an urge to touch people's heads, but still I can safely see a ten-year-old back to his room. It bothered me that I needed to prove something this elementary. And prove it to people whom I could never hope to convince.

62 "This is it," Michael said. From the other side of the door I heard the sound of a television. It was one of those Sunday-morning magazine programs, a weekly hour where all news is good news. Blind Jimmy Henderson coaches a volleyball team. An ailing groundhog is fitted for a back brace. That type of thing. The boy inserted his card key into the slot, and the door opened onto a bright, well-furnished room. It was twice the size of mine, with higher ceilings and a sitting area. One window framed a view of the lake, and the other a stand of scarlet maples.

63 "Oh, you're back," a woman said. She was clearly the boy's mother, as their profiles were identical, the foreheads easing almost imperceptively into blunt freckled noses. Both too had spiky blond hair, though for her I imagined the style was accidental, the result of the pillows piled behind her head. She was lying beneath the covers of a canopy bed, examining one of the many brochures scattered across the comforter. A man slept beside her, and when she spoke, he shifted slightly and covered his face with the crook of his arm. "What took you so long?" She looked toward the open door, and her eyes widened as they met mine. "What the . . ."

64 There was a yellow robe at the foot of the bed, and the woman turned her back to me as she got up and stepped into it. Her son reached for the coffees, and I tightened my grip, unwilling to surrender what I'd come to think of as my props. They turned me from a stranger to a kindly stranger, and I'd seen myself holding them as his parents rounded on me, demanding to know what was going on.

65 "Give them to me," he said, and rather than making a scene, I relaxed my grip. The coffees were taken, and I felt my resolve starting to crumble. Empty-handed, I was just a creep, the spooky wet guy who'd crawled up from the basement. The woman crossed to the dresser, and as the door started to close she called out to me. "Hey," she said. "Wait a minute." I turned, ready to begin the fight of my life, and she stepped forward and pressed a dollar into my hand. "You people run a very nice hotel," she told me. "I just wish we could stay longer."

66 The door closed and I stood alone in the empty corridor, examining my tip and thinking, *Is that all?*

RESPOND

Write a paragraph or two that describes Sedaris' ethos. What qualities does he possess? What quirks does he want you to know about? Why do you think he wants to reveal his sometimes odd characteristics? How do these help him make his claim?

Notice the shift in perspective when Sedaris gets into the elevator to help the boy with the cups of coffee. What is the effect of this perspective shift, and why do you think Sedaris makes it? How does this lend itself to Sedaris' overall purpose?

DISCUSS

Why do you think Sedaris titled this piece "Chicken in the Henhouse"? Who is the chicken in the henhouse in this essay, and why? How is this significant given Sedaris' purpose in the essay?

ARGUE

Write a rhetorical analysis of "Chicken in the Henhouse" that focuses on how Sedaris uses the appeal to ethos. Of course, your analysis should include an account of what you take to be Sedaris' overall purpose and argument, and it should narrowly focus on the ways he uses the appeal to ethos to achieve this goal.

"My Amendment," by George Saunders, is a satire modeled after the greatest satirical work in the English language, Jonathan Swift's "A Modest Proposal." Like Swift, Saunders proposes a "solution" to a hotly debated issue—in Saunders' case, same-sex marriage. Saunders, who teaches creative writing at Syracuse University, has published two collections of stories, Pastoralia *and* CivilWarLand in Bad Decline, *and a children's story,* The Very Persistent Gappers of Frip. *This essay appeared in the March 8, 2004 edition of the* New Yorker.

MY AMENDMENT

George Saunders

[1] As an obscure, middle-aged, heterosexual short-story writer, I am often asked, George, do you have any feelings about Same-Sex Marriage?

[2] To which I answer, Actually, yes, I do.

[3] Like any sane person, I am against Same-Sex Marriage, and in favor of a constitutional amendment to ban it.

[4] To tell the truth, I feel that, in the interest of moral rigor, it is necessary for us to go a step further, which is why I would like to propose a supplementary constitutional amendment.

[5] In the town where I live, I have frequently observed a phenomenon I have come to think of as Samish-Sex Marriage. Take, for

example, K, a male friend of mine, of slight build, with a ponytail. K is married to S, a tall, stocky female with extremely short hair, almost a crewcut. Often, while watching K play with his own ponytail as S towers over him, I have wondered, Isn't it odd that this somewhat effeminate man should be married to this somewhat masculine woman? Is K not, on some level, imperfectly expressing a slight latent desire to be married to a man? And is not S, on some level, imperfectly expressing a slight latent desire to be married to a woman?

[6] Then I ask myself, Is this truly what God had in mind?

[7] Take the case of L, a female friend with a deep, booming voice. I have often found myself looking askance at her husband, H. Though H is basically pretty masculine, having neither a ponytail nor a tight feminine derriere like K, still I wonder: H, when you are having marital relations with L, and she calls out your name in that deep, booming, nearly male voice, and you continue having marital relations with her (i.e., you are not "turned off"), does this not imply that you, H, are, in fact, still "turned on"? And doesn't this indicate that, on some level, you, H, have a slight latent desire to make love to a man?

[8] Or consider the case of T, a male friend with an extremely small penis. (We attend the same gym.) He is married to O, an average-looking woman who knows how to fix cars. I wonder about O. How does she know so much about cars? Is she not, by tolerating this non-car-fixing, short-penised friend of mine, indicating that, on some level, she wouldn't mind being married to a woman, and is therefore, perhaps, a tiny bit functionally gay?

[9] And what about T? Doesn't the fact that T can stand there in the shower room at our gym, confidently towelling off his tiny unit, while O is at home changing their spark-plugs with alacrity, indicate that it is only a short stroll down a slippery slope before he is completely happy being the "girl" in their relationship, from which it is only a small fey hop down the same slope before T is happily married to another man, perhaps my car mechanic, a handsome Portuguese fellow I shall refer to as J?

[10] Because my feeling is, when God made man and woman He had something very specific in mind. It goes without saying that He did not want men marrying men, or women marrying women, but also what He did not want, in my view, was feminine men marrying masculine women.

[11] Which is why I developed my Manly Scale of Absolute Gender.

[12] Using my Scale, which assigns numerical values according to a set of masculine and feminine characteristics, it is now easy to determine how Manly a man is and how Fem a woman is, and therefore how close to a Samish-Sex Marriage a given marriage is.

[13] Here's how it works. Say we determine that a man is an 8 on the Manly Scale, with 10 being the most Manly of all and 0 basically a Neuter. And say we determine that his fiancee is a –6 on the Manly Scale, with a –10 being the most Fem of all. Calculating the difference between the man's rating and the woman's rating—the Gender Differential—we see that this proposed union is not, in fact, a Samish-Sex Marriage, which I have defined as "any marriage for which the Gender Differential is less than or equal to 10 points."

[14] Friends whom I have identified as being in Samish-Sex Marriages often ask me, George, given that we have scored poorly, what exactly would you have us do about it?

[15] Well, one solution I have proposed is divorce—divorce followed by remarriage to a more suitable partner. K, for example, could marry a voluptuous high-voiced N.F.L. cheerleader, who would more than offset his tight feminine derriere, while his ex-wife, S, might choose to become involved with a lumberjack with very large arms, thereby neutralizing her thick calves and faint mustache.

16 Another, and of course preferable, solution would be to repair the existing marriage, converting it from a Samish-Sex Marriage to a healthy Normal Marriage, by having the feminine man become more masculine and/or the masculine woman become more feminine.

17 Often, when I propose this, my friends become surly. How dare I, they ask. What business is it of mine? Do I think it is easy to change in such a profound way?

18 To which I say, It is not easy to change, but it is possible.

19 I know, because I have done it.

20 When young, I had a tendency to speak too quickly, while gesturing too much with my hands. Also, my opinions were unfirm. I was constantly contradicting myself in that fast voice, while gesturing like a girl. Also, I cried often. Things seemed so sad. I had long blond hair, and liked it. My hair was layered and fell down across my shoulders, and, I admit it, I would sometimes slow down when passing a shop window to look at it, to look at my hair! I had a strange constant feeling of being happy to be alive. This feeling of infinite possibility sometimes caused me to laugh when alone, or even, on occasion, to literally skip down the street, before pausing in front of a shop window and giving my beautiful hair a cavalier toss.

21 To tell the truth, I do not think I would have scored very high on my Manly Scale, if the Scale had been invented at that time, by me. I suspect I would have scored so Fem on the test that I would have been prohibited from marrying my wife, P, the love of my life. And I think, somewhere in my heart, I knew that.

22 I knew I was too Fem.

23 So what did I do about it? Did I complain? Did I whine? Did I expect activist judges to step in on my behalf, manipulating the system to accommodate my peculiarity?

24 No, I did not.

25 What I did was I changed. I undertook what I like to think of as a classic American project of self-improvement. I made videos of myself talking, and studied these, and in time succeeded in training myself to speak more slowly, while almost never moving my hands. Now, if you ever meet me, you will observe that I always speak in an extremely slow and manly and almost painfully deliberate way, with my hands either driven deep into my pockets or held stock-still at the ends of my arms, which are bent slightly at the elbows, as if I were ready to respond to the slightest provocation by punching you in the face. As for my opinions, they are very firm. I rarely change them. When I feel like skipping, I absolutely do not skip. As for my long beautiful hair—well, I am lucky, in that I am rapidly going bald. Every month, when I recalculate my ranking on the Manly Scale, I find myself becoming more and more Manly, as my hair gets thinner and my girth increases, thickening my once lithe, almost girlish physique, thus insuring the continuing morality and legality of my marriage to P.

26 My point is simply this: If I was able to effect these tremendous positive changes in my life, to avoid finding myself in the moral/legal quagmire of a Samish-Sex Marriage, why can't K, S, L, H, T, and O do the same?

27 I implore any of my readers who find themselves in a Samish-Sex Marriage: Change. If you are a feminine man, become more manly. If you are a masculine woman, become more feminine. If you are a woman and are thick-necked or lumbering, or have ever had the slightest feeling of attraction to a man who is somewhat pale and fey, deny these feelings and, in a spirit of self-correction, try to become more thin-necked and light-footed, while, if you find it helpful, watching videos of naked masculine men, to sort of retrain yourself in the proper mode of attraction. If you are a man and, upon seeing a thick-waisted, athletic young woman walking with a quasi-mannish gait through

your local grocery, you imagine yourself in a passionate embrace with her, in your car, a car that is parked just outside, and which is suddenly, in your imagination, full of the smell of her fresh young breath—well, stop thinking that! Are you a man or not?

28 I, for one, am sick and tired of this creeping national tendency to let certain types of people take advantage of our national good nature by marrying individuals who are essentially of their own gender. If this trend continues, before long our towns and cities will be full of people like K, S, L, H, T, and O, people "asserting their rights" by dating, falling in love with, marrying, and spending the rest of their lives with whomever they please.

29 I, for one, am not about to stand by and let that happen.

30 Because then what will we have? A nation ruled by the anarchy of unconstrained desire. A nation of willful human hearts, each lurching this way and that and reaching out for whatever it spontaneously desires, trying desperately to find some comforting temporary shred of warmth in a mostly cold world, totally unconcerned about the external form in which that other, long-desired heart is embodied.

31 That is not the kind of world in which I wish to live.

32 I, for one, intend to become ever more firmly male, enjoying my golden years, while watching P become ever more female, each of us vigilant for any hint of ambiguity in the other.

33 And as our children grow, should they begin to show the slightest hint of some lingering residue of the opposite gender, P and I will lovingly pull them aside and list all the particulars by which we were able to identify their unintentional deficiency.

34 Then, together, we will devise a suitable correction.

35 And, in this way, the race will go on.

RESPOND

How does Saunders define "Samish-Sex Marriage"? How does he use the term in his argument?

ANALYZE

Many satirists rely on tone, among other literary elements, to help convey their purpose. How would you characterize Saunders' tone? Point to some examples in the essay to show how he establishes his tone.

DISCUSS

In the third paragraph of his essay, Saunders writes, "Like any sane person, I am against Same-Sex Marriage, and in favor of a constitutional amendment to ban it." Do you believe him? In explaining your answer, point to specific passages in his text to support your position.

ARGUE

Write a satirical response to Saunders' proposal. Remember: You'll really be arguing *for* a same-sex marriage ban, but you should seem like you're arguing *against* it.

In a note companying this essay when it first appeared March 11, 2007 in the Washington Post, *Belén Aranda Alvarado described herself as "a brunette marketing manager in New York City, where she lives with her daughter, Natalia—also a brunette." As you read her essay, pay attention to how Alvarado connects with her audience and advances her argument.*

FADE TO BLONDE

As an experiment in ethnic identity, a proud, political Latina reaches for the bleach.

Belén Aranda Alvarado

[1] When I think of the space where Latinas and blondness meet, I always remember Iris, a Puerto Rican classmate from my days at Columbia University. Iris was one of those women whom men generally like and women generally don't. She was more comfortable with playful banter than serious exchanges, and it was rumored she liked flirting with other women's boyfriends. But to many of the other Latinas in our class— at least those newly politicized and hyper ethnically aware, like me—she was guilty of larger crimes. Iris once infamously represented the Puerto Rican student group by offering free salsa lessons while wearing a white ruffled peasant blouse, hoop earrings and bright red lipstick. She never disguised her love of traditional, totally un-PC frat parties, the kind where they played AC/DC's "You Shook Me All Night Long" to pack the dance floor. And she dyed her hair blond. An orange-y, brassy blond.

[2] At the time, my biggest desire was to make my light-skinned Chilean self look as identifiably Latina as possible. Saddled with a hair texture that was, at best, ethnically ambiguous and, at worst, simply wavy, I coveted Iris's naturally tight, corkscrew curls. It was the kind of mane I would've described as "Jewish hair" when I was still going to high school in Rockville, but now it seemed to be Caribbean-beauty perfection. Iris's decision to color it was unfathomable, a sure sign of succumbing to mainstream "white is right; blond is better" beauty standards. It couldn't have puzzled me more if she'd slapped on some blue contact lenses and asked us to call her Madison. Didn't she love her brown self?

[3] I solved my own hair dilemma by visiting the JC Penney salon while on a trip home and getting the chunky white girl behind the counter to give me a spiral perm. She botched it enough that I got my money returned, but, to my elation, people back at school let me know that they thought this—my botched perm—was my true hair. They assumed I'd been blowing it straight until then. Joy! My ethnic identity unmistakably announced.

[4] After our 1995 graduation, more than 10 years would pass until I would see Iris again. It would be at a reception hosted by Columbia's Latino alumni group, and, in the weeks before, I would think of Iris frequently. She would show up brunette. But there would be another blonde in attendance—me.

[5] A few weeks before the reception, I was asked to go blond for this article. The editor

FIGURE 11-2

In her essay "Fade to Blonde," Belén Aranda Alvarado cites a study showing that, "given a choice of hair color, most men making more than $75,000 a year would pick blond partners." How does Alvarado use this and other research about hair color and standards of beauty to advance her argument? How does she blend this data with her own story? In explaining her "experiment," Alvarado wonders if she can be "a righteous, fierce, representin' Latina, and yet go blond." Does she succeed?

was looking for someone politically aware and proud of her Latina looks. I literally wrote the book on Latina beauty. (Really. It's on Amazon.com.) What's more, I just happened to have already marked on my calendar a perfect testing ground for this change-of-tresses: the reunion, where friends would be receiving awards for going on hunger strikes and taking over buildings to persuade the university to add a Latino studies major. Imagine the escandalo when I walked in blond.

⁶ My former classmates, I imagined, would think I'd done it for the usual reason: to snag a little of the love our society ladles on blondes. Consider a study cited in the *Chronicle of Philanthropy* last year: When the researchers sent a bunch of undergrads out collecting donations door-to-door, pretty girls unsurprisingly brought in the most money—but blondes far out-raised equally fly-looking brunettes. Yet another study related that, given a choice of hair color, most men making more than $75,000 a year would pick blond partners. A scientific article by a McGill University anthropologist posited that the reason there are so many flaxen-haired Europeans may be that during the Ice Age, when successful male

hunters were in short supply, women with eye-catching blond hair had a mating-game advantage over their darker peers.

[7] Latinos come in all colors, but our standard mix of European, African and indigenous heritage means that naturally golden hair, while it does occur, is rare. So any bonus blondness brings is beyond pretty much the whole ethnic group—which, on some level, feels unfair and infuriating. No wonder so many of us turn to chemicals: Across the board, Latinas buy more hair care products—including dyes and the attendant deep-conditioning treatments—than women in any other ethnic group. And no wonder the Latinas who equate going blond with changing your name from María to Mary disdain their frosting cap-, highlighting brush-wielding sisters.

[8] I'm aware of all this. And I love being Latina: I'm convinced that, at some point or another, everyone who isn't part of our cool cultural hybrid secretly wishes they could be. But 10 years past college, I craved another sort of privilege: that of unburdened whimsy. If white women can change their hair color the way they change their lipstick—with complete impunity and no worries over "correctly" representing their community—why couldn't I? Even women's studies majors now march on Washington in tight pink baby-tees that scream, "This is what a feminist looks like!" So had enough time gone by that I could be a righteous, fierce, representin' Latina, and yet go blond?

[9] I told the editor I'd do it.

[10] As soon as I got off the phone, I went out and bought the beauty bible for Latinas on the lightening path: *Us Weekly*, the supermarket rag that regularly features photo after photo of dyed and highlighted Latina celebs. Jessica Alba, Jennifer Lopez, Shakira, Eva Mendes—they're all there, having gotten lighter-haired as their stars rose. (Cameron Diaz is claiming she's going to stick to her new brown locks, but I suspect it's a post-breakup dye job—meant to shock, not to stay.) In the issue I bought, practically the only Latina celeb missing was beautiful, intelligent, raven-tressed Salma Hayek. I love Salma. I bet she'd kill in a big-budget superhero flick (like Jessica) or as the girlfriend to corrupt cop Denzel Washington (like Eva). But instead she seems—to me at least—to be one of the most underappreciated Latina actresses out there. Why don't we see her more? I wasn't even sure what new movie Jessica Alba was in, but there she was full-page in another tabloid, getting her nails done at a charity event. Maybe if Salma got highlights . . .

[11] I called various salons in town and started getting an education in the economics of blondness. While the women's magazines I read as a teen promised easy blond streaks via lemon juice, the truth is that taking hair from jet black (that's me) to something approximating blond requires many chemicals, many salon hours and many dollars. The cheapie drugstore, do-it-yourself route isn't available, as the chemicals needed to strip dark hair of its pigment aren't legally sold to anyone without a beautician's license. (And with good reason. The smell alone is enough to cause tears.) Salons around town gave me preliminary estimates starting from $250 to $500—emphasizing that the bill was liable to grow once the stylists actually got a look at my hair. And that was without the expensive conditioning shampoos and weekly deep-conditioning treatments I'd need afterward, to prevent my ends from splitting, frizzing and breaking off completely.

[12] I decided that I'd go to a Dominican-owned salon I'd seen close to my home in Wheaton. A Latina hairdresser, I reasoned, would have experience taking a client with chemically relaxed hair like mine from one end of the color spectrum to the other. And the salon would do it for the bargain-basement $250—all *The Washington Post* was willing to spend.

13 It took not one, but two days of six-hour sessions to get to a passably blond hair color. At the end of the first, I left thinking I looked strawberry blond. At home, my neighbor set me straight: My hair was actually Irish-jig red. I could have auditioned for "The Lord of the Dance." After much on-the-phone complaining—and then begging—with my stylist ("You were happy with it when you left," she kept saying, impatiently, in Spanish), she took me in for another session, gratis, to add blond highlights. And that, she told me, was as blond as I was going to get. My hair certainly didn't look God-given, but at least it could reasonably be described as blond.

14 When I got home, my sister, her boyfriend, my neighbor and my boyfriend gathered around. The unanimous verdict: a thumbs-up. Only one person registered disapproval: my 5-year-old daughter, Natalia. "Mami, you painted your hair," she said, running her hands over my tresses. "Your hair is dark like mine."

15 I've always been the culturally conscious parent, making sure she had plenty of "Dora the Explorer" DVDs to offset the glossy, blond perfection of Cinderella, Sleeping Beauty, Barbie and countless other mermaids and fairies. But in my rush to seize my blond moment, it hadn't occurred to me that my daughter might connect my change to her own stunning, raven hair. I'd be going back to my real hair color soon, I told myself.

16 In her book Blonde Like Me, author Natalia Ilyin describes the blond effect as "a gentle rise in the tidewaters of public friendliness." In her brightest moments, the blond Ilyin reports, she was the recipient of impulsive marriage proposals and the cause of minor traffic accidents; at times she felt like "power and sex personified"—exactly as I'd always thought blond life would be.

17 My expectations for myself were more modest. A compliment—or a drink?—from a stranger. Salesclerks with suddenly improved attitudes. A heightened interest in what I had to say.

18 In the first few days, my new hair color definitely gave me a little buzz. At brunch, my family suggested that it flattered my skin tone, maybe even more than my natural color did. And my boyfriend's growled comment, "You look gooood," had me feelin' frisky. We were both getting a nice boost from my frosted tresses.

19 But there were unexpected bumps along the way. The day after my initial salon visit, my reflection caught me by surprise as I came out of a bathroom stall. What I saw in that unself-conscious moment: bland, blah, like-everybody-else-ness. I'm light-skinned, with what can be described as Caucasian features. To many people—Latinos and Anglos alike—I don't "look Latina." Until that moment, I'd had no idea that I wielded my black hair in the same way that I use the accent in my first name and my long, vowel-ending hyper-ethnic last name: as a banner, letting people know in no uncertain terms "Sí, soy Latina!" Without it, I felt erased.

20 Entire books have been written about blondness. Ilyin's made the biggest impression, because there I found a perfect description of my motivations: I was what Ilyin calls an "ironic blond," someone making a statement with an overt appropriation of a style not originally intended for her. Think Madonna, Li'l Kim or RuPaul, who, when questioned about the politics of his wigs, said, "I'm not going to pass as white, and I'm not trying to . . . [but] I want to create outrageous sensation, and blond hair against brown skin is a gorgeous, outrageous combination."

21 Gorgeous outrageousness was also what I was after, especially as I prepared to attend the Latino alumni reception at my alma mater. Imagining gasps and looks of horror, I planned ahead, getting a spray

tan and even considering (briefly) wearing the blue contact lenses that would create a perfect fake hair/fake eyes/fake tan triumvirate of wildly inappropriate personal grooming choices for a politically correct college-educated Latina. Oh, the whispers, the stares, the scandal!

22 But when I arrived at the dinner and met friends I hadn't seen in years, they embraced me and said... "Hi." I felt the need to explain my experiment, but if the women said anything about my hair, it was that they really liked it. That threw me off. They weren't supposed to actually like me as a blonde, much less tell me I looked better. I waited expectantly for the reaction from one friend in particular, Jenny. An architect of the hunger-strike-building-takeover-sparking-massive-national-media-attention endeavor, she was Puerto Rican, worked for a nonprofit and lived in a predominantly Latino section of town. In other words, homegirl was down. When she saw me she said, "Oh, you changed your hair." I complimented her on her 'do, and I'm pretty sure that after that we went and got a drink from the open bar. Nothing else. Nada.

23 There was only one friend, a black woman, who told me she thought I looked "less Latina." On a black or darker-skinned Latina woman, she said, blond was okay; they'd never be mistaken for either being white or wanting to look as if they were. But on me, with my fair skin and straight hair, it was too close to "passing" for her comfort. The closest I can get to blond-on-brown outrageousness is to get a fake tan. But no one would think I was embarking on a subversive beauty experiment. They'd just assume I was trying to get a job at Hooters.

24 Iris was now a brunette working for the Cleveland port authority. She'd attended this Latino alumni event every year since its inception, she said, flying in from Ohio for the weekend. She seemed amused that I remembered her as a blonde.

25 "It was such a short time in my life," she told me later. She said there'd been a price to pay for the color change at the time. From Latinos of both genders, she said, "the reaction was, 'You're too whitewashed.'" But it had been worth it. The change had allowed her to step out of the stereotyped role of the submissive Latina. "It was like Mariah with Mimi, like Madonna with Dita," she said. "I felt like I was a different character, more free, more daring."

26 Who knew? Iris had been an ironic blonde, too.

27 According to Iris, Latino men had been particularly disapproving of her change. I'd had a different experience. About a week before, on a weekday afternoon, a guy probably 10 years younger than I had sidled up as I was waiting to cross a street and said: "Hey, ma, you look good! You got a man?" At the time, I was pushing my sleeping daughter in her stroller—a scenario that, in my experience, deters most men. But not this guy. He even worked her into his whole approach: "She yours?" he asked. "Aw, she beautiful just like you." Either he was really, really hard up, I'd thought, or the blond hair really was working a mojo of some kind.

28 But the men at the Latino reunion—the same Ivy Leaguers who had known Iris years before—ignored my blondness completely. Forget any ramped-up flirtatiousness, it was hard getting them to talk to me at all. When I finally approached one and asked point-blank, "Do you notice anything different about me?" he got such a panicked look on his face that I thought maybe, by accident, I'd asked him if I looked fat. "You changed your hair. It's what women do," he practically wailed.

29 A few weeks later, Jenny and I had brunch, and I broached the topic of blondness again. "I only heard from someone

else later that you were doing it for an article, and I have to say I was relieved," she told me. A-ha! Here it was: the "What were you thinking?" discussion, the outrage at a hegemonic white-dominant concept of beauty that left all non-blondes to feel marginalized. Heated debate! Emotional exchanges!

30 "I think it was the wrong tone of blond, and I think that is a mistake a lot of Latina women make," she explained. "I've been thinking about going blond, too, and I wanted to figure out how to get the right blond, instead of that orangy blond so many of us get that I just think looks so tacky."

31 Afterward, I e-mailed around to see how many of the women I'd seen or talked to since changing my hair color shared Jenny's caveat. A number of them e-mailed back in the affirmative. Going blond was fine, but the wrong shade? Eeewww. So we can be upper-crusty Bergdorf blondes, but not drugstore blondes?

32 Apparently so.

33 There had been a time, in the early, giddy days of my blondness, when I'd considered keeping the new color, at least for a while. *The Post* had promised to take me back to my natural black, but maybe, I'd thought, it could be persuaded to pay for a touch-up instead? In the name of research? Now, despite tons of conditioner, my hair looked dried, frizzy and beat. I'd tried re-dyeing my eyebrows myself, to match my tresses, and that looked terrible, too. It's not that I didn't want the kind of hair my friends were saying was "the right kind" of blond. I just didn't have the money. And it wasn't worth it to spend any of my own funds on coloring.

34 If the experiment had ended there, it might have left me with the impression that all you need for politically liberated, whimsy-inspired blondness is fistfuls of cash. But then came the wedding.

35 A Latina friend was getting married. The reception was held in a funky loft space, and I was full of the pleasure of attending—until I found my table. There, accompanied by her preternaturally tan, distractingly handsome Latino boyfriend and sporting both a short aqua mini-dress and a head of perfect, white-gold hair, sat my doppelganger, another dyed Latina. She was talking—no joke—about vacationing in St. Barth's. Far from the only rubia at the party—there's a saying that Latinas don't go gray, we go blond, and the older generation at this shindig bore that out—she was the only one who rankled me.

36 With astonishing quickness, I made a series of decisions about who she was. I decided that if I settled down next to her and asked her how she kept her double-processed ends from splitting or what conditioner she used, she'd probably whip out a much-handled photo of a blond baby, swear it was her and insist that she was "simply going back to nature." She probably tries to live her life as a real blonde, I thought. And gets away with it, too. Because she probably has the money and time that can give anyone a swinging, shiny Pantene ad head of hair. She wasn't an ironic blonde like me.

37 I ended up leaving the wedding early. On the way home, though, a thought struck me. About a week before, I'd been on the phone with one of my Latino friends from business school, and told him I'd gone blond. "Then you can get a job at Sin City," he joked, referring to a local strip club frequented by young, working-class Latinos. We had both laughed. Being compared to a stripper hadn't bothered me—there's something so unapologetic and edgy about the stereotypical stripper look. But the idea of being confused with a blonde who might be trying to pass was horrifying. The problematic blonde, for me, was the woman at my table, who, despite my own complicated feelings about being blond,

I immediately assumed was trying to hide her ethnicity. But then, where did that leave the bleached-blond Latina? If your hair is "not the right tone," then you're tacky, cheap, orange. And irony, as Iris's experience showed, is no protection. But if your privilege—both of skin color and of wallet—allows you to execute the transformation too well, you're trying to pass?

[38] Damned if you do; damned if you don't.

[39] After the wedding incident, it was all work and no fun, as my poor locks strained under too many chemical processes. I wasn't sure I'd really gotten to the bottom of the blond conundrum, but I knew I'd had enough. A second wedding gave me just the push I needed to go back to brunette. My roots had long been showing, as my boyfriend himself had pointed out. The blond hair had to go.

[40] I did what many a Latina has done in moments like this: I called my cousin. As a real-life hairdresser, she's subjected herself to various hair color incarnations. When she came to save me with a color rinse and shag haircut, she herself was sporting a tongue-in-cheek platinum mullet with deep purple on the sides. "You'd better really be ready to go back to being brunette," she scolded me. She said she'd had too many clients come in claiming to want some change, only to end up crying in her stylist's chair. "These women," she sighed, shaking her head. "In the end, they just can't handle it."

[41] And there it was. I, in fact, do have a deep connection with her customers, Latina and non-Latina alike. I didn't like this change. The change in status from being more Obviously Hispanic to Ethnically Ambiguous, at best. The misinterpreted intentions. It was all too stressful.

[42] I'll stay brown and proud, *muchas gracias*.

[43] Though I'd still love to try those blue contact lenses . . .

SUMMARIZE AND RESPOND

In a paragraph or two, define what Belén Aranda-Alvarado means by "ironic blonde." How does this category of blondeness play into her overall claim about cultural identity?

ANALYZE

Not all instances of humor are of the "laugh out loud" variety, and in her piece, Aranda-Alvarado's opts for a more subtle approach for amusing her audience. What elements of humor can you identify here? Look for the humorous phrases, anecdotes, and imagery she provides for us and describe them. How do these examples lend themselves to her overall claim?

DISCUSS

Alvarado writes, "If white women can change their hair color the way they change their lipstick—with complete impunity and no worries over 'correctly' representing their community—why couldn't I?" Based on your reading of the essay, what is Alvarado's point here? How does she reconcile the dilemma she presents?

Using the narrative of a developing relationship as a framework, novelist Kim McLarin explains in the following essay why she feels compelled to "engage with race." She wrote this piece for the September 3, 2006 edition of the New York Times.

RACE WASN'T AN ISSUE TO HIM, WHICH WAS AN ISSUE TO ME

Kim McLarin

[1] His name was Jerry. A nice man, late 40's, funny and smart, divorced with two grown children, a social worker who had dedicated his professional life to working with troubled kids.

[2] He was also—let's be honest—the first to come around. He was the first man after my own divorce to raise an eyebrow, to take an interest after my ex not only moved out but moved on. Funny and smart and dedicated to troubled kids is all admirable, but in truth I would have said yes to a drink with a four-foot gap-toothed troll had one smiled my direction. The self-confidence of a 40-year-old divorced mother of two is a shaggy thing.

[3] So the fact that Jerry was also white I noted but decided to file away for now. Why worry about it right out of the gate? Yes, race had been an issue in my marriage—not *the* issue perhaps, but an issue nonetheless. What I did not know was whether race arose as a problem because I am black and my ex is white or because I am a person who grapples with race and he is not.

[4] That my ex does not grapple with race he would not dispute; he does not care to read, think or talk about it, and he wondered why I did. My ex believed I always went looking for race, but I didn't; race came looking for me.

[5] And when it did, I would stand and call its name: when officials in our inner-ring suburb talked about closing our "borders" against a wave of nonresident students sneaking into our schools; when a white woman at my gym reached up, uninvited, and petted my locks like she was petting a dog; when my sick mother received one level of medical care and my ex's sick sister received another. At such times he tried to understand my feelings, but he did not share them, and even talking about it made him uncomfortable.

[6] It's a dividing line as real as any in America—those who grapple with race and those who do not. But like most dividing lines, it's impossible to tell on which side a person stands by looking at them, or at least that's what I thought at the time. So why get ahead of myself with Jerry? Why dig for land mines when I may not make it past the way he slurps his beer?

[7] We met for drinks. Sparkwise, I felt little, but we ended up talking and laughing easily for more than an hour. I told him I was a writer; he told me his five favorite books and how they had shaped his life. He told me he had gone to a seminary as a boy but eventually left the Catholic church; I told him I'd been raised a Pentecostal but mellowed into Methodism as an adult. We talked about our children, travels, mutual love of the blues and mutual dislike of the cold, and then he said he would like to read my books; he thought he would like them. I said he well might not.

8 "How do you deal with it when people you know don't like your work?" he asked.

9 I quoted a playwright whose name I could not remember who admitted in an interview that he told his friends if there was a choice between being honest and being kind in talking about his work, they should choose to be kind. "Don't value your opinion over my feelings," the playwright said.

10 Jerry nodded. "Some people use honesty like a weapon."

11 "Like a switchblade," I said. "Like a bayonet. They slice up your heart with all these ugly, hurtful words and then, while you're bleeding on the floor, they hand you a Band-Aid: 'I was only being honest.'"

12 "Honesty is overrated," Jerry agreed.

13 So the following day, when he e-mailed his attraction, I tried to be both honest and kind. No spark, I wrote, but he was great, good company. If he was looking for "the one," I was probably not going to be her. But if he simply sought intelligent dinner companionship some Friday evening, I'd be more than game.

14 Not a bayonet, I thought, but a butter knife. And still it hurt.

15 "Ouch," he replied, and disappeared.

16 By the time he resurfaced a few months later, I had suffered through two terrible blind dates, joined an online dating service, carried on several e-mail conversations that died, actually talked on the phone with a few men, met three for drinks, backed away carefully from each, then canceled the service.

17 A few of these men were black, the others white, and in no case did I find anything remotely resembling chemistry. In fact, so utterly lacking in connection were these encounters that it made me appreciate anew how rare is connection. In the face of human isolation, race seemed to retreat a little.

18 So when Jerry called again, I decided to let the spark thing coast, because at least he and I could talk. "My wounds are licked," Jerry said. "Have dinner with me."

19 "Why not," I said. Maybe, in time, the spark would come.

20 We talked and laughed for four hours, then necked like teenagers in the parking lot in the rain. The next day we e-mailed and text-messaged each other. It was all so much fun, such a heady relief after the months of loneliness.

21 But then, on our third date, things changed. First, he was late and I was irritable. Earlier, I'd had a frustrating discussion with several white undergraduates in my Literature of Slavery class. All semester I had struggled to teach them to think critically about race and slavery and history, to have them challenge their assumptions. They insisted, for example, that racial divisions were as old as time and that the myth of African inferiority preceded slavery, not, as I suggested, the other way around. And they argued that racial genetics were more than skin deep, whether I wanted to believe it or not. How else to account for the way black athletes dominate some professional sports?

22 That evening, when I shared my frustrations with Jerry, he wondered if the students didn't have a point. "What about all those Kenyan marathon runners?" he asked. "Isn't it possible there's some genetic reason for that? Isn't it possible blacks are just better athletes than whites?"

23 A perfectly innocent question. Yet something small and painful flickered inside my chest. Logically, if one accepts a genetic physical superiority of blacks, one must also accept the possibility of intellectual superiority in whites. Did he not consider that notion? Did he reject it out of hand, or subconsciously believe it? And if I wondered these things aloud would he, like my ex, judge me bitter or oversensitive?

24 I mentioned an essay I'd given my students in which the anti-racism advocate

Tim Wise suggests that no one brought up in America can claim to be free of racist indoctrination, that doing so only perpetuates the crime. "What Wise says is that we all must recognize and confront the legacy of the past," I explained.

25 "I don't think everyone is racist," Jerry said. "Maybe racialized. But that's not a bad thing."

26 By now my hands were trembling, so I did not ask what he meant by that. I had the feeling that even if he tried to explain I would not understand. James Baldwin said being black in America is like walking around with a pebble in your shoe. Sometimes it scarcely registers and sometimes it shifts and becomes uncomfortable and sometimes it can even serve as a kind of Buddhist mindfulness bell, keeping you present, making you pay attention.

27 This is why, among other reasons, I engage with race, but not all black people do. I know several interracial couples in which both people swear race is never an issue, almost never comes up at all. I believe them, but it amazes me. And I know one thing: I can never join that pack.

28 My ex did not grapple with race, at first because he did not have to, being a white man in America, and later because it frightened him. This difference was a small but steady river that ran between us, and the more he tried to ignore it the more I clawed at the banks, and the more I clawed at the banks the larger the river swelled until, at last, we were engulfed. A black person who grapples with race cannot be with a white person who doesn't. Whether a black person who grapples with race can be with a black person who doesn't is a different and unresolved question for me, but on the first point I'm solid.

29 So when Jerry called and asked if I would meet him for a drink, I agreed, but this time I went only to tell him. We met a bar with billiard tables. He wanted to teach me to play but I said we wouldn't have time.

30 "I can't see you again," I said.

31 He blinked with surprise. "Why?" he said, finally.

32 I used my bayonet: "Because you're white, and it costs too much for me to date a white man. It cost me to be married to a white man for 13 years. I can't do it again."

33 "That's ridiculous," he said, after a minute. "That's the most ridiculous thing I've ever heard."

34 "Which proves my point," I said. "It's not ridiculous."

35 "You can't be with any white man?"

36 "No, I don't think I can."

37 I may as well face it. Because, after all, Jerry was a good man who worked with troubled kids and lived his life open to relationships with people of different races. And yet I couldn't be with him, even though, unlike my ex, he did seem willing to grapple with race.

38 But he was nearly 50 and his grappling apparently was just beginning, whereas mine started at 5. For nearly 50 years he'd lived in America and yet it surprised him that race might even be an issue for us. There was an innocence in this, an innocence born of being white. An innocence I could neither share nor abide.

39 "It costs me too much," I repeated.

40 We were silent for a minute. Behind us balls clicked and people laughed.

41 "And now," Jerry said, "it's costing me."

SUMMARIZE AND RESPOND

Write a 100-word summary of McLarin's essay, taking care to portray her central argument accurately. Then, respond to the following quote from the author: "A black person who grapples with race cannot be with a white person who doesn't."

Using evidence from her piece to support your response, explain how you think McLarin wants to be perceived by her audience. Do you think she succeeds?

Compare McLarin's argument with the one made by Justin Britt-Gibson in "What's Wrong with This Picture?" (in Chapter 9). Whose position do you find to be most like your own? Why?

In the following essay, Washington Post *writer Joel Achenbach presents a humorous argument for limiting the use of the F-word so that its raw obscenity and shock value remain intact. His piece appeared in the June 25, 2006 edition of the* Post.

DROPPING THE F-BOMB

Joel Achenbach

[1] The most versatile word in our language can do almost anything, other than be printed in a family newspaper. It can be a noun, a verb, a gerund, an adjective or just an expletive. It can be literal or figurative. Although it has an explicit sexual meaning, it's usually used figuratively these days, as an all-purpose intensifier.

[2] The F-word remains taboo. But just barely. We may be entering an era in which this fabled vulgarity is on its way to becoming just another word—its transgressive energy steadily sapped by overuse.

[3] From hip-hop artists to bloggers to the vice president of the United States, everyone's dropping the F-bomb. Young people in particular may not grasp how special this word has been in the past. They may not realize how, like an old sourdough starter, the word has been lovingly preserved over the centuries and passed from generation to generation. For the good of human communication we must come together, as a people, to protect this word, and ensure that, years from now, it remains obscene.

[4] Our leaders aren't helping. Before he was elected president, George W. Bush used the word repeatedly during an interview with Tucker Carlson. Dick Cheney on the Senate floor told a Democratic senator to *eff* himself. Presidential candidate John F. Kerry said of Bush and the war, "Did I expect George Bush to [mess] it up as badly as he did? I don't think anybody did." No one is shocked that these people use such language, but as statesmanship it's not exactly Lincolnesque.

[5] More generally, the word is imperiled by the profusion of communications technologies. Everyone's talking, e-mailing, blogging and commenting on everyone else's comments. Combine that with partisan rancor and a general desperation to get one's message across, and naturally the

word gets overtaxed. In Blogworld there are no idiots anymore, only [blithering] idiots. The most opportunistic move in the corporate realm may have been the decision by a retailer to call itself French Connection United Kingdom, which allowed it to put the company's initials on T-shirts everywhere. Jeepers, that's clever!

6 I don't want to make a federal case out of all of this—but that's what the government is doing. The Federal Communications Commission in recent years has cracked down on "indecency" in general and this word specifically. The FCC's fines for indecency have risen steadily: a mere $4,000 in 1995, then $48,000 in 2000, then $440,000 in 2003 and finally a whopping $7.9 million in 2004. President Bush signed a bill last week increasing by tenfold the maximum fine for indecency on radio or TV, to $325,000. Broadcasters have sued to overturn recent FCC rulings, arguing that broadcasters shouldn't have to abide by laws that don't affect cable and satellite providers (which is why HBO's "Deadwood" can clock, by one Web site's calculation, 1.48 F-words per minute). The inability to be indecent is, for broadcasters, a competitive disadvantage.

7 In any case, government fines for indecency are something of a rearguard action, unlikely to stem the tide. It's like trying to fight rising sea levels one sandbag at a time.

8 A landmark case revolves around the word used by Bono, the rock star, at the 2003 Golden Globe Awards. He blurted out that winning an award was "[bleepin'] brilliant." The FCC first ruled that his comment wasn't indecent, because it didn't describe a sexual act. But in 2004, after the Janet Jackson breast exposure during the Super Bowl halftime show, the commission reversed the Bono ruling, saying the singer's comment was indeed profane and indecent.

9 The FCC's logic, however, was a stretch. It argued that any use of the word "inherently has a sexual connotation." But that's just not true. In fact, the reason it is used so often is because it has escaped the bonds of its sexual origin. It's now used as a generic intensifier. It makes plain language more colorful and emphatic.

10 The reason it must be suppressed in polite society is not because it's a bad word, but because, in certain circumstances, it is a very good word. It is a solidly built word of just four letters, bracketed by rock-hard consonants. It is not a mushy word, but one with sharp edges. Consider how clunky the term "the F-word" is. The authentic article, by contrast, explodes into space from a gate formed by the upper incisors and the lower lip. Then it slams to a dramatic glottal cough.

11 I'd even argue that it has therapeutic properties. Ponder, if you will, how critically important this word can be when you stub a toe. It serves as an instant palliative. It's like verbal morphine. You can't hop around the dining room, holding your foot, shouting "Drat!" or "Dagnabbit!" or "Heavens to Betsy!" Those words don't work.

12 "It's a sexual word in origin but it's not used that way very often," says Jesse Sheidlower, editor at large of the Oxford English Dictionary and editor of the 1995 book "The F-Word," a 224-page dictionary in which some of the permutations of the word are absofreakin'lutely ridiculous.

13 "It does not have the sting that it used to," he says. "For young people, it just doesn't have that much power for them."

14 The word has been around since at least the 15th century. The English word with which we are familiar is related to similar words found in the Germanic languages, such as Dutch, Norwegian, Swedish and German. These words meant "to thrust" or "to strike" or "to copulate." The first known printed appearance, Sheidlower says, comes from a text around 1475, in a poem that more or less said the monks of Cambridge did not go to heaven because of their sexual dalliances with women. For

the next four centuries it was almost always used in a literal sexual sense. The figurative uses so common today didn't arise until the late 19th century, Sheidlower says.

15 The word was not openly printed in the United States until 1926, when it appeared once in Howard Vincent O'Brien's memoir "Wine, Women and War," according to Sheidlower's book. After World War II, writer Norman Mailer negotiated his way around the taboo by using the made-up word "fug" in the dialogue of the book "The Naked and the Dead." This spring, Andrew Crocker, a Harvard senior, turned in his thesis on the use of the word in post–World War II America, and he relates the famous story that Tallulah Bankhead (or, in some tellings, Dorothy Parker, or Mae West) said to Mailer at a cocktail party, "So you're the man who can't spell f—." Nice line, though Crocker says it's apocryphal.

16 James Jones used the word in his 1951 novel "From Here to Eternity." Like Mailer, Jones was reflecting the speech of American soldiers during the war. This point is key: The word was routinely used by real people, it just was rarely published and never broadcast. It was still taboo.

17 Liberating the word became a dubious triumph of the 1960s counterculture. At Woodstock, Country Joe and the Fish led a rousing cheer that began with "Give me an F!" and continued on through "K," finally asking, "What's that spell?" Now it sounds silly. Wow. They said a bad word out loud! What revolutionaries!

18 Soon, the word became common in popular culture, but still retained some of its sizzle. Consider the classic line by Otter in the 1978 movie "Animal House" after the fraternity brothers have wrecked Flounder's car: "Flounder, you can't spend your whole life worrying about your mistakes! You [effed] up—you trusted us!" Drift a few years forward to 1989, and Spike Lee's "Do the Right Thing," and the word gets a real

workout in the mouth of Sal, who at one point uses it six times in the space of five sentences.

19 Today it still has enough power to be memorable, as when Jack and Miles in the movie "Sideways" discuss the possibility of drinking merlot:

20 Jack: "If they want to drink merlot, we're drinking merlot."

21 Miles: "No, if anyone orders merlot, I'm leaving. I am NOT drinking any [expletive deleted] merlot!"

22 Just to clarify: This is funny not because Miles used a bad word, but because of the juxtaposition of the bad word with the one that follows. We do not expect to hear a person express such strong feelings—to the point of vulgarity—when discussing a particular kind of grape.

23 We must not overharvest the swear words that are part of the commons of our language. It is an adults-only commons, of course. Kids need to be told that they still can't use it. How can a 13-year-old be transgressively vulgar with the word if his 5-year-old sister already uses it? This word is supposed to be a reward of adulthood. We have to conserve it, so that our children and our children's children can use it when we're gone.

24 There is a wonderful scene in the 1987 movie "Hope and Glory." A gang of boys is rambling through the rubble of London during the Blitz. The new boy, Bill, wants to join. They ask if he knows any swear words. He says he does. Say them, the boys insist. He hesitates. He admits finally that he knows only one swear word. After much delay and agonizing, he says it, loudly.

25 The word.

26 The other boys are shocked into silence. "That word is special," the gang leader finally says. "That word is only for something really important."

27 Precisely.

SUMMARIZE AND RESPOND

Summarize the reasons Achenbach gives for wanting to "preserve" the F-word. Do you agree with his argument?

ANALYZE

Though he's writing a humorous essay, Achenbach makes a clear appeal to the audience's intellect. Write a brief analysis in which you trace his use of logos to persuade readers. Do you think combining humor—itself a pathetic appeal—with logos is an effective argument strategy? Explain your answer.

DISCUSS

Do you think certain words should be off limits? Or should we be able to say whatever we want whenever we want? If you answered "yes" to the first question, explain why and discuss who should decide which words are banned. If you answered "yes" to the second, discuss the possible consequences of a world in which no words are taboo.

Charlotte F. Allen, author of The Human Christ: The Search for the Historical Jesus, *uses the following essay to state her very strong opinions about living wills and the "right-to-die" movement. As you read, notice how she uses her own experience to open the essay and introduce the issue, and then presents evidence from other sources to support her position. Allen wrote this piece for the October 14, 2007 edition of the* Washington Post.

BACK OFF! I'M NOT DEAD YET

I Don't Want a Living Will. Why Should I?

Charlotte F. Allen

[1] Do I have to have a living will? Last year, I had an experience that gave me the distinct impression that if I didn't have one, my life was hardly worth, well, living.

[2] A routine mammogram had revealed that I had early-stage breast cancer. This kind of cancer is noninvasive and thus not particularly life-threatening if promptly attended to, and the required outpatient surgery isn't especially risky. Nonetheless, one of the shoals I had to maneuver through at the hospital (which otherwise afforded me excellent care) was a series of efforts to persuade me to sign on to the currently fashionable notion of a "good death."

[3] Those efforts came in the form of a living will, one of those advance directives on end-of-life care that are currently urged

upon us all by such high-minded organizations as the American Medical Association, the American Bar Association, state laws and an array of policymakers, bioethicists and advice columnists. Even this newspaper ran a long article in its business section this year advancing the notion that you haven't got your life in order without a living will. Whether to have a living will is presumably up to the patient. But I've developed a sneaking suspicion that someone else may be hoping to call the shots. After three attempts to induce me either to sign up or to state my refusal to do so in writing, I had to wonder how voluntary a living will really is in many cases. In my case, I started to feel ever-so-slightly harassed.

4 When I showed up at the hospital for some pre-surgery medical tests, one of the receptionist's first questions was, "Do you have a living will?" The form she gave me after I shook my head was as complicated as a tax return. There were numerous boxes for me to check specifying a range of conditions under which I might like to have a Do Not Resuscitate order hung over my hospital bed, whether I would want to be denied "artificial" food and water under some circumstances, what I thought about being taken off a ventilator, and so forth.

5 Furthermore, I found something weasely in the way all those options were presented, as though my only real choice were between being dispatched into the hereafter at the first sign of loss of consciousness or being stuck with as many tubes as needles in a voodoo doll and imprisoned inside a ventilator until global warming melts the ice caps and the hospital washes out to sea. I found the box on the form that said "I decline a living will" and checked it. Right now, my husband is my living will, and after we spent 13 days observing Terri Schiavo exercise her "right to die" by being slowly dehydrated to death after her feeding tube was removed in 2005, he knows exactly how I feel about such matters.

6 A few days later, when I returned to the hospital for the surgery, a different receptionist handed me a second living will. "I've already gone through this," I said, handing it back. After the operation, I was back to begin six weeks of daily radiation. A third receptionist pulled out the very same form and asked the very same question: "Do you have a living will?" At least I knew where to find the "I decline" box fast.

7 Now, I'm sure that all three receptionists were just doing their jobs. A 1991 federal law requires hospitals and other healthcare facilities to make their patients aware of living wills. Yet the repeated experience of being given 30 seconds in a busy lobby to read and sign a complex document that cast a negative pall upon positive efforts to keep me alive did not inspire my confidence in the living-will industry.

8 In fact, when I contemplate the concept of "dying well," I can't avoid the uneasy feeling that it actually means "dying when we, the intellectual elite, think it is appropriate for you to die." Consider what's happened in recent years: The classic Hippocratic Oath and its prohibition against physicians giving people a "deadly drug" has collapsed with the growing acceptance of such notions as physician-assisted suicide, the "right to die," and even giving some very sick, disabled or demented people a little push over the edge, as seems to be the case in the Netherlands. People facing end-of-life decisions may well feel subtle pressure from the medical and bioethical establishments to make the choice that will save the most money, as well as spare their relatives and society at large the burden of their continued existence. A "good death"—that's the English translation of the Greek word that begins with an "e." You know, euthanasia.

9 Even the hospice movement, which has historically opposed anything that smacked of euthanasia, has become tainted by this

thinking. Hospices and home hospice care had always sounded wonderful to me: providing a comfortable place for the hopelessly ill to die with sufficient pain medication and no burdensome and futile efforts to prolong their lives.

¹⁰ Then, seven years ago, I paid what I thought would be a last visit to my 93-year-old father, who was dying of prostate cancer at home with round-the-clock nursing care. The phone rang, and I picked it up. On the other end, a middle-aged male voice inquired about my dad's condition. "Sooner or later he's going to go into a coma," said the voice, which never got around to identifying its owner but was presumably a friend of my parents'. "Then, what you have to do is take him to a hospice. That's what we did with my mother. They'll put him on a morphine drip, and he'll be gone in a few days. They know what to do." I was too dumbfounded to ask the obvious question: Why would someone in a coma need morphine? (My father, by the way, died at home some five months after that visit.)

¹¹ Certainly not all hospices engage in practices that deliberately hasten death. But in February the American Academy of Hospice and Palliative Medicine reversed its long-standing opposition to physician-assisted suicide (which is legal in Oregon and said to be quietly practiced by many doctors elsewhere) and adopted a new set of rules that effectively endorsed the practice. The academy even decided on a new euphemism for the procedure: "physician-assisted death." Even where assisted suicide is illegal, many hospices now endorse "terminal sedation," the ethically murky practice of anesthetizing terminal patients, then cutting off their nutrition and liquids.

¹² The problem is that nowadays there is simply no societal agreement on how people who are sick or disabled beyond hope of cure ought to be treated. Many people, especially highly educated, nonreligious people, think that "physician-assisted death" is exactly the right way to go—or to send off your unconscious mother. If you think that bioethicists will erect safeguards against this sort of thing, think again.

¹³ As far as I can tell, bioethicists exist for the most part to do some moral chin-pulling before giving the green light to whatever consensus the rest of the elite have reached. If you believe, as the Dutch do, that it's fine for a children's hospital to euthanize severely disabled infants, you can always find a bioethicist to give you a stamp of approval. If you want to harvest the organs of dying people without waiting for brain death to occur, you can probably find a bioethicist to sign on to that, too. Myself, I'm with Slate blogger Mickey Kaus. In 2003, as the Schiavo controversy was raging and Yale surgeon Sherwin Nuland, author of "How We Die" and an advocate of limited assisted suicide, was pontificating on National Public Radio about her low quality of life, Kaus wrote: "If I'm ever in Terri Schiavo's situation, and not in any pain, please follow these simple steps: Keep the feeding tube in, and keep Dr. Nuland out."

¹⁴ It's not surprising that many people have reservations about theories of "dying well" that always seem to involve not staying alive. In 2004, the Hastings Center Report, a journal that focuses on bioethics, reported that despite decades of aggressive promotion of living wills, only 18 percent of Americans of all races had them, including only 35 percent of residents of nursing homes. Those most suspicious of the talk about "dying well" are African Americans and members of other minority groups. African Americans are only one-third as likely as whites to have a living will, and only one-fifth as many blacks as whites sign DNR orders.

¹⁵ According to the article's authors, it seems that people talk a good game about living wills, especially when they're

healthy, but when their health begins to fail, they often have very different ideas about what they would be willing to undergo to stave off death for a little while. Furthermore, according to a 1990s study by the National Institutes of Health, even when patients have living wills, if those wills contain directives with which doctors and hospitals disagree (such as, I myself suspect, prolonging the patient's life instead of terminating it), many doctors simply ignore the patient's desires. Living wills, it would seem, are effective only if they happen to comport with doctors' and bioethicists' own theories about what is best for the patient anyway. For this reason, the authors of the Hastings study propose that instead of filling out a living will, people execute a durable power of attorney, a simple document that entrusts decisions about end-of-life care to a relative or friend who shares the signer's moral beliefs about death and dying. That sounds about right to me.

[16] A year ago, I received the gentlest of shoulder-taps from the man with the bony fingers, though he'll inevitably be back. I wish we lived in a different kind of society, one with agreed ideas about what a "good death" means—but we don't, at least not now. So I say: Go ahead and sign a living will if you want. Have your doctor pull out your feeding tube or inject you with cyanide or do whatever fulfills your idea of death with dignity. But count me out. I don't want to "die well"; I just want to die in peace.

SUMMARIZE

Write a 100-word summary of Allen's central claim.

ANALYZE

In her essay, Allen writes: "In fact, when I contemplate the concept of 'dying well,' I can't avoid the uneasy feeling that it actually means 'dying when we, the intellectual elite, think it is appropriate for you to die.'" And later in the piece, she refers to the "intellectual elite" again. Who do you think she is talking about when she uses this phrase? How would you characterize her feelings about this group of people? What does this say about Allen's ethos?

DISCUSS

Allen states that "nowadays there is simply no societal agreement on how people who are sick or disabled beyond hope of cure ought to be treated." Do you think our society will ever reach agreement on this issue? Explain your response.

from reading to writing

1. Several of the writers in this chapter incorporate humor into their essays. What makes humor a useful tool for getting people to think and talk about difficult or uncomfortable subjects? Are there issues that we should never use humor to discuss? Explain, using at least one of the essays from this chapter in your response.
2. Working with a partner or in a small group, choose one essay from this chapter that you found to be funny and explain why it was humorous and how the author used the humor. Be specific in your response.
3. First-person essays depend on a strong ethos, but effective use of the other rhetorical appeals can make these kinds of arguments even stronger. Select two essays from this chapter and compare how the authors make appeals to pathos and logos to strengthen their arguments.
4. Though they are often compelling and effective, first-person essays sometimes fail—to connect with or interest readers, to support their argument, or to make the issue at hand seem larger than the author. Think about the essays you've read in this chapter and discuss any weaknesses or failures that come to mind. What could the authors have done to prevent these problems?

appendix 1

A RHETORICAL APPROACH TO RESEARCH

"[R]hetoric we look upon as the power of observing the means of persuasion on almost any subject presented to us; and that is why we say that, in its technical character, it is not concerned with any special or definite class of subjects."

—Aristotle, from *Rhetoric,* Book 1, Chapter 2

Aristotle's point in this quote is that rhetoric is not the study of any single thing—it's not just about politics or law, art or business, sports or fashion; in more immediate terms, it's not *only* about reading and writing arguments. Rhetoric can be about any and all of these, and just about anything else—including research. In Chapters 2 and 3, we talked about the generative possibilities of the rhetorical situation for both your writing and your reading. In this appendix, we want to show you how to apply what you've learned about the rhetorical situation to the process of finding and using sources that will help you produce successful writing projects.

We'll start with a caveat: This is by no means an exhaustive guide to research and documentation. There's much more to each of those subjects that we can deal with here, and there are lots of good writer's handbooks and websites you can turn to for that. What we want to do is give you a few strategies, rooted in the rhetorical situation, for thinking about and completing research-oriented writing assignments. We'll do that in four brief sections, and then we'll show you what a completed research project looks like in Appendix 2. Here are the topics we'll cover in this appendix:

- **Posing Research Questions:** an explanation of how to develop and use questions to guide your research and your argumentative writing.
- **Finding and Evaluating Sources:** a few thoughts about figuring out what you need from your research, where to start looking, and how to evaluate sources based on what you know about their rhetorical situations.
- **Incorporating Sources Rhetorically:** a guide to using sources effectively and responsibly in your writing.
- **Documenting Sources:** a brief discussion of the MLA citation and documentation system, which is used in many writing classes, and a list of links to websites that provide examples of MLA formats and information on other systems of documentation.

But first things first. Before you do any work whatsoever on a writing assignment—especially one that requires hours of research—you should make sure you understand exactly what it is you're supposed to do. In other words, you need to think about your own rhetorical situation—specifically, about the requirements of the assignment you've been given and the precise nature of your audience.

Let's start with the assignment. There's a big difference between a researched report, a researched argument, and an exploratory essay; although they all require research, each incorporates that information in different ways. And audience expectations will be very different for each kind of assignment. That's why you need to make sure you know exactly what kind of project you're supposed to complete. If you're required to work on a researched writing project in a composition class, you're likely to encounter some or all of these common assignments:

- *an annotated bibliography* (a list of sources, each with a brief summary and account of its relevance to your larger project);
- *a literature review* (a more detailed narrative account of a collection of sources related to your topic);
- *an exploratory essay* (a paper that examines several perspectives on a narrowly defined issue and that may or may not include your own point of view);
- *and a researched argument* (an argumentative essay in any of the genres we outlined in Chapter 4—definition, evaluation, causal, or policy).

Of course, the exact nature of your research and writing tasks will depend on the assignments you get from your instructor. Just remember that it's your job to make sure you understand what *kind* of researched argument or project your instructor wants you to complete.

The other part of understanding an assignment is knowing your audience. Sometimes, that audience will be your instructor and no one else. If this is the case, you should think—and ask—about your instructor's expectations. What does she want to know? What does she expect you to include in your argument? And how will she evaluate your work? In other cases, your teacher might ask you to write for a different audience—a local newspaper or campus website, for example. The same rules apply: You need to think about precisely who this audience is, what they might expect, and how you can appeal to them (see Part 2 below for a more complete discussion of how to assess audience expectations).

With a clear understanding of your assignment and audience in mind—and after you've worked with your instructor and classmates to choose an appropriate topic—you'll be ready to get to work on your project.

Part 1: Posing Research Questions

If your class is using this textbook, your teacher is going to want more from you than a generic "research paper"—a collection of information from sources cobbled together into a narrative. You're more likely to be asked to write a focused, thesis-driven argument that brings your reasoned and well-researched perspective and insight to your topic. So how do you get there? Diving right in with your mind made up is one option, albeit an ineffective one. A more productive route is to start with questions. What is simultaneously rewarding and challenging about doing research is that the process itself shapes your thinking as you go. What this means is that you don't—in fact you shouldn't—start with answers. Rather, you should ask questions to help you develop your focus and, eventually, your claim. Let's look at an example to see how asking questions can help guide a research project.

In the spring of 2008, according to news reports, one house of the French Parliament passed legislation to ban the promotion of anorexia and other eating disorders. The *Guardian* newspaper reported that the law specifically targeted "pro-ana" websites that "support anorexia as a lifestyle choice rather than a medical disorder." These news reports caught the attention of one of our students, and she decided to do her research project—an annotated bibliography and a policy argument—about these "pro-ana" websites. With the help of a group of classmates, the student developed a handful of questions, listed below, to guide the early stages of her research. As you read them, notice how they mirror the stasis questions outlined in Chapters 3 and 4.

- **Questions of definition:** What are "pro-ana" websites? Who are their authors? What is their purpose? Who is their target audience?
- **Questions of evaluation:** Is there any evidence to suggest that these websites do harm? Are they morally or ethically wrong? Are these websites legal in the United States?
- **Questions of causality:** Why did these websites spring up? What effects do they have on girls and women of different ages? What might be the effects of banning them? Is banning them even feasible?
- **Questions of policy:** Do governments have the responsibility (or capability) to monitor and regulate such websites? Are there better ways to combat the influence of these websites? Can something be done at the campus level to educate women about the dangers of these sites? Should people who contribute to these sites be punished?

As she conducted her research, our student explored these and other questions before deciding on her ultimate claim: She wrote a policy argument on the need for education and intervention as an alternative to the influence of "pro-ana" websites.

Your list of research questions may be longer or shorter, and they may be organized differently. Using the stasis questions—as our student did in the previous example—is just one way to help you get started. The point is, beginning your research by asking questions will give you the latitude to fully explore your issue even as it allows you to focus in on your own argumentative claim.

Part 2: Finding and Evaluating Sources

Once you've decided on some research questions, you'll be ready to start your search for sources. As tempting as it might be at this point to Google your topic to see how many hundreds of thousands of hits you get, you should resist that urge and spend a little time thinking about what you need to know. Otherwise, with the vast amount of information out there, you might find yourself overwhelmed with possible sources. And even though you might find some of these useful, chances are you'll spend a lot of unproductive time scrolling through websites with questionable information from hard-to-identify organizations. To make your searching more efficient, we suggest that you begin by setting up three lists:

- First, jot down things you know about your topic, especially as they relate to your assignment. Think about why you chose the topic. Did it sound interesting to you? Do you have some experience or expertise in the area? Have you read about or researched the issue before? Taking inventory of information you know already—things such as background, anecdotes, and personal experience—will help you do two things: see where you stand as you begin the research process and figure out what to put on your second list (things you need to learn about your topic). And keep in mind that no matter how much you *think* you know about an issue, there's always plenty more to learn.

- Second, make a list of things you need to know. As you examine your first list, you should start to formulate questions based on your assignment and the other elements of your rhetorical situation. At this point in the process, thinking about your purpose and your audience will prove especially useful. With those two elements of the rhetorical triangle in mind, here are some questions you might consider as you try to figure out what kinds of sources will help you:

  - **Do you know enough background about your topic?** Is there relevant history you need to learn and share with your audience to help them understand the issue and your position on it?
  - **Can you put the topic in context?** How, for example, has the issue played out in the past? Has it been the subject of public debate or of legislative action? And where do things stand now? Are there current efforts to deal with the issue you're researching? Are people speaking publicly about it now? What are they saying?
  - **What does your audience know about the topic?** What do they need to know in order to understand your argument? Obviously, you'll never know for sure exactly what your audience knows or how it feels. But making some informed assumptions—about political leanings, interests, and emotional investments, for example—is more useful than flailing away in the dark.
  - **Do you need help figuring out how to make your audience care about the topic?** This is especially important if you know your audience is hostile, skeptical, or apathetic. In any of these cases, you might need to find source material that will help you connect with your readers and make them care long enough to read and consider your argument.
  - **Do you need data, statistics, or other "hard" evidence to help persuade your audience?** Yes, your argument likely will be rooted in opinion, and that's fine. But no matter how eloquently you state your opinion, most audiences will need other reasons—often including statistical evidence—to accept your position.
  - **Are there other perspectives on the issue that you might not have considered?** Remember the old saying, "There are two sides to every story"? Well, the truth is there are usually more than two sides. Although politicians, special-interest groups, journalists, and talk-show hosts make it seem like just about every controversial issue breaks down into two camps—those who are for it and those who are against it—more often than not there are multiple perspectives that require more than a thirty-second sound bite to understand. Your research can help you find, understand, and figure out how best to incorporate these points of view in your argument.

- And, third, leave room for a list of things you haven't thought of yet. Obviously, this one will be blank for a while. But once you get started, it could fill up fast. You might discover data that shows something unexpected about your topic or perspectives you hadn't considered. You might even find yourself asking new research questions and heading off into different directions. And that's fine—as long as you have the time to spend. Remember, research can be a slow process. But keeping an open mind as you work through your project, and being willing to go where the most interesting research takes you, can be rewarding.

With these lists in hand, you'll be ready to search more efficiently for the kinds of sources that will help you learn about your topic and compose an argument that successfully appeals to your audience. So, where should you look? As we've said before, there are other places where you can get much more detailed guidelines for doing effective research—writer's handbooks, your campus writing center, and the reference department of your library are your best bets. That said, we do have a few specific ideas about where you can start looking for general-information sources (things like newspapers, magazines, journals, and online news and opinion sites) and about how to gauge the credibility and usefulness of the sources you find. We base our recommendations on the rhetorical situations our students face—the nature of and audiences for the research assignments they have to complete—and on the types of issues our students have written about in the past.

- **Where to start looking:** Because our students like to write about issues that affect their lives, either directly or indirectly, and that are featured in the news media, we suggest they start looking for sources in the electronic databases available through the university library. (Please don't think that we have anything against books. We love books, and sometimes our students use them as sources. But because most of the issues our students like to research and write about are current, the publication time lag for books can be a problem.) Unless they're working on a project in a specialized field—such as electrical engineering or nursing—we steer them toward general-information databases that archive articles, opinion columns, and essays from newspapers, magazines, and some academic and professional journals. They've found these databases to be especially useful because they are relatively easy to search and because they include the full text of most articles (rather than citations for sources available elsewhere). Most academic—and many public—libraries offer access to these databases (or similar ones). The descriptions are from the databases themselves:

  o **LexisNexis Academic:** Provides access to more than "6,000 news, business, and legal sources. These include regional, national, and international newspapers, news wires, broadcast transcripts, . . . magazines, trade journals, business publications," and more. The database is updated daily.
  o **Academic Search Complete:** "Contains the full text of more than 4,000 scholarly publications. . . . The database covers the social sciences, humanities, education, computer sciences, engineering, physics, chemistry, language and linguistics, arts & literature, and more."
  o **Expanded Academic ASAP:** Includes "more than 3,500 indexed and full-text titles . . . in all disciplines with more than 20 years of backfile coverage. It offers balanced coverage on a wide-range of topics."
  o **Readers' Guide Full Text & Readers' Guide Retrospective:** The Full Text "indexes and abstracts articles from more than 240 of the most popular general-interest magazines published in the United States and Canada," whereas the Retrospective contains "comprehensive indexing of the most popular general-interest periodicals published in the United States and reflects the history of 20th century America."

- **Searching the Internet:** Obviously, databases that collect information from the mainstream news media and from scholarly journals aren't the only good sources out there. We've explained why we encourage students to start with these kinds of sources, but we also know that the Internet is an unbelievably powerful—and tempting—database in its own right. Our best advice here is pretty basic: Search with skepticism and patience. One advantage to searching databases such as LexisNexis is that the articles and essays have been through some kind of vetting and editing process. That's not the case for many websites that you'll find when you search the Internet. Of course, this doesn't mean the information you find on the Internet is always suspect; we simply suggest that you to think rhetorically about the sources of information you want to use

- **Evaluating sources:** How can you know if the information you find from any sources is reliable? Your best bet is to make informed judgments based on what you know about the rhetorical situations of the sources you're interested in. Here are some questions you can ask about sources to help you decide whether you feel comfortable using them:

    o **Author:** Who wrote the text you want to use? Does the text reveal anything about the author? Many publications—in print and online—include brief biographies about their authors. If no author is listed, you should ask yourself why (most newspaper editorials are unsigned, for example, because those texts represent the voice of the entire editorial board; but an openly racist anti-immigration text with no author should raise a red flag). Does the author have any particular expertise on the issue at hand? Does the text express a particular agenda that the author is working toward?

    o **Publication:** Who is publishing the text? Is it an established magazine such as *Vibe* or *Newsweek*? Or a well-known newspaper? Is it a university or a research lab? Or a special-interest group such as the National Rifle Association? Does the publication accept advertising? What kinds of ads does it run? Here again, thinking about the companies and people behind the text—and their purposes and agendas—can help you make informed decisions about which sources to use and which to leave alone.

    o **Target audience:** Who is the text trying to reach? Why? Does the text seem to exclude any potential readers? What do the text, author, and publication want from the audience?

    o **Purpose or agenda:** You should think about purpose at every stage of the evaluation process. Why has this text been written? What is the author trying to accomplish? Is the author open about the purpose or agenda? Or does the reader have to infer it? What might a hidden purpose or agenda say about the author's reliability?

Thinking critically and rhetorically about potential sources can help weed through texts, websites, and other material to find the kind of information you need—and feel confident using—to make your argument and persuade your audience.

Part 3: Incorporating Sources Rhetorically

Now that you've explored your topic and selected some sources that you think will help you connect with your audience, it's time to start thinking about precisely how—and where—to incorporate these ideas into your argument. Certainly this task is not as simple as dropping in a quotation here and there. If you've committed enough energy and thought to your research, your own argumentative claim will be informed and improved by the reading and analysis that you've done. And to complete your task, you need to carefully consider how you'll responsibly, persuasively, and smoothly weave your research into your writing.

To strike just the right balance between others' claims and your own, you should always keep your audience and purpose in mind. How much outside research will your audience need to understand and be persuaded by your claim? Is your audience aware of different perspectives that you'll need to account for? What progression of outside research (followed by your explicit analysis) will most effectively move your readers?

You know by now that there's no single answer to these questions, but if you keep your audience and purpose in mind while you work, you can find the most effective way to respond, with the necessary research, to your rhetorical situation. Think of it like this: The way you frame your research is just as important—and it can be just as persuasive—as the way you develop your appeals to ethos, pathos, and logos. As a matter of fact, you can't separate your research from these artistic proofs. To help you decide how best to use your sources, we've put together a list of questions to keep in mind about your audience:

- How much does your audience know about your topic? Are you going to need to provide background information to educate them, or can you move ahead to specific perspectives related to your claim?
- Is your audience likely to be receptive to your claim? If that's the case, you won't need to spend as much time backing up your position, but you will need to find a way to demonstrate its significance.
- Is your audience likely to be skeptical of or indifferent to your claim? In either case, you can use outside sources to dramatize the exigency of the problem and to support the validity of your position.
- Will your audience demand statistical data and "factual" information? If so, you'll need not only to include it, but you'll also need to make clear that it comes from a respectable source.
- Or, will your audience be more receptive to expert opinion, anecdotal evidence, or narrative? If this is the case, you should make these kinds of sources prominent in your project.

Once you've considered what your audience knows and might expect, you should think about what kinds of sources will help you develop your appeals to ethos, pathos, and logos. Remember that the appeals always work together, but as we've done elsewhere in this book, we're talking about them separately here to help you understand how different kinds of sources might work in your argument. In your final project, the way you have collected, arranged, and presented your research will speak volumes about who you are as an author. This work can also appeal to your audience's emotions, and, of course, help your argument make sense.

With that in mind, here are some ideas—arranged by rhetorical appeal—to help you use your research persuasively:

- **Ethos:** By considering what your audience knows and how it feels about your topic as you look for sources, you've already taken the first step toward making an effective ethical appeal. Why? Because the sources you draw on and the way you analyze and present them will send a strong message about your credibility and authority. Citing relevant statistics and presenting them with insight, for example, will establish your expertise on the topic, while accurately summarizing several perspectives on your issue will send the message they you're fair-minded. But making a mistake like dropping in a long quotation without analyzing it, resting your claim on an unreliable source, or not properly referencing material can cost you your audience's trust, so you must incorporate your research with diligence. The good news here is that handling these challenges capably can make you appear as a trustworthy expert whose claim is difficult to deny. And beyond speaking to your credibility, your research and the skill with which you work it into your argument can shape your authorial persona—as, for example, an expert, or a fair-minded guide, or, as in the case of James Poniewozik, a funny and knowledgeable critic. Think about the way that Poniewozik, the author of "Ugly, the American" in Chapter 2, speaks with insight about the television comedy *Ugly Betty* and about the immigration debate to make his claim that Betty Suarez is more American than most characters on TV. Not only does he come across as someone who knows a great deal about the show, but also as a person fully invested in the positive influence television can have in public policy debates.

- **Pathos:** Using sources to push your audience's buttons is easy—but it's also irresponsible and, more often than not, counterproductive. Yes, you could present a heart-breaking anecdote for no other reason than to catch your readers' attention and make them feel guilty, but once they realized this manipulation, you more than likely would have lost them for good. Instead of slipping into obvious and off-putting manipulation, you should strive for the subtle use of pathetic appeals. You can see one successful example of this in "Walking a Thin Line"—about the pressures of the modeling industry—in Chapter 8. Here, author Rebecca Johnson uses pathos to make an emotional connection to her audience. She opens her piece with a brief narrative about a model's casting call (evidence gathered from the author's primary research). She makes us feel what the 16-year-old model is going through as she stands before a casting agent to be judged, in less than two minutes, on her height, weight, and body type. By opening her piece in this way, Johnson frames her research to, as journalists say, "put a face on the issue." Because of her light touch, this example doesn't cross the line into manipulation or offend the audience through implication. Instead, it evokes a subtle sense of empathy and brings the audience into the story. Though Johnson makes us feel sympathy for the young girl in her story, your appeals to pathos don't have to evoke sadness or pity. You can even appeal to the audience's sense of humor to make them more receptive to your claims. Let's say you want to argue that there's unacknowledged racial tension on your campus. Because this is an issue that many of your readers might be reluctant to talk about, you could incorporate a description and analysis of the "Racial Draft" sketch from *Chapelle's Show* in order to engage your audience with humor while you simultaneously ask them to consider difficult questions.
- **Logos:** No matter how strong your opinion about an issue, and no matter how well you articulate it, you'll find that many audiences (your instructor included) will expect you to offer other kinds of evidence to support your claim. Perhaps the simplest way to think about appealing to logos is with so-called "hard" evidence like statistical data and the numeric results from surveys and polls. On almost any given topic, such data abounds, but you need to be careful—and selective—in your use of it. Filling your paper with lots of numbers is a sure way to lose readers, and although they're often presented as "facts," statistics can be interpreted in many different ways and are just as open to manipulation as words and phrases. For this reason, when you choose to incorporate statistics, you need to consider your sources carefully and present your data as fair-mindedly as possible. Doing so can help you persuasively take your audience through the logical steps of your argument. Of course, there are other types of evidence—beyond data and other numbers—that can help you bolster your claim. These include anecdotal evidence (the recollections of events that someone reports having happened) and informed or expert opinions that either take a position similar to your own or radically opposed to it. It may seem obvious that citing an expert who agrees with your claim (or even one small element of your claim) can help you support your argument, but keep in mind that you should continually analyze and make explicit how this information fits in with

your larger purpose. You must always make a space for your own argumentation so that it stands beyond what an expert has already said. And don't rule out a source simply because it stands in disagreement with your claim. Arguing against positions different from your own can be a sophisticated and effective way of persuading your audience. Done properly and fairly, it shows that you're open to different ideas and not afraid to show why your position might be more reasonable (or effective).

Although we've cited specific types of evidence in these sections on ethos, pathos, and logos, you should keep in mind that the way you incorporate your outside research will have an effect on each of these rhetorical elements of your project. Your sophisticated and even-handed use of statistics can successfully appeal to ethos because your writing demonstrates that you think carefully and fairly about your issue. Likewise, a pointed example that evokes sympathy in your audience can simultaneously help you demonstrate that there exists a logical need for change. If you take only one thing from this section on research, let it be this: Research is rhetorical. The way you incorporate your source material can make or break your persuasive efforts, and so you should always be thinking about how outside material can best help you achieve your purpose given the audience to which you appeal.

STRATEGIES FOR INCORPORATING SOURCES

Artfully working outside source material into your own writing isn't a natural skill, but with a bit of practice—and an idea about how and when to take on one of three specific approaches—you can manage this task effectively. In this section we'll discuss three basic techniques for incorporating outside source material—quoting, summarizing, and paraphrasing—and we'll give you some advice about when each might be the most appropriate choice. Always keep in mind, though, that your rhetorical situation should help you to decide which technique you'll ultimately use.

- **Quoting:** You want to be selective when it comes to quoting outside sources, and you should always have a rhetorical reason for doing so. Perhaps you'll be analyzing the language of a film critic in your evaluative argument about the top three film adaptations of comic books, or maybe the author you're planning on quoting makes a claim that is so extreme you think your audience members need to read it for themselves. For the most part, you should use a direct quotation only when the author's style or words are vital for you to accomplish your purpose. The quotation might say something truly profound, or the author might say it in a striking way. When you're trying to decide whether you need to directly quote from an outside source, keep the following guidelines in mind:

  - You should use quotations sparingly. This way, when you do use them, they'll be more effective.
  - You don't have to quote full sentences; you can use partial quotations to emphasize material

that works best for you and to help keep the focus on your argument.

- You should use long quotations (more than three lines) infrequently. When you overuse these, it's easy for your outside research to take over your own claim.
- You should always keep the focus on your voice. Accomplish this by introducing your quotations and following them up with an account of why they're useful to your argument or how they're situated in relation to your claim.

- **Summarizing:** Summaries are useful when you want to provide your readers with a broad overview of one or more of your sources without attending to too many small details from the original texts. What makes a summary such a powerful tool in your writing is that it allows you to distill a large amount of material into a small amount of space. Because of this, you're able to quickly move ahead to positioning the outside information in relation to your own argument. If you plan to summarize texts in your writing, keep in mind some of these ideas:

  - You must be sure that you have a full and correct understanding of the source's main idea before you summarize it in your paper.
  - You should write summaries that are in service to your overall purpose and are appropriately situated within the trajectory of your argument.
  - You should build on your summaries so that the audience has no doubt about the significance of the material you've covered.
  - You must appropriately cite your summaries (both in the text and on your Works Cited page).

- **Paraphrasing:** It's useful to paraphrase when the content of your source material is important for your claim but the author's style and words are not essential in what you're trying to accomplish. When you paraphrase, you put the pertinent information from a narrowly defined section of your source material into your own words and structure. That the section be "narrowly defined" is crucial because the power of paraphrasing is that it allows you take the time to go into plenty of detail about the pertinent information. This is unlike a summary, which recounts rather quickly the main idea of a whole piece. Not sure if you should paraphrase a portion of your outside source material? Here are a few thoughts to consider:

  - You should paraphrase to elaborate fully on one particularly useful section or element of a text. Follow up your paraphrase with an explanation of how this information is important in terms of your overall claim.
  - You should use paraphrases to keep yourself from over-quoting your sources. This practice not only helps you grasp important elements of the sources you're using, but it also helps you keep your paper in your own voice and focused on your own purpose and claim.
  - You must carefully document when you paraphrase (both in the text and on your Works Cited page), even though you've put the outside material into your own words. When you're paraphrasing, you're writing about another person's ideas, and you must acknowledge them appropriately.

Part 4: Documenting Sources

The reasoning behind proper documentation is not complicated: If you use words, information, or ideas from a source, you need to let your readers know what those outside elements are and where you got them. Why? First of all, if you don't do this—if instead you present someone else's words or ideas as your own, even accidentally—you'll have committed plagiarism, the academic equivalent of a serious crime that warrants severe punishment. Beyond the disgrace of being labeled a cheater, however, there are more interesting and instructive reasons to learn how to credit your sources properly:

- Though it might not feel like it when you're slumped over your laptop, alone, struggling to finish a paper in the wee hours of the morning, most writing is a social activity. More often than not, we write for an audience. And we read what others have written as members of an audience. These communication transactions—much like the private and public discussions we engage in daily—create a community of discourse, an ongoing conversation of sorts about anything and everything in our lives. And like any community, this one depends on the ethical behavior of its members to flourish. So, when we join the conversation, whether orally or in written texts, we have a responsibility to acknowledge words and ideas that aren't our own. To do otherwise could undermine the community by creating suspicion, resentment, and other feelings of ill will.
- Then, of course, there is the rhetoric of citation and documentation. Like every other element of your writing projects, the way you cite and document your sources says something about you to your audience. If your readers suspect that the words or ideas you're presenting aren't your own, you could lose their trust to such a degree that they won't even consider your position—indeed, they might not even finish reading your paper. On the other hand, by gracefully integrating your sources and clearly giving them credit, you can establish yourself as a credible and authoritative voice, one that even skeptical readers will find it difficult to ignore.

You'll learn the mechanics of proper citation and documentation though practice. Depending on your instructor's preferences and your field of study, you'll use any one of several documentation systems. The most commonly used in English classes is the MLA style, a system developed by the Modern Language Association to bring consistency to articles and essays written in the humanities, especially languages and literature. Another widely used system is the APA style, developed by the American Psychological Association for authors writing in the social and behavioral sciences. The most comprehensive guides to each of these systems are the stylebooks the two organizations publish:

- *MLA Handbook for Writers of Research Papers* (for high school and undergraduate college students);
- *MLA Style Manual and Guide to Scholarly Publishing* (for graduate students and academic professionals);
- the Publication Manual of the American Psychological Association.

You can also find excellent explanations of when and how to use these documentation systems in writer's handbooks and online. One of the best sites we've found is published and maintained by Purdue University's Online Writing Lab. Descriptions of and links to Purdue's site and other sources follow:

MLA Style

- **The Modern Language Association (MLA):** "What Is MLA Style?" This page on the MLA's website offers a brief explanation of the MLA citation and documentation system, but no examples.

  - <http://www.mla.org/style?>

- **The Purdue University Online Writing Lab:** "MLA Formatting and Style Guide." This is an extensive and easy-to-use website that offers explanations and lots of examples of how to use MLA style.

  - <http://owl.english.purdue.edu/owl/resource/557/01/>

- **The Purdue University Online Writing Lab:** "Works Cited: Electronic Sources." This page from the Purdue site listed above deals exclusively with sources you'll find using databases and on the Internet.

  - <http://owl.english.purdue.edu/owl/resource/557/09/>

APA Style

- **The American Psychological Association (APA):** "APA Style." The APA's style homepage offers background and explanation but few examples.

  -

- **The Purdue University Online Writing Lab:** "APA Formatting and Style Guide." Like Purdue's MLA website, this one is clear and easy to use.

  - <http://owl.english.purdue.edu/owl/resource/560/01/>

appendix 2

COMPLETING A RESEARCH PROJECT

We know from experience that, no matter how well a teacher explains an assignment, many students like to see examples of what they are expected to do—or at least of what a successful version of the assignment might look like. With that in mind, we have compiled a package of material that you might find useful as you contemplate your own research projects. The first part of the package is an abbreviated assignment sheet for a multipart research project that our students usually complete over the final two to two-and-a-half months of the semester. In this sheet, we try to cover all of the key elements of the assignments' rhetorical situation, with an emphasis on audience and purpose. (As you'll see, we leave it to our students to decide their ethos, or how they want to present themselves as researchers and writers in these assignments.) The other parts of the package are one student's completed assignments—his annotated bibliography, exploratory essay, and policy argument.

Jason Walker, the student who wrote the annotated bibliography and essays, was enrolled in a composition course at Louisiana State University in the Fall of 2008 when we asked the class to complete the following research project. Because, as he indicates in one of his assignments, Jason has studied geography, he decided to research and write about the causes of and problems associated with Louisiana's rapidly vanishing coastal wetlands. He explains his interest and findings very eloquently. But before we get to that, let's look at the assignment sheet for the project (we've included only the main elements of the assignments so that you get an idea of Jason's rhetorical situation).

RESEARCH PROJECT ASSIGNMENT SHEET

Your final three major assignments—the annotated bibliography, the exploratory essay, and the policy argument—will all focus on the same issue. You'll spend a couple of weeks researching the issue and compiling an annotated bibliography of useful and reliable sources. Then, you'll write your exploratory essay as a way to help you decide what specific problem associated with your issue you want to address in your policy argument. Specific instructions for each element of the project follow.

Rhetorical situation

As we've discussed many times, you need to think about your rhetorical situation as you select your research topic. Here is some information about your purpose, audience, and ethos:

- Purpose: You're preparing your two essays for inclusion in a hypothetical special edition of the *Daily Reveille,* LSU's campus newspaper. This collection of essays, called "Whatever Matters," is designed to counter the widespread perception that college students are becoming less willing to engage in public debate about issues of importance to them.

- Audience: This special edition will not only be published on campus and online, but will also be mailed to parents, alumni, and potential students and their families. In short, it will be used as a recruiting tool to show people that LSU students are informed, engaged, and willing to get involved. So, your audience is the usual readership of the campus newspaper, plus parents, alumni, and potential students and their families.
- Ethos: Since your essays are going to be part of this special edition, it will be clear that you are a student at LSU. Beyond that, the ethos you choose to present is up to you.

Finding a topic

Your first task is to select an issue to research and write about. The issue you choose must fit all of the following criteria:

- It must interest you (remember, you'll be spending the rest of the semester researching, thinking, and writing about it).
- It must involve a public problem that needs to be addressed (for example, the rising cost of higher education).
- It must be controversial. In other words, there must be disagreement over what to do about the issue.

Annotated Bibliography Assignment

Using the research topic you have selected, you are to compile an Annotated Bibliography of eight sources that will help you think and write about that topic later in the semester (in the exploratory essay and the policy argument). Keep in mind that the annotated bibliography is a tool for you to use as you work on your final two essays. The information you include in your annotations should help you figure out at a glance how the sources might be useful to you.

Guidelines

- You must write a one-page (300-word) introduction in which you explain your interest in the issue and what you're covering in your annotated bibliography.
- Your bibliographic entries must follow MLA formatting guidelines and must be listed alphabetically by author or title.
- Each annotation should be about 100 words long and must summarize and evaluate the source.

Questions to consider as you write your annotations

- Positioning the text:
  a. Where was the text originally published?
  b. What do you know about this author and publication? What can you tell from the text?

    c. What are the author's or publication's biases? Do they have any apparent agendas?

    d. Who is the target audience?

- Summarizing the text:

    a. Is the information current or too old to be useful?

    b. What are the main ideas?

- Responding to the text:

    a. What did you learn from the source?

- Evaluating the text as a source:

    a. How might it be useful to you?

Exploratory Essay Assignment

You are to write an essay in which you explore and explain your research topic—what it is, why it matters, and what people are saying and doing about it. The purpose of this assignment is twofold: First, it will give your audience an overview of your topic; second, it will help you identify a specific problem related to your topic that you want to write about in your policy argument.

Research

You must use at least three (but no more than six) outside sources in your essay. These sources must be properly cited using MLA format, and you must include a works cited page.

Writing Tips

- Your paper should include the following:

    a. An introduction that provides background and context on the topic; explains why you're interested in it; and explains why the audience should care about it.

    b. Summary and explanation of different perspectives on the issue.

    c. Transitions that lead the reader smoothly from one idea to the next.

    d. A conclusion that sums up what you've learned from researching the issue and writing this essay. You might also include other things you feel like you still need to learn and/or a statement of your position on the issue.

- Remember that you are not writing an argumentative essay (that's your next paper). You should focus on presenting a clear and fair discussion of the state of the topic.

Policy Argument Assignment

You are to write an argumentative essay in which you identify a problem associated with your research topic and propose a course of action to deal with the problem. As you do this, you'll need to give your audience ample reason to believe that the problem you're addressing is worth their attention and that your proposal is valid. You also may need to address and rebut alternative courses of action.

Research

You must use at least three (but no more than six) outside sources in your essay. These sources must be properly cited using MLA format, and you must include a works cited page.

What follows are the three papers Jason wrote in response to these assignments. As you read each, notice how he attends to the requirements of the assignment as well as the needs of his audience.

ANNOTATED BIBLIOGRAPHY

Losing Ground: Who is Responsible for Protecting
Louisiana's Disappearing Coastline?

Jason H. Walker

I have been a student of geography for nearly ten years now and a resident of the state of Louisiana my entire life. So it wasn't a surprise that I found the subject of my research paper while making my daily commute across the Atchafalaya Basin. The topic I was looking for was directly below my feet. It was clear. Okay, the water wasn't clear on that particular day, but what I wanted to research was. I began by asking questions: What is the status of Louisiana's disappearing coastline? How much have Hurricanes Katrina, Rita and Gustav accelerated the problem? More importantly, is anyone doing anything about it?

I assume that most people agree that Louisiana is rapidly losing its coastline. Just ask any native who has grown up fishing the coastal bayous and swamps of our state. From a scientific standpoint, this topic has been researched for decades now, and the findings are pretty unsettling. According to a study conducted by the Louisiana Department of Natural Resources, Katrina and Rita "caused 42 percent of the damage that scientists had formerly predicted would occur in the next 50 years through non-storm events" (Green 1). How much land are we actually losing? Here comes the staggering figure...an area the size of a football field is lost every 38 minutes. At this point, I was easily convinced that the state of Louisiana has a serious problem on its hands.

There are many efforts being undertaken to protect the coastline. Groups range from the Federal Emergency Management Agency (FEMA) to citizen-driven non-profit organizations. And in 2006, 155 coastal wetland restoration projects had been approved by Congress. These preventative measures were at least temporarily reassuring. But the more I researched the topic, the more I found mention of "political hurdles" and "political red tape." With the national attention that Hurricane Katrina received, with the overwhelming volunteer and government assistance that New Orleans has deservedly been the recipient of, why isn't more attention being turned toward our coastal land loss problem?

The purpose of my research project is to uncover how efficiently and cooperatively our national and local governments are working to address and solve the issue at hand. Maybe ensuring the future of the Louisiana coastline falls not on the shoulders of politicians, but on the residents themselves. Or maybe while the presidential election and energy crisis are fresh on everyone's mind, we can grab the attention of our politicians and remind them that 27% of the nation's oil supply is being piped onshore in areas that may be under water within the next 25 years. While compiling sources for my Annotated Bibliography, I've realized that these issues are very real and very time sensitive. Perhaps by the time my research is concluded Louisiana will have gained some ground.

Boruff, Bryan J., Christopher Emrich, and Susan L. Cutter. "Erosion Hazard Vulnerability of US Coastal Counties." Journal of Coastal Research 21-5 (2005): 932-942. BioOne eJournals. Middleton Library, Louisiana State University, Baton Rouge, LA. 28 Oct. 2008 <www.lib.lsu.edu/databases>.

This article was published in 2005 in the scholarly *Journal of Coastal Research*. Based on the source of publication I would assume that the target audience is students, research institutes, and possibly governmental organizations. The purpose of the article is to examine the vulnerability of the three major coastlines in the continental United States (Atlantic, Gulf of Mexico and Pacific). The information will be useful in my research because it compares and contrasts these coastal counties/parishes. Specifically, the authors take a look at the reason these particular areas are vulnerable, based on physical and socioeconomic characteristics. However, the data collected in this research was collected before the devastating hurricane season of 2005. The authors of this article were, at the time, from the Department of Geography at the University of South Carolina.

Bourne, Joel. "Louisiana's Vanishing Wetlands: Going, Going..." Science New Series, Vol. 289, No. 5486 (Sep. 15, 2000): 1860-1863. JSTOR. Middleton Library, LSU, Baton Rouge, LA. 28 Oct. 2008 <www.lib.lsu.edu/databases>.

This article discusses a $14 billion coastal restoration plan (Coast 2050) and the scientific and political hurdles that it may face. Although published in 2000, this article will be useful because it can be compared with some of the more recent information that I have accumulated in my research. The subject of the text, Coast 2050, appears in many of the articles listed in this bibliography and seems to be one of the front running efforts to protect the Louisiana coastline. I am specifically interested in the political red tape that author expects Coast 2050 may endure. The article was published in a nationally distributed science periodical that may target a wide range of readers.

Dorell, Oren and Tom Kenworthy. "La. Coast No Longer as Nature Intended." USA Today 3 October 2005: 9A. LexisNexis Academic. Middleton Library, LSU, Baton Rouge, LA. 21 Oct. 2008 <www.lib.lsu.edu/databases>.

This newspaper article discusses how Louisiana's coast no longer provides a natural storm shield, protecting cities and communities from hurricane force winds and tidal surge. It was published in 2005 and provides a current snapshot of the status of Louisiana's coastal areas. The article was printed in one the nation's largest newspapers and includes insight from a couple of LSU oceanography and coastal studies professors. The target audience of the article is very broad, ranging from daily subscribers of the newspaper to anyone with interest in coastal erosion. The text is somewhat brief but contains staggering figures on the severity of this issue. The article also provides personal perspectives from natives living in the affected areas. This article will be useful in my research project because it provides a vivid picture of the current status of the Louisiana coastline and the potential threat that may result from loss of these natural buffer zones.

Green, M. M. <u>Coastal Restoration Annual Project Reviews: December 2006</u>. Baton Rouge, LA: Louisiana Department of Natural Resources, 2006.

This is a public document that was funded by the State of Louisiana. The purpose of the text is to provide information about previous and current projects that exist in the state of Louisiana whose efforts are to combat the coastal land loss problem. This book will be useful in my research because it provides a current snapshot of all the projects being conducted to research and protect the coastline. In particular, I will be able to use this information to break down who is funding a majority of these projects. Only 1,000 copies of this document were originally printed, so I would assume the target audience is very small. The distribution was likely within various state departments as well as local research institutes.

National Research Council of the National Academies. <u>Drawing Louisiana's New Map: Addressing Land Loss in Coastal Louisiana</u>. Washington, D.C.: The National Academies Press, 2006.

This is a post-Katrina and post-Rita book that takes a look at the disappearing coastline of Louisiana. It is the result of research conducted by the Committee on the Restoration and Protection of Coastal Louisiana and the Ocean Studies Board. The study was supported by several organizations, including the U.S. Army Corp of Engineers and the State of Louisiana. Based on the committees and organizations involved in the development of this text, I would assume the target audience is politicians, scholars, and the individuals directly involved in the conservation efforts. The text will be extremely useful, not only because the information is current, but because a variety of subject matter is covered, ranging from the social and political constraints that restoration efforts will face, to a historical review of the Mississippi River over the last 20,000 years.

Streever, Bill. <u>Saving Louisiana? The Battle for Coastal Wetlands</u>. Jackson: University Press of Mississippi, 2001.

This book covers various topics related to Louisiana's diminishing coastline. I'm specifically interested in the chapter titled "Good Business," which addresses what actions non-profit and non-governmental agencies are taking to study and combat the problem. The author is a research biologist in Alaska; however, he was formerly employed at the Waterways Experiment Station (Wetlands Branch) in Vicksburg, Mississippi. The book is relatively current, but was published before the Louisiana coast was hit by Hurricanes Katrina and Rita. Still, it will be valuable because it contains chapters that touch specifically on the subjects of subsidence, the Atchafalaya, multi-dimensional thinking about the coast, life on the bayou, and lessons that can be learned from our situation. The target audience for the book appears to be scholars, environmentalists and individuals interested in Louisiana's current coastal crisis.

Varchaver, Nicholas. "The Next Energy Crisis." Fortune Vol. 156, Issue 4 (20 Oct. 2007): 80-85. Academic Search Complete. Middleton Library, LSU, Baton Rouge, LA. 29 Oct. 2008 <www.lib.lsu.edu/databases>.

This article, originally published in *Fortune* magazine in the fall of 2007, addresses the subject of oil production and the vital role that Louisiana plays in the petroleum industry. Specifically, the text focuses on Port Fourchon and how this land (the site of a major oil pipeline) is in danger of eventually subsiding into the Gulf of Mexico. The target audience, based upon the place of publication, is anyone who has interest or ties to oil production in the Gulf. This article will provide an interesting angle to my research because it ties together coastal land loss and the oil industry. The text may also clue me in on why big business and the government should/may be interested in protecting our coastline.

Walker, H. Jesse, James M. Coleman, Harry H. Roberts and Robert S. Tye. "Wetland Loss in Louisiana." Geografiska Annaler. Series A, Physical Geography Vol. 69, No. 1 (1987): 189-200.

This academic article provides detailed information on the causes of wetland (coastal area) loss in Louisiana. It was originally published in 1987 in a journal that specifically addresses the subject of physical geography, and the authors were, at the time, from LSU. The target audience of the article is specifically for geographers, scientists and students. Although the text is relatively old, the subject matter is still pertinent to my research project. The article breaks down the causes of wetland loss—specifically the geologic, catastrophic, biologic and human factors. The text is very well structured and gives the reader a clear understanding of the forces at work behind Louisiana's coastal loss. It will provide the background information I need to establish the problem addressed in my research papers.

EXPLORATORY ESSAY

Proving Ground: Who Is Responsible
for Protecting Louisiana's Coastline?
Jason H. Walker

Fact or fiction? Louisiana is losing an area of wetlands roughly the size of a football field every day. Fiction. Actually, a section of marsh that size is lost to the Gulf of Mexico every 38 minutes. So it would be more accurate to say that Louisiana loses more than 37 football fields of coastline every day. These coastal zones support unique plants and wildlife, economically vital onshore oil pipelines, and thousands of citizens. What is being done to protect and restore this land? As of 2006, 155 projects designed to study, preserve and protect the coast had been approved by Congress. However, of the approved sites, only 77 had been fully constructed (Green 1). In this essay, I will explore the numerous and often complex reasons that are causing our coastline to disappear and attempt to shed light on the most effective way to gain some ground on the issue.

Basically there are two major forces at work behind this disappearance: human activity and Mother Nature. But Mother Nature's hands are tied from being able to naturally replenish the lost soil, so it is up to human beings to find a solution. Who is up to the task? Who is going to fund this massive undertaking? There are a variety of organizations and individuals currently working to address the issue. Some of these groups include the Federal Emergency Management Agency (FEMA), the Environmental Protection Agency (EPA), the Louisiana Department of Natural Resources, and citizen-driven non-governmental organizations (NGOs). The individuals that represent these organizations have had to clear hurdle after hurdle in order to secure funding and gain the support of state and federal legislators. But each hurdle takes time, and time is of the essence. The loss of Louisiana's coastline affects more than just the citizens that live along the Gulf; it has the potential to be a detriment to the already declining national economy.

Many factors have caused the Louisiana coastline to diminish and subside. For our purposes, these can be broken down into two categories: human impact and natural impact. Let's start with the human causes. Up until the nineteenth century, the Mississippi River naturally ran its course, shifting from east to west. Imagine laying a garden hose stretched out on your driveway, turning the water pressure all the way up and leaving it unattended. Without someone holding the hose, it will continuously snake back and forth. This is similar to how the Mississippi River once flowed; but unlike a garden hose, rivers are constantly depositing soil throughout the surrounding delta plain while in motion. In the nineteenth century, however, when the Mississippi delta became more heavily populated, the inhabitants began to construct artificial levees and dams along the length of the river. These structures were necessary for humans to establish large, permanent settlements in this region. The dams and artificial levees were built in order to prevent flooding, to supply water for irrigation, and, later, to produce electric power (National 33). While these structures remain vital for supporting human life along the Mississippi, they are also a major reason that Louisiana's coastal environments are disappearing. Dams, while beneficial for a number of reasons and common throughout the world, act as artificial barriers that stop the flow of sediment to the mouth of a river. And their counterpart, levees, prevents the introduction of new sediment, which would naturally accumulate as the river meanders during its life cycle (National 33). Over the past 200 years, these two feats of engineering have greatly contributed to the increased rate at which Louisiana is losing its coastal areas.

The second factor involved with the disappearance of Louisiana's coastal wetlands is Mother Nature. Still fresh on the minds of the nation and particularly the citizens of the Gulf Coast is the hurricane season of 2005. Hurricanes Katrina and Rita both made landfall along the coast of Louisiana, producing massive storm surges that pushed a wall of water deep into the interior coastal regions of the state. While some of the water retreated after the storms moved inland, much of it stayed behind. This new supply of water covered low-lying areas and resulted in the creation of new lakes and marshes. According to studies collected by the Louisiana Department of Natural Resources, these two hurricanes "caused 42 percent of the damage that scientists had formerly predicted would occur in the next 50 years through non-storm events" (Green 1). The same studies estimate that Hurricanes Katrina and Rita transformed 217 square miles of marsh into open water (Green 1). With a predicted increase in the occurrence of highly active hurricane seasons and, as a result, more and more major storms, Louisiana needs to act as quickly as possible in its efforts to restore these coastal marshes. The marshes and barrier islands of Louisiana act as natural buffer, slowing down and breaking up storm surges. These protective buffer-zones play a vital role in the protection of the state's major cities as well as numerous coastal communities. Another natural process that is contributing to the loss of coastline is subsidence, or the sinking of the land. Subsidence can occur for a number of reasons, including the introduction of saltwater. When saltwater concentration increases in the marsh, it disrupts the brackish (salt and freshwater) environment that is essential for supporting native vegetation. These plants and their root systems hold together the soil, creating stretches of land. If saltwater continues to overcome the environment and plants continue to die, the land will sink and eventually succumb to the Gulf of Mexico (Bourne 1861). The final straw that breaks the proverbial back of Louisiana's efforts to restore its coastline is global warming. Made recently popular by former Vice President Al Gore, global warming has the potential to cause globally catastrophic events. Whether or not humans are responsible for the current rise in temperatures isn't up for debate in this essay. Let's save that for another day. But the fact is, if the average global temperature increases by several degrees, polar ice caps will melt, resulting in a dramatic rise in sea levels. As you can imagine, this scenario would not bode well for the citizens of Louisiana.

So now that we have established the problem of coastal loss and outlined some of the contributing factors, we need to find a solution. More importantly, we need to find a person or organization willing to lead the effort. There are currently many organizations and individuals working to research and combat the issue. The most important and vital supporter of coastal restoration is the United States government because protecting Louisiana's coastline will be a massive undertaking that will cost millions, ultimately billions, of dollars to finance. Without the financial assistance of the federal government, efforts would be impossible and futile. In 1990, Congress recognized the national significance of wetland loss in Louisiana, passing the Coastal Wetlands Planning, Protection and Restoration Act (Green 3). In 2004, Congress extended the act for an additional 15 years and appropriated roughly $40 million dollars annually to fund coastal restoration projects. As previously mentioned, there are currently 155 projects funded by this particular legislation. Now that we have the attention of the government, who is going to supervise the various wetland protection projects and continue to seek financial support? This task will likely fall into the hands of Louisiana's sometimes notorious state politicians.

Actually, contrary to popular belief, there have been great strides made by Louisiana's elected officials. The driving forces behind Congress' Coastal Act of 1990 were Louisiana Senators J. Bennett Johnston and John Breaux. These senators were successful in the first ever appropriation of government funds to address Louisiana's coastal issues. In 1997, following the actions of Johnston and Breaux, local and state government officials were responsible for the implementation of "Coast 2050," a program than concentrated all previous and current restoration efforts into one collective and comprehensive planning effort. This $14 billion dollar plan, intended to protect more than 10,000 square kilometers of marsh, swamp, and barrier islands, was also supported by Congress and is funded by a portion of royalties collected from federal oil and gas leases (Bourne 1860). In addition to the implementation of congressional acts and financial plans, many of Louisiana's state agencies and departments have the responsibility of monitoring these federally funded projects. It's important to keep in mind that the achievements of local politicians were not made without some political resistance and clearing of red tape.

We all know that our local politicians wouldn't be elected to office without the support of the citizens. This democratic empowerment gives non-governmental organizations, academic communities, and the average citizen a voice in the Louisiana coastal discussion. There are numerous concerned individuals and citizen-driven groups that have relentlessly worked to help in the restoration/preservation efforts. After all, these are the people who live or enjoy recreation in the affected areas. Many of the citizens who live in these coastal areas are employed by the oil industry or make their living through agriculture. And while they may not have the means to stop the invading Gulf of Mexico, they can provide important and valuable insight. They can also provide the media and local nonprofit organizations with the ability to make the issue personal, to put a face on the problem. In 2006, *USA Today* published one of many articles written after Hurricanes Katrina and Rita showing how the diminishing coastline has directly affected the local population. After losing his home to Hurricane Rita, Lucious Thibodeaux, a retired oilfield worker, explained why he can no longer go home: "There's nothing to stop the waves…the Gulf is in our backyards" (Dorell). This statement is simple but poignant. The Thibodeaux family is only one of many that have or will eventually fall victim to the side effects of coastal land loss, but it's important to remember that these issues are real and have already impacted numerous communities.

After exploring the issue of Louisiana's disappearing coastline, I believe that efforts to protect this irreplaceable environment will have to be collective and cooperative. The federal government must help fund any viable program, and local politicians and state agencies must be involved to find a successful course of action. And it's up to volunteer organizations, the media, and the citizens of Louisiana to keep the nation's eye focused on our vanishing coastal. Without the combined efforts of many, without a cooperative angle of approach, Louisiana will only continue to lose ground. That, unfortunately, is a fact.

Works Cited

Bourne, Joel. "Louisiana's Vanishing Wetlands: Going, Going…" Science New Series, Vol. 289, No. 5486 (Sep. 15, 2000): 1860-1863. JSTOR. Middleton Library, LSU, Baton Rouge, LA. 28 Oct. 2008 <www.lib.lsu.edu/databases>.

Dorell, Oren and Tom Kenworthy. "La. Coast No Longer as Nature Intended." USA Today 3 October 2005: 9A. LexisNexis Academic. Middleton Library, LSU, Baton Rouge, LA. 21 Oct. 2008 <www.lib.lsu.edu/databases>.

Green, M. M. Coastal Restoration Annual Project Reviews: December 2006. Baton Rouge, LA: Louisiana Department of Natural Resources, 2006.

National Research Council of the National Academies. Drawing Louisiana's New Map: Addressing Land Loss in Coastal Louisiana. Washington, D.C.: The National Academies Press, 2006.

POLICY ARGUMENT

Standing Ground: Louisiana's Push to Protect Its Coastal Wetlands

Jason H. Walker

In case you haven't already heard, Louisiana is disappearing. The Gulf of Mexico is engulfing the coastline at an average rate of 37 football fields per day (Green 1). It's only a matter of time before areas like Lafayette and Baton Rouge are converted to beachfront property. Okay, maybe the latter statement is a little extreme. But the truth is that Louisiana has a major problem on its hands and it's ultimately up to the citizens of the Pelican State to do something about it. Why should anyone care if the marshlands, swamps, and barrier islands are lost to the Gulf? The answer is pretty obvious. This vast stretch of land is home to irreplaceable, culturally unique communities, and thousands of species of fish, wildlife, and vegetation; it is the economically vital site of onshore oil production and transportation; and it provides a natural buffer that helps to weaken hurricanes and absorb tidal surges. Over the past couple of decades, federal funding has been allocated to begin the protection, preservation, and restoration of these coastal environments, but as of 2006 only about half of these coastal research and development projects had been fully realized (Green 3). Time, unfortunately, is not on the side of the countless organizations and individuals fighting to protect Louisiana. If the state is on the receiving end of another catastrophic hurricane season similar to 2005, the result, without a doubt, will be devastating. In only a matter of hours, a Katrina-like hurricane could exponentially increase the rate at which this valuable land is lost. And the damage could be irreversible. For all of these reasons, there needs to be a greater sense of urgency behind these protective efforts, and Louisianans need to help expedite the process.

Louisiana's coastline is vanishing for a number of reasons, some rooted in human activity and others in natural events. Often, the causes involve a combination of the two. These range from the construction of levees and dams to an increase in sea levels. The rate at which the coast is subsiding and eroding varies from year to year, with hurricanes acting as the greatest catalyst. Researching the causes of this problem and, more importantly, finding solutions is an ongoing affair. So who is working to resolve the coastal crisis? Congress, through the efforts of Louisiana politicians, has allocated more than $14 billion to research and combat the issue of coastal wetland loss (Bourne). The actual implementation of these projects is decided by an arranged partnership of federal and state agencies, among them the Army Corps of Engineers, the Environmental Protection Agency, and the State of Louisiana (National). As of November 2006, these organizations had mutually approved 177 coastal restoration projects. But, unfortunately, only 77 have been fully constructed.

It has taken the greater part of three decades to recognize that Louisiana's coastal problem is of national significance. During that time, funding has been provided, legislation has been implemented, agencies have been united, research has been conducted, data has been collected, and projects have been approved. This may make you wonder, especially after the devastation of Hurricanes Katrina and Rita, why every effort is not being made to complete construction of these projects? Why does there seem to be an air of complacency? Have the citizens of Louisiana already suppressed the terrible memories of people stranded on roof tops, homes and personal belongings succumbing to the Gulf of Mexico, familiar hunting and fishing grounds being converted to open water? Not likely. The people of Louisiana are some of the most passionate in the world. They are passionate about their food and culture, passionate (borderline obsessive) about their sports teams, and passionate about their pursuit of having a good time. If they can redirect some of this passion and energy toward the coastal restoration efforts, I believe that tremendous ground can be gained. After all, the issue isn't whether Louisiana is losing its wetlands and marshes to the Gulf of Mexico. That has been confirmed, time and time again. The issue is the urgency with which the problem is being addressed. Working together with state and local governments, the citizens of Louisiana can help speed up the restoration efforts.

How can the residents of Louisiana contribute to the coastal preservation and restoration efforts? One of the easiest ways is by supporting their congressional delegation and taking part in the public discussions of the issue. Many of these lawmakers have fought tirelessly through the endless bureaucracy that accompanies passing most legislation—especially when the proposed legislation, as in is this case, comes with a price tag in excess of $40 billion dollars. It sounds like a lot of money, but relative to the damage caused by the hurricanes of 2005 (roughly $200 billion), it is only a few drops in the proverbial bucket. Before each election, the voters of Louisiana should research where their candidates stand regarding the issue of coastal preservation so they can cast informed ballots. Another way ordinary citizens can get involved is by contacting the offices of their legislators directly, to voice support, to offer suggestions, or simply to find out where the lawmakers stand on the issue. Contact information for state representatives and officials is easily accessible and available through government websites. Correspondence can be made via phone calls, letters and emails. Finally, people can show their interest in the issue by attending public hearings, town hall meetings, and other open forums for discussion and deliberation. Feedback from those who live in the afflicted areas can be extremely useful and persuasive because it shows everyone that real people are being affected.

For those who aren't interested in the politics of coastal preservation and restoration, there are other ways to get involved. As with all environmental causes, volunteers are always needed. There are numerous local and national organizations committed to the effort of protecting Louisiana's coastal marshes and wetlands, among them the Coalition to Restore Coastal Louisiana, America's Wetland Foundation, Restore or Retreat, Lake Pontchartrain Basin Foundation, and Parishes Against Coastal Erosion. Each of these groups has a website that details its mission statement, ongoing efforts, and well as other useful resources. With a little research, interested individuals can determine which of these groups most closely addresses their personal concerns. If unable to donate your time and labor, you can always donate money to help facilitate the operational costs that are associated with the conservation efforts.

The State of Louisiana can also help its own cause by raising public awareness about the issue. One useful tool available to state legislators is public service announcements (PSAs). PSAs similar to "Smokey the Bear" or "McGruff the Crime Dog" can help educate the public and send a clear and direct message to children as well as adults. The cost of producing these advertising campaigns would also be relatively insignificant compared to the overall cost of coastal restoration efforts. If the public develops a greater sense of awareness, it can create a ripple effect. And that ripple could make its way to Washington D.C. and encourage additional financial support from the federal government. Another way to raise public awareness would be to designate a particular day of the year to help promote and gain support for wetlands protection. This tactic would be similar to Arbor Day or Earth Day, just on a smaller scale. Designating a public awareness day can be accomplished city by city, not necessarily having to be a statewide affair.

In order to expedite the process of protecting Louisiana's coastal areas, the citizens of the state need to stay informed and support the efforts of local politicians and environmental organizations. They and the state government need to spread the word about this pressing and far-reaching problem. This issue is vital to the sustainability of life and economy along the shores of Louisiana and to the economic well-being of the nation. Preserving the coast, preventing erosion, protecting the natural environment isn't a matter of how, it's a matter of when.

Works Cited

Bourne, Joel. "Louisiana's Vanishing Wetlands: Going, Going..." Science New Series, Vol. 289, No. 5486 (Sep. 15, 2000): 1860-1863. JSTOR. Middleton Library, LSU, Baton Rouge, LA. 28 Oct. 2008 <www.lib.lsu.edu/databases>.

Green, M. M. Coastal Restoration Annual Project Reviews: December 2006. Baton Rouge, LA: Louisiana Department of Natural Resources, 2006.

National Research Council of the National Academies. Drawing Louisiana's New Map: Addressing Land Loss in Coastal Louisiana. Washington, D.C.: The National Academies Press, 2006.

index

differences, discussion of, 4–8

disagreements, 4–8. *See also under* arguments

Dispatch from the Department of Human Behavior (Vedantam), 89

Dixie Chicks, 12

Dobson, James, 12

"don't ask, don't tell," 112

Dorfman, Ariel, 101

Do Smart Girls Finish Last in Love? (Vanderkam), 256, 271

Dropping the F-Bomb (Achenbach), 341

Dubner, Stephen J., 104

The Dumbing of America (Jacoby), 135

Easterbrook, Gregg, 189, 203

eating disorders, 223, 231, 235

Eating Disorders: Not Just for Women (Boodman), 223, 231

Elamawy, Shirien, 3, 5, 18–20

Elmer Fudd, 10

emotion *(pathos),* 26, 28, 68, 70–71

Encomium of Helen (Gorgias), 39, 64

The End of Literacy? Don't Stop Reading (Gardner), 119, 125

environmentalism, 212, 215

Ephron, Nora, 107

Eratosthenes, 62, 74

ethical evaluations, 97–98

ethopoeia (character of the speaker), 63

ethos (character), 26, 28, 67–69

Euphiletus, 62, 74

evaluative arguments, 74, 82, 93–99

evidence to support evaluations, 96–97, 106

exploration in argument, 13

exploratory essay, 350, 361–62, 367

Facebook, 71, 258–259, 268

fact, questions of, 74, 81

Fade to Blonde (Alvarado), 337–338

faith on campus, 178

fat. *See* obesity

The Fat Girl's Guide to Life (Shankar), 70

Finder, Alan, 178

finger-pointing, 6–8. *See also* blaming

first person writing, 324

For Clues on Teenage Sex, Experts Look to Hip-Hop (Parker-Pope), 310

Ford, Glen, 316

formal definitions, 85, 88–89

Fountain, Henry, 256

Franco, James, 28

Franken, Al, 5–6

Franklin, Benjamin, 13

Freakonomics (Leavitt & Dubner), 104

friendships, 256, 258, 260

Friends Indeed? (Garreau), 258

From 'fat' to Fat (Shankar), 245

F-word, 347

Gardner, Howard, 119–120, 125

Garreau, Joel, 258

gay stereotypes, 273, 275, 327

gays in the military, 112

generous reading, 34–35

genus definitions, 85

Gen Y's Ego Trip Takes a Bad Turn (Gordon & Sahagun), 164

Glick, Jeremy, 4–5

global warming, 74–76, 82–84, 189, 190, 192, 193, 196, 203

Global Warming: Who Loses—And Who Wins? (Easterbrook), 189, 203

The Godfather, 12

Going Nuclear: A Green Makes the Case (Moore), 218

Goldberg, Jonah, 174

Google, 138

Gordon, Larry, 166

Gore, Al, 12, 82

Gorgias of Leontini, 39, 64–65

graffiti, 69, 70, 72

Greenpeace, 192

greenwashing, 212, 215

Handler, Nicholas, 176

Hagstette, Todd, 125, 145

Hauck, Charlie, 294

Heavy Habits (Roan), 224

Heavy Suit, Light Touches (Scott), 99

Helen of Troy, 39

Hermagoras of Temnos, 72–74, 83

hip-hop music, 29, 310, 316, 319

Hip-hop Profanity, Misogyny and Violence: Blame the Manufacturer (Ford), 316

Hirschorn, Michael, 293–294

Homer, 39

Humane Society of America, 88

Iliad (Homer), 39

immigration, 38, 72, 87

Imus, Don, 27, 312

Independent Nation (Avlon), 8, 10

Indiana Jones, 89, 91

Iraq War, 7–8, 12, 55, 66

Iron Man, 98–99

Is Google Making Us Stupid? (Carr), 138

Isn't That Special? (Goldberg), 174

Isocrates, 13–14, 45, 65

Is Persuasion Dead? (Miller), 3, 16–17

Jacoby, Susan, 135

Johnson, Rebecca, 235

Johnson, Steven, 284, 293

Jones, Indiana, 89

Joubert, Joseph, 8

Just, Richard, 181

kairos (timeliness), 64

Kakutani, Michiko, 158

Kavulla, Travis, 73, 268

Kennedy, George A., 63–64

King, Stephen, 23–24

Kitman, Jamie Lincoln, 215

Kluger, Jeffrey, 196

Leavitt, Steven D., 104

legal oratory, 73

Liberal Arguments: Still a Quagmire (Coulter), 6

Lies and the Lying Liars Who Tell Them (Franken), 5–6

Life Begins at Conversation (Quindlen), 14

Life in the Green Lane (Kitman), 215

literacy, 119, 122, 125, 128, 149, 152. *See also under* reading

Literacy Debate: Online, R U Really Reading? (Rich), 128

living wills, 350

logos (logic), 26, 28, 71–72

The Lonely American Just Got a Bit Lonlier (Fountain), 256

LOOK@Me: Generation Next is Living Out Loud and Online (Ludwig), 157, 168

Love in the Digital Age (Mathias), 251–252, 264

love relationships, 256, 273

Ludwig, Melissa, 157, 168

Lukas, Carrie, 108

Lysias, 62–63

credits